COUNTERATTACK

BATTLECORPS ANTHOLOGY VOL 5

EDITED BY JASON SCHMETZER

An Imprint of InMediaRes Productions, LLC.

COUNTERATTACK: BATTLECORPS ANTHOLOGY VOL 5
Cover art by Anthony Scroggins
Edited by Jason Schmetzer
Design by Matt Heerdt

Published by Catalyst Game Labs,
an imprint of InMediaRes Productions, LLC
PMB 202 • 303 91st Ave NE • E502 • Lake Stevens, WA 98258

http://bg.battletech.com
      (official BattleTech web pages)
http://www.battlecorps.com
      (BattleTech subscription fiction web pages)
http://www.catalystgamelabs.com
      (Catalyst Game Labs' web pages)
http://www.battlecorps.com/catalog
      (online ordering)

Catalyst Game Labs is dedicated to producing high-quality games and fiction that mesh sophisticated game mechanics with dynamic universes—all presented in a form that allows beginning players and long-time veterans to easily jump into our games and fiction readers to enjoy our stories even if they don't know the games.

Catalyst Game Labs is an imprint of InMediaRes Productions, LLC, which specialized in electronic publishing of professional fiction. This allows Catalyst to meld printed gaming material and fiction with all the benefits of electronic interfaces and online communities, creating a whole-package experience for any type of player or reader. Find Catalyst Game Labs online at www.catalystgamelabs.com.

BattleCorps is a subscription-based website actively supporting the *BattleTech* universe with new art, fiction, and a dynamic community. Under license from WizKids, Inc, we deliver new material every week, keeping fans and readers entertained with the ongoing politics, battles and technological development of the 31st century. Find BattleCorps online at www.battlecorps.com.

FOREWARD

JASON SCHMETZER

Welcome to the counterattack.

The stories in this volume are taken from the fifth year of publication on *BattleCorps*, a time when the site and the new stable of authors it had grown were continuing to really push the boundaries of what *BattleTech* fiction was and could be. It was a year of exciting firsts and triumphal returns, and it demonstrated that whatever else was happening, *BattleTech* fiction was going in surprising and unexpected ways.

A number of exciting returns happened on the site, but the first thing you'll likely notice about this collection compared to volumes one through four is fewer authors and fewer stories. There are several reasons for this, but the most obvious—and most telling—is that during 2008 *BattleCorps* published more and longer stories than ever before.

In fact, we serialized and published several novels!

Chris Hartford's excellent *Fall from Grace* finally saw serial publication in English—it had been previously published in German—in the latter part of the year, offering readers an in-depth look at the Star League-era Free Worlds League and Magistracy of Canopus. Also in 2008 were two parts of Randall N. Bills' heretofore-unseen *Founding of the Clans* novels. As exciting as those two projects were, however, they were far from the only exciting returns.

Fan-favorite mercenary regiments saw significant attention during this year, with new stories appearing about the Jihad-era Crescent Hawks as well as the Succession Wars-era Wolf's Dragoons. Popular

FOREWARD

writers like Steven Mohan, Jr., and Phaedra Weldon continued to turn in stories that could only be described as tours de force; indeed, in this collection you'll find Weldon's "With Carrion Men," which returns readers to the popular character Aris Sung while he's in more danger than ever before!

Powerful as those stories are, though, there was one story that was just too large to include here, but which appeared in 2008 and must be mentioned: "Not the Way the Smart Money Bets," marked the first short fiction New York Times Best Selling author Michael A. Stackpole had written for *BattleTech* in years. In it, Stackpole took readers back to the foundations of one of his most compelling and cherished characters: Morgan Kell, and the Kell Hounds.

We opened this foreward by saying "welcome to the counterattack," and while what we've told you so far is certainly powerful, we don't want you to think you've already heard about the best. There are other, smaller stories included here that simply demand your attention, written by both new and familiar authors. They range across centuries of the thousand-year *BattleTech* fictional history.

These stories tell the tales of infantrymen and vacuum marines; of mighty MechWarriors and lowly tankers. These stories present the horror of the Word of Blake's Jihad and the soul-wrenching betrayals of the fall of the first Star League. They are stories that put relatable, interesting characters into terrible stress and watch how they react. They are stories that demonstrate to readers the best and worst of the *BattleTech* universe, the events and battles and heartbreak of that thousand-year history.

We said "welcome to the counterattack," and we meant it. Welcome to the stories that, by theme and nature and simple storyline, demonstrated the resolve of *BattleTech* characters fighting back against oppression, against defeat, and against each other.

Walk the deck of a gunboat in "Blue Water," and trace the machinations of the Word of Blake in "Office Politics." See the bonds between common soldiers in "Godfather," and the deep bond of loyalty between charismatic leaders and their men in "Feral." Witness the double-crosses of merciless pirates in "Unholy Union."

Welcome, again, to the counterattack.

CONTENTS

CONTENTS

AN ILL-MADE HOUSE

JASON SCHMETZER

PART ONE

Hasse Plateau
New Vandenburg
Taurian Concordat
4 April 2765

The sound of groans and catcalls limped through the gap between the floor and the door panel. Captain Aaron Dane stood at attention before the major's desk, waiting for the field-grade officer to acknowledge him. Major Talbert was studiously engrossed in his paperwork. At the noise he looked up, his eyes focused past Aaron at the door.

"They must be playing it again," he murmured, and went back to his requisitions.

Aaron clenched his jaw but made no other move or sound. He'd been standing motionless for two hours. The backs of his thighs and his forearms were burning, but that was pain he could deal with. He'd once spent twenty straight hours at attention in Aphros. He was a Gunslinger. He wouldn't give in to discomfort.

"All right, Captain, you can sit," Talbert said, without looking up. The major was a spare man, a centimeter or so over two meters. His dark hair stood up in the front. His mouth, although supple, was perpetually frowning. In effect, as Aaron saw it, he was the perfect superior: condescending; supercilious.

Distasteful. Aaron sat down.

"We stand on enemy soil, Captain," Talbert said. "New Vandenburg," he gestured at the walls with his free hand, "has decided it can manage its own affairs without us. So they announce to the galaxy with that broadcast they keep airing."

Aaron said nothing. If the major wanted to monologue, he wasn't going to stop him.

"The General's at Fort Gorki right now, trying to get things figured out." Talbert looked up then, as if to see whether or not Aaron would react to the presence of General Kerensky, Commanding General of the Star League Defense Force. When he didn't react, Talbert blinked and kept talking.

"Which is what we're doing here," he said. "Do you understand?"

"Sir?"

"I asked if you understand, Captain."

"Sir, yes sir. I heard you. I understand that some rebels have decided they have a death wish. I understand that the General is on the other side of the planet, trying to calm them down. I understand that we're out here on the ass end of nowhere, instead of being where we matter."

Talbert set down his requisitions. The papers settled loosely on the cluttered composite desk. Aaron felt a breeze as a small electric fan washed air across him. He smelled Talbert's sweat, carried on the air.

"Free-thinking people who decide they don't want people a thousand light years away making their decisions for them don't have a death wish, Captain." He folded his hands on the desk in front of him before leaning over them. "And as for your assessment of our position, I think you need some perspective. Why don't you take your company out on patrol?"

Aaron blinked, held it. "Is that an order, sir?"

Talbert smiled. "It is, Captain."

Aaron sighed. "Sir, yes sir," he said, and stood. He drew himself to attention and waited until Talbert waved a dismissal at him. The door opened in instead of out. When he released the flimsy panel, the breeze from the fan was enough to slam the door against the frame after he left.

He didn't look back.

▲▼▲

The *Thug*'s sensor console beeped negative again. Aaron ground his teeth and tried not to imagine Major Talbert's smug grin again. Instead, he guided his *Thug* back around to the north, toward the Bridge Pass. The rest of the company followed.

"Still nothing, Captain?" Lieutenant Brake asked. His olive-painted *Thug* shadowed Aaron's. The eighty-ton machines were identical, save

for the crossed six-shooters painted on Aaron's 'Mech. Those pistols had bought him a lot of drinks in Haganau over the last few months.

"What do you expect?"

"The news from Fort Gorki doesn't sound good," Brake said. "I don't want to see that sort of thing here, is all."

Aaron sighed. He was on the wrong side of the world. After Petain's screwup outside Fort Gorki, the Taurians had pulled a whole battalion from between the sheets and thrown it at General Kerensky himself. He was a Gunslinger. He should have been with the General.

His sensor board pinged again, a more strident note than before. Aaron looked down through his neurohelmet's visor. He frowned.

"Contacts on the other side of the river," he said.

"Three Lance, break right," Brake ordered, not bothering to acknowledge the transmission. As company XO, it was his job to move the other two lances around. "IDs? My screen isn't painting anything."

Aaron slowed his *Thug's* walk and turned it east, toward the river that separated the Hasse Plateau from the Haganau Plains. Fort James Miller, the newly-built SLDF outpost on the Plateau, overlooked the city itself. There was a Taurian militia base in Haganau. His HUD painted three light hovertanks cruising along the riverbank. Schematics and other data flickered across the lower-right corner of his display. They mounted short-range missiles only. They were no threat to him or his 'Mechs.

"Little toys," Aaron said. He brought his *Thug* back around to the north. The rest of the company followed suit, falling into a rough triangle formation, with each lance diamond-shaped in its position. Brake ordered the transition without Aaron noticing. He was a good troop, too good to be stuck out here with Talbert as a CO.

It was six kilometers up the River Road to Bridge Pass. It was named because the single bridge across the Elbe River faced the only pass that led onto the Plateau. Star League planners had laid claim to the mesa as soon as they'd seen it, although Fort James Miller had only been constructed a year ago. Aaron looked down at his map display, noting the dozen green icons representing his company of *Thug*s and the blue line of the river. They were probably five klicks from the bridge. Not long at this speed, but probably still too quickly for the major.

"Captain Dane?" Brake asked. A red icon burned to life on Aaron's communication board, signaling that the lieutenant was on a discrete channel.

"Lieutenant?"

"I just wanted to say that no one misses Captain White. All of the troopers, sir, they're behind you." The lieutenant's *Thug* shifted its torso slightly until it was facing Aaron's. He saw it in his HUD. "It's an honor to have a Gunslinger as our CO."

"That's good to know," Aaron said, before severing the connection. The weight of his neurohelmet pressed even more heavily on his head as the *Thug*'s wide-legged gait rocked him in his cockpit. White was not someone he wanted to think about.

White had been relieved for cause. White was the reason he was out in this backwater. When the previous company commander was arrested for conspiring to turn over SLDF materiel to pro-Taurian rebels, Aaron had been the only supernumerary company-grade officer on-planet. The orders had been cut and signed before Aaron even had a chance to talk to the division commander.

White reminded him that he was out here with people who valued money more than loyalty. The Star League deserved better. Aaron clicked his com system to the company frequency. Several of the company's troopers were talking.

The first voice he identified was from Blakely, in B Lance. "We should be pounding these Tauries back into the Stone Age," he said.

"Enlightenment from the Sphere, Blakely?" asked Hernandez, who ranked as the best gunner in B Lance. He was also from the Outworlds Alliance. "And people wonder why we didn't want to join."

We? Aaron made a mental note to look more deeply into Hernandez's record.

"We've done it once," Blakely said.

"And it took twenty years and a million or so casualties," a woman put in. Aaron searched his three-sixty HUD until he found Sergeant Grover's *Thug*. She was the only woman from Rim Worlds space in the company. "You want to be here for twenty years, Blakely?"

There was long break in the conversation after that. Aaron turned the volume of his helmet speakers down and let himself go. His hands knew how to keep the *Thug* on course, and his eyes were aware enough to make the marked turns. He could march his *Thug* for hours like that, another trick learned on Venus.

"Contact!" Brake called. An alarm pinged on Aaron's console. He jerked himself aware and scanned his boards. All of his weapons were hot: the Tiegart PPCs charged and ready, and missiles in the tubes of his Bical racks. The threat board on his tactical display was clear; the alarm had come from Brake, cross-loading across the company channel.

"Report!" he said.

"Multiple bogeys north," Brake said. His voice was even, but taut. Aaron squeezed his control yokes. Bogeys, not contacts. Which meant the young lieutenant had some idea of what he had.

"IDs?"

"'Mechs," Brake said. "And they're not ours."

▲▼▲

The *Thug*'s computer finally stopped flashing through BattleMech schematics and displayed a high-resolution image of the leading 'Mech of the Taurian company. Aaron glanced at it and immediately sent it flashing to the rest of his *Thugs*.

"Where the hell did they get that?" Blakely asked.

A reinforced company of Taurian BattleMechs stood a hundred meters from the mouth of Bridge Pass. The trailing lance—the lightest lance, from what Aaron saw—was still near the bridge itself. Most of the 'Mechs were heavy designs, older models that the Star League had been phasing out in favor of newer machines. Aaron bet there wasn't a single one of the designs still represented today in any of the Royal divisions.

Except for the lead 'Mech.

"It's an *Emperor*," Blakely said.

"No kidding," Hernandez said. "I saw one on New Earth. I thought those only went to the Royals."

"Apparently not," Aaron said, cutting into the chatter. "Damp it."

At ninety tons, the *Emperor* outmassed Aaron's *Thug* by ten tons. It was far more heavily armed and armored. In a straight-up contest, Aaron's *Thug* wouldn't last more than a minute.

Gunslingers didn't believe in straight-up contests.

Aaron tapped his com system. "Brake. Right now, get through the Pass and report to the major. Taurian BattleMechs at the Bridge." He kept his eyes on the *Emperor*, but his peripheral vision kept watch for motion.

"You're going to need me here, Captain," Brake said.

"I gave you an order, Lieutenant," Aaron said. "Carry it out!" He toggled the microphone off and waited. A few heartbeats later Brake's *Thug* moved, stepping around its lancemates and starting toward the Pass. None of the Taurian 'Mechs moved. Aaron toggled his radio back on.

"Watch them," he said on the company channel. "If they're going to do something, it will be before we have a chance to warn the Fort."

"Why aren't we just radioing the report?" Blakely asked.

Aaron flicked his eyes to his ECM screen. "Look at your ECM, Sergeant." The long-range communications were jammed.

"Do we fire?" asked Hernandez.

"Not first," Aaron said softly. He stepped his *Thug* forward, moving it away from the rest of the company. Brake's *Thug* disappeared into the Pass. Aaron took a deep breath, held it. He exhaled. A finger opened the general channel.

"I am Aaron Dane," he said. "Captain of the Star League, commander of these 'Mechs." He drew in another breath. "I am a Gunslinger."

An amber light burned on his HUD. "And I am not," a scratchy voice said, "and yet I am here." The *Thug*'s computer painted a caret over the *Emperor*, identifying it as the sending unit.

Aaron smiled. "So you are." He waited, but nothing further came across the airwaves.

"I have to ask your intentions," he ventured.

The *Emperor* shifted, moving a step backward and turning to face Aaron's *Thug* head-on. Aaron held very still, his fingers light on his controls. The instructors at Aphros had pounded this into the trainees. The moment before battle was joined was electrical, tangible. You could feel it in the wind, in the air. Even in the cockpit. On the back of your neck, the small of your back. Taste it in your sweat.

Anticipation.

"The Elbe is the boundary," Aaron said. "No Taurian military unit is to cross the river without escort and permission." He risked a glance down, judging the position of the rest of his company. Gunslingers learned to fight alone, to duel. To trust themselves and their 'Mechs.

No one moved. On either side.

"You shouldn't believe everything you hear on the HV," Aaron said.

Nothing.

"The Star League is not your enemy," he whispered, just loud enough for the microphone to pick up.

Sound sparked to life in his helmet speakers. Static hissed and popped across the open line, punctuated by short crackles. The other man had his microphone engaged, but didn't speak. Aaron waited, tense.

"You would ignore Fort Gorki?" The scratchy voice was soft, filled with emotion.

"Gorki was a mistake."

A short bout of harsh, pain-filled laughter echoed across the empty space between the two 'Mechs. "Tell that to my daughter."

"You have my sympathies," Aaron said, sincerely. "Consider that Star League troopers died too." He swallowed and spread the *Thug*'s arms wide. "We've already had blood for blood."

The light lance near the bridge burst into motion, sprinting forward. The *Emperor*'s arms rose, spilling raw light deeply into the maws of the huge autocannons mounted there. The *Thug*'s sensors screamed for attention as targeting systems swept across the 'Mech. Every Taurian BattleMech on the field shifted, bringing weapons to bear.

Aaron triggered the PPCs filling the *Thug*'s bulky forearms. Crackling whips of artificial lightning flailed the horizon. Fresh static washed across the radio, and the burning scent of ozone crept between the *Thug*'s parts to trickle into the cockpit.

"Challenge!" he shouted.

"I am no samurai," the Taurian said.

"And you're no soldier," Aaron spat, his attempts at diplomacy abandoned. "I challenge you for that 'Mech. Somewhere a Royal is without his 'Mech because of you."

"Captain—" Hernandez began.

Aaron toggled the company channel. "If he accepts my challenge, no one interferes. If not, we fall back to the pass and hold them until Brake gets back with the rest of the battalion."

The *Emperor* didn't move. The trailing lance slowed and then stopped just behind the bulk of the Taurian 'Mechs. No one fired. The *Thug*'s alarm continued to wail at Aaron; all of the enemy 'Mechs were still painting him with their targeting scanners.

But they weren't firing. Every second he held them here was another for Brake to warn the major.

"We will fight, you and I," Aaron said, after he switched back to the general frequency. "And when I beat you, I'll have that 'Mech and the name of the man who sold it to you. You'll take your force back across the bridge, and you'll abide by the terms of the Accords." He stopped talking, waiting.

"And when I win?" the *Emperor*'s pilot asked.

"You won't."

"Nevertheless."

Aaron's lips drew back from his teeth. "Then you'll have killed a Gunslinger. How many Tauries can claim that?"

For most of a minute no one moved. Aaron watched the *Emperor*, watched its shoulders, trying to see the bunching of the myomers beneath the thick armor. If the Taurian decided to rush him, it would begin in the big 'Mech's broad shoulders.

The *Thug*'s alarms quieted. The Taurian BattleMechs relaxed, many of them settling back into still postures. Aaron released the breath he hadn't realized he was holding.

"I accept," the *Emperor*'s pilot said.

▲▼▲

Lieutenant Thomas Brake swore as his *Thug* took a final ponderous step inside the perimeter. He slapped the standby switch and dragged the heavy neurohelmet off his head. Normally it took several minutes to bring the assault 'Mech to a slumber, but Brake expected to be back in his cockpit quickly.

Major Talbert was waiting at the bottom of the chain ladder when Brake reached it. The officer had even held the bottom steady, making it easier for the MechWarrior to clamber down. Brake dropped the last meter to the ground and brought himself to attention. Two infantrymen, weapons at the ready, stood behind the major.

"Sir. As I reported by radio, there is a reinforced company of Taurian BattleMechs at the Elbe River Bridge. Captain Dane remained behind with the company to delay them while I warned you."

Talbert narrowed his eyes. "Is that so?"

"Major, we don't have time. I need to get back out there." Brake restrained himself from frowning. The rest of the battalion was already drawn out. The infantry squads were in formation off the side of the parade ground. The heavy rumbling of their APCs shook loose gravel on the field.

"Was there fighting?" Talbert asked.

"Not by the time I had left, sir," Brake said. He clenched his fists instead of frowning. His fingers, slick with sweat, slid along his palm until his fingernails cut painfully into the thick calluses on his hands.

"Then maybe there's still time," Talbert said. "Sergeant?"

The two infantrymen each took one step away from Major Talbert and snapped their rifles level. Brake did frown then, staring down the barrels of two assault rifles.

"Major?"

Talbert reached across delicately and slipped the compact laser pistol from Brake's holster. "You'll be detained, Lieutenant," he said. "Unless you choose to do something foolish."

"You're with *them*?"

AN ILL-MADE HOUSE

Handing the pistol to one of the infantrymen, Talbert stepped back and smiled. "I was born on New Vandenburg, Lieutenant, did you know?" The smiled slid away into a sneer. "I've been in this Army all my life. I've seen what's happened to my world. It can't be allowed to continue. If the Lords of the Inner Sphere can't be trusted to do right by us, we'll do right for ourselves."

"You swore the oath, Major," Brake said. "You know the motto. *I am the defender of the Star League; my strength is in loyalty.*"

"That's the thing, Brake," Talbert said, laughing. "The Star League didn't defend me."

▲▼▲

They faced off at three hundred meters, near the base of the floodwall at the edge of the river. Aaron held his *Thug* steady. His grip on the controls was firm. He'd turned the radio off, leaving only the gentle background hum of the *Thug*'s fusion engine. He breathed in, held it.

"See the enemy in front of you," he whispered. "Face him, and him alone. When he is defeated, then you may consider the next."

The *Emperor* raised both its arms and flashed ruby laser pulses to the sky. It was a show of bravado that Aaron didn't care to match. The *Thug* was a powerful 'Mech, but it surrendered ten tons to the *Emperor*. The Tiegart PPCs were some of the best in known space, but the *Emperor*'s big autocannon easily matched them. The pair of Bical short-range missile racks embedded in the *Thug*'s broad chest were reliable launchers, but the paltry missiles would merely pock and score the *Emperor*'s thick armor.

Aaron spread the *Thug*'s arms wide, held them there for a three-count, then let them fall to the *Thug*'s sides. He didn't waste his energy or his heat sinks in pointless displays.

"See the enemy in front of you," he whispered.

The *Emperor* stepped to the right and brought its arms up together. The large lasers mated to the cannon barrels flared to life, washing coherent light across the armor over the *Thug*'s left leg and left torso. The cannon remained silent.

Aaron leaned the eighty-ton assault 'Mech forward and charged off to his right. He brought his left arm to bear and fired. The PPC bolt scored high on the *Emperor*'s chest, splashing melted armor to the dusty ground and sending silver-white static discharges snaking over the *Emperor*'s shoulder. Already the *Emperor* had the better of the exchange, but Aaron remained confident.

The rest of his company stood half a kilometer back, in front of the Pass. The sole remaining officer, Lieutenant Velasquez of C Lance, stood at the forefront. Aaron knew she wanted to be Gunslinger. She'd be watching.

The Taurians had formed a half-circle. The light lance was actually standing on the Bridge, but the heavier units were spread in an arc in front of it. The lead 'Mech was a flat-black *Guillotine*.

A burst of cannon fire skittered across the *Thug*'s left side, probing. A few of the heavy slivers gouged divots from the tough armor, but the majority missed the moving 'Mech and dug into the ground. A single laser flickered past, refracting in the thrown dust.

Aaron dodged the *Thug* left, back toward the *Emperor*. He triggered both SRM racks, more to keep the *Emperor*'s pilot occupied than to cause any damage. He wanted the Taurian overconfident, thinking he had the Gunslinger in the lighter 'Mech on the run.

He had the edge. The *Emperor* outmassed him. The *Emperor* outgunned him. Those were Aaron's *advantages*. He was faster. He ran cooler. The *Thug* was packed with heat sinks, enough to cool even the ravenous heat loads of dual PPCs.

"Face him," Aaron whispered.

Inertia shoved him against his five-point harness as he stopped the *Thug* in its tracks. The *Emperor*, tracking him as he moved, stumbled and turned ponderously, trying to correct its aim. Aaron snarled and squeezed his triggers.

Both PPCs unleashed their azure fury against the thick torso armor over the *Emperor*'s heart. Aaron shouted in triumph and shoved the *Thug* into motion. That was his target.

The price the *Emperor* paid for all those weapons was the massive extralight engine buried beneath all that armor. Breach any one place and he could knock the bulky shielding away.

A double-blast of discarding-sabot autocannon shot scraped at the armor over his *Thug*'s right side. A yellow warning indicator flashed to life on his wireframe schematic. One of the shots had breached his armor, but luckily missed hitting anything vital.

"Deal with him," Aaron ground out, tugging the *Thug* into a staggering zig-zag. "Before he deals with me."

▲▼▲

For the seventh time Brake glanced to either side, judging the odds of getting one of the infantryman's weapons. His *Thug* stood motionless

on the parade field, still active on standby. Talbert had no MechWarriors to put in it.

"Damn," Talbert said. Silver light reflected off of the low-hanging clouds toward the Bridge Pass. The rumble of cannon fire echoed up the fissure. "He's fighting."

"He's doing his duty," Brake said.

They were on the parapet overlooking the main gate to Fort James Miller. Talbert turned away from the vista and faced Brake.

"I wanted to do this without bloodshed, Lieutenant," Talbert said. "There is more than enough force in Haganau to force our 'surrender.' No one at Division would fault an infantry battalion and a detached company of 'Mechs for giving in to a full 'Mech battalion."

"Thanks for the intel, Talbert," Brake said, forcing himself to smile. "I'll be sure to tell the S-2, when I see him."

The infantrymen shifted, taking a step back. Clearing a field of fire, Brake realized.

Talbert stepped close. "Careful, League man."

Brake forced another grin. He hoped it hid the shaking in his hands.

▲▼▲

The *Emperor* stepped close and hit Aaron's *Thug* with its lasers. The two large beamers on the *Emperor's* arms dug deeply into the already-pitted armor over the *Thug's* chest. The mediums dug and needled and succeeded in penetrating the last bit of protection over his left arm. Warning alarms announced the immobilization of his left elbow actuator.

Aaron clutched in his controls and twisted the *Thug* as far as its waist would pivot. At the apex of the turn he rippled both his SRM racks. The fat-bodied missiles barely cleared the launch frame before detonating against the shredded armor over the *Emperor's* heart. Explosions added scorch marks to the already-PPC-blackened tatters.

A flicker in the corner of his eye caught Aaron's attention. He glanced right, at the secondary display he'd set to thermal imaging. A new point of light blossomed and began leaking wispy trails on the *Emperor's* left side.

"Finally," Aaron muttered. He charged the *Thug* past the staggering *Emperor*, trying to get behind it. He wasn't trying to get at the weaker rear armor—by now, he'd smashed the frontal armor to practically nothing—but just out of the Taurian's zone of attention for a moment.

Dazzling light flickered in his display. Aaron looked behind him. He cursed. His right hand dove for the throttle even as his left was shoving forward.

The *Emperor* jumped.

In SLDF circles, it was called a "death from above," or sometimes a Highlander Burial. The 90-ton assault 'Mech called a *Highlander* was famous for leaping into the air and smashing unwary foes to the ground by simple mass. It was one of the most dramatic and damaging attacks a 'Mech could make. It played wonderfully on entertainment holos across known space.

It was one of the first maneuvers Gunslingers were taught to counter.

The Taurian pilot twisted his battered 'Mech in the air, bringing the *Emperor*'s still-imposing front to bear. He feathered his jets, accounted for the *Thug*'s speed, and cut the power. Ninety tons of BattleMech fell out of the sky from almost sixty meters in the air.

The *Thug* stopped moving. Aaron let his 'Mech fall to one knee, dragging it against the ground to slow the fast-moving machine. It appeared as though the *Thug* stopped and knelt, as if in supplication. Aaron used his momentum to pivot the *Thug* on its knee. The action shredded armor, but brought the 'Mech around enough that he could bring one arm to bear.

The *Emperor* sailed overhead and landed where the *Thug* should have been.

"Deal with him," Aaron whispered, "and then move on to the next." His hands moved, whip-like.

The *Thug* leapt upright as if propelled by rockets. The battered left arm came up with the 'Mech, burying itself in the *Emperor*'s right chest. The already-savaged armor over the *Emperor*'s heart shuddered, stressed, and shattered. The *Thug*'s fist sunk into the *Emperor*'s chest cavity.

Aaron's thermal display flashed white and then faded. Other sensors sounded as the *Emperor* began to collapse. With the loss of its shielding, the fusion engine had gone into emergency shutdown.

It was over.

"I want you across the river as soon as you've recovered this man," Aaron sent to the black *Guillotine*. He used the *Thug*'s right fist to point down to the *Emperor*'s cockpit, where the Taurian pilot was clambering out of a battered cockpit hatch.

"You're letting them go?" Blakely blurted.

"At ease, Sergeant," Lieutenant Velasquez said, before Aaron could answer. "The Challenge is over."

"We'll just be back tomorrow," the *Guillotine*'s pilot said.

"We'll still be here," Aaron said. He waited, his *Thug*'s armor still smoking and pinging, until the last Taurian BattleMech crossed the bridge. Then he turned his 'Mech toward the Pass.

"Where the hell is the cavalry?" he asked.

▲▼▲

Brake saw the motion at the mouth of the Pass, but someone pointed it out to Talbert almost immediately. The major leaned across the parapet, holding a pair of rangefinder binoculars to his eyes.

"Dane," he spat, and turned away.

The wide shoulders of the captain's *Thug* gradually rose above the level of the ground. Even from a kilometer away Brake could see the damage to the Gunslinger's 'Mech. Its armor was blackened and its left arm hung at an angle. The assault 'Mech's stride was off, but Brake couldn't tell if that was actuator or myomer damage.

"What now?" he asked.

Talbert turned back. He handed the binoculars to a nearby infantryman and pulled his helmet on. "Now we move ahead of schedule."

Brake smiled, a real smile, not a false one like he'd worn before. "You laid the odds out earlier, Talbert. A battalion of infantry against a company of 'Mechs." The rest of the company appeared behind Dane's *Thug*. They were trailing at a respectful distance, keeping their speed down to match their commander's. A lump rose in Brake's throat, full of pride in his troopers.

"We may be infantry," Talbert said, "but we've got big guns." He brought his communicator around and adjusted it. "Welcome the conquering heroes, Captain," he said.

The rumble of ferrocrete moving on ferrocrete was all the warning Brake had to steel himself before the massive quad PPC turret atop the wall pivoted and fired.

▲▼▲

"Jesus Christ," Hernandez shouted. "I've got red lights everywhere! Cease fire, you idiots!"

Aaron was adjusting the frequency on his radios. He began to broadcast on the emergency channel. "Cease fire! Blue on blue! Cease fire!" He checked his transponder, saw that it was broadcasting his SLDF identification codes.

The rest of the company slowed to a halt, each *Thug* reacting according to its pilot. Blakely's arms were leveled. Velasquez saw it almost as soon as Aaron did and began shouting at him on the lance channel.

"Fort James Miller, Fort James Miller," Aaron said. "Hold your fire, we're friendlies." His fingers brought his targeting system online without having to be told. He frowned at the targeting reticles that appeared on his HUD. He reached for the control to turn them back to standby.

The Fort fired again.

Hernandez swore. Aaron looked for him in his HUD. The *Thug* was down, struggling to rise. The act was made more difficult by the lack of its right arm. The limb had been severed cleanly at the shoulder. It was sparking on the ground a few meters from Hernandez's thrashing feet.

"Back to the Pass!" Aaron ordered. His hands steadied on the weapons controls. He centered his target pipper on the turret and waited, controlling his breathing.

"It's got armor," he told himself, and fired his right-arm PPC. The ion packet wasn't as dazzlingly brilliant as the fort's fire, but it spent itself on the turret's thick frontal armor.

Velasquez had most of the rest of the company already retreating down the incline. Aaron turned his *Thug* and brought it to where Hernandez was still trying to rise. He reached down and grabbed the damaged *Thug*'s shoulder. A wrenching lift that made his actuators scream brought the recalcitrant machine to its feet. He shoved it toward the rest of the company.

"Captain Dane," a voice said.

"Major Talbert?" Aaron twisted his *Thug*'s torso. Magnification showed him people on the Fort's parapet, but he was too far away to identify faces without more magnification than he had time for. "Sir, the eastern PPC turret is firing on my company!"

"Do not approach this fort, Captain," Talbert said.

"Our transponders are active," Aaron said. "Just order them not to fire."

"Any Star League forces that approach this Fort will be fired upon."

The sounds of his cockpit fell away. The blood drained from his face. Aaron leaned closer to his screen, adjusting his magnification. Talbert's face swam into view. He saw the officer holding a field communicator.

"As of this moment, Fort James Miller is a Taurian Defense Force facility. The Star League is no longer necessary nor welcome."

The smug son of a bitch was smiling.

"You traitorous bastard," Aaron said. "You think you can hold that box from me and mine?" His hands twitched on the controls. The *Thug* took a half-step forward.

Alarms sprang to life again as long-range missile batteries swept targeting scanners across him. A small indicator on his HUD showed the estimated recharge time for the quad-PPC battery almost expired. Rage filled his heart but his fingers obeyed his mind.

The *Thug* stepped back.

▲▼▲

Thomas Brake watched the captain's *Thug* begin to retreat. He'd heard Dane's voice, tinny as it was over the major's communicator. The anger was palpable. Deep in his mind something clicked.

Taking a long step to the side, Brake brought his right arm up and dove his elbow just beneath the helmet of one of the infantrymen. The trooper gagged as his trachea was bruised, dropping his rifle and grabbing his throat. Brake caught the falling weapon and stabbed the butt-end back into the trooper's face. The man fell back, his body blocking two more infantrymen who were just starting to move.

Dropping to one knee, Brake reversed the rifle. The stock fell into his shoulder as the barrel came up, and he snugged it tight. Talbert was turning, the communicator still held by his ear. His eyes were widening.

Brake brought the sights up. He notched the forepost between Talbert's eyes. His finger squeezed, gently, as he'd been taught in basic training.

Another rebel infantryman tackled him from the side. The three-round burst missed Talbert's head and instead simply plucked at the sleeve of his uniform. A rough-callused hand pushed his face to the cool ferrocrete while more hands pulled the rifle away from him.

"Stand him up," Talbert said. He lowered the communicator and stuck a finger through the tear in his sleeve. His eyes almost glowed when he looked up, staring at Brake as four infantrymen lifted him to his feet.

Brake sighed, a soft exhalation that took with it all the tension in his body. He blinked, held his eyes closed, and opened them slowly. The mesa was beautiful, he realized.

"Watch this," Talbert said into his communicator. The laser pistol he'd confiscated from Brake appeared in his hand. Brake stared at it. He focused his eyes on the needlepoint-sized aperture. He thought of his wife and daughter. In his mind he felt the smoothness of his wife's skin. He smelled the soft soapy musk of his daughter fresh from the bath.

There was a flash of light.

▲▼▲

Aaron's knuckles were white on the *Thug*'s controls. His throat was raw, burning with each breath as his chest heaved. The cockpit still rang with the echoes of his scream as the rebels pushed Brake's body over the parapet. It slithered like a limp doll down the wall and out of view.

"Captain," Velasquez said, "we have to go. There are still 'Mechs in our backfield."

"Sons of bitches," Blakely said. His voice was trembling.

"Accept that you can't deal with me and escape, Dane," Talbert said. "I control the Fort and the Plateau. My compatriots control Haganau. Withdraw." The carrier-hum popped as the rebel officer terminated the connection. Aaron watched them file off the parapet and into the fort.

He brought his *Thug* around, turning his back on the fort. The missile-tracking alarms were still blaring, but he knew he'd have sufficient time to get his stronger armor toward the missiles before they reached him. The screech of the *Thug*'s damaged actuators echoed though the 'Mech's body.

"What are you doing, sir?" Blakely asked. With Brake's death, he was the senior sergeant in B Lance. Aaron found the correct *Thug* in his wraparound display and stared at it for a moment.

"There's a satellite relay in Haganau." The *Thug*'s first few steps down the Pass were prophetic. He stumbled, straining his already-weakened knee actuator further. Too much more stress and the joint would seize. "We're going to get word of this to the Fleet."

With the General himself on New Vandenburg, the SLDF Navy presence in-system was huge. Aside from the General's flagship, there were three more *McKenna*s present, and a host of frigates and support craft. A signal strong enough to bounce out of the atmosphere would reach one of them.

"What about the Fort?" Hernandez asked.

Velasquez answered before he could. "We'll be back, Sergeant." Her voice was even but tight with emotion. "Count on it."

The company cleared the Pass in short order. A Taurian salvage crew had already descended on the corpse of the *Emperor*. They looked up when Velasquez's *Thug* marched into view. By the time Blakely was leading B Lance out of the Pass, they were scrambling toward their hovercraft. Aaron exited the Pass in time to see the light craft racing down the river, its huge fans ripping roostertails from the shallow wavetops.

"Across the bridge and into town," Aaron said. The *Thug*s queued up; the bridge wouldn't support their mass together. In pairs they dashed across the span, carefully out of step to avoid any resonance.

"And then?" Blakely asked.

"We split up. Half of you will come with me to the Civic Center. There's a transmitter at the militia base on the other side of town. They'll expect us to try for that one. They won't know about the back-up in the Civic Center." Aaron waited until the rest of the 'Mechs were across and then crossed himself.

"Unless Talbert told them," he whispered. As a field-grade officer, Talbert had the clearance to know about the backups; whether or not he'd ever looked it up or shared it with his Taurian friends was another matter.

"Velasquez," he said, stepping onto the Taurian side of the river, "take your lance and Harlow and Garrett from Blakely. I want you to roam about town, watching for flankers. I'm going to drive right to the Center. They'll know where we're going once they spot us. It's your job to slow the reaction." He paused. "Blakely, you'll come with me." The eleven *Thug*s stood still for a moment. "We'll get word to the General about Talbert's treachery," Aaron said. "Once we've got some support, we'll go back and root that bastard out." He started his *Thug* moving. The tracks of the 'Mechs that had retreated earlier mixed with his. The buildings of Haganau loomed in the distance.

"Simple orders, troopers," he said. "If it moves on you, kill it."

Haganau
New Vandenburg
Taurian Concordat
4 February 2765

Zoning in Haganau had limited the buildings to a height of thirty meters. Aaron Dane's slender column moved slowly down an avenue, the ferrocrete crunching beneath their feet. He'd let Blakely lead, knowing that the hothead would have a light finger on the trigger but not caring. No one else was trained, and his *Thug* was in no condition to flush an ambush after the duel with the *Emperor*.

The streets were deserted. It was early evening. Aaron has spent several nights just like this one in town, carousing with the locals and enjoying some rest. It was strange to be on the same streets without the people. He imagined they'd heard the sounds of the battle earlier and fled inside the shelters.

"No contacts, Captain," Blakely reported. His *Thug* was paused at an intersection. "Two klicks to the objective."

"Keep moving," he said.

They'd gone a half a kilometer further before the sky lit up to the east with reflected weapons fire. Aaron turned his head in time to see a barrage of PPC fire lance skyward. Several of the beams must have intersected a low-flying aircraft, because a yellow-white explosion lit the clouds.

"The word's out, Captain," Velasquez said. Her transmission was splotchy, reflected through so many buildings and alleyways in spite of the Taurian jamming.

"Shoot and scoot, Lieutenant," Aaron said. "I want them chasing you, not me."

"Roger that, sir."

"Almost a klick, sir," Blakely said.

The last kilometer passed without incident. From the direction of the lights, Aaron figured that Velasquez was leading her pursuers around to the north, toward the small spaceport. He smiled, envisioning the six *Thug*s lumbering down the narrow streets, Taurians in pursuit.

"Here's the plan," Aaron said, planting his *Thug* in front of the Civic Center and beginning his standby checklist. "Blakely will accompany me into the building. The rest of you stay buttoned up and scanning. If you're attacked, hold this ground until we get back."

As soon as he got the neurohelmet racked on the shelf above his head, Aaron slapped his five-point harness and climbed stiffly out of his command couch. He pulled a flat olive vest from beneath his seat and slipped it over his cooling suit. A web belt with a pistol and two fragmentation grenades went around his waist. He adjusted the pistol until it was near his right hand and then climbed out onto the *Thug*'s shoulder.

Blakely was waiting for him when he reached the ground. The other MechWarrior was dressed the same, but he carried a small sub-

machine gun instead of a pistol. When Aaron raised an eyebrow at it he shrugged.

"Quantity over quality," he said. "Shall we?"

The Civic Center was a squat gray building with a marble façade, the sort of building that had been built during the Reconstruction to house the Bureau of Star League Affairs offices during the Occupation. The eighty-meter-square building projected a squat but permanent presence. It fit the surrounding architecture enough to blend, but its sheer monolithic size made it stand out, exactly as its designers had intended. It was more than twice as tall as any other building in the city; Star League planners didn't care about zoning.

The double-glass doors on the front were locked, but they had missed the carousel. Blakely led, holding his submachine gun muzzle-up while the glass frame spun him through. No one waited inside as Aaron stepped through, but yellow emergency lights were flashing sickly shadows against the wall.

"Where to?" Blakely asked. He had the extendable stock of his gun braced against his shoulder, but the muzzle pointed safely at the floor.

Aaron pointed. "The stairs. The relay will be in the basement, in the chapel." The pair started toward the stairs. They eschewed the elevators, as they'd been taught, mindful of being trapped in a steel box suspended by cables.

"The chapel?" Blakely asked.

"The SLDF always hid transmitters in the BSLA buildings," Aaron said. They took the metal-grate stairs as quietly as their heavy Mech-Warrior boots would allow. "In case a garrison got overrun during the Occupation. Units trapped without orbit coms could infiltrate the Affairs buildings and get help."

"I never heard that," Blakely said. He reached the bottom stair and held up a clenched fist, listening. The only sounds were the gentle echoes of their footsteps going up the stairwell. "You think it's still here?"

Aaron drew his pistol and motioned at the door. "No reason it shouldn't be." He held a finger to his lips until Blakely nodded, then cracked the door.

Air rushed into the stairwell, damp air heavy with the cloying dankness of mold and office detritus. Aaron leaned out and looked both ways, but the corridor was deserted. A small white cross, half the fluorescent bulbs flickering, flashed at them from halfway down the corridor.

"Let's go," he said.

Blakely followed him through the door, watching the corridor behind them. Aaron waited as the sergeant turned back to latch the door behind them, gently pushing it shut with the clasp held open.

A door slammed from around the corner at the end of the corridor.

"Move," Aaron snapped. He sprinted toward the chapel, pistol at the ready. The floor was thick with scattered paper and slick spots of fungus. He shouldered the door to the chapel open and lunged in, Blakely right on his heels. Aaron slid down the wall beside the door, holding the pistol at his side.

"Two people," Blakely whispered. He pulled the bolt of his submachine gun just far enough to see a bullet chambered before sliding it closed with a gentle snick.

Footsteps echoed, the sounds sharpening and the fading as the two people walked past. Aaron closed his eyes and sighed, letting the pistol fall to his lap. Blakely relaxed from his crouch on the other side of the door.

"They'll see the 'Mechs," he said.

Aaron grunted and shoved himself to his feet. He holstered his pistol and pulled the two grenades from his belt. Blakely reached out and grasped them like they were eggs. "Watch the door," Aaron said, and turned into the chapel proper.

"Hurry," Blakely said.

A small altar stood at the front of the room. Alcoves littered the walls, each of them devoted to a particular faith. The Star League allowed religious freedom, and the Camerons had wisely built pandenominational chapels. One alcove in each, however, boasted no icons or idols; only a simple Cameron Star mounted on the wall, a place for men and women of no firm religion to contemplate their place in the galaxy. To ask a higher power for help, if need be. Aaron touched the points of the Star in a precise order. He had a very specific higher power to speak with.

The Star slid silently into the ceiling, revealing a small dust-covered screen and keyboard. The screen flickered to life, scattering green raster lines across its surface before settling on a blinking cursor.

▲▼▲

Gabriella Velasquez tasted blood on her lips and laughed, imagining what she must look like. When she'd been a teenager, her friends had always dressed her up like a vampire. With her full lips and pale skin, it had taken very little makeup. She licked the coppery taste away and swallowed.

"Two more, from the west," Hernandez said.

"Grover, Paulson," she said. "Take them."

The two least-battered *Thug*s in her force turned left, toward the still-glowing sky where the sun had set, and rippled off four PPC shots in as many seconds.Their cyan brightness illuminated the slinking forms of two Taurian medium 'Mechs. One pair of lightning strikes found the lightly-armored torso of the left *Sentinel*, burying themselves deeply in the Defiance-built 'Mechs's heart. The other pair missed, exploding the hardened ferrocrete a dozen meters behind. One of the Taurian 'Mechs raised its right-arm autocannons and fired. Grover's *Thug* took the full barrage in the chest. He stutter-stepped the eighty-ton 'Mech and shook off the damage.

The *Sentinel*s split down opposite side streets.

"How bloody long does it take to send a message?" Garrett asked. His *Thug* was backstopping the force, two blocks behind them and backing slowly their way.

"As long as it takes," Velasquez said. She wondered the same thing.

"I read two more lances coming behind the skirmishers," Hernandez said. He'd climbed his *Thug* up a parking structure to give his sensors greater range. With one arm—and one PPC—gone, he was more useful as a spotter than a shooter.

Velasquez called up a map of the city and squinted at it for a moment. "Shift west six blocks." Her finger traced a route through the buildings. "There's a viaduct that runs right past the Civic Center and out of the city. We'll pick up the Captain and get out of here."

"There are rebel 'Mechs to the west," Paulson said. Static slithered through the signal as he fired his PPC. "Two *Sentinel*s, plus whatever Hernandez is scanning."

Velasquez turned her *Thug* down an alley. The last of the sun's light faded from the sky, leaving only the gray overcast sky that hid the stars above them. Her 'Mech's broad shoulders scraped gouges in the buildings to either side. A fire escape squealed and fell.

"Like the captain said," she murmured. "If it gets in our way, put it down hard."

▲▼▲

The error tone beeped again. Blakely hissed at him from the door. Aaron turned away from the screen, muttering a curse under his breath, and watched Blakely pull the door open a crack and peek out.

"Company," Blakely mouthed.

Aaron tapped in a final code and twisted away from the console. His pistol slid silently out of its holster. He crouched, the pistol muzzle-down between his knees, with his thumb on the safety.

"-League 'Mechs outside," Aaron heard a woman's voice say.

"We should call the base and let them know," a man said.

Blakely gently slid the door closed and shuffled backwards, keeping his submachine gun pointed at the door. The sound of the pair's footsteps echoed again, rising in sharpness and decibel. Aaron held his breath, willing them to walk past.

The console behind him pinged with an open channel.

"Shit," he whispered, turning away from the door. A green cursor was blinking again, waiting for him to type his destination and message. He holstered his pistol and spun in place.

The door latch clicked. They were coming in.

"Don't shoot," Aaron said. He looked around, his head swinging back and forth, until he found what he was looking for. He dove across the dirty floor, sliding on the dust and debris, until he reached his objective.

A slender man in a red jogging suit leaned through the door. He frowned, peering around, until he looked at the Cameron alcove. The console's green screen was casting bilious light across the chapel.

"What's that?" he asked, and stepped inside. A slender woman in a matching outfit followed him in. Blakely didn't move, hidden behind the door. He poked it with his toe as soon as the woman cleared it, starting it closed.

Aaron waited until they were halfway down the aisle. He nodded to Blakely and stood up, pistol leveled. "Don't move," he said.

To their credit, neither made a sound. The woman gasped and took a step back. The man stepped protectively in front of the woman, keeping an arm behind him while he held her wrist. "Who are you?" he asked, his voice sharp.

"Captain Aaron Dane, Star League Defense Force," he said. The door clicked closed behind the couple. The woman jumped, still holding her hands in front of her face. The man glanced behind him. He saw Blakely.

Aaron tossed the electrical extension cord he'd found to Blakely. "Tie them up," he said, and turned away. The open connection cursor blinked steadily at him.

Hernandez died when the black *Guillotine* found them. They were six blocks from the Civic Center, close enough for the green icons of the rest of the company stationed around the squat building to appear on Velasquez's tactical display. Hernandez was just behind Velasquez in the center of the column when proximity alarms squealed to life. Warnings from the rest of the company were too late; the heavy Taurian 'Mech dropped from the sky on flaming jets, its lasers and missiles already firing as it fell.

Hernandez tried to turn, but the damaged *Thug* was too slow. Hungry red lasers cut deeply into the already-shattered armor on his side. Velasquez brought her own 'Mech to a halt and yanked on her controls. Eighty tons of BattleMech didn't turn on a dime.

"Damn it," Hernandez said. His remaining PPC flared to life, driving a sizzling ion lance down the empty street. It was nowhere near the attacking 'Mech, but it showed his struggle.

The *Guillotine*'s missiles tracked where the lasers had already stalked, disappearing into the gaping wound on the *Thug*'s torso. Smoke and debris exploded outward when the warheads detonated, one after the other. A rippling, crackling screech of pain rang across the radio, and the *Thug* exploded.

"Take him down!" Velasquez shouted.

The *Guillotine* shrugged off the shockwave of Hernandez's death and twisted its torso to face Velasquez. The shutters over the six-round missile launcher flicked open again, white-painted warheads prominent. Wisps of bone-white steam leaked from the laser apertures. Velasquez snarled, holding her controls hard over, willing the ponderous *Thug* to turn.

Four PPCs took the *Guillotine* clear in the back. Garret and Grover, who'd been bringing up the rear of the column, caught the Taurian killer in a deadly web of fire. Velasquez shouted in triumph as her targeting crosshairs finally crept across the staggering 'Mech. She squeezed all her triggers.

The *Guillotine* jumped.

"Damn you!" she called as the black 'Mech disappeared back the way it had come. Her fire destroyed the façade of a building behind the *Guillotine*'s last position.

"Do we pursue?" Paulson asked.

"We do not," Velasquez said. She said her next words through grinding teeth. "We keep moving."

Hernandez's shattered *Thug* lay across the pavement, half buried in a collapsed building. Smoke belched from half a dozen places, sweeping down the avenues in death-colored whorls.

The *Thug*s marched past.

▲▼▲

Location received, the green-tinted screen read. *Situation*?

Aaron closed his eyes briefly. The officer on the other end of this communication sounded like he was in a hurry. Opening his eyes, Aaron swallowed the lump in his throat and typed a single word.

Turncoats.

"You can't just keep us here," the woman in the red jogging suit said. She and the man were tied roughly together, back to back, on the floor in the aisle. Blakely stood near the door, his weapon pointed toward them but his attention on the corridor. "We're just civilians."

Aaron ignored them. He watched the screen. *Understood*, it read. *Rendezvous resupply these coordinates.* Aaron read off the string of numbers and concentrated. That was back across the river, at the base of the plateau, almost exactly where he'd begun this hellish day. Another short order appeared, and Aaron nodded. It made sense.

Aaron pondered asking for more information for a moment, but then decided against it. If the other end had more information to offer, they'd have sent it. He bent to the keyboard and typed another parting word.

Strength. The reply came back almost immediately.

Loyalty.

"Let's go," Aaron said. He left the alcove open and walked past the two civilians without pause. Blakely raised an eyebrow, but Aaron shook his head. "Leave them," he said.

The woman's shouts echoed in the corridor as they ran for their 'Mechs.

▲▼▲

There were nine other green icons on Aaron's display as he settled his neurohelmet back onto his shoulders. He did a quick headcount and toggled a discrete channel to Velasquez. "Hernandez?" he asked.

"Dead," came the wooden reply.

Aaron clenched his jaw. "Let's go," he said, after a pause.

"Where are we going, sir?" Blakely asked. The sergeant's voice was tinny; he must still be getting his own helmet settled. His *Thug* lurched into motion, its limbs moving with an ungainly lack of coordi-

nation; characteristic signs that the pilot had pushed the machine into movement while his neurocircuits were still warming up.

"Back the way we came," Aaron said. He started his own *Thug* into motion. The company fell into a rough column of march, with the relatively unscathed A Lance 'Mechs in the lead. "Back across the river to a meet with a resupply ship, and then we're going back to the Fort."

"What about the Taurians?" Paulson asked.

"Burn 'em," he said. "We look to our own house first."

No one asked what would happen if the rebels tried to stop the SLDF company from crossing the river again. By now everyone knew the orders for that situation.

The arches of the Elbe River Bridge appeared out of the inky darkness after what seemed too short a time. Garret, in the rear of the column, reported in-and-out sensor contacts with trailing Taurian 'Mechs, but none of them came close enough to engage. Even battered as they were, ten Star League *Thug*s were a force too strong to attack piecemeal. Aaron knew they'd wait until the SLDF troopers had crossed the bridge, and then try and rush them *en masse*.

Again, Aaron was the last one across the bridge. His creaking *Thug* shuffled across the mighty span and stepped around the banking abutments. He stopped, and the rest of the company stopped around him.

"They're coming," Velasquez said. Her voice was weary, as if the thought of another combat so soon weighed on her. It had been almost twenty hours since they'd left on patrol.

"Company," Aaron said, on a general frequency. Unencrypted, so any Taurian listeners could hear. "Volley fire, PPC," he ordered. The remaining *Thug*s raised their arms.

"Target the bridge," he said, and fired.

Every trooper shifted aim and fired before their brains caught up with the order. In *Thug* battalions, the volley-fire order was ingrained in every trooper from day one. Seventeen PPCs struck at the thick bridge members. The heavy steel and ferrocrete deformed beneath the barrage, shaking and groaning until it collapsed into the steaming waters of the Elbe.

"Company," he said after the rumbling subsided, "volley fire, cease fire."

"Jesus, Mary, and Joseph," someone muttered on the company channel.

"I guess we're not going back that way," Blakely said.

Aaron checked to make sure he was still on the open frequency. "When we go back," he said, "we'll have company."

By the time the Taurian BattleMechs made it to the wreckage of the bridge, the company was half a kilometer away.

▲▼▲

The *Union*-class DropShip the fleet had sent had repair berths and technicians for a full BattleMech company. The lack of a full complement meant that Aaron Dane's company was repaired and rearmed slightly ahead of schedule. The MechWarriors, Aaron included, had caught a precious ten hours of sleep while the technicians repaired the 'Mechs. All ten were now ready.

It was up to Aaron to make the troops ready. The nine MechWarriors of the company were drawn up in a line in the main 'Mech bay. Behind them, the technicians were sealing a final armor plate back onto Aaron's *Thug*.

"It's flaring up," he said. He stood in front of them, in a fresh jumpsuit taken from the DropShip's lockers. It was an empty jumpsuit, with no rank insignia, no decorations, not even a name tape. The only marking on its drab-green surface was a Cameron Star on the shoulder. It suited Aaron perfectly.

"Right now, rebel Taurian troops are overrunning our positions in Vandenburg City and all across the planet. Current intelligence estimates two full divisions of Taurian 'Mechs are on-world." He paused for a moment to let that sink in. A full division of BattleMechs would be nine regiments and change; two divisions meant the rebels had almost two thousand BattleMechs on New Vandenburg.

"We don't know where they came from," he said. "Secret factories deeper in the Periphery would be my bet." He sniffed and rolled his shoulders. "I don't really care."

"What concerns me most are the traitors in Fort James Miller. The bastards that shot Thom." He saw the body slip down the wall again in his mind. "We've got our orders from Division; we're going to take out Talbert and his men, and deny the fort to the rebels."

"Take out?" Velasquez asked.

Aaron looked her in the eye. "We're to reduce the fort to slag, Lieutenant. We won't be reoccupying it."

"Then we've lost? We're pulling out?" Blakely asked.

"No," Aaron told him. "We're moving on. Once we've dealt with Talbert, the rest of the battalion will be dropped in." He rubbed his

hands together, looking each of his MechWarriors in the eye. "Then we're going after the rebels."

An hour later, the *Union* was nothing more than a rapidly-diminishing spark in the sky, and ten Star League *Thug*s were marching toward the Bridge Pass.

▲▼▲

Major Talbert stood on the parade field, looking up at the empty *Thug* still idling there. The irony of the situation did not escape him. Despite his preparations, there was no one available who could pilot the powerful machine. Not even the Star League technicians, who'd refused to even shut down the machine.

Even after he shot three of them.

"Sir!" He turned at the shout. "'Mechs!"

He reached the parapet in less than a minute. By the time he could see over the lip of the armor, there were ten *Thug*s standing at the edge of the Pass. He snatched the binoculars from a sentry.

Fresh welds gleamed from several of the 'Mechs. Talbert played the binoculars across each 'Mech, hoping, until he came to the assault 'Mech in the center.

Paired six-shooters gleamed in the afternoon light.

"Damn it," Talbert whispered.

▲▼▲

"I can see the quad PPC," Blakely said. "It's active." His *Thug* was the closest 'Mech to the Fort. The technicians on the DropShip had tested each 'Mech's sensor suite carefully, and Blakely had come back the best. He was the company's eyes.

"There's no reason to think any of the active defenses are down," Velasquez said. "Talbert was always a stickler for maintenance." Aaron heard the snarl in her voice. "We'll have to take down the whole Fort."

Aaron relaxed a moment in his cockpit. A touch on his triggers bounced a rangefinder laser off the Fort's thick walls: 902 meters. Well beyond range of everything except artillery, and there were no cannons at Fort James Miller. He closed his eyes, centering himself. He touched a control.

"Talbert," he said.

Nothing.

"You know you can't escape."

Static screeched across the frequency. The quad PPC turret erupted in scintillating light, but the burst was tens of meters off; the *Thug*s were too far away.

"It'll cost you to come and get me," Talbert said.

Aaron grinned inside his neurohelmet. "Not as much as it'll cost you." He straightened in his seat, adjusting the tension on his five-point harness until he was snug. "The Star League does not tolerate traitors," he said.

Talbert's mocking laughter filled the frequency. Alarms pinged mutely at him—he'd disabled the audibles—with multicolored lights as distant targeting scanners played over him. "Is that all you have? Rhetoric?"

Aaron reached forward and took the controls of his assault 'Mech. The machine trembled with controlled power. The technicians had done a good job. The fresh-burnt tang of new lubricant penetrated his cockpit, but he ignored it.

"I've finished the formalities," Aaron said. "You will pay for Brake. You will pay for what's about to happen." He pushed the *Thug* into a slow walk. The rest of the company moved to follow.

"Goodbye, Talbert," he said, and cut the connection.

▲▼▲

Talbert looked at the handset for a long moment. The heat shimmering across the plateau hid the advancing *Thug*s for instants at a time, making the ten hulking 'Mechs look like a wavering horde of SLDF hardware.

"Orders, sir?" The lieutenant standing next to him asked.

"Full commitment," Talbert said, still watching the advancing *Thug*s. "Everything that shoots better be shooting." He turned away from the view and retreated down the parapet. "I'm going to the TOC."

Engines roared in the parade field, kicking up swirling dust storms like half-made dervishes. Talbert shielded his eyes and found the man he was looking for. He made a ring motion with his left hand, and pointed toward the pass.

The wind intensified. The dust pattered against Talbert's back until the sentry pulled the heavy armored door closed behind him.

▲▼▲

"I'm getting something new," Blakely called.

"Ignore it," Aaron ordered. The range counted down to seven hundred meters. "Company, volley fire, PPC!" The Tiegarts came up.

"Target the quad," he said. He indicated the deadly PPC turret with his targeting pipper and then shot the image to the rest of his company. "Here's your point of aim."

Turrets on the flanks of the fort disappeared in clouds of dirty white smoke. Alarms blinked at Aaron from his console. "Incoming missiles," he said.

The *Thugs* continued their steady advance. The range fell down, six fifty... six hundred. The missiles barrage repeated, striking at the armor of *Thugs* all along the line. None of his troopers faltered.

This was what assault 'Mechs were made for. The *Thugs*' heavy armor shed the missile warheads with minimal damage. The slow-moving assault 'Mechs stayed in step. "Sixty meters to range," Aaron said, watching the numbers fall.

Five-fifty. Light autocannon fire began to scratch at the *Thugs* now, from turrets supporting the missiles. The quad PPC tracked left, until it seemed that all four barrels were peering into Aaron Dane's soul.

Five hundred forty meters. His targeting reticle flickered from black to gold. He squeezed the triggers.

Twenty Tiegart PPCs vented their master's fury on the most dangerous weapon in Talbert's arsenal. The heavily-armored box-shaped turret drank in the crackling particle streams. It glowed with an unholy light for what seemed like an eternity.

The turret exploded.

"Volley fire, cease fire!" Aaron called. "Independent fire! Silence the turrets, people!" He shifted his aim to the left, reaching for a smoke-shrouded missile launcher.

An alarm flashed at him. Aaron slapped the override without looking, reactivating the audible tones. Alerts shrieked at him. A scourge of red icons flashed at him from his tactical display.

"Choppers!" someone called on the company channel.

▲▼▲

The Taurian helicopters had flown in overnight, once the 'Mechs had reported the destruction of the bridge. Talbert had asked for reaction forces in case the SLDF made a push for the fort, and the squadron of VTOLs was all he got.

Twelve stolen Cyrano attack craft.

"Order the troops into the APCs," Talbert told his aide. He leaned over the plot table in the TOC, watching the repeaters as the SLDF 'Mechs broke their formation and began striking at the defense turrets.

He hadn't expected the concentrated attack on the quad PPC. The rest of the turrets were designed to supplement that heavy battery.

"You're not going to order infantry into that open field to face troops, Major!" the lieutenant said. Yet his mouth formed the orders as soon as he'd spat out that sentence, but still the disbelieving look stayed on his face.

"We're abandoning the fort," Talbert told him. "We'll use the hovers to cross the river and join the units in Haganau." A shudder shook dust free of the ceiling. It wafted through the thick air inside the TOC, glistening in the harsh fluorescent lighting.

"Then why send the helicopters?"

Talbert sighed and pushed past his aide, headed for the door. He'd seen all he came in to see. The ionization track on the evening's log was clear; a DropShip had come down during the night. That was where Dane had gotten his resupply. That meant the fleet knew of his defection. Which meant it was time to go, before the heavy forces fell from the sky to crush him in the open like an insect.

Behind him, speakers broadcast the first screeching scream of pain and told him the helicopters had engaged the Star League BattleMechs.

▲▼▲

Ruby-red light glared through the polarized ferroglass of Aaron's cockpit. He blinked steadily, trying to clear the afterimage from his eyes even has his hands brought the *Thug*'s big cannons to bear.

"A cannon to kill a fly," he muttered. A tone sounded in his helmet; gold flashed on his HUD. Aaron's finger drew in the slack on the trigger.

Blue-white lightning scoured the Cyrano from the sky.

"The gates are opening!" Velasquez shouted.

The heavy armored doors were indeed sliding apart. A slender hovercraft darted between them as soon as there was space, its fan screaming and kicking up a cloud of dust behind it. The APC dashed toward the Pass, ignoring the battle raging around it.

"Fort defenses neutralized," Paulson reported. A small, angry black-orange cloud billowed into the sky at the Fort's south point,

where a short-range missile battery had been worrying the *Thugs.*

"Rally on the gate!" Aaron called. He jerked his *Thug* away from the pyre of the Cyrano and pushed the throttle to its stops. "They're trying to break out!"

"Let them," Blakely said. "We've got the fort back."

Aaron lowered his targeting pipper on the speeding APC. It was almost out of range. The huge fans pushing the air-cushion vehicle across the plateau made it oscillate, giving the hovercraft a natural defense against fire. Aaron bobbed his head, tracking his guns back and forth.

He found the rhythm. He waited, half a breath held, and fired. One PPC, the opposite weapon from the one that had smashed the Taurian helicopter to the ground.

The bolt missed, leading the speeding APC by a dozen meters. The rocks absorbed the PPC bolt's tremendous heat and kinetic energy and promptly did what any matter given that much power would do. The rocks exploded.

Just as the hovercraft slipped over them.

"Watch for others," he said, watching the damaged APC spread itself across the landscape like a meteor fallen to the ground.

From the maw of the gate more hovercraft appeared, weapons blazing.

▲▼▲

"Go!" Talbert shouted. He leaned closer to the radio as the ramp at the rear of the APC rose, crowding the infantry squad packed in with him. "Get us moving, damn it!"

"They're waiting for us," the driver said.

Talbert dropped his handset and shouldered his way toward the front driving compartment. He drew the laser pistol at his waist and leveled it at the driver's helmeted head.

"Get us moving," he said. "Right now."

The deck shifted as the driver increased thrust to his fans. The APC lurched into motion and fell into line, the third vehicle from the end in the queue of screaming hovercraft waiting to run the gauntlet of Star League 'Mechs.

Talbert holstered his pistol and snatched at a radio handset. He twisted the dial until he found the channel he wanted. A roar cut through the keening wail of the fans as one of the Cyranos swooped low, lending its support.

"All choppers," Talbert said, craning his neck to peer out a gun slit. "Aim for the leader! Concentrate your fire and we might have a chance to get out of here.

"Kill the Gunslinger!"

▲▼▲

Aaron brought the *Thug* to a halt as he reached the halfway point between the Fort and the Pass entrance. The wreckage of half a dozen APCs was strewn behind him, the victims of deadly PPC fire from the other *Thug*s still converging on the area. He turned the *Thug* around and watched as the last three APCs exited the gates.

"Halt!" he broadcast. He brought the *Thug*'s arms up and spread them wide. "You can't get past me." He released one yoke and tapped a command into his weapons panel. Scatter shields on the *Thug*'s chest snapped open, unmasking the short-range missile launchers embedded there. The steady beeping of their seeker-heads searching for a target filled his cockpit.

New alarms screamed. Aaron looked up, blinked. There was a crashing roar, like a series of hammer blows against his 'Mech. He felt the *Thug* shift.

Darkness.

Only a moment's darkness, and he was rocking the *Thug* upright. His tactical display showed the nine remaining Cyranos banking around behind him for another pass.

"They're after you, Captain," Blakely said. His *Thug* was closest, and his Tiegarts threw great static-belching gouts of charged ions across the sky. "All of them."

Aaron sneezed, spattering blood in a fine mist across the faceplate of his helmet. He swung the fogged visor up in time to see the final trio of hovercraft bearing down on him.

He jerked his yokes, fighting the *Thug* to one knee. The beeping of the SRMs became a steady wail. He looked in his screen, eyeing the Cyranos. They were still closing. Aaron looked back at the hovers. Close enough. He squeezed the triggers, felt the telltale shiver as the missiles' exhaust washed across the *Thug*'s broad chest.

Then he stomped on his foot pedals and gritted his teeth, trying to throw the *Thug* out of the Cyranos' path. Red light flared in his HUD. The *Thug* shook. Something snapped in his cockpit, shooting sparks across his bare arms and exposed face. He felt the skin on his cheeks sting.

Then the *Thug* struck the ground, and the darkness rushed up to meet him.

▲▼▲

Talbert saw the wave of laser wash across the *Thug*'s chest. It rocked as armor exploded away from it beneath the lasers' caress. He clenched a fist and pounded it on the seat in front of him. His shout filled the APC as Dane's *Thug* fell.

"Not yet," the driver said, twisting his wheel.

Dane's *Thug* shuddered and sat up, bracing itself on one PPC-arm. Talbert screamed in frustration and raised the radio. "Hit him again!" he shouted.

"Two platoons report reaching the river," his aide said, listening to a slender handset that he held cupped on his shoulder. "The rest didn't make it."

"We'll make it," Talbert snarled. He dropped the handset and gripped the back of the driver's seat with both hands. "Get us past him, Sergeant," he said.

"Almost there," the driver whispered.

The *Thug* had made it to one knee. Through the windscreen Talbert saw the needle-shapes of the Cyranos banking around, diving toward the Gunslinger's 'Mech. Talbert's lips drew back in a snarl of contempt. The hubris it took to paint a giant target on a 'Mech amazed him. He stared at the crossed six-shooter insignia, burning it into his memory. He wanted to be able to recall it later, the exact details of seeing that famed art flash past, helpless to stop him.

His eyes narrowed. Something was wrong, different. The six-guns didn't have any barrels. Where the barrels should have been gaped a pair of black caverns. The light shifted just enough for Talbert to make out the white-painted tips of short-range missiles. He cursed.

The *Thug* fired, both racks. It disappeared behind the cloud of exhaust, only to reappear as it threw itself out of the helicopter's line of fire. The Cyranos adjusted easily, stabbing laser fire into the *Thug*'s exposed back. The eighty-ton assault 'Mech shook with a spasm and half-curled into a ball.

Talbert squeezed the seatback even harder, jubilation filling his soul. The Gunslinger couldn't stop them now.

He was still thinking of his freedom when the *Thug*'s final flight of missiles corkscrewed in and flipped the hovercraft like a child's toy.

▲▼▲

Aaron Dane woke the third time Blakely shook him. He came awake suddenly, disoriented. His hand snatched at the empty holster on his hip. What had happened to his pistol? He looked around, eyes searching for a weapon, before his mind registered that it was one of his MechWarriors standing next to him.

"It's okay, sir," Blakely said. "Relax. It's over."

Aaron sat up. He was lying on the ground. To his right lay the ruin of his *Thug*. Flames licked at the destroyed torso. Thick black smoke belched into the sky, but it was quiet.

"Report, Sergeant," Aaron said. His voice was scratchy, as if it were fighting its way out of his chest. He looked around again. The Fort smoked in the background, but the rest of the view was dominated by the comforting shapes of *Thug* BattleMechs silhouetted against the sky every so often.

"Three APCs of rebel troops made it across the river," Blakely said. His voice was heavy with regret. "We couldn't stop them all from getting away." He held out a plastic bottle, which Aaron took.

"Losses?" he asked, before uncapping the bottle and drinking deeply. The water was tepid, and filled with the dryness of distilled water, but it was wet. He held in a mouthful, letting the water soak into the soft tissues of his cheeks and gums before he swallowed. He capped the bottle and handed it back to Blakely with a nod of thanks.

"Your *Thug* is the only 'Mech with major damage," he said. "Lieutenant Velasquez is holding the plateau and the Pass, but the Taurians have made no attempts to attack."

Aaron rolled his head around on his shoulders, listening to his neck sinews cracks. "Talbert?"

Blakely smiled and reached to his belt. He removed a blackened and twisted laser pistol and presented it. "That last hover you destroyed, sir. It was his."

Aaron looked at the destroyed weapon in his hand. After a long moment he tossed it away and laid back. The rough rocks cut at his skin, poking through the tears in his cooling suit, but he ignored them. The sky was blue but deepening as the sun set. A star flashed at him, slowly moving.

"What's next, sir?" Blakely asked.

"Our house is clean," Aaron said. He squinted at the moving star. "It's time to go and remind the Taurians who's boss." He grunted and pushed himself up. Blakely helped him stand. Aaron leaned back,

shading his eyes with a hand. "At least we won't be alone this time."

Blakely looked up and grinned. "The rest of the battalion?" he asked. The star took on the elongated shape of a comet, revealing itself as a DropShip braking from orbit.

Aaron nodded. He looked away from the sky and down to his *Thug*, shattered and smoking on the ground. A pang stuck in his chest, realizing how close he'd come to dying in that 'Mech.

"I'm sure they'll get it repaired soon enough," Blakely said, seeing where Aaron was looking.

Aaron shrugged. "It's probably scrap this time," he said. He clasped Blakely's shoulder, squeezed, and let go. He pointed the sergeant to where his *Thug* stood silent. "Best get mounted up, Sergeant," he said. He started walking toward the Fort.

"Sir?" Aaron turned. Blakely was standing at the foot of his 'Mech, one hand on the chain. "It was an honor to fight alongside you."

Aaron laughed. "We're not done, Blakely," he said.

"But your 'Mech-"

"Is trashed," Aaron said. "I know." He waited, but Blakely just stared at him. Aaron pointed toward the Fort, and the shadowed hulk standing a meter higher than the lip of the walls.

Brake's *Thug*.

Blakely smiled and turned to climb his 'Mech. Aaron watched the young sergeant for moment and then resumed his shuffling walk. It would take a while for the ground to cool once the DropShip landed. He'd have plenty of time to get into Brake's cockpit.

"Talbert is dead," he whispered to the shadows. He looked again at Brake's *Thug*, still waiting for a MechWarrior.

"Now to kill the rest of this cancer," he said.

UNHOLY UNION

CHRIS HUSSEY

ONE

Raider's Roost
Butte Hold
14 September 3028
1930 hours

"He wants me to do what?" Redjack Ryan slammed his glass down on the worn ceramic table as he jumped to his feet. "That fat bastard has finally lost what is left of his addled mind if he thinks I'm going there!" Spit and beer flew from his lips as the pirate shouted at the man in front of him.

Kelly Hunt cowered as shouts and curses of agreement came from the other pirates in the room, but quickly recovered. He stood up straighter and wiped Ryan's spittle from his face. "Ryan, you know Grimm has always been a bit—" Hunt looked down while he tried to find the right word. When it came to him, his head snapped up and he smiled. "—idealistic. That's why the two of you never got along. This time though, he seems very serious. He wants you to come to Oberon."

A chorus of laughter erupted. Hunt ignored it. He was just the messenger, after all. On the surface, being the messenger in the Periphery often earned you their traditional fate; you got shot. Still, Hunt knew he had an edge that would likely prevent Redjack Ryan from taking that route. As a reliable free trader, Hunt had carved out a nice niche for himself as one of the few brave enough to ply the routes in this neck of the Periphery. On top of that, he knew a few secret places that had saved a pirate's butt when the Lyran Commonwealth or the Draconis Combine decided to get aggressive. He'd given that information to Redjack Ryan

more than once, so the two had a bond in that regard. At least, Hunt was hoping they did.

Ryan glared at Hunt. "Not quite. Hendrick Grimm and I never got along because he didn't like my command style." He paused and then continued sarcastically, "He wanted someone with class." More laughter.

Hunt stepped forward and reached into the left breast pocket of his coat. A chorus of steel sliding on leather answered the gesture as every man in the room unholstered his gun and pointed it at Hunt. Ryan himself had taken a step back and was resting his hands on his guns.

"Relax, boys." The merchant spoke soothingly as he produced a portable holo-player and held it out to the bandit. "Grimm knew you wouldn't believe just me, so he wanted you to watch this."

Ryan cautiously leaned in toward Hunt's outstretched hand, easing his grip from the pistol at his hip. The rest of his crew followed suit. The pirate stared at the player for a long moment before taking it and setting it next to his half-filled glass on the long table in front of him. Dropping back into his chair, Ryan pressed play.

The unit whirred quietly as a glowing three-dimensional image crackled into view. Looking out at Ryan was the round, bald, scarred and multi-chinned face of Hendrick Grimm III, bandit king of Oberon VI. The fat man's eyes looked off to the side, then back at Ryan. Grimm smiled.

"Ryan. If you've kept your attitude in check, you haven't killed Mr. Hunt. Good boy. Now just sit back for a moment, try not to be a sonofabitch and listen to me, before you decide to shoot a hole in the player.

"Odds are you haven't heard what is happening of late. Let me fill you in. The Steiners and the Davions got married, my friend. And to celebrate, they're kicking the living snot out of the Liaos right now. And the Lyrans are tearing big chunks out of the Dragon's hide." Grimm smiled, his chins lifting nearly to his cheeks. "It's quite amusing, actually. Nice to see those Drac bastards running scared for once."

"So what the hell does this have to do with me?" Ryan shouted at the player.

"I suppose you're wondering what the hell this has to do with you, aren't you?" Grimm looked away again, moving his arm as if reaching for something. He produced an optical disc. "This is what it has to do with you, and me." Grimm paused. "And Maria."

Ryan's eyes narrowed, and he shot an angry, skeptical look at Hunt.

Grimm continued. "Now stay focused, son. This disc was secured for me by one of my contacts in the Combine. It's intel on the Lyran's deployment along our border, and their push into this theatre of the Combine." Grimm leaned in. "The Dragon's running scared right now. They're desperate. The Commonwealth is riding roughshod over their border, and Drac regiments are falling like dominoes. They want some of the pressure taken off, and they've asked me for help." He leaned back in his chair. "I'll be honest with you, son. I can't do what they're asking me to do alone. There're too many worlds to hit in too short a window, and I won't stretch myself that thin."

"And you're asking me to help you?" Ryan spat.

"And I need your help. Yours and Maria's. Between the three of us, we can rain down such fear and pain on the Lyrans, they'll have to pull back. That'll give the Dracs time to regroup and counterattack, which will guarantee our safety in all this. There'll be no time for Lyran retaliation." Grimm raised a sausage-like finger. "Now, I'm sure you still don't believe a word I'm saying, so I'm putting the dragon's money where my mouth is. Hunt has with him ten thousand in C-bills as down payment, courtesy of ol' Takashi himself." Grimm paused once more, smiling his fleshy smile. "There's two million more where that came from as soon as you arrive on Oberon. Plus any salvage you acquire once the attack begins. I'll see you in a couple of weeks."

The image on the player faded to black, and then disappeared.

Ryan leaned back in his chair, propping his boots on the edge of the table, and pushed a hand through his short-cropped hair. Agnar Haggerty leaned on the table next to Ryan. "He can't be serious, can he?"

Ryan turned to look at his second-in-command. "Grimm's as snaky as he is fat, that's for damn sure."

Agnar nodded. "That's true. But is he right? Could we really be facing trouble from the Lyrans if the border gets too far from us?"

Ryan thought about that for a moment. There was a certain advantage to having both the Draconis Combine and the Lyran Commonwealth so close. It allowed him and other pirates, like Grimm and Maria, to flip-flop between nations. To lose one of the nations from that balancing act would leave the pirates with only one target and increase the likelihood that they themselves would be the target of revenge. Pirates were a tolerable nuisance only when you had another Successor State breathing down your neck.

The one thought Ryan didn't want to dwell on much was Maria being part of the operation. The emotions that churned to the surface whenever he thought about his former lover always clouded things

for him. He had to banish her from his head for the moment.

Ryan leveled a stern glare at the merchant. "So what are you getting out of this?"

Hunt snorted. "Not a damned thing. Grimm just asked me to deliver the message as part of my normal trade run."

"Don't bullshit me, Hunt."

The merchant smiled ruefully. "I may have gotten a better deal on a few items in return for talking to you, but that's all." Hunt winked at Ryan. "Besides, Redjack, you know that when it comes down to it, I'm with you."

"What about Maria?"

"I can't say. I'm not delivering her message. She's got no love for Grimm either, but if I was betting, I'd say she'd do it."

Ryan closed his eyes and laced his fingers behind his head. Several moments passed before Agnar spoke up again.

"So, what's it going to be, Boss?"

The pirate rocked his chair down hard, slapped his hands on his thighs and stood. "Mount up, boys! We're headed to Oberon."

▲▼▲

Redjack Ryan crossed the cracked ferrocrete landing pad toward his DropShip, *Summoner's Gale,* taking stock of the activity around the port. His men were loading up the last of the unit's 'Mechs, as well as other supplies and stores for the journey. The pirate spotted Kelly Hunt across the landing pad, watching his own ship be loaded. A sudden thought struck the pirate, and he changed direction to walk toward the merchant.

"Hunt! Hold up!" Ryan shouted and waved the man down.

Kelly Hunt gave a few final instructions to a crewman before turning toward the pirate. "What is it, Ryan?"

The blond-haired brigand came to a stop and looked down at Hunt. "Tell me, what was Grimm's mood when he told you about all this, and gave you that recording?"

Hunt stroked his chin. "He seemed pretty serious about it to me. Told me this whole Lyran-Davion alliance had him worried. Worried about his future. Worried that the Dracs could fall like I hear the Liaos are." The merchant looked over at the crew loading his ship. "I think he's worried about the playing field. Right now, you've all got it good. Hell, I've got it great." Hunt's expression darkened. "But if one of the big boys tips the scales too far one way, that could mean bad news for people like you and Grimm. And me."

Ryan snorted. "He didn't think I'd do it, did he? Didn't think I'd take him up on his offer?"

Hunt laughed. "He told me it was more likely Kerensky would return to the Inner Sphere than you would team up with him."

Ryan laughed and slapped Hunt on the shoulder. "Well, I guess that fat bastard is in for a surprise, isn't he? Are you coming?"

The merchant shook his head. "No. I'm going to planet-hop over to the Grennids settlement first." He was referring to the settlers who lived on the southern continent of Butte Hold. They were a small group and presented no threat to the pirates, so the two societies left each other alone. "Then I'm off to Crellacor. The ale there fetches me a good black market price on Icar." Hunt started to walk away from the pirate. "Besides, why would I want to be witness to all the bloodshed when the three of you get together?"

Ryan laughed again and headed back toward his ship. *You've got the right idea, Hunt. There'll be plenty of blood, especially if I'm forced to drain it out of the fat man's carcass.*

TWO

JumpShip **Hath No Fury**
Zenith jump point, Blackstone
1 October 3028
0900 hours

"Radio those paranoid assholes one more time. Tell them Maria Morgraine says once again that her forces are not going to raid the world. We're only here for a recharge, and at the invitation of Hendrick Grimm III. Tell them if they send one more panicked transmission off-planet, our plans *will* change."

Maria Morgraine looked at the captain of *Hath No Fury.* "I'm not joking. If those idiots do any more saber rattling, I'm going to personally go down there and stuff their transmission gear down their throats!" She made her way to the bridge doors. "I'll be in my cabin."

Maria snaked her way through the cramped confines of the *Fury* until she reached the hatch connecting the *Fury* to her command DropShip, the *Sigrun.* It was a silent walk; her crew didn't speak to her unless she spoke to them first, and the system worked well for both sides. It didn't take long for new recruits to stop saluting.

COUNTERATTACK
BATTLECORPS ANTHOLOGY VOL 5

She keyed the lock on her cabin, but the door didn't open. Maria punched in the passcode again, but the door didn't budge. Muttering a curse and slamming her fist against the bulkhead, Maria knelt down and pumped the manual override to slowly crank open the door. With each pump, she could feel her anger and tension rise higher.

Once inside her cabin, Maria tried the passcode again. The door efficiently slid shut. The pirate shot the door a baleful look and moved to her desk. She took out the holo-recording from Grimm. The plastic casing felt cool in her hands as she turned it over. *What do you* really *want, Grimm? "Too many worlds for you to hit alone" my ass. I don't doubt the Dracs are paying you to cause some sort of problem, but there has to be more to it than that. There's no other force around to challenge you, unless the Belt Pirates have stumbled upon something. No, you're looking to get rid of one of us.* Maria stood up and moved to the wall next to her bunk. A two-dimensional map of the Inner Sphere was overlaid on a vid screen that hadn't worked in months. Maria stared at it. *You can't be looking to get rid of me. Our forces don't cross paths often enough. Sure, we've no love lost after what you did to Ryan back in '17, but what point would revenge serve after all these years?*

The thought of Ryan gave her pause. *Ryan.* She hadn't been there that day more than ten years ago when Grimm banished him from Oberon. By the time she finally returned to Oberon, she'd heard dozens of stories of how it all happened; destruction of a Free Worlds League city; caught sleeping with Grimm's daughter, Ella; killed a Lyran ambassador from Icar; the list went on and on. Maria never was able to find out the truth. Grimm refused to tell her what happened, saying it was a matter between the two of them alone. But Grimm went too far when he forbade her to mount a mission to find Ryan, and her relationship with Grimm never was the same.

She had loved Ryan; despite her best efforts to contact the pirate, however, he couldn't be found. Maria had turned her anger over losing her lover against Grimm in the years following, eventually taking those loyal to her away to strike out on her own. *Grimm was probably happy to have me out of what was left of his hair.* If she were honest with herself, she had to admit it still bothered her that she didn't know what had happened. The most persistent rumor was that Ryan had slept with Grimm's daughter. Maria knew it was possible, given the kind of man he was, but she secretly hoped that wasn't the truth. She could more easily stomach Ryan killing innocent civilians on some world she'd never been to, than being betrayed in such a way.

Maria finally discovered Ryan's whereabouts two years ago, but by then it had been too long; it was unlikely they'd ever have any resolution to their relationship. She knew this was true when, just last year, a company of Ryan's men hit the Valkyrate world of Last Chance, damaging several factories and making off with an entire year's harvest. That attack had made the past year a tough one. Losing so much food had caused a lot of people to starve. Her Valkyries demanded blood, but Maria knew vengeance wouldn't put food in their bellies.

After all that, the thought of possibly seeing Ryan again made Maria sick to her stomach. Then the realization struck her. *It's Ryan you're after, isn't it, Grimm?* Maria grimaced. *And you want me to do it.*

Maria lay down on her bunk. Everything was starting to make sense. In the holo-recording, Grimm expressed sadness over losing Maria and her loyalists years ago, but congratulated her on the progress she'd made in establishing the Valkyrate, hinting at what could be an even brighter future.

Maria had to admit, with Ryan out of the picture the idea of an alliance with Grimm had merit. It wouldn't take much to roll over Von Strang. *We'd have our own mini-state. Those Spheroid bastards would have to take us seriously then.* Maria sat up and cut off her reverie. *Be careful, Maria. Getting in bed with Grimm could make you become what you hate the most. You've never wanted to be anything like the Successor Lords. The freedom you have now is what you've always craved.*

Maria got out of bed and returned to looking at the map. She studied it closely once more and then slowly smiled as her finger tapped on the worlds of the Oberon Confederation. *Still, there is an appeal to ruling my own bandit kingdom.*

THREE

Grimfort, Oberon City
Oberon VI
8 October 3028
1130 hours

Redjack Ryan made his way along the hallway leading toward Grimm's Grand Hall. *Hasn't changed much.* Ryan assessed the drab, worn décor as he walked through Grimm's palace. Though the hallway was clean, the windows were smeared and dust-covered, allowing only a hazy view of the outside. The walls were equally stained, from smoke,

spilled alcohol, bodily fluids, or hell knows what else. At Ryan's side stalked his lieutenant, Agnar "Satan's Son" Haggerty.

The arrival on Oberon had gone smoothly enough. Grimm's forces let Ryan's men land without a challenge, though the Bandit King had insisted that Ryan keep his crew on board their DropShips until the deal had been sealed. The last thing Grimm wanted was the two sides tearing each other apart in some drunken brawl in one of Grimfort's taverns.

Ryan reluctantly agreed. While the Butte Hold pirates either feared or respected their leader, bowing to his authority was never their strong suit. Ryan knew he'd be lucky to keep them on board for a couple of hours at most, but he did his best to give his orders to stay put as thoroughly and menacingly as possible. *Grimm won't be able to tell whether my troops are acting with or without my permission, but he'll know I'm not rolling over and playing dead for him.* Finally, Ryan made sure that the DropShip's cannons were armed and ready and that the aerojocks were primed. There was no way he was going to be caught flat-footed.

"You're pretty quiet, Boss," Agnar observed.

Ryan laughed ruefully. "I'm just waiting for Grimm's men to come around the corner and open fire."

Agnar shared his laugh. "You know that won't happen. That would deprive him of the satisfaction of killing you personally."

Ryan nodded. "That makes sense."

"You know, I'm impressed that you remember your way around this place so well."

"You're not the only one. Most of the time I roamed these halls, I was drunk off my ass. I was happy if I was able to make it back to anyone's quarters, let alone mine. If I didn't end up passed out on the floor in some hallway, it was a good night."

Agnar laughed again. "Those were some good times."

"Don't wish too much for the past, Ag. I'll strand your ass here and take bets on how long you'll last." Ryan smiled fiendishly.

They rounded a corner, spotting a pair of armed men standing by a lift. "This must be the place, eh boys?" Ryan shouted to the guards, whose only answer was to open the lift doors. "Humorless as always. Tell Grimm I think you should be paid more." Ryan patted each man on the shoulder, and was answered with disinterested grunts.

The pair entered the lift and the doors closed behind them. It jerked to life, taking them up, squealing and creaking the entire time. About halfway into the journey, the lift stuttered, shaking both occupants. Ryan shook his head. *When these doors open, I'll be setting foot in a place I haven't been in over ten years.* He reached for the pistols strapped to each hip, making sure they were in place, unsnapping the catch on one out of reflex—a habit he made sure to practice before joining any large gathering. He'd had his Sternsnacht Python for as long as he could remember and it'd saved his life more than once. After physically checking his main weapons, Ryan mentally checked off the other forms of insurance he'd hidden in his leathers. Short blades in his boots and belt, as well as a spring-loaded version in his left sleeve. "You ready?" he asked his lieutenant.

Agnar nodded, mocking. "Locked and loaded, sir. Do you really think they'll open fire on us?"

Ryan shook his head. "No. Not right away at least. Fatboy's going to want to gloat a bit first, then let me have it."

"You think he'll do the same to Maria when she arrives?"

Ryan shrugged. "We'll see. I heard she popped in at a pirate point only two days out. She should hit planetside tomorrow. Bitch always liked to make an entrance. If we're lucky, we won't have to see her at all."

Agnar smiled.

The lift jerked to a stop and gave a groan of welcome as the doors slid open.

The room had changed little since Ryan had been here last. Divided into three sections by support pillars, the room still wore its drab gray furnishings, with long stretches of sun-faded silks doing their best to bring a splash of color and life to the space. The left and right sections of the hall could be set up to serve refreshments when there was a band or other performers on a makeshift stage on the opposite side. Couches, benches and chairs filled out the rest of the side areas; Ryan remembered that those with the torn translucent curtains were often used by couples wanting privacy. The windows with views to the grounds below and the doors leading out to the balconies were surprisingly clean. Ryan noticed that the hardpoint mounts for anti-personnel or anti-'Mech weaponry were still stationed on some of the outer edges. *Nice to see they aren't being used at the moment. Maybe Grimm does trust me.*

The center section remained open to allow Grimm's guests to mingle, his troops to assemble, or for the occasional audience from the population or worlds beyond. Grimm's personal area occupied the stage at the far end of the hall. His throne was more a bowl than an actual chair, built to accommodate his expansive girth. An array of

ripped, faded and stained cushions huddled around the seat, which was where advisors, concubines and others usually reclined.

Even though currently empty of guests, the room smelled strongly of stale sweat with an underlying current of alcohol and a weed of some sort. A lone figure stood looking out a window at the far end of the left side of the hall.

"I'm happy to see you made it, son." Grimm's gruff voice was low as he turned toward Ryan.

"What the hell is this, Fatboy?" Ryan strode confidently into the room, Agnar four paces behind him. "No welcoming party? I come a dozen light years and all I get is just you, in this shithole that hasn't been cleaned since I was here last?"

Grimm chuckled as he turned away from the window. He was dressed in loose, bright blue silks that rested gently on his belly. Baggy white linen pants, with only a hint of dust from the dry, summer-baked ground outside draped over scuffed black boots. "Nice to see you haven't changed, Ryan." The bandit king made for a bench and gestured toward another. "Sit down. Relax for a moment." He nodded to Ryan's lieutenant. "Agnar. It's good to see you as well. Why don't you help yourself to some drinks?" Grimm gestured toward one of the bars. Agnar changed course and began a search for alcohol.

Ryan sat on the bench opposite Grimm, then slowly slid down into a relaxed pose, placing his hands behind his head. "I'm not even going to try and shoot you dead where you stand. I know you're not stupid enough to really be here by yourself."

"Good. Glad to get that out of the way. Besides, you may change your tune after I lay out the full deal. Hell, you might even want to kiss my ass in apology."

Ryan let out a loud laugh as Agnar returned with a whiskey bottle and three shot glasses.

Grimm shared his laugh as he took a shot of whiskey from Agnar. He downed the drink with a quick snap of his head, then focused his gaze on Ryan, who had also thrown back his shot. "I'll be honest, Ryan. I didn't tell you the whole truth."

Ryan faked surprise. "I expected as much. I know you always have something going."

Grimm nodded. "I wasn't lying when I told you about the Lyrans hitting the Dracs hard. This Steiner-Davion marriage is going to change things. What I hear about the Liao worlds falling makes me believe the Dragon won't be far behind. It'll survive, no doubt, but the yard we play in won't be the same in a couple years. Once the Steiners secure the worlds they've taken, they'll be turning their attention toward us. People like you and Maria won't last long." Grimm rubbed his bald head in a gesture of exhaustion. "And I may not be far behind you. I don't think Katrina wants to conquer us, but she'd smash us all good and hard, to the point where there's no coming back." Grimm's eyes narrowed. "But it doesn't have to be that way."

Ryan cocked his head and took another shot of whiskey. "Go on."

Beads of sweat popped out on Grimm's head as he began to pace back and forth. "The Combine does need some pressure relieved, and they have asked me to hit the Lyrans, but they also want *you*. They didn't even bother to try and contact you. Frankly, they told my agent they didn't have the time, and they knew we had history."

Ryan scrunched his face in skepticism. "You really expect me to believe that?"

"No." Grimm said flatly. "That's why I made them provide proof of what they're offering you." Grimm reached into his pocket and produced a small data disc and reader and handed them to Ryan. He closed his plump hand quickly around the items as Ryan reached for them, denying him access. "There's one more thing."

Ryan rolled his eyes as he looked over at Agnar.

"I need you to get rid of Maria."

Ryan's gaze turned cold.

Now it was Grimm's turn to look skeptical. "Don't give me that look, son. You haven't seen or heard from her in years. Don't you think that if she truly loved you, she would have found you a lot sooner?" Grimm stood up and walked back toward the window. "Hell, she stayed here for almost three years before she'd finally had enough of me and left. Doesn't sound like true love to me."

Ryan spoke through gritted teeth. "Why?"

"Why get rid of her?" Grimm turned back toward the pirates. "She's a problem, frankly. She's too uncontrollable. You're bad, but at least you know when to back off from the Spheroids. She doesn't care. She'll keep hitting and raiding, attracting too much attention. She always has. You eliminate her, and her forces will either fall in line, or scatter to the four winds. Either way she'll be gone, and I'll let you have her worlds. Form your own state."

Ryan scoffed. "They're not yours to give."

Grimm smiled. "They will be." He tossed Ryan the disc and reader. "You'll be impressed with the Dragon's gifts for you, but since I'm bigger, I get bigger presents. If we're successful, we'll come out of this with enough hardware and cash to make sure we can weather

any revenge the Lyrans might take." The bandit's smile grew wider. "Plus, consider me the middle man in all this, which means I'll be holding your gifts until after the raid. If you don't play by my rules, your gifts become mine." Grimm's expression turned more sinister. "Then I'll just take you out myself." Grimm walked back toward Ryan, his face softening once more. "I don't want to do that, son. You've always been a loose cannon, but I've always liked you, even if you did sleep with my daughter. You're a helluva MechWarrior, and with the proper motivation I know we can trust each other enough to get through this, especially when you think about the brighter days we could have ahead."

Ryan steeled his own gaze. "You sure about that?"

Grimm nodded. "Absolutely. Ryan, you value what you can hold in your hand more than anything else. When it comes down to it, you've always taken the cold cash in your wallet over the warm body in your bed." Grimm chuckled to himself. "Go back to your ship. Take a look at the disc. We'll discuss battle plans in three days."

Ryan looked over at Agnar, who'd remained silent the entire time. His lieutenant shrugged in response. Ryan rolled his eyes. "You're a shitload of help." Ryan cocked his head at Grimm. "You know where to find me." The pair turned away from the bandit king and strode out of the hall.

FOUR

Grimfort, Oberon City
Oberon VI
11 October 3028
1130 hours

Maria Morgraine glared menacingly at the rotund face of Hendrik Grimm on the viewscreen in her cabin. Grimm answered her glare with a devilish smile.

"Give me one reason why I shouldn't have my Valkyries unload and smash this city right now. I'd sooner see the Archon on Gotter-dammerung than kill Ryan."

"Maria. You and I both know that simply isn't true. Don't think for one second that there's some romantic notion in Ryan's heart. He never returned for you, never tried to find you. In fact, if I heard the stories right, some of his men hit one of your worlds."

Maria looked away, then back to the screen. "I should kill you where you stand, you sonofabitch."

Grimm chuckled. "But you won't, my dear. You may want to retain a romantic notion that the pirate still loves you, but deep down, you know it isn't true." Grimm held a data disc up to the screen. "I'll soothe your wounded heart. As I said, the Dragon needs the Lyrans off their backs, and they've put their money where their mouths are. They've given you a lovely assortment of munitions and other supplies, including a shiny new lance of 'Mechs. When it's all over, you'll be getting more. Enough to withstand any Lyran counterattack, though I'm wagering there won't be one." Grimm's expression turned more cordial. "I'll even sweeten the deal. When Ryan is gone, we'll divide the spoils. I'll take the world, and you can have his men, including those who dared to strike at the Valkyrate. And just to show you I'm not the monster you think I am, I'll help you replenish your food stores." Grimm smiled. "I'd never be so bold as to suggest an alliance, but I see no reason why the icy mountains of Gotterdammerung cannot warm just a bit."

Maria knew she needed to change the subject. "How are we proceeding from here?"

Grimm's smile widened. "Once you make planetside, your ships can resupply, and I'll deliver the first portion of your payment. You'll need to turn around immediately. I've already given Ryan his orders, and he's on his way. He thinks that none of our forces are working together, so you'll have surprise on your side. Once you've completed your mission and the smoke has cleared with Ryan's subordinates, bring me back proof, and I'll get you the rest of what I owe you."

"Fine with me." Maria leaned in toward the monitor. "Don't double-cross me, Grimm. You don't want the vengeance I will unleash upon your blubbery hide."

Grimm chuckled once more. "My dear, I know well the phrase, 'Hell hath no fury.' If anyone should be fearful, it's Ryan."

▲▼▲

The screen went black as Maria's image faded away. Hendrik Grimm III leaned his bulging frame back into his throne and sighed. Running a beefy hand over his bald head, he looked out over the still-empty hall. His troops were busy making a good show of loading up his own raiding forces for their part of the plan.

"You sure this is all going to work?"

The voice came from the darkness across the grand hall. A lone figure stood in the open doorway leading toward one of the many balconies. He slowly moved toward Grimm.

"I didn't see you there. You really should remain in the quarters assigned to you until Maria has come and gone. The less suspicion you raise, the better our chances of success."

The man stepped from the shadows into the light surrounding Grimm's throne. Even though the bandit king towered above him on the converted stage, the man had a presence that placed him on equal footing. "You still haven't answered my question, Grimm."

Hendrick Grimm sighed. "It will work. Maria will arrive on Toland first, engage the token militia there, and wipe out the supply depot. Ryan will arrive two to three days behind. Maria's forces will be hidden and in position by then. When Ryan makes planetfall, it won't take long to finish them. My agent will take care of Ryan or Maria, whoever is left. Your men can mop up the rest. Just like that, two large thorns will be removed from your side."

The man rubbed his chin. "What makes me think I can trust you?"

Grimm chuckled. "Quite frankly, you can't." The bandit king shifted his weight. "I will tell you this, though. I've got no love for Redjack Ryan or Maria Morgraine. I do love my throne, however, and I can see the writing on the wall. Better to back a winner, if you ask me."

The man's eyes narrowed slightly. "Well said. But what about your agent?"

Grimm nodded. "No worries there. I assured him he'd be allowed to escape once you move in." He shrugged. "But if that does not happen for some reason, it doesn't concern me. He'll have served his purpose."

The man shook his head. "You'd discard someone so easily. That does not give us much hope for our future together."

"You misunderstand my motives. I can trust him in this mission, as he sees a chance to advance his own position. If he survives and returns to Oberon, I will have to start watching my back more closely. I have no desire for such machinations. And fret not over our future. When this is all resolved, my men will be happy to turn their attention toward the Combine." Grimm pointed a stubby finger at the man. "You just be sure to stick to *your* end of the deal."

The man smiled, turning back toward the shadows and the hall's exit. "Never fear, King Grimm. The Lyran Commonwealth never abandons a good deal."

FIVE

Cantor Canyon
Toland
11 November 3028
1430 hours

Maria maneuvered her *Grasshopper* into position on the top of a rise overlooking the supply depot, which was built into the wall of one of the steep, rocky ridges of Cantor Canyon. As Grimm promised, the militia resistance was small. She found it reassuring that he'd kept his word so far.

Maria knew there was no way her Valkyries could keep the secret that they were really here to take out Redjack Ryan and his command; the token force here on Toland helped maintain the illusion. If her warriors didn't have anything to engage on this world, there would be too much suspicion.

"That's the last of them." The voice crackled in Maria's neurohelmet. "They're all turning tail."

"Good work, Randi," Maria answered, as she eased her 'Mech down the hill. She had to work hard to keep the machine upright, as the rocky soil gave way easily under the 'Mech's weight. She could see what was left of the militia tanks and 'Mech forces racing away from the depot and base. "Send a few of the ladies in to scare away any stragglers and secure the munitions. Once we get everything taken care of here, we might make a small hop to Toland City. I have an old debt I'd like to repay." Maria lied, but knew she had to keep the show up for a little longer.

▲▼▲

Two hours later, the pirate leader had assembled her senior officers around the large faux-wood table in the small depot's command center. The air felt wet from the humidity, and everything Maria was wearing stuck to her body, sweaty from the summer heat. Maria could feel the tension in the room. She'd known that as soon as she ordered her troops to leave the munitions and all prisoners behind that her officers would become suspicious. They'd protested both orders, but obeyed them.

"So, you want to tell us what this is about?" Randi, her second-in-command, spoke with obvious anger. "We never take anything and just hold it. Now you have us *locking up* Lyran soldiers in their own cells, instead of taking hostages."

Shar, Maria's support company commander, jumped in. "And why the hell are we leaving those munitions in storage? They should be on the ships, and we should get out of here. That's what Grimm wanted. Let's get what we came for and move!"

Maria held up her hand and nodded. She was getting angry herself, but she kept it in check; her officers didn't have all the details, and she couldn't expect them to understand. "This supply depot isn't our only mission. We've got a second task that'll be on us in a couple days, most likely." Maria paused for effect and then continued. "The game is changing, ladies. The latest war in the Successor States is going pretty well for the Lyrans. This means that we could have some real trouble once matters settle down." Maria could see some of her officers' eyes narrow. "To protect our interests, we're entering into a strategic alliance with Grimm." Maria heard the gasps of disgust but pressed on. "Redjack Ryan's troops are being led here in an ambush that we'll spring. I'm going to kill Ryan and take command of his forces."

Stunned silence answered Maria. Then Randi broke it. "You can't be serious!" Her other officers joined in the protest.

Maria glared. "Just think for a moment. If we don't have a Combine border close to us, keeping the Lyrans honest, we'll never survive. No pirate force as large and active as ours can exist for long without a border shared by two or more Successor States." Maria could feel a small twinge of complaint in her gut as she spoke the next words. "If we get rid of Ryan, take his troops and ally with Grimm, we will be able to stave off a Lyran counterattack. Plus, Grimm is hitting Steelton right now. Once we get rid of Ryan, we'll rendezvous with Grimm and hit Apollo, where the real Lyran supply depot is. That should hurt their war effort enough to give the Dragon time to recover, and hopefully counterattack before it matters to us."

Shar shoved back from the table, shouting, "You know you can't trust him, Maria! Grimm has something else going on. This plan of his is far too risky. We're your command staff—this is the kind of decision we make together! You should have consulted us." Murmurs of agreement followed her outburst.

"Every plan's risky, Shar. Besides, I've got a way to deal with Grimm in case he tries any treachery. I've got *Winged Vengeance* waiting on Lackhove. If they don't hear from one of us within a month, they've standing orders to start leapfrogging across all Grimm's worlds except Oberon and cause as much damage as possible." Whenever it was feasible, Maria kept a company or so of 'Mechs and other combat units behind her main force to use as her ace in the hole. She didn't have to use them very often, but they always proved their worth when they were needed.

"The *Vengeance* isn't going to do us a whole helluva lot of good if Ryan gets the better of us," Shar shot back.

Maria's self-control slipped a little. *She never gives me credit for knowing the score. Too bad—you can't command by committee.* She pinned Shar with a steely look. "It's covered. The *Sigrun* is set to lift within the day. They're taking up a position on the other side of the third moon in-system. Nice hiding place there. They'll shadow in behind Ryan's forces; that should be enough insurance for those with little faith." She looked away from Shar in dismissal.

Shar pressed the attack. "And how do you plan to deal with Ryan's men after he's dead? Those pirates have no love for us. Hell, Maria, they *attacked* us last year, damn near starving us to death in the process. And now you want to let them sign up?"

Maria waved her off. "They'll have two choices. Either be disarmed and sign up with the Valkyries, or stay here and spend the rest of their days in a Lyran prison. Choice seems obvious to me."

Shar spat on the floor. "This is foolishness! We should have had a say in this plan. Instead you've signed our death warrants!"

Maria drew her pistol and took aim at Shar. "I can put my signature on yours right now, if you like." Shar stopped cold and stared back at Maria. "Get it through your head, right here, right now." Maria looked at each of her officers in turn. "This goes for all of you. We're throwing our lot in with Grimm—for now. Once we see what happens with the Spheroids, things will change. I have no plans to become his bitch. That fat bastard lost my loyalty years ago. I know he's shifty, but where we sit now, we're safe. First sign I see of things changing, the Valkyries will bring unholy hell down upon him. And with Ryan out of the way, we have one less loose cannon to worry about."

Silence fell across the room for a moment. Maria lowered her gun, but did not holster it. "Now get the hell out."

"You'll never do it." Shar mumbled as she made for the exit.

"What did you say?" Maria shot back, freezing everyone in their tracks.

Shar turned to face her commander. "You'll never kill Ryan. You've never stopped loving that bandit. Grimm knows it too, and he's using it against you."

Maria raised her pistol once more and gritted her teeth. "I'll kill him as easily as I could kill you right now."

"Do it." Shar challenged flatly.

"Wait!" Randi shouted, as Maria cocked her head in response to the challenge and pulled the trigger.

The clap from the pistol brought screams of surprise and a howl of pain from Shar as she collapsed to the ground, clutching her thigh. When Maria stepped forward, some officers cleared away, while others knelt by Shar to attend to her wound. The Dominatrix of Gotterdammerung dropped to her haunches by the wounded captain. "You're too good of a MechWarrior to kill outright, Shar. Especially now." Maria chuckled a bit. "I guess you've called my bluff on that. How about we consider this a warning shot?" Maria slapped Shar on the wounded leg, eliciting another yelp, stood up and walked out of the room.

SIX

Cantor Canyon
Toland
13 November 3028
1700 hours

"Looks like we got an *Enforcer, Assassin, Trebuchet* and a *Valkyrie* on the perimeter of the compound, Ryan. We can tell there are a few more 'Mechs inside the wall, but they're not moving."

Redjack Ryan keyed his commlink. "Do they belong to the Thirtieth Lyran?"

"Nope. They're not Lyran. I can't tell the designation, but they must be mercs like Grimm's intel indicated."

Another truth. So far, everything Grimm had given Ryan was true. There was a supply depot on Toland. It was lightly guarded by mercenaries. Ryan was late in arriving on Toland and making the drop zone, but Grimm wouldn't know that. Ryan had initially decided to go straight for Toland, but Agnar wanted to know why they weren't caching the initial payment from the Combine that Grimm had given them. It was mostly cash rather than munitions or supplies and he would hate to lose any of that money, but Agnar was right—he should stick to his usual routine. Ryan had made a habit of burying much of his treasure over the years, like the pirates of ancient Terra. Most of the goods were on dead, abandoned or uncolonized worlds between Butte Hold and the Lyran border. Only Ryan knew the exact hiding places. Dropping off this treasure had cost them two days, but Ryan saw no problem with that.

The pirates of Butte Hold had committed two companies to this raid. Ryan's company led the direct assault on the compound, while the other split wide to both flanks to flush out any hidden units. Ryan hoped that one company would be enough to scare off the mercs, but the second one could be called in quick enough to seal the deal. Either way, he wanted to use as little firepower as possible. He knew from Grimm's instructions that Maria's troops were hitting Wotan, where resistance would be heavy enough to cause her problems, but not heavy enough to stop her from hitting her second target here on Toland. Ryan had to make sure he'd eliminated the mercs here and then set up his ambush for Maria. *If you can actually go through with it.*

"All right Agnar, let's move in. Target the *Assassin* and *Trebuchet* first. I don't want these guys to have the advantage in either speed or range." Ryan pressed down on the foot pedals of his *Quickdraw,* engaging the 'Mech's jump jets. The force of the launch pressed him into the command couch and drove the worn pads of his neurohelmet into his shoulders. The 'Mech cleared the hill he was concealed behind and Ryan guided the machine to land on the crest. As he tracked downward, he keyed the crosshairs of his Delta Dart long-range missile pack onto the *Trebuchet.* When the crosshairs pulsed red, the pirate let fly with a volley.

The battle had begun.

The battle had begun. Ryan's men had started their advance toward the compound. Maria watched as the three lances pushed toward the entrance. She could see a *Trebuchet* taking a heavy pounding from one lance, while an *Assassin* scrambled to shake the missiles and autocannon fire chasing it down. *He's only committed one company. Odds are he's got his other two hiding or flanking.* "Randi, bring your company around. Watch for hidden units."

Static crackled in Maria's ear. "Understood. We've spotted two lances already."

Maria chuckled. *This is going to be easy.* "Excellent. Keep the damage to a minimum. Those machines will be ours within the hour. Shar. Bring your company up. There may be another lance or more on your flank."

A flat acknowledgment was Shar's only reply.

"The battle has begun, sir."

Kommandant Harris Ivor nodded. "Good. We'll hold for the moment. Give these bandits a chance to diminish each other first. Then we'll move in for the kill." Kommandant Ivor didn't know all the intimate details of his mission, but that didn't make his battalion of the Thirtieth Lyran Guard any less prepared. When the orders came in a month ago from HQ on Icar, it was obvious they were important. Intelligence had indicated that an attack was imminent by not one, but two pirate bands. The Valkyries of Maria Morgraine and Redjack Ryan's pirates from Butte Hold. The intel had been detailed enough to indicate that it was very likely the Valkryies would arrive first, followed by Ryan's forces within a week's time. The intel went further to say that they would not be working in concert, and would likely engage each other. The Kommandant had been instructed to activate an old supply depot in Cantor Canyon, setting it up as a false target with minimal defenses.

Harris was no fool. He knew some deal was going down. There'd been plenty that had changed in the last year, so to see something like this on the heels of the invasion into the Combine, coupled with the wedding of Hanse Davion and Melissa Steiner—the Kommandant knew this had to be part of the plan. He was more than happy to have the chance to attach his name to part of history by eliminating two of the more notorious pirate bands in the Inner Sphere.

Harris had followed his orders to the letter. The depot had long ago been used by the Rim Worlds Republic. A secret network of caves had been carved out of the bluffs and ridges surrounding the depot, probably to hide units being manufactured by the Republic. Both the caves and depot fell into disuse during the early Succession Wars. Only in the last five years had Lyran engineers begun working to return the caves to a usable state. They were still lacking many important facilities, but they served just fine to hide Ivor's battalion.

The Kommandant turned toward the exit. "Alert the company commanders. I'm heading for my lance. We'll be departing in twenty minutes." Ivor left the command center and strode toward his *Zeus*. He let a smile play on his lips. *These pirates won't know what hit them.*

SEVEN

Cantor Canyon
Toland
13 November 3028
1730 hours

Ryan steadied his *Quickdraw* against the beating being given to it by the particle cannon of an enemy *Vindicator*. The artificial lightning bolt had seared off most of the armor on the *Quickdraw's* right leg, melting a huge gash from hip to calf. Taking a half step to the side, Ryan quickly centered his crosshairs on the 'Mech and keyed his firing sequence. Matched Omnicron medium lasers on each arm pulsed and speared the *Vindicator* in the chest, while a quartet of missiles followed in their path, with three striking near the same spot as the lasers. The fourth missile took an odd arc and struck the shoulder of the *Vindicator*, triggering a propellant flare, which sent it spiraling out of sight. The burst of flame scored the 'Mech's chest, melting off some of the insignia. The *Vindicator* took a half step back from the impact, but remained on its feet.

Ryan scanned his three-sixty visual display as he prepared to engage the jump jets again. A flash of blue to his left caught his attention as particle cannon fire struck the *Vindicator* in its already damaged leg. The bolt tore through the myomer muscles that powered the huge machine, vaporizing the skeleton underneath, snapping the leg clean off. The warrior struggled to remain upright but failed miserably, with the overcompensation to its left causing the 'Mech to fall on its side, crushing the left arm underneath its body.

Ryan saw Pers Stromsky's *Griffin* give a salute with its non-gun hand. "Thanks much, Pers," Ryan said. "No need to finish this one off, I've got it." Ryan cut short any potential for Stromsky heading over to the downed 'Mech. He knew the warrior had a penchant for kicking in the cockpits of fallen foes. While it didn't really bother Ryan all that much, today he had no time for his troop's theatrics. The battle had started off well for his pirates, but it quickly turned sour when the forces on the other side of the depot's wall joined the battle. They were a bit more determined than Ryan expected, and were using the twisting narrows of the canyon to better advantage than were his men. Things got worse when Ryan tried to call in reinforcements and found them already engaged and on the run. *A lot more than the company-sized unit Grimm said was here.*

Ryan brought his *Quickdraw* about, as a twinge of doubt about Grimm entered his mind—*betrayal*? "Agnar, can you help my sorry ass?"

Static answered the pirate, then Agnar's voice. "Sorry, boss. We've been playing cat and mouse with a *Grasshopper* and her lance. It's not easy. Whoever is in there, she's good."

Ryan nodded. "Try and hold there. I guess I need to help your sorry ass." Ryan took one last look at the downed *Vindicator* and noticed an odd mark on the disabled machine. The pirate keyed in on the torso of the *Vindicator* where the errant missile had struck and zoomed in. The image of the double spear and shield they had chalked up to being the mercenary unit's logo had been melted away, revealing a half-charred female warrior, sword held high, wings on her back spread wide. Ryan's jaw clenched. *Did Agnar say* Grasshopper? A second disturbing realization quickly followed. *Did Agnar say "she?"* His stomach lurched as the realization hit him. *She's not supposed to be here yet!* As another unimaginable thought raced into his head, Ryan tapped a few commands near his comm and shouted into his mic.

"Maria?"

▲▼▲

Maria Morgraine's *Grasshopper* broke to a full run. Her command lance had been intercepted from engaging Ryan and taking him down. A trio of 'Mechs was keeping her lance occupied and pulling her away from her target. She raced to get a better angle on the *Orion* currently giving her fits. She was almost positive it was Agnar Haggerty. *I always hated you. You always were Ryan's biggest ass-kisser, with a cruel streak that would make a serial killer blush. You're called "Satan's Son" for good reason. Perhaps I'll do Ryan the favor of killing you first, so he can have one small satisfaction before I put a laser in his brain.*

She twisted left, panning the crosshairs over her opponent. As she reached to press her firing stud, her neurohelmet barked a high-pitched screech, followed by a short burst of static. Then an angry voice. "Maria. What the hell is going on? Why are your Valkyries here?"

Heat flushed Maria's face. *He knows. Somehow he figured it out. Dammit.*

The voice persisted. "You frozen bitch! I don't know what the hell you think you're doing, but this is our target. Grimm sent you somewhere else.

"Unless I was your target." Maria could hear the anger in Ryan's voice. "What did he offer you, *lover*?" Ryan's voice dripped scorn.

Anger boiled up inside Maria as she slammed her comm. "Don't even start, Ryan! Now just wait there so I can come and kill you!" Maria skidded to a stop and hit the jump pedals on her *Grasshopper*. The 'Mech shot backward into the air over a small rock mound. The *Orion* that had been tracking her was caught off guard and continued moving in its original direction. Maria married her Conan five-pack missile launcher to her Diplan heavy laser and depressed the firing stud. The *Orion*'s right arm was bathed in steam as the laser vaporized the plating along the upper half. The missiles struck lower, ringing against the 'Mech's right thigh. After her parting salvo, Maria rolled her 'Mech mid-flight and landed with a confident thud, quickly resuming her run.

She could see Ryan position the strong side of his 'Mech to face her troops and take aim. The loping gait of her *Grasshopper* made it tough to draw a solid bead when using her long-range weapons. Maria began to feel doubt as the 'Mech just stood there. Her headset crackled.

"This isn't right, Mar."

Maria winced at Ryan's pet name for her.

"It's fine if you want to hate me. Even kill me. But do you really want to have it on your conscience that Grimm put you up to this?"

Maria began to slow her 'Mech slightly. "What the hell are you talking about?"

"Think about it. Grimm screwed us both over. Now he's coming to you and giving you the opportunity to kill me, when it was Grimm that caused both of our problems in the first place. You think you've been free from his grip all these years, Mar, but Fatboy still has control over you."

Maria pulled her *Grasshopper* to a stop. She took a moment to center her crosshairs on Ryan's *Quickdraw*. From this range, she could unleash everything she had and hit—especially if he continued to stand still. Maria's grip tightened on the joystick, her thumb hovering just above the firing stud. What seemed like an eternity passed before Ryan spoke again.

"Look, Mar. If you're going to kill me, do it to my face. You owe me that, at least."

"No, I don't." Maria pressed the firing stud, launching a full salvo. With the extra time to solve the firing solution provided by them both standing there and because neither 'Mech was moving, all weapons struck true. A quartet of Diplan medium lasers struck the knee joint on the already damaged left leg of Ryan's *Quickdraw*. The remaining armor plating vanished in a loud hiss accompanied by blue and black smoke. Maria could see myomer fibers snapping free from the skeleton be-

UNHOLY UNION

neath. Her heavy laser and three of her missiles finished the job, separating the two halves of the leg. Ryan made no attempt to avoid getting hit, and his 'Mech fell to the ground like a chain-sawed tree.

▲▼▲

Redjack Ryan saw stars when his neurohelmet struck the wall of his cockpit in the impact from the fall. Anger fueled his adrenaline and kept him from losing consciousness. *Okay, maybe she does hate me,* Ryan joked to himself through the pain. He could see Maria's *Grasshopper* moving cautiously toward him. *This is just great, Redjack. Not only has Grimm betrayed you, but it looks like he got your former girlfriend to do his dirty work. Well, honey, you want me? You've got me, but I'll be damned if I let you take us all.* Ryan switched frequencies from broad band to tactical. "Boys, this is Ryan. Give it up. We're fighting Maria's Valkyries. I'm down and they've got us outgunned."

Agnar replied, "You sure, Ryan? We could run interference, give you a chance to get out."

"No way. Get out, and I'll see if I can get us out of this mess." *C'mon Ag, you know what to do.*

Ryan unfastened his safety harness and slid his helmet off. He hustled to get out of the 'Mech's cockpit. *If she sees me, she might hesitate, give my men time to make an exit. Maybe even give me a chance to get out of this alive. 'Course, she didn't hesitate to blow off my 'Mech's legs, did she?* Ryan popped the hatch on his *Quickdraw* and scrambled out. *If I get out of this Grimm, somehow I will get back to Oberon, kill you and spit on your carcass.*

Maria's *Grasshopper* stood there, the arm-mounted lasers pointed squarely at Ryan as he emerged. He thought could feel menace in the 'Mech's posture, and he wondered if it was from the pilot or just the ordinary anxiety of a man facing a killing machine. *I thought I had gotten through to you.* Ryan lowered his head. *Maybe not.*

He looked back up at the 'Mech and the weapons targeting him. "Is this how it's going to end, Mar?" Ryan shouted as he drew his pistol and began firing futilely at the 'Mech. "I thought we loved each other as much as we hated, but I never expected one of us to kill the other!" Ryan emptied the clip and finished by throwing the pistol, which clanked harmlessly against the *Grasshopper*'s torso. Maria's 'Mech remained motionless.

Ryan's face burned as the betrayal and the apparent hopelessness of his situation sank in. *Grimm, you sonofabitch. I swear I will come*

back from the grave and haunt your dreams. He waved his arms wildly and continued to shout at the *Grasshopper.* "This wasn't exactly how I was expecting to go, Mar. But so be it! What are you waiting for? Get it over with! What do you want, Maria? What the hell do you want?!"

The external speakers of the *Grasshopper* crackled to life with Maria's voice. "To know that I beat you."

Ryan cocked his head at the words. *What the hell does that mean?*

Seconds later, the hatch in the *Grasshopper*'s head flipped open and a knotted rope ladder tumbled down. It was followed by the stocky form of Maria Morgraine. She descended quickly and ran to Ryan when she reached the bottom. Ryan watched in confusion as she approached. *Should I have saved one last bullet?*

Maria climbed up on the toppled *Quickdraw* and stood face to face with Ryan. "I also want to tell you that I still love you."

Ryan smiled.

EIGHT

Cantor Canyon
Toland
13 November 3028
1745 hours

Kommandant Harris Ivor sat in the cockpit of his *Zeus* studying the visual feed from the recon lance several kilometers ahead. The images seemed to reflect exactly what the scouts had reported. A definite cease-fire had occurred. It looked as if Ryan's forces had surrendered, but Ivor could see no signs that the pirates were being forced from their 'Mechs. Indeed, it seemed as if everything had simply stopped. Either way, Ivor liked the situation less and less.

Ivor keyed his comm. "Can you discern what is happening near the depot?"

The Alpha lance commander answered. "Negative, Kommandant. There is a small grouping of 'Mechs around a downed *Quickdraw.* We can see some activity, but can make out no detail. Beta lance is reporting that a small group of pirates that were fighting have disengaged and are converging on the depot."

Something clearly is not right. Things never are right when bandits are involved. "Hold your position, Alpha lance. We're moving out." Ivor switched his comm to unit-wide. "Attention, all units. The pirate forc-

es around the depot decoy have disengaged. They could possibly be developing an alliance. Everyone up to 40 k-p-h. Let's get these brigands." Ivor lurched his *Zeus* forward and was on his way to the depot.

▲▼▲

Agnar grabbed Ryan's shoulder and spun him around, glaring. "Ryan, you can't be serious! When Grimm catches wind of this, he's going to come down on both of you like a hurricane."

"Not if we hit him first." Ryan flashed an arrogant smile. "I've always liked the way 'Redjack Ryan, King of Oberon' rolls off the tongue." Ryan shook free of Agnar's grip and stepped off toward where Maria was conferring with her commanders. Agnar didn't let him get far, coming right up behind the pirate and hissing in his ear, "No, Ryan. You need to kill her now. My lance is ready to back you up. We can take out all her commanders at once. Get control of this. You'll have the Valkyrate and more," Agnar persisted. "Think of all the munitions and other weapons Grimm has waiting for you. Don't let your groin think for your head again."

Ryan spun on Agnar and went nose to nose, letting his rage show in his eyes. "Don't you ever say that again. If I hear one more word from you, I'll make it so *your* groin can't do any more thinking." Ryan spat on the ground. "Don't you get it? Grimm *betrayed* us. There are no extra munitions. No more cash. No bonuses. He sent us out to be killed by my old girlfriend. I'll give the fiend credit for the idea, but that plan is over. In fact, I'm going to get Maria to help me take Grimm's little plan and shove it down his throat!"

Agnar shook his head. "Ryan, you can't trust her."

"I trust her more than I trust Grimm, that's for sure." Ryan squinted his eyes. "Whose side are you on, anyway?" The pirate turned sharply away and stalked off to join Maria.

A gust of wind kicked dust into Agnar's eyes. He blinked away the grit, then turned toward the members of Ryan's command lance. All four of the MechWarriors had disembarked from their machines, just like Maria's command lance. Things were not working out at all. Agnar had expected either Ryan or Maria to be dead by now, making it easier for him to finish off the survivor. He sucked in a breath through his teeth. *You damn fool, Ryan. I knew that if you figured out she was here, you'd do this to me.*

Agnar had known that, despite many angry tirades directed against Maria over the years, Ryan never really stopped loving her.

A relationship I never understood. Agnar had tried his best to get the two of them to kill each other, even launching a devastating raid on one of Maria's worlds last year, but the Ice Queen refused to chase them down. *Damn bitch.* When that ploy failed, Agnar knew that his chances at a coup of Butte Hold had faded.

The recent message from Grimm renewed Agnar's hope. The Lyran Commonwealth wanted insurance against "a possible Combine incursion," and Grimm saw the chance to forge a better, more stable state of his own. The Lyrans promised hardware and munitions, but wanted proof that they could rely on Grimm to act in their interests. Agnar had long been in Grimm's camp, and the bandit king knew he could count on Ryan's second-in-command to turn over Redjack to the Commonwealth. Being able to bring Maria's Valkyries in on the deal was just icing on the cake. That was the seed of their plan—a plan that was about to fail spectacularly, unless Agnar acted fast.

"What's the plan, Boss?" asked the scruffy-faced Tack Hadder, one of Ryan's personal lance.

Agnar practically spat the words. "They're going through with it. We shouldn't have to give up everything just because Ryan wants a lover's reunion!" Agnar drew his pistol, turned and started back toward Ryan; he heard the men fall into step behind him.

Ryan and Maria seemed to be arguing about something and were oblivious to Agnar's intent, but one of Maria's Valkyries pointed and uttered a panicked gasp.

"It's over, Redjack! Grimm sends his regards, and thanks." Agnar raised his pistol as Ryan turned to face him.

Agnar smiled, then without warning, blood, brain and bone burst from his forehead. The traitorous officer collapsed lifeless to the ground.

Maria was quick to draw her own weapon, and aimed it squarely at the remainder of Ryan's command lance.

Ryan stepped forward, a smirk on his face. "Good job, Tack. Always knew I could count on you." He slapped the MechWarrior on the shoulder.

"What the hell is going on?" Maria yelled.

Ryan turned back and smiled. "No need to worry. That bastard Agnar has been spying on me for Grimm for the past several years. I was beginning to wonder if he would ever betray me."

"You mean you knew this was going to happen?"

"Like this? Hell, no." Ryan laughed. "Like I told you, Grimm wanted me to kill you, and had me thinking you'd be showing up after

we'd secured things here. As soon as I realized you were already here, I suspected something deeper was up. I knew my only chance was to get you to not kill me."

Maria moved closer to Ryan, gun still drawn. "So you were just trying to save your own ass?"

Ryan closed the distance between them and gently pushed the hand holding the pistol so that it was pointing at the ground. "Honestly, Mar. Would you expect anything less?"

Maria Morgraine dropped her pistol, and with her free hand slapped Ryan hard across the face. "Not at all." Standing on her toes, she pulled the pirate's head down and kissed him.

A beeping alert sounded. Randi shouted, "Hate to break this up, you two, but we've got trouble."

▲▼▲

"Ryan, move your ass! We've already engaged their first line. Their 'Mechs are fresh and pushing us hard."

Ryan keyed his personal comm. "I'm working on it, Tack. Get the rest of the men back toward the drop point. I'll be there soon enough."

"Like hell. Maria and the rest of the Valkyries are covering us, but they can't hold out forever."

Ryan was working as fast as he could. He was trying to bypass the lockouts and other security measures Agnar had programmed into his *Orion* to prevent anyone else from piloting his ride. Ryan had forbidden these common precautions long ago, for precisely this situation; the pilot was dead, and Ryan needed the machine. Obviously, Agnar had had a good reason for disobeying. The *Orion*'s cockpit had quickly become a mess of hanging wires and exposed circuit boards as Ryan tried to patch into the brain of the machine. Every member of Ryan's command lance had offered him a ride, but Ryan couldn't bear to leave behind a perfectly good 'Mech—it had too much value, especially to a pirate. There was just no choice. If you could take it, you had to. In the distance, he could hear the dull thuds and booms of combat. Agnar, Grimm and the Lyrans had laid the perfect trap; now it was up to Ryan to fight his way out of it. He was counting on Maria's forces to help him, but there was still some nagging distrust in the back of his mind. *She's a pirate just like me. I'd expect her to cut and run, or at least her Valkyries.* Complicating the situation was that the two forces' DropShips were in different locations, so their troops would be forcibly divided.

Ryan completed his latest splice and then hit a row of switches. A shower of sparks burst from the numerous reroutes he'd made, but the command screens flickered to life. The pirate howled in victory while pulling on the bulky neurohelmet. Ryan multitasked between bringing the 'Mech online and strapping in. Within moments, the fusion reactor hummed to life.

"Tack, I'm in. Tell everyone to pull back!" Ryan shouted into his mic. He swung the *Orion* around and it responded, but sluggishly. *It'll have to do.*

▲▼▲

Maria Morgraine pressed the firing stud on the targeting joystick in her *Grasshopper*. The red beam from her heavy laser struck a Lyran *Shadow Hawk* squarely in the chest. Armor plating bubbled away, but the 'Mech remained largely unharmed.

An indicator light on a port panel flashed from red to green. *Good. Let's get the hell out of here!* The pirate was growing rapidly dissatisfied with the situation. Her battalion and nearly two companies of Ryan's men outnumbered the Lyran units with which they were engaged, but Maria knew the Lyran 'Mechs were fresh and had better tactical coordination: *too many people on my side out for themselves.* Maria's hope was to keep the Lyrans at bay long enough for Ryan to get moving. Part of her still wondered why she was even doing this. *Because that bastard Grimm betrayed us both.* Maria shook her head at the way she found herself thinking of Ryan—as part of a team ... as one half of a pair.

Maria keyed her comm. "Attention all. We're good to go. Valkyries, with me. Rebels, you're back with Redjack. We'll see you at the rendezvous point." Maria hit her jump jets and shot the *Grasshopper* into the air. Her crosshairs centered on the *Shadow Hawk* once again.

▲▼▲

"They're splitting off, sir. The majority are breaking east, with the rest coming back toward your position."

"Copy. Keep up the pursuit. I don't want any to get away." Kommandant Ivor could see the pirate forces on the edge of his radar image quickly moving to their DropShips. The tunnel network in the canyon had allowed Ivor to place his command company only a short

distance behind what recon had pegged as the likely command lance for one of the pirate bands on Toland. Though he was unsure which pirate leader it might be, Ivor was giddy at the prospect of nabbing a well-known thorn in the Commonwealth's side. "Alpha company, move out. We don't want them to enjoy any reinforcements. I want them alive to face Lyran justice."

▲▼▲

The *Orion* lumbered along, tight with the rest of the lance. Ryan had compensated as best he was able for the imperfect sync between the hijacked 'Mech's sensors and his brain. He only had two more kilometers to go before reaching the *Leopard* and *Union* DropShips that awaited him.

A loud yelp over his comm system was the only warning Ryan received before his klaxons sounded. He checked the display as it lit up with a dozen enemy 'Mechs literally coming out of the sides of the canyon walls that dotted the landscape around him. Cries of ambush announced the volleys of missiles that arced toward the lance. Within moments, the entire quartet was covered in flame and smoke as the destructive rain covered them.

"Dammit!" Ryan fought hard to keep the 'Mech on its feet while his lancemates returned fire in random directions. "Pull back! Pull back!" Ryan shouted. The pirate quickly began a retreat of his own as laser bursts and particle cannon fire sniped just overhead. He keyed his comm to reach the rest of his forces. "This is Ryan. We've been ambushed by a whole damn company. We need backup, now! We're making for the drop zone, but I'm only so good." The *Orion* rocked again as autocannon fire from a *Centurion* pounded into the 'Mech's chest.

▲▼▲

Karen Grander sat in the pilot's chair of her *Leopard* class DropShip, *Summoner's Gale.* As Ryan's command ship, she'd earned the pirate's trust and respect over the years, thanks in large part to her skill as a pilot and captain.

She barked orders to the rest of her crew as she prepped the *Gale* for a hot take-off. It was a drill she and her crew had done many times before—probably too many.

"*Bonny T, Black Caesar,* this is the *Gale.* We're hot-lifting. Ryan needs his ass saved—again."

Karen's comm crackled in return. "We hear ya, *Gale.* You want backup?"

"We've got this one, *Caesar.* Besides, you need to get everyone else. Stay prepped to support when they're in range, and keep an eye on the sky."

▲▼▲

Ryan locked onto the *Centurion* with his KaliYama missile system and let fly with a massive volley that covered the head and shoulders of the 'Mech. *Nice shooting, but you're not going to make it,* he told himself. *There's too many of them.* Ryan took stock of the forces against him. Nothing he saw made him happy, but the paired *Catapult*s and *Hunchback*s were the 'Mechs that worried him the most. Ryan was doing what he could to keep the canyon walls between him and those large cannons. The largest Lyran 'Mech was a *Zeus,* and even though the lightest in Ryan's lance was Dag Staham's *Thunderbolt,* there would be no way they could last long enough for help to arrive. *Unless ...*

"Target the *Zeus.* It's got to be their command 'Mech. Let's see if we can bend their morale a little." Ryan tied in all his longer-range weapons and centered his crosshairs on the *Zeus'* chest. Tack's *Stalker* had already laid down a barrage of missile and laser fire, all while taking a beating. Ryan was happy to see the Lyran 'Mech bathed in smoke and fire. Ryan's own missile volley overshot the 'Mech, tearing up the ground nearly sixty meters behind it. His autocannon struck true, however, pounding the left leg of the machine. The pilot showed his mettle as he kept the 'Mech on its feet, even as more missile and laser fire from Dag's *Thunderbolt* covered it. The pair of particle-cannon blasts from the *Awesome* piloted by Kate Malger proved to be too much. The *Zeus* rocked forward and dropped to its knees, and its massive arms stopped its descent.

Not so easily cowed, the Lyran 'Mechs returned fire. Dag's *Thunderbolt* had played too close and bore the brunt of the assault. The 'Mech disappeared in a hail of missile, laser and autocannon fire. Ryan could hear Dag's screams as he tried to weather the storm, but it was too much. The tattered remains of the *T-bolt* wavered slightly before collapsing lifeless to the ground.

That was enough for the other two 'Mechs in Ryan's lance. Both broke formation and ran in opposite directions. "Tack! Kate! Get back here!" Ryan's orders went unanswered. Weapons fire chased after the fleeing 'Mechs, but also had the unintended effect of drawing

off a lance of Ryan's pursuers. Unfortunately for him, a lance still remained, led by the *Zeus,* which had regained its footing. The 'Mech stood with its left arm pointed straight at Ryan, as if to command him to stop, while the other three 'Mechs spread out, trying to surround the pirate.

Ryan did his best to angle away from the closing circle, checking the ETA of the rest of his forces, but knew he was finished. *They're not firing. They want me alive.* Ryan checked his display. Tack and Kate seemed to be facing the same scenario, but they were trying to fight their way out. *And losing.*

Ryan raised the hands of his *Orion* in surrender but continued to back up, preventing himself from being surrounded. The *Zeus* responded with a laser shot directly over the cockpit of Ryan's 'Mech. The pirate slowed to a stop. *Message received, Mr. Zeus.* Ryan saw Kate's 'Mech go down on his display. *That's about it, then.* "Maria, this is Ryan. I can't escape my ambush. Looks like Grimm is going to get part of his wish."

"Not yet, sir!" a crisp voice crackled over Ryan's headset.

Ryan checked his display again to see a *Leopard* DropShip angling in for a strafing run. The Lyran 'Mechs saw it as well, but too late to do any real damage to the massive ship. A Lyran *Warhammer* cracked off both its particle cannons, which struck home, but it wasn't enough to change the outcome. Two-score missiles, multiple lasers and a pair of PPCs tore into the lance. The *Zeus* toppled in a hail of explosions, while the *Warhammer* that had struck the craft rocked back as it took a heavy laser strike to its cockpit. The other two 'Mechs, a *Hunchback* and *Griffin* took only minor damage, but turned their attention away from Ryan.

It was the break the pirate needed. Resuming his retreat, Ryan tied all his weapons together and centered on the *Hunchback.* A hail of missile and autocannon fire ripped into the 'Mech's right arm, tearing it clean from the body. The 'Mech staggered but kept its footing as it turned its back to Ryan.

The *Griffin* tried to avenge his partner, but its particle cannon shot wide left, while a decade of missiles exploded harmlessly around the *Orion*'s feet. Ryan backed around the side of a small hill, which put him out of sight of the enemy 'Mechs. "Karen, you're a lifesaver. Don't come around for another run. Kate's done, and Tack's not looking much better. Drop in behind me and let's get the hell out of here." Ryan turned tail and kicked his *Orion* into a sprint toward another hill.

▲▼▲

The black fog in Kommandant Ivor's head started to clear, allowing him to open his eyes. His *Zeus* was barely functional. He checked his tactical displays and saw that the fleeing *Orion* was breaking for a clearing in the canyon, where the *Leopard* was intending to land for a hot pick up. The *Awesome* was down, and the *Stalker* wasn't too far behind. *We'll never get the* Orion, *but we got some of the bastards.* Ivor checked his long-range scans and saw the remainder of the pirate force closing fast. They outnumbered his command company, and their DropShips were too close. "Command, this is Ivor. Pull back. Disable that *Stalker*, but let the *Orion* go. I don't want any losses going up against that *Leopard,* or anything else they're liable to bring over."

Ivor carefully got his *Zeus* to its feet and watched as the *Leopard* came in slowly for the fleeing *Orion*. "Damn pirates."

NINE

JumpShip **Hath no Fury**
Uncharted world, Periphery
1 December 3028
1930 hours

Maria looked at Ryan's naked, scarred and tattooed back as he stood at the opposite end of her cabin, staring at her map of the Inner Sphere. Ryan was drawing a circle around the worlds of the Valkyrate, and expanding it to include his own world of Butte Hold.

"The Greater Valkyrate, huh?" Ryan asked without turning around. "That's what you want to call it?"

Maria sat up in her bed, pulling the blankets up to just above her breasts. "It's better than saying 'The Bigger Butte.'" She chuckled, purposefully mispronouncing 'Butte' as 'Butt.'

Ryan turned, a fiendish but playful grin on his face. "It would match yours." A pillow from Maria's bunk was his answer. Ryan tossed the pillow back. "My men will hate it."

"There's not much left of your men to complain, from the way I see it."

Ryan laughed, but it hurt to admit she was right. He'd lost about forty percent of his force between Maria's attack and the Lyran follow-up. The Valkyries, on the other hand, had lost only a few 'Mechs

and still had a company in reserve. Ryan knew he was outgunned if he tried to make any power plays. *Choose your battles, Redjack.*

"Greater Valkyrate it is, then." He smiled and launched himself across the room toward Maria.

Maria yelped as she put up her arms and legs to both block and catch Ryan's playful leap. The two wrestled for a moment before Ryan finally pinned her. Maria struggled half-heartedly. "What do you want to do about Grimm?"

Ryan sighed. "There's not much we can do, love. Our force is far from cohesive, Grimm has more firepower than we do, and he might still be in bed with the Lyrans for all we know. It's not safe. We can't take him on directly."

Maria nodded, but did not look happy. "We can't let him get away with it. We have to do something."

Ryan thought for a moment. "If we do what you had planned with the *Winged Vengeance,* all we'll do is bring down his fury on us. We need to hit him somewhere it'll hurt, but not hard enough to force him to come after us. We need to send a message." Ryan got out of bed again and returned to the map.

"You have an idea?"

"Two, actually." Ryan tapped his finger on a world within the Oberon Confederation. "First, I think I know where we can hit him, but I need to find a certain merchant." Ryan smiled.

"And two?" Maria asked.

Ryan walked slowly back toward the bed, his devilish grin returning. "If we're going to rule the Greater Valkyrate together, we're going to need an heir."

TEN

Grimfort, Oberon City
Oberon VI
25 December 3028
2315 hours

Dual shafts of moonlight laid shadows across the face of Hendrick Grimm III as he stared at the datapad in front of him. The report contained little good news. The supply depot he had hidden on Placida had not only been looted clean, it had been utterly destroyed. Razed to the ground, with very few men left alive. The survivors had identified both Redjack Ryan and Maria Morgraine in the invading force.

Grimm had known for a while now that the trap he and Agnar laid had failed. Though he didn't know the details, the news he'd received via ComStar had told him plenty. Elements of the Thirtieth Lyran Guard had engaged pirates on Toland, suffered minor losses, and captured several bandits in the process. The bulk of the raiders had escaped. Because none of those pirates ever showed up back on Oberon, Grimm knew that Agnar had failed. *Worse than failure: it seems you brought the two of them together.*

That, and the strike at Placida, made him angry. He clearly understood the message Ryan and Maria were sending him, and in fact was oddly comforted by the fact that this was the only world that had been hit. After the collapse of his plan, the last thing he needed was facing off against vengeful pirates and a possibly angry Lyran Commonwealth.

Aside from those who worked at the depot, only his senior staff and a few select couriers knew about the facility. It was more than just a depot—it was also a munitions factory that supplied slightly less than half of the ammunition for his infantry troops and also some of his 'Mech units. There was no way Ryan or Maria could have known about the facility unless someone had squealed.

This was not turning out to be a merry Christmas.

Grimm sighed and rubbed his heavy hand over his bald head. He played the scenarios quickly through his mind, trying to assess who would most benefit from betraying him in this way. One by one, he eliminated his senior staff from suspicion. All of them had been with him a long time, and their loyalty was unquestionable.

Grimm employed three different couriers to travel to the facility, but none of them were fully aware of what the bandit king hid there. Grimm eliminated one, then another, as he calculated how long it had been since each had traveled to Placida.

That left him with one. *Of course. It makes sense for it to be you.* In that moment, he vowed to find the traitorous rat and string him up alive. *I'll show you the meaning of justice in the Periphery. And when I'm through with him, Ryan, I'll make sure you and Maria know what it means to anger the king of Oberon.*

Grimm pressed the comm button on his desk. "Get me the merchant, Kelly Hunt."

ABANDONMENT

BLAINE LEE PARDOE

Drop Zone Theta Alpha
The Attore Bluff
Ford
Lyran Commonwealth
April 10, 3022

Lieutenant Charles "Charlie" Vincent Bane stepped over the crest of the bluff in his *Dervish* and braked to a full stop in stunned disbelief. There was supposed to be a DropShip there. This was the right coordinates, he checked his secondary display again. *No way in hell I'm off–I've been tracking my position for four days.* It had to be a mistake.

There were *signs* a DropShip had been here recently. The grass and brush were burned clear and the ground was caked from the intense heat of the fusion engines. There were four massive depressions in the ground, perfect circles 20 centimeters deep, from left by the DropShip's gigantic landing feet. There was debris, the kind of garbage and trash usually left behind when a ship departed. But there was no DropShip at the top of the bluff. None. Two hours of climbing Attore Bluff and no ride offworld. He swept the entire bluff with his long-range sensors, but found nothing more than a faint radioactive signature about a half-kilometer from the charred ground. He tagged the image on his display as the reality soaked in.

They had left. There was no wreckage from a DropShip in the area. There may have been some sort of a fight here, but the ship had not been destroyed, at least, not here. They had simply left.

Bane pounded his command console. *How could they have left him?* He felt a stinging around the edge of his eyes and fought back tears. It had been a long week of hard travel to reach the drop zone, only to find it empty. They had taken off early, *he* was on time. They weren't supposed to leave a man behind, that was part of the code. MechWarriors didn't do that, not House Marik MechWarriors, anyway. The Lyrans, well, that was a different story. He knew them to be a heartless crowd, but not the Captain General's men. His comrades had a sense of honor. But the absence of the DropShip told him a different reality, one that he was suddenly forced to deal with.

Perhaps the sensor reading could tell him more. He angled his battered *Dervish* to the northeast and pushed across the charred ground. As he got closer, he saw lots of burn marks in the grass, the occasional crater, telltale marks of errant expendables fired in battle. When he saw the charred hulk of the Mobile HQ, the purple eagle of the Third Sirian Lancers, he realized the drop zone had been overrun.

Idling his *Dervish*, he climbed out of his cockpit, pulled out his needler, and trotted to the blackened hulk of a vehicle. *Something destroyed this entire HQ and I'm thinking a needler is going to help...I must be crazy or stupid or both.* Holes stitched along the side in a diagonal pattern showed several autocannon hits. The air stung his nostrils, a hint of sweat, charred armor, even rotting flesh—most likely from the crushed remains of the HQ's mangled cockpit. The side door was half-cracked open. He touched it quickly, half wondering if it was hot, but he only felt cold, broken metal.

Climbing inside, he saw the interior of the HQ was a wreck, but had not been badly burned. It appeared that the armored exterior had bore the brunt of the damage. A salvage crew had made quick work of anything worth taking. The remaining consoles were shattered; two of them were broken off their mountings and hanging by strands of wires just over the floor. The long range sensors had simply been removed, right down to the wiring. He stepped over a cracked, dried brown stain on the floor—blood, proof of the fight that had doomed the vehicle.

The primary battlerom was gone. Most likely the victors of the battle had pulled it. It made sense, who knows what kind of military secrets they might find? *None, if I know Colonel Zander. He would never send us in with any data that might be turned against our people.*

Charlie moved over a fallen chair and to the tactical feed. He opened the access port, reached in and extracted the small, circular chip—the backup battlerom for the HQ. Perhaps it might tell him what had happened here and where the DropShip had gone. He descended from the HQ and sprinted to his *Dervish*. He had to find some cover to sort through everything, then decide what his next move would be.

▲▼▲

The copse of trees provided ample cover for his tiny camp. He'd built the fire against a large boulder that blocked most of the light it gave off. Dinner was a rations pack, old and cold, the way he liked it. He'd rigged his *Dervish's* sensors to alert him if anyone approached. In the meantime, he got some much needed time out of the cockpit.

The backup battlerom hadn't offered much in terms of hope or good news. Using his battlecomputer, he had had been able to re-cover enough to piece together what happened. Three days ago, the Ford Planetary Militia had swept up this plateau and overran the land-ing zone. The Mobile HQ had fallen to the rear of the column and was finally overrun. The DropShip, *The Liberty Bell*, had been given orders to depart. They were the last orders that the Mobile HQ had sent, and the ship had apparently obeyed.

This had been the secondary drop zone, his last hope for a ride offworld. The raid by the Third Sirian Lancers had been a QCCF, a quasi-controlled-cluster-fu** from the moment they had landed. The overrunning of the drop zone by planetary militia had been the icing on the proverbial cake.

Charles leaned against his sleeping bag and stared up at the stars. Some of those stars were those of his home, the Free Worlds League. He wondered if he was ever going to find his way back to those stars now. When the operation had started his mission was simple, take his lance of 'Mechs about 100 kilometers from the landing zone and take out a munitions plant near the city of Gunster. Ford's position along the border made it a tempting target, and the Lyran Commonwealth made sure that the world was heavily garrisoned. They had landed with a full battalion, usually more than enough for a lightning raid.

Someone had tipped off the Lyrans, at least that was Charlie's thinking. They had popped up with at least twice as many troops and from the way they fought, they were anything but local militia. *Military intelligence had screwed the pooch on this one.* Every one of the raiding parties had run into well-placed, highly-organized resistance. House Marik had not planned on taking Ford from the Commonwealth, they just wanted to make sure it was of no value to the Lyrans. But the Lyrans had been there, waiting, more than prepared to face them. *If I ever get off this rock I'm going to kick our regimental intelligence officer in the balls...*

Most likely the defenders were some frontline Guards units painted up to look like the locals. As Charlie and Bravo Lance of the Second Company reached the outskirts of their objective, he started to get communications feeds from the other officers. Every raiding unit had stumbled into some sort of trap. Captain Foster had taken two lances of heavies into a swamp that had been sewn with vibramines. What the mines didn't destroy, the lance of aerospace fighters had bombed into oblivion. A classmate and comrade of his, Bucky Barrington, had been sent to take out a key switch station on the mag lev line. Finding it heavily defended, he had barely escaped with his life.

Their warnings prepped Charlie. He sent out a light *Stinger*, Lieutenant Christi Parker, to scout. She'd barely managed to bark a warning before the enemy was all over her. The lance of assaults and heavies had hit them hard. Charlie had accounted for one, a nasty old *Catapult*. The remains of his lance, against his orders, had charged towards the plant, firing as they went. They drew the rest of the defenders with them. By the time Charlie had finished the *Catapult*, the rest of his MechWarriors were dead and the defenders were heading his way. He had been hopelessly outmanned and outgunned.

So, he ran. It shamed him, but he ran away. The choice was life or a brief but lonely death, and at the time, that didn't seem reasonable. Bane's *Dervish* pulled away from the Lyrans and he kept going. After a while, the Lyrans broke off their pursuit. After all, he was a lone BattleMech, already damaged. How much trouble could he cause? Charlie shook his head. He didn't know the answer to that question even now, days later.

As he stared up at the stars he wondered, *what now?* If *The Liberty Bell* was gone, then so was the rest of the Third Sirian Lancers. He wondered if there were others like him, abandoned on Ford, left to fend for themselves. If there were others, how could he contact them? Using the secured channels might work, but it would still alert the Lyrans that he was still on Ford. With the other members of the Free Worlds League raiding party gone, they would be free to hunt him down like some wild animal.

He pulled out his survival kit, unrolling it in the fire's dim light. The usual implements were there; a large knife, a fishing kit, a small, pen-size power pack, some emergency ration bars that were probably vintage First Succession War, from the look of the labels. A fire-igniter, which he wished he'd found before he spent thirty minutes trying to light the fire on his own. There were emergency flares, a tissue-thin thermal blanket, an emergency pulse communicator—all good to have, but worthless in his current situation.

There was some money there too. About fifty C-bills, some Marik dollars, and a few Lyran minted coins. Enough for a good night on the town, but hardly enough to scrape together a living. As he studied the contents of the survival kit, he realized just how bad things were for him and how limited his options were. He rolled up the kit carefully in its tube and leaned back to stare up at the stars again.

Surrender? He looked up at his *Dervish* and cringed. The BattleMech was old, not like the newer model Davion *Dervishes* they were allegedly making. This one dated back generations. It had been his grandmother's BattleMech, and his father's and had been in the family way before they had piloted it. Surrender meant that the 'Mech would become spoils of war. The Lyrans would take it, refit it, and use it—*against* the Free Worlds League. His 'Mech might very well kill members of his own family.

And if he did surrender, then what? Prisoner of war camp? He had heard the stories about the Lyran camps, of the torture and mistreatment. Some of that had to be propaganda, but even those lies started with a grain of truth. Would they try and squeeze military secrets from him? He chuckled at the thought. Charles Vincent Bane didn't know any useful secrets. The shame of surrender would stain him for the rest of his life, even if he managed to get exchanged and sent home. Worse, he would be dispossessed. Being a MechWarrior carried status, and that was hard to let go.

If surrender wasn't an option, he wondered what was. Could he use his money to book passage on a commercial DropShip offworld? Probably not. He could possibly send a short message via HPG, but he had no idea what to send and to whom. The money wasn't enough and as a world on the border, the officials of Ford were going to be looking for proper paperwork and identification. False IDs could be purchased, but Charlie realized that he didn't have the kind of connections needed. And, even if he could get passage offworld, what about his 'Mech? He would return in disgrace and dispossessed. They would never give him a military command again, there would always be some concern if he had been turned by the enemy and sent back as a mole.

Ford was a large planet with plenty of terrain for hiding. Perhaps he could conceal his 'Mech and get a job, blend in. Over time he might earn enough money to book passage off-planet. Would he be able to take his 'Mech then? Was it a matter of money? Yes, there were unscrupulous merchants with DropShips, but how would he arrange for transport of a 'Mech off a Lyran world, bound for the Free

Worlds League? There was no amount of money he could earn that would pay that kind of bill. Each option he explored offered less appeal. No matter how well he hid the 'Mech, there was a risk that someone would find it. BattleMechs required maintenance and his had already been in a fight. Without proper supplies, maintenance, and the gear to mothball his ride properly, his 'Mech could soon be rendered useless. Bane didn't have the equipment or money necessary to keep the machine operational indefinitely.

He closed his eyes for a moment and drew in a deep, sighing breath. There was something else nagging at him as his options seemed to evaporate. He, Lieutenant Charles Bane, had fled his last engagement. He felt his face flush with the memory. When he realized his lance had stumbled into a trap, he'd ordered them out, but they had not obeyed. The cost had been their lives. Bane had run. In the face of the enemy, he had turned his back and run to save his own life. The mission had not mattered, nor had the fate of the rest of his lance. Charlie had run. Even if he did return to the Free Worlds League, the truth would come out. Charlie had never been a good liar. They would interrogate him and learn that he had fled the fight. With the losses and ambushes, chances are they would label him as the scapegoat.

The shame welled up in him and he crossed his arms, hugging himself tightly in the cool evening chill as if to ward against it. Charlie felt he could handle the disgrace, but he knew his parents couldn't, nor could his brother. His brother, Drake, served in the Second Sirian Lancers regiment. If it became known that Charlie had run in the face of battle, his career would be damaged as well.

He opened his eyes and stared upward at the stars. Surrender was not an option. Hiding or attempting to go home was not possible either. Where did that leave him? Lieutenant Bane stared up for a long time before he found his answer in the stars. It was not a perfect solution, but it was the best he could hope for. It was the only path that did not offer shame...he would have to complete his original mission.

▲▼▲

Charlie had no intention of a suicide run against the munitions plant at Gunster. His intent was to sweep in, destroy the facility and get out. If there was a strong defense, he would slug it out with them and punch-out before his BattleMech was destroyed. He might end up dispossessed, but his loyalty and honor would not be questioned when—if—he someday returned home. The stain of his flight from the

last battle would be erased if he was successful. Dispossessed with dignity; that was how he mentally framed the idea.

There were many issues with his plan. Gunster was days away and the last time he was there the munitions plant was heavily defended. Taking out a munitions factory was no easy task. Large earthen berms divided the facility, each one very high and sloped. This helped contain industrial accidents. Where one or two buildings were destroyed, the blasts and fires would not easily spread to the other nearby structures. This meant that he would have to open fire on each part of the plant. Only by saturating the area with fire could he ensure that the facility would be destroyed.

Preventing that would be the defenders. It had been a lance of heavy and assault 'Mechs the last time he was there. The *Catapult* had been destroyed, but the others had survived. It was possible that they had assume that he had either been destroyed or evacuated with the rest of the Sirian Lancers; but that was not something he could rely on. The munitions plant was still a tempting target, especially given Ford's position along the border. Even if there wasn't a full lance of BattleMechs there, it was possible that there would be other defenders.

His *Dervish* was still in one piece, but had been damaged in the ambush. Charlie had taken a few hits to the upper torso and right side of the 'Mech. He'd fired off half of his long-range missiles, which worried him. A *Dervish* is a good close-support fighter, and once he ran out of LRMs, he would only be able to engage the enemy up-close and personal.

Charlie had spent hours looking over the terrain around Gunster on his tactical display, carefully studying his objective. Now that he'd seen the area first hand, he understood the subtlety of the terrain that the maps didn't reveal. His lance had come in along the main road leading towards the plant. There had been nothing subtle about the approach, nothing devious. The defenders had positioned themselves perfectly and wiped his force out. *This time I won't make the same mistake.*

Charlie allowed himself a wry grin at the thought. When the Lancers had come it had been a raid that was to surprise and stun the local militia on Ford. This time they probably didn't know he was still there, in an operational BattleMech. Their intelligence leak didn't know about Charlie either. *Maybe this time I can achieve real surprise.* The route he chose was long, curvaceous, and far from settlements. It would take a week to reach the point he planned to use to mount his attack. He only hoped that his *Dervish* held together long enough to get there.

Eight Days Later...

Charlie slid from his cover behind the boulder and looked out at the plant. Using his enhanced binoculars, he surveyed for heat sources and enlarged the images. The plant bristled with personnel and activity. The sight of people didn't surprise him, but it did unnerve him a little. If he was successful, many of them would be dead, victims of his attack. *No, not victims...simply dead Lyrans.*

He had left his *Dervish* in a small forest three kilometers away. As he surveyed the munitions plant he saw signs of the defense. Two Galleon tanks protected the main gate. The Galleons were light tanks but could still provide a nasty punch. He didn't see any BattleMechs, but assumed they had some nearby.

The key was getting close to the plant before being spotted. With all of the trees cleared around the facility, any direct approach would give the defenders plenty of warning. But, near the planet was the Cuyahoga River. A murky, fast-moving river, the plant tapped it as a source of cooling water. That was the key to his plan.

Charlie paused for a moment, lowering the binoculars. This was what he had planned a week ago. Now the question was would he have enough nerve to pull it off? Gulping in air, he tucked the binoculars in his haversack. Yes, it was time for him to redeem himself.

Making sure he hadn't been spotted, he withdrew and jogged back to his 'Mech. Settling into his command couch, he secured the safety harness and donned his neurohelmet, the coolant vest gurgling to life as he turned on the system. Looking around the cockpit, he wondered if this was indeed the last battle he would be fighting in the family's BattleMech. The centuries-old cockpit showed signs of age. There was the replacement targeting and tracking system his father had installed. The burn marks that had been painted over on the top of the canopy from a fight that his grandmother had survived. It was said that during the First Succession War, the entire cockpit had been replaced when his great-great grandfather had been killed during a battle with the Lyrans—the same people he was now facing. One more time the Bane family legacy was marching off against the enemies of the League.

The *Dervish* moved gingerly towards the bend in the river. The Cuyahoga was wide here, nearly three-quarters of a kilometer across, and deep. He slowly walked into the water. In just a minute the river washed over the top of the cockpit glass. The murky liquid was so thick it was nearly impossible to see, so he relied on his tracking system to help guide him. Charlie fought the strong current and made his way, one slow plodding step at a time, upriver.

It took two long tedious hours to reach the edge of the plant complex. Fighting the constant push of the river with the controls made his arms and legs ache. He crossed the river bottom and from what he could tell, he was just about to break the surface. Charlie reached out and patted the main display once. "One more fight pretty lady—that's all I'm asking for." With those words he leaned back and throttled the 'Mech forward and up—out of the water.

It was obvious that the civilians and the defenders were stunned, but Charlie wasn't. He fired his medium lasers at the closest Galleon, hitting it on the flank. Long crimson beams cut a pair of nasty scars along the side of the tank. He stood knee-deep with the *Dervish* in the running brown river water, letting the river cool his 'Mech.

The tank he hit stayed still, the other one burst into movement, almost blindly, charging away. Charlie fired two salvos. One a pair of short-range missiles aimed at the tank he'd already hit, the second pair into the factory complex itself. One of the SRMs plowed into the tank, the other blew up the guard shack. The pair fired at the factory hit buildings but he could see little results other than their wispy trails of smoke.

Charlie unleashed his long-range missiles at the Galleon making a break for it. The missiles twisted through the air and engulfed the tank's side and rear armor just as it begin to turn. Armor plating flew off in all directions, but the tank was still in the fight. The first Galleon aimed one of its lasers at him, striking his *Dervish* in the right thigh. Steam rose from the water, a mix from the hit and from all of the weapons fire that he was unleashing.

Charlie danced the targeting reticule on the first Galleon and be-gan to move up river slightly, straining against the current. He fired his lasers again. The hits were deep this time, burrowing deadly holes into the side of the light tank. The Galleon seemed to rock for a mo-ment, obviously the result of some sort of internal blast. Smoke bil-lowed out of every hatch as the crew abandoned it.

The other Galleon fired, but both of the shots missed by a mere meter or two. His sensors came to life as he detected another target, this one more dangerous—a BattleMech. The seventy-ton *Grasshop-per* was a nasty battler. It was at the far end of the plant, but was al-ready breaking into a full run around the edge of the factory complex.

He twisted his *Dervish* towards the last tank. The battered Gal-leon was still smoking from the rear as it turned to face him. Its lasers fired brilliant red beams at him, tearing at his torso armor. The *Dervish*

sagged, fighting the current and the impact. Charlie let loose with a long-range missile salvo, then turned, firing another wave of missiles into the middle of the factory complex.

Most of the missiles hit the tank. Its left side turret caught the brunt of the blast and was so badly savaged it was left sagging, gouging the barrel into the ground as it drove. The driver stopped and tossed the tank into a bucking reverse.

The missiles aimed at the factory hit all over the complex. He saw a secondary blast in the distance; something vital had been hit. Charlie checked the *Grasshopper* on sensors and saw it closing in from the north, nearly at the edge of the plant.

He stopped fighting the current and turned back, towards the tank. To the tank driver this had to have looked like his worst nightmare. The *Dervish* came out of the water and fired short range missiles at it as the 'Mech broke into a charge right at it.

The missiles finished the tank, hitting the less-protected top of the vehicle, ripping holes into the armor. Flames emerged from one hole, then every hatch seemed to pop at once as the crew bailed. *Great!* Charlie rushed past it and turned to the south end of the plant just as the *Grasshopper* let loose with four of its medium lasers. Two of the lasers found their mark on the legs of his *Dervish*, searing off chunks of armor as they struck. The other two shots went high and wide. Charlie rounded the corner so that the building blocked another immediate attack.

Now that he was out of the water, the *Dervish* was running much hotter. He fought the heat and kept going. Charlie unleashed his short-range missiles as he ran. Buildings were hit and he could feel the blast of each explosion. He kept making his way at a full run past the front of the plant complex and then around the corner again.

The *Grasshopper* was not so forgiving. A wave of long range missiles streaked in the air, locking on him mid-flight, testimony to the skill of the MechWarrior. The missiles ate into the *Dervish*'s thin rear armor and nearly tumbled him face-forward. From his cockpit he saw a piece of his rear armor splay in the air overhead and land in front of him as he lost his stride.

At the corner of the plant's perimeter, he stopped and twisted his torso around forty-five degrees. Locking onto the *Grasshopper*, he let go with his long-range missile racks. He didn't wait to see if they found their mark, juking around the corner. There was as deep rumble like thunder as one of the buildings out of his field of vision exploded. *Good!* If nothing else, his raid had already been successful.

The *Grasshopper* fired regardless, hitting the building he was next to and spilling a grinding chunk of the brickwork into his *Dervish*. It didn't do much damage, but it surprised him. This MechWarrior was willing to risk hitting one of the buildings to stop him. It was an unnerving realization.

Time to up the ante. Charlie rounded the building and ran between the buildings, firing his lasers as he went, searing two more buildings. He was charging into the middle of the complex. *Let's see if he's willing to play on my terms.* In the tight quarters of the industrial complex every missed shot stood the chance of doing damage.

As he passed on building, a pair of medium lasers hit him on the side. The armor there was gone, and all that stopped the lasers was the long range missile rack. It was nothing more than melted slag now, that's what the damage display told him anyway.

Ahead was a large, five-story building. The moment he thought he had cover, Charlie fired a wave of long-range missiles into it. The structure half-crumbled towards him, flames bursting out of the interior. *Burn baby–burn!*

Another wave of long range missiles came in around him. Three hit his arms and back. Spinning, he saw the *Grasshopper* land nearby. Jump jets! *Damn.* He toggled his medium lasers and fired at it as it landed. One laser missed, hitting the building behind the Lyran BattleMech. The other hit it square in the chest armor. The massive 'Mech didn't even look as if it had felt the impact. The large laser in its torso fired back. This time the hit was devastating. Charlie felt a rumble in the bowels of the 'Mech as ammo cooked off, probably the last of his long-range missiles. His head felt as if he was cast into the bowels of the worst hangover he ever experienced—the nightmare of neuron-feedback from the internal blast. Nausea swept over him to the point where he popped the faceplate open on his helmet in case he had to vomit. The feedback had dulled the violent shake and rattle from the hit, but his senses emerged from the haze of sickness as he regained control. The missile rack that remained went off-line as well, either from the laser hit or from the internal blast. Smoke rose from the torso of his 'Mech in front of the armored cockpit glass.

He ran around a corner to put the structure between him and the *Grasshopper*, using one of the earthen berms for partial cover as he moved. For the first time the *Dervish* seemed sluggish, as if it was fighting him. The engine was running hot, he didn't need a display to tell him that. The sauna all around him told him more than the readouts. The heat told him the internal damage had been bad, worse than he thought. Still, he kept going, pushing the old BattleMech further and harder. He fired short-range missiles into a pair of storage tanks. They went up in thunderous explosions, and burning fluid poured out. Alarms went off in the planet complex and he saw people running in every direction.

The *Grasshopper* rounded a corner and fired a snapshot with its medium lasers. Three hit, one blew up a car that was parked next to him. His leg armor bore the brunt of the assault. He lumbered his *Dervish* out of line of sight again and glanced at his damage display. The movement of his 'Mech was worse than ever. It moved as if it were drunk, half running, half staggering with each step.

He fired a pair of short range missiles off at a building that had a lot of pipes leading into and out of it. Flames roared up. It had to be driving the *Grasshopper* MechWarrior insane. He was not fighting him, he was trashing the plant instead. With his last round of SRMs he saw the heat indicator reach the redline. Time was running out. He slowed slightly as he ducked between two low buildings that only offered cover to his legs. The Grasshopper lined him up and fired his long range missile rack.

Whoever that is, they're good! The missiles hit on the right arm of the *Dervish*, blasting off the remains of the armor there. He looked over and saw only jagged strips of armor and exposed myomer bundles where the arm had once been. More importantly, the medium laser there was nothing but a blackened piece of scrap metal now. His short-range missile rack was still operative, but he doubted it would last very much longer. While the damage display still showed it as online, he knew it was gone. The sensor must have been fried as well.

This is almost over. His *Dervish* was dying around him. He passed the two low buildings and came to a large complex near the heart of the munitions plant. Charlie stopped and switched his short-range missiles online. He fired them all at the building right in front of him. Shrapnel in the form of pieces of mortar and brick rained down on him.

The heat rose even further into the red zone and suddenly he heard a shudder as the fusion reactor tripped into shut-down mode. Target warning came into his ears as the *Grasshopper* moved into position for the killing shot to his rear. Lieutenant Charles "Charlie" Vincent Bane did something he swore he would never do. He reached out, grabbed the ejection bar, and pulled it towards him. There was a blast of cool air and a roar filled his ears. Disorientation overcame him and he remembered laughing right before everything went dark.

ABANDONMENT

Dearborn City
The Eastern Expanses
Ford
Lyran Commonwealth
Two Days Later

Charlie sat in the chair and watched the interrogation officer pace back and forth on the far side of the table, like a cat waiting to pounce. "You caused quite a stir, Lieutenant," the man said in a thick Germanic accent, using the Lyran form of his rank. "Nothing we cannot repair, but you have taken the plant off-line for some time."

He wanted to smile, but held back. He didn't want to give this man any reason to punish him. His arm was in a cast from the ejection seat landing hard on the ferrocrete at the plant. His hair had been singed to the roots on his scalp, which supported a field dressing which still stung when he shifted in his seat. "I did my duty."

"The Third Sirian Lancers left this world weeks ago," the man replied coolly. "You claim to be one of them, but they left. So tell me, who are you and what unit are you with? Where are your comrades hiding? What are your mission objectives? Surely a minor munitions plant cannot be your only target, Herr Bane? Who is working with you? What other units are on Ford right now? I need a list of targets, Herr Bane!"

Charlie let go the urge to smile. The frustration of his interrogator gave him a sense of comfort. He rose in his seat and grinned broadly. "I told you already, I was with the Third Lancers. You want to go looking for my unit, go ahead, you won't find them."

"You were left behind to destroy that plant?"

"I was abandoned," he proclaimed proudly. "The destruction of that plant was the fulfillment of my mission. You can believe that if you want or not. I don't care."

"I find it hard to believe that such a skilled MechWarrior was abandoned. You must be lying," the man accused.

Lieutenant Bane smiled. That was the best compliment he could have hoped for.

WITH CARRION MEN

PHAEDRA M. WELDON

Jakarta City, Ruins
Farandir
Magistracy of Canopus
2 February 3072

The *Wraith* stumbled to the side, momentum as combined with a well-placed shot into his already damaged left knee joint working against the Warrior's ability to keep balance. Unable to maintain stability, the 'Mech toppled over—its own mass and velocity Aris Sung's worst enemy. He yelled as his body was thrown hard against the harness and felt something crack inside his chest as his *jian* flew from the floor where he'd tossed it and slammed into the HUD platform. He also glimpsed his needler flying past as well and heard it strike something just as hard and unforgiving.

The 'Mech rolled twice, the ferrous glass cracking, shattering, but staying in one piece as it struck rock and ruined buildings alike. Another ER PPC hit from the enemy and the torso shuddered a final death throe. Aris held on until the ride stopped. When it was done he hung upside down, wheezing for breath. He fought to stay conscious, but thinking felt like moving through deep water.

The impact of the center buckle against his chest caused enough pressure to send shock waves through his diaphragm, which now seized, making it difficult to breathe. Aris gasped as he fumbled with the buckle, trying to release the pressure.

With a grunt he managed to flip the catch and fell out, landing on the back of his neck and left shoulder. Aris would have cried out at the jarring impact if he'd been able to pull air in to start with.

His vision dimmed—not enough oxygen to his brain. It was shutting down. He didn't need to see through the shattered ferrous to

know his attacker was approaching. The rhythmic tremors beneath him announced its presence.

I've got to get... out...

He stumbled trying to right himself, massaging his diaphragm with his left hand as he pulled himself into a kneeling position with his right. It was a trick he'd learned in battle once, taught by his House Master. Massaging the muscle should stop the spasms so he could pull air into his starved lungs—but would it be in time?

There... a bit of air came in and he gasped.

With his right hand he yanked at the buckle to his neurohelmet and it fell away. His hair was plastered to the sides of his head and the sudden open air was icy against the tips of his ears.

Out... I've got to get out... It was the one driving thought in his mind as he kept rubbing his diaphragm. More air escaped through the tension in his chest, and his vision improved.

Stumbling in the wreckage of his cockpit, Aris found his *jian*, pulled it on over his shoulder and looked for the needler. When he didn't find it, he looked for the emergency backpack he always kept, all the while absently rubbing at his chest. More air slipped through, he could breathe shallowly. To anyone else would sound as if Aris was gasping for breath.

And he was.

There was no sign of the backpack. Aris looked up to see the approaching 'Mech through the broken ferrous glass and smoke.

It was an *Atlas*, its face painted like a white, bone skull, grinning at him as it came in for the kill.

Still wheezing, Aris yanked at the hatch release, crying out as the movement jarred his ribs.

The hatch wouldn't move. He moaned and staggered as wrenching pain shot through his chest. He coughed, but it sounded more like choking.

Damnit!

With no other option, he crawled over the debris and leaned onto his right side. Grabbing what had been the overhead computer deck, he kicked against the glass. Normally, he would have broken both legs, as ferrous glass is armor tough. But the glass was shattered into thousands of tiny fragments already, and gave way with a few good blows.

But when it did, the snow and cold wind came in with it. Aris had no time to consider the dangers of his less than amply-clothed body—or the fact he had to climb through a small hole bordered with jagged glass.

Sharp edges gashed his shoulders, sides, and legs. One piece cut deep into his left thigh and he screamed as he pulled himself out, only dimly aware of the fire on his left cheek. He could only assume he'd sliced it as well.

He fell forward into the snow, an icy, shocking wake-up to the pain in his chest, thigh, and upper arms as his boots sank in to his mid-calves. The ground vibrated harder as the *Atlas* approached, and Aris ran as fast as he could toward the nearest building, leaving a faint trail of pink, bloodied snow with every step.

It was only the sound of bending metal that caused him to pause and turn. He watched with grim horror as the *Atlas* actually stomped on his cockpit, as if squashing an annoying bug. The hull screeched and gave out an angry death toll as a part of Aris' life died in front of him.

Another explosion somewhere in the city ruins caused him to turn again. He knew on instinct his partner had just lost his *Phoenix Hawk*.

But had the pilot, Mikhail Chess, escaped?

Shivering, Aris wound his way deeper into the city's ruins. Every breath he took felt as if a knife were being driven into his chest. His ragged breathing resounded like thunder in his ears, his muscles burned, and his chest ached as he stumbled over the frozen, destroyed city of Jakarta. Everywhere he looked, for kilometers on either side, all he could see were gray broken buildings, their still standing foundations jutting into the white sky above like broken bones.

It was a wasteland of broken dreams—a monument to the arrival of the Word of Blake.

It was cold here, below freezing. The beaded sweat from his and Mikhail's hurried escape from the spaceport turned to ice on his forehead, arms and thighs. He had to keep moving. Find shelter. Warmth. Or all the effort he'd put into arriving on Farandir was for naught.

Already he felt his core temperature war with the elements—the need to generate heat in order to move tempered by the lulling snow that fell so gently around him, coating his dark, thick hair with a thin powder.

No, not snow.

Ash.

So much ash that it mixed with the snow.

'Mech fire rumbled behind him and to the right, near the space port where his *Leopard* DropShip, *Midnight's Call*, had been ordered down.

It had all happened so fast—a mission that started as dangerous—but simple. They were to land on Farandir where the Chancellor had received word a resistance cell had survived.

Magestrix Centrella wanted to depart Sian immediately to investigate, but Sun-Tzu convinced her he could send in a small unit to gather intel and send word back. House Imarra was assigned the task—but none of the operatives sent ever reported in again. It was as if their existence had been wiped away. Not one record of them, and no witnesses to their whereabouts.

Aris had kept himself abreast of the situation through his own channels in the palace, and once House Imarra had been dispatched, he'd sent his own team into Word-occupied space near Canopus. A group of five, broken into two parts.

Raven Clearwater, Shindo Rosenberg, Quinn Tudors, Lynn Trahn and Yan Lu. Raven paired up with Quinn, while Lynn took point with Rosenberg and Lu. Raven and Aris had mapped out how and when to enter the territories, their identities, and when to make contact.

Lynn Trahn made contact with Aris a few weeks before the news about the disappearance of House Imarra's team reached Sian, reporting their team was in position. Two days after Imarra's disappearance Aris received word from Raven confirming evidence of a resistance cell working clandestinely on Farandir.

Aris had finally confided in Ty Wu Non that he had two teams stationed on Farandir.

"I know," the House Master had said with little to no smile. "I helped Clearwater fund the operation."

Aris hadn't been surprised—Raven very rarely acted without the House Master's approval. It was the opposite of what Aris was known for—believing too much that asking for forgiveness was better than begging for approval.

Aris recruited Mikhail Chess, his long time friend and comrade and one of House Hiritsu's newest MechWarriors, and made arrangements for a rendezvous on Farandir with Raven Clearwater, Lynn Trahn and their teams. Aris' job was to make contact with the cell and offer the Magestrix's aid.

"They're allowing transports and cargo vessels into occupied territories of the Magistracy," Ty had said during their briefing. This was as much as Aris had known and used as his people's entry into the occupied territories. "Their forces, along with the Word of Blake supporters, need supplies, and there are runners and crippled mercenary units who need the protection and money given to them to transport these items. A small DropShip should slip through unnoticed."

But in a universe turned upside down, unnoticed could get one killed...

He'd stopped running, though he couldn't remember doing it. Fatigue, pain, and the constant cold wore him down. He was losing seconds—brief periods of vacant thoughts.

It was cold. Too cold.

Aris shivered just inside the ruins on the outskirts of the city and faced a bleak expanse. The forests he had hopped to hide in had been laid to waste. He and Mikhail had had no time for aerial shots of the surface before the Blakist temporary government had ordered them down.

There was nothing left of Farandir's beautiful Layla trees, with their legendary and sought after pearl wood. Aris had cherished the few pieces he'd seen at the palace on Sian—an armoire and a small table—the latter he'd commandeered for his own office.

There was nothing left but burned, charred stumps. A smoking hillside that framed a sinking sun.

Oh no...

The sun was setting faster than he'd realized. He was going to freeze if he didn't find shelter of some sort and a place to build a fire, unnoticed. Maybe, if he could wait them out, he could build a small one within the ruins and the smoke would be masked by the burning 'Mech kilometers away.

A movement out of the corner of his eye caught his attention. Crouching low, he turned and looked around him, but nothing moved other than the lightly falling snow.

Yet...

But there was something there, in the ruins behind him. A ghost on the fringes of his senses.

He'd only had this feeling once before.

Years ago, in another ruined city.

Hustaing.

Another lifetime ago, as it seemed, to rescue a princess who no longer graced the palace but had found kindness and solace in the arms of a prince of the Federated Suns.

A shiver rocked Aris on his heels and he turned, still unsure if the cold was from the falling snow or from the overwhelming sense he wasn't alone.

And he was sure he hadn't been alone in the ruins for some time.

It has been with me since I started on foot...

He stood as still as his shivering body could and listened, quiet-

ing his breathing and closing his eyes. He tuned out his other senses and only focused on his hearing, his awareness of the surroundings, pulling in his *chi* so that he could become one with the surrounding buildings.

Pushing away the ghosts of the city's pain, as well as the sting and ache of his own wounds, he heard a noise. A footstep. So slight. Only a whisper. As if a soft leathered boot had brushed against sand and concrete.

Automatically his hand reached behind him and grabbed the hilt of his *jian*. Slowly he slid the blade free of the scabbard, his body descending into a crouch, his left knee bent upward, his right leg extending to deepen his kneel.

There was no light, no cold, no uncontrollable shivering.

There was only... the sound.

His body reacted before his mind could counter with doubt. He spun to his right and brought the sword up high, his right foot acting as a brace against the rocky ground as his sword blocked something metallic as it swung down to greet him. His chest screamed at him and it felt as if his ribs had wrenched free of his chest and were now poking through his flesh—but he made no sound. If he'd not stopped to listen—it was possible the weapon could have removed his head.

He hissed as he dodged and rolled, his movements made sluggish from the pain and the half-frozen condition of his body, coming up into a crouch to face—

Nothing.

There was no one there.

He looked left, then right, moving back as he tried to sense where his attacker could have gone without him seeing. Or at least caught a glimpse of him.

The light hadn't reached the tops of the mountains—it was the only light Aris had to see with—but to see what?

Nothing moved, except for the snow.

His eyes widened as a soft movement caught his eye—just to his right. Where it looked as if the snow had settled in mid-air, on top of something solid—

The movement shimmered and Aris again parried the attack, blocking the sound of a blade through wind, then spinning and striking below the first attack and striking—

Nothing. There was nothing there!

Except the shimmer and the crunch of boots on snow.

A scuff.

A familiar feeling of dread. An all too familiar sensation of being watched.

No... it couldn't be.

Was this—was this the same stranger he had faced on Hustaing? The thing that had killed Richardson? The thing that had watched him but had not killed him as it had killed the others, both man, woman, and child alike?

Was it a ghost?

A demon that chased him through time to face him again?

He took a step back and listened, realizing too late that whatever it was had the advantage, because he hadn't been alert to its movements.

Unless—

There! The image shimmered again, the snow giving away its position. Aris didn't know when it would strike, but could only guess at the sound of metal cutting through air.

He parried again and stumbled back on debris hidden by a bank of snow. The light was fading, casting everything in a monochromatic glow.

He remembered the precision his demon—if it was the same creature—had killed with in the warehouse on Hustaing. He'd seen it move swiftly behind its opponents and cleanly slice open their necks.

Aris couldn't allow it to move out of his vision. He couldn't run from something he couldn't see. Back then, he'd believed whatever it was had saved him, yet now it toyed with him, somehow wanting and yet prolonging his death.

There was sound again—a slight hiss—and then fresh pain. Red fire shot from somewhere in the shimmer, a beam of laser light that sliced a small hole clean through his upper left arm. He cried out, hissing as the cold air made his teeth ache.

Aris took several unsteady steps back, almost falling over the uneven ground. Agony lingered in his shoulder and it was difficult to lift that arm. His chest tightened again, the cracked ribs protesting the sudden movements.

He breathed hard—now shivering uncontrollably. This wasn't good. His body temperature was dropping rapidly even with the activity. Hypothermia was setting in.

That is, if this creature didn't slice his throat first.

But creature or not—he glanced at the cauterized wound. Definitely a laser, which meant the wielder was human.

Something caught him across the left cheek, snapping his head to the side as he fell back and landed painfully on his backside, but

keeping a firm grip on his *jian*. Scrambling back, he realized the shimmer was more solid now, the image reflecting light so that he could make out a distinct shape in the drifting snow.

His opponent wasn't as tall as he'd assumed, standing perhaps even with Aris' own height. But it was broad shouldered—and he could make out a hood, and a cloak in the snow. Ah... was it the cloak that bent the light?

Was it possible that if he damaged the cloak he could make the enemy fully visible? But even as he moved upward in a single, fluid motion, sweeping the sword from left to right with the intent of slicing into what he believed was his opponent's right arm, something heavy, hard and sharp knocked his sword arm back, deflecting it with the power of twenty warriors.

Seconds became minutes as the world tilted and warped. The snow blurred for an instant as Aris Sung's senses steadied enough for him to realize what had happened.

He was no longer standing, but lay at an angle on his back, propped up into an almost sitting position, bolstered by the stack of cobbled rubble beneath him.

He blinked several times to clear his vision as he stared down at something on the ground, lying in a pile of snow.

Bloody snow.

He recognized his *jian* where it lay, gleaming on the ground. under the filtered moonlight that peaked through a small hole in the sky. It was as if the sky wanted him to see.

To see what was on the hilt.

Then the pain came—devastating at first—taking the breath from his already punished lungs as his muddled and frozen brain realized he was staring at his hand—still clutching his sword.

My hand.

Is on the ground...

And then the light was gone, blocked out by the enemy, now fully visible before him. The creature was just perceptible in the shadow of a pristine white robe, and something gleamed just inside, catching the lights of the setting sun.

"Warrior," came a soft voice. Sensual. Accented.

Feminine.

Aris wanted to look down at his arm—needed to see his right arm to know that it was indeed his hand lying on the ground behind his enemy. But he couldn't look away from the silver points that revealed themselves to be eyes, peering out at him from beneath the hood.

A soft, slender, uncovered hand emerged, followed by an equally beautiful arm, and reached out to him. A finger caressed his jaw. He shivered uncontrollably now, unable to quiet his body. His teeth chattered.

"Beautiful warrior," came the voice again, and there was a richer accent. One he couldn't place. "Prince... "

He saw the embroidered emblem just inside the cloak. The sword of Blake. Silver eyes. Another hand emerged from the cloak, this one made solely of smooth silver, a robotic monstrosity that imitated the same sensual, graceful movements of its living counter part, and moved the hood away from the face.

She was beautiful—exotic to behold—with Eurasian features and short, close-cropped black hair. Her face was thin, elfin, and her lips ruby red. The only thing that looked out of place, and yet fit her best, were her eerie, silver eyes.

She smiled down at him. "Beautiful prince—do not weep," she said again in a voice that Aris would hear only in a parent placating a child. "This was not an honorable death—I have an advantage, you see. I have seen the sweet warrior fight before."

Aris blinked, unable to control the shivering, much less move his arms, or his body. She was before him, looming closer as she knelt down to him and reached out and pressed her palm flat over his upper chest. He could feel the metal—cold ice against his skin.

He stared at her, unbelieving the mixture of beauty and horror in the image he beheld. Maiden and monster.

Angel and demon.

He tried to pull away, though he couldn't be sure if it was from revulsion or from shaking. She almost purred as she spoke. "I admired how you moved... and I... Setiwah... am honored to be the one to take you."

Admired how I moved?

Was it possible? Aris frowned up at her, lost in the silver eyes. Was this the same individual in that warehouse? He had only been speculating before, but to be confronted with the reality of her was beyond coincidence.

"Wh—" the shaking was unbearable, more so than the dull ache and throb from his right stump. The cold had numbed it, yet the pain of its loss was fresh. "Wh—wha—at-t-t ar-re yu-yu-you... "

"I am Setiwah, Precentor Delta of the Manei Domini."

The Manei Domini.

The cyborg soldiers of the World of Blake. He had read of them, heard the reports, but he had never seen one up close.

In all of the intel he'd read—of the to-the-last-man slaughter of the Shin Legion and the Home Guard to the eradication of Necromo's shipyards—he really had not allowed the knowledge of what the Word of Blake was capable of to sink in—until now.

As he looked into the face of death, and she smiled at him.

How... Aris shivered. *How can we fight such a monster?*

"You can't," she said in her silky voice, and it made up his world. "You will fall."

The sound of metal sliding against metal startled him seconds before he felt the icy cold of something in his chest. She was smiling, still. Aris tried to breathe—but he coughed instead.

He tasted blood and realized it was welling up from his throat. Flooding his esophagus, filling his lungs and stomach.

No...

He blinked several times and looked down. He saw her metallic hand pressed on his chest, but just beneath her wrist he could see a sword, extending directly out from beneath her forearm, buried to the hilt into his flesh.

Into his chest, easily cleaving through bone and muscle.

She had pinned him to the rock beneath him, piercing his heart.

Blood welled over his lips. He felt his lungs collapsing inside of him. Aris fought to take air in even as he saw spots before his eyes.

Soft fingers lifted his face below his chin and she was close to him again, leaning in so that she filled his world. "You were so brave, warrior prince. And the Master was happy with you then. But now, your time is at an end. His progeny lives, thanks to you... and I."

He tried to breathe again but couldn't, and more blood welled into his mouth. The light faded away.

What did she mean?

"She lives. The Master's progeny is strong. You are a hero, little Aris Sung."

Setiwah leaned in closer to him and touched her cold, ruby red lips to his cheek. "Beautiful... Aris Sung... " she whispered in his ear as she brought her face closer and pressed those lips to his, running her tongue over his lower lip, licking the blood from his flesh.

But even as he died Aris' thoughts were far way from where he lay, pinned to the broken rubble of a once great city in the Magistracy of Canopus.

He thought of Isis.

The Master's Daughter?

And then the world became a lot colder.

Unknown
Farandir
Magistracy of Canopus
8 March 3072

Dark.
    Light.
    Voices.
    "... til it's out!"
    "It's not moving—is it dead?"
    "How do we know for sure?"
    "I say we take it apart, limb from limb."
    Quiet.
    Cold.
    "So how do we know it's dead?"
    "Beats the hell out of me. Burn 'em."
    Noise.
    Movement.
    Heat.
    "Blake's balls—he's alive—what the hell were they doing to him?"
    Pain.
    Always pain.

Unknown
Farandir
Magistracy of Canopus
19 April 3072

Sound returned first, followed quickly by nausea. He coughed—no, no, no. He can't cough. He'll give away his position.
    Why can't I move my arms?
    "He's waking."
    "Is that wise? I mean... he's not close to being ready."
    "I have to know there's no permanent brain damage. I can repair limbs—but the mind?"
    Mind? Where was my mind? Why can't I move? It's cold. And dark.
    He heard something—soft. A moan?
    "I think he's trying to talk."
    Ahhh... that was me. He tried again to open is eyes. But when he did, the light blinded him and he winced, closing them again.
    "Move that lamp away—it's too much too soon."
    The light vanished from his eyelids and he opened them again,

blinking. The images were blurred. Black and white. Two people. They were close. One wore glasses.

"Am I... " he heard himself say in a whisper. He cleared his throat but there wasn't much he could do to improve his voice. His throat ached. Raw. Tender. "Am I alive?"

The image of the person closest to him, the one with glasses, smiled. Color returned slowly and he saw she was female. Thick, yellow hair with brilliant, green eyes. Her glasses were silver framed. There was a mole on her left check, just above her lip. "Yes, you are alive."

He tried to move again, but found he couldn't. "Where?"

"Where are you?"

He couldn't nod. He couldn't move anything.

She looked away and the other face came into view. This was also a woman, with short, dark hair and dark eyes. He thought of Setiwah and cringed briefly. "Are you in pain?"

Her voice wasn't as soft. But he sensed authority, mixed with a little concern. *For me?* "I—no. No. Where am I?"

"You're in a care facility." She looked away, her expression frowning before she looked back at him. "We found a sword stored in the same lab we found you—did you use a sword?"

Sword. Aris tried to recall memories. Things were clouded, sluggish. He remembered seeing something fly through the air as his 'Mech fell forward. "I—I had a *jian...* "

The woman nodded and looked to her side again. Aris assumed she was talking to the woman with the mole and glasses. "You were right. Though I don't understand why they actually preserved his hand still attached to the sword."

"A trophy maybe?" came the other woman's voice. "It's sick."

My hand... A fuzzy memory sharpened abruptly. He'd been pressed against the rocks, but through the snow and the fog in his mind, he could see his hand... on the snowy ground.

Oh god no...

He tried to move again.

"Mister," the woman with the authority said. "You're going to have to be still. Marina is doing her best to reattach your hand. Do you understand me?"

He stared at her, his surroundings sharpening. "Reattach?"

"Yes. Ebon medicine has come a long way, sword user. Which is why I was asking if the sword was yours—I'm not sure you're going ot be able to use it quite the way you did before."

My hand... Aris tried to flex his fingers. But there was nothing. No feeling. No sensation. Not anywhere in his body. The memories came back, abrupt and unfriendly.

There had also been a cold inside of his chest. And the smile of a demon staining his lips. He remembered seeing a sword—through his chest.

"She stabbed me... "

"She?" the woman frowned. "I don't know who she is, but yes you suffered extensive damage in your heart. Which is why you've been immobilized. Part of what remains of your heart is being maintained by machines. We can repair that damage as well."

She seemed to settle her position, as if she'd suddenly sat on something. "But first I have to know who you are. Why you were here, and are you worth the total cost of manpower I lost to wrench you out of that lab?"

He could see her from the waist up now. Brown shirt, coat, with gold bars on the left shoulder. A makeshift epaulet. "You—why would you risk anyone to find me?"

"Because I found it very interesting that the Wobbies would send so much firepower after two 'Mechs. I figured you were pretty important." She folded her arms over her chest. "And you weren't on their side. Are you important?"

He smelled apricots. Burning oil. "No."

"We know who the other MechWarrior was," she said.

He looked at her. "Was?"

"He was killed, in the ruined city. They destroyed his 'Mech with him inside. His name was Mikhail Chess. Part of House Hiritsu, Third Company.

"Now I have a pretty good idea of who you are, but I want to hear it from you. Name, soldier. Or I'll have these nice people pull the plug on the machine that's pumping your blood for you."

Pumping my blood?

He remembered polished silver. Blood. A sword through his heart. *They killed my heart.*

"Marina," the woman said to someone out of his sight.

"No," he said and cleared his throat again. "I am... *Lien-Zhang* Aris Sung, Third Company, House Hiritsu."

"I told you he was a Cappie," said a new voice. Deeper. Huskier.

The woman with the short hair arched an eyebrow. "Tris, I can tell he's a Capellan by looking at him. He's one of Sonny's boys. I just needed to know which one." She fixed him with a very serious look.

"*Lien-Zhang* Sung, I am Commander November Talliard, Magistracy Armed Forces, Ebon Magistrate, and I run this crazy little shop of horrors. If you are who you say you are, and I do believe you, and I am who I say I am, which I also believe, I need to know why a Capellan soldier is here on Farandir causing so much chaos?"

Aris fought a sudden fatigue, blinking rapidly.

"Sir, he really needs to sleep. All this talk—the emotional battle—it's putting a strain on what's left of his heart. It's only been six weeks... "

Six weeks?

He looked to his right to see the woman with the glasses. Marina? "How... long?"

"It's been six weeks since we found you in that lab," she said and smiled at him again. It wasn't a condescending smile, but he did feel like a child. "I'm not sure how long you were there before then. I'm assuming you were taken the day you landed, so I'm guessing you've been out of commission for—about eleven weeks. About three months."

His mind lurched trying to process the dates.

Lab. They found me in a lab.

So... she didn't let me die after all.

Setiwah.

Warrior.

Manei Domini.

"Aris Sung," November said, bringing his attention back to her. "I need to know why you're here. Why come to this world and risk death or a fate worse than death? What is a Capellan doing here?" She leaned close to him, her voice low. "I have to know why you're here, and whether or not I can trust you. Lives depend on me—non-Blakist lives, Aris Sung. Citizens still loyal to the Magistracy."

Could it be? Was this the resistance? The cell Raven had reported to him? Was it his own failure that in essence brought him directly into the hands of the very people the Magestrix wished to find?

It seemed too coincidental. But then again, he had created quite a noise when he landed. Which brought attention to himself.

A great deal of attention. Which meant if Commander November had risked her own people to retrieve him from a Word of Blake lab, she must have been desperate to learn his identity.

Which might mean they need him or what he might represent.

He looked at her and tried to muster as much authority in his voice as possible before answering. "I bring word from the Magestrix and his Celestial Wisdom: You are not forgotten."

There was little else he could say after that as darkness over took him once again and he drifted away, Setiwah's laughter echoing in the dark.

Unknown Resistance Cell
Farandir
Magistracy of Canopus
3 May 3072

A wave of nausea forced Aris to brace himself against the carved rock. It was damp and cold, the snow from above the underground bunker melting, the water sieving down into the tunneled mines beneath. The coolness felt good against his forehead as he closed his eyes.

He knew the nausea would pass. But it would take some time as his body adjusted to the changes.

The implanted changes.

A new heart.

"Sung?" came a familiar voice to his right. He turned, rolling his head against the rock and saw Marina standing a few centimeters away. "You shouldn't be up. I can't stress enough that your body needs time to adjust to the heart—the cyberware has to learn your body's needs before you can effectively—"

She paused and looked away.

He swallowed. "Before I can effectively walk down a hall without getting sick?"

There was a nod before she reached out to him. Five centimeters shorter, she had to push up on her toes to touch his forehead. "You have a fever again."

"I can't lay in bed all the time," he said, though he felt fatigue mingle with the nausea and wanted nothing more than to lay down on a soft bed and rest.

Thirsty.

He was always so thirsty.

"You'll have to for a while," Marina said and pulled at his arm. He came willingly, with no other choice. He was bent at the waist as the nausea threatened to push everything he'd managed to eat back up. "I am sorry—I don't know why it's been so hard for you."

Could it be because I wished I had died in that city? Aris closed his eyes as they moved slowly down the dimly lit corridor to the infirmary.

WITH CARRION MEN

Yes, he had found the cell. And he had been surprised to find it was backed by the Ebon Magistrate, a branch of the Magistracy military that very few knew of. On the one hand, it was a miracle they had survived away from Canopus and managed to create a covert cell of resistance fighters. But if word of their existence leaked out, there would be—complications.

Yet if it had not been for the Ebon's excellent medical treatment, he wouldn't have survived.

Aris clenched his right hand, felt the knuckles move. And yet... he had so little strength in it. He could feel with it—though the sensations were weak, distant, more like a ghost of what they were.

Will I ever be able to fight with it?

A door on his left opened and November stood there, her expression less than friendly. But then, she'd looked like that since he'd first opened his eyes.

She reached in and helped Marina wrestle him back to his bed where he collapsed in a heap on his back. His breathing was ragged again and before he could protest Marina had pulled his shirt away from his chest and once again pushed plugs and wires into the holes that laced the center of his torso.

Where his heart should be.

"We didn't replace your heart," Marina had told him when he'd finally been able to stay awake. The drugs they used made him sick upon waking and November insisted he be kept as immobile as possible. "We repaired and improved on it."

Improved on it.

Half was no longer flesh and blood, but metal and synthetic. It refused to pump his blood at times and left him on the floor, light headed and unable to speak or move.

Aris felt the bolt of electricity as it was fed into the chest connection. He grunted at the pain, but he was getting accustomed to it. The pain meant life.

Through gritted teeth he said, "Will it always... be like this?"

November shook her head as she moved to the other side. She was dressed more formally today than he'd seen her in past weeks. And it was odd that she was here where he had been confined since his arrival.

For his safety, he'd been told.

"Eventually your heart and your body will synchronize. And they'll work as one, just as your hand has now re-bonded to your neural network."

Marina had told him the connections looked good—but the question they avoided was whether or not he could still fight with that hand, with a *jian*, a pistol, or even a 'Mech.

She smiled at his expression. "Soon you won't even notice the difference. Your heart will beat stronger, and you will be stronger for it. You'll be able to endure more than you did before."

He looked at her, his eyes narrowed. "You have a cybernetic heart."

"Yes," November nodded. "I do. The Ebon found me much as they found you, in a Blakist lab. They patched me back up when they learned who I was—who I had been—and I was given a new life."

Aris closed his eyes. The nausea was overwhelming.

There was a warm hand on his left arm. He knew it was November's. She touched him often—softly at times. "You will get better, Aris Sung. And you will fight again." She squeezed his arm.

He nodded but kept his eyes closed as the nausea induced by the drugs Marina pumped into his system washed over him and he fought to keep his dignity.

New Serang
Blakist Stronghold
Farandir
Magistracy of Canopus
3 May 3072

If it weren't for the increased Wobby security officers present, or the numbers of Blakist supporting pins on citizen's lapels—like the one decorating her own—no one would really suspect the city to be controlled by the Word of Blake.

Sure. No problem.

Raven Clearwater sat in the window of the cafe, a cooling cup of coffee on the Layla wood table in front of her. Young people, dressed in grays and browns seated at other tables, talked in low whispers.

This was a college cafe, sandwiched between the old school where freedom had been taught, and the newer educational buildings, where the New Thought was introduced.

The Word of Blake.

She'd donned her business day casual, a pantsuit of indistinct gray, a fitted suit-jacket and boots. She felt naked without her *jian*, or even a nakjama or needler, but Ordinary Citizens were not permitted

weapons because they were blasphemous against the good and kind nature of Blake.

The cafe's speakers, though muted, constantly played the soft-voiced speaker for the Word, easing in platitudes of the mercy of Blake, and of a bright future of peace and atonement.

If I hear this schlock one more time I'm going to puke.

Raven's forged papers granted her a temporary business license to monitor and ship in mechanical parts to fix the continuously failing heaters along the city's high walls—the barrier that kept the cold of Farandir on the other side of the wall. Little did those employing her realize that the problems were the work of Raven's other shadow team, headed up by Lynn Trahn.

Lynn had served in Raven's lance in the Third Company of House Hiritsu for over a decade, one of the few survivors retained after the retaking of Kaifeng. She and her people, Rosenberg and Lu, hand chosen by Aris Sung, were good at what they did. Not only skilled 'Mech Warriors, but damned fine saboteurs.

Raven checked her chronometer.

She was waiting for her student.

And he was late.

Again.

A student. *I have a student.* She gave a short sigh. In all of her years serving House Hiritsu, she would never have imagined being assigned a student. *I'm a Warrior, not a house-mom.*

But when asked about the experience of teaching—Raven would on any occasion say it had been—interesting. Quinn Tudor wasn't the average student—all bent on proving honor and kowtowing it to all the nobles.

No—Quinn's problem had been *not* following the rules. He'd been a problem child from the start—having been pulled from the infantry ranks—too small, clumsy and weak to be effective.

Or so they'd believed.

At first she'd considered the addition of Quinn in her life a punishment, or a cruel joke played by the House Master. In her opinion if someone couldn't make it in the House Ranks, send them on their way.

Why give them special attention?

Yet once given that special attention, Quinn had blossomed into one of the best communication and special ops agents House Hiritsu could ask for.

With his looks and his youth, very few people suspected him of any other talent.

By her side for nearly two years now, she'd insisted he be brought along on this job. Aris had been against it in the beginning, insisting he was too young and inexperienced.

"So you're doubting my ability to train properly, Aris?"

Her old friend had looked more than a bit puckish at her statement and bristled. "That's not what I meant and you know that."

"You want to know what Quinn can do? You're looking for brute strength and cunning. But just set up a session. You choose the mat. He'll be there."

She'd been a little surprised when Aris took her up on her challenge. And he'd been more than surprised when he was almost bested by a young man a good five centimeters shorter than him and with a slighter build.

Aris had approached her then, mopping up the sweat on his brow with a towel. "I will never doubt you again, Clearwater." He nodded. "So what are you training him on? *Jian*? Knives? Battle-armor? 'Mech?"

She'd smiled. "Yes."

Raven checked her chronometer again. Ten minutes past their original meeting time.

Being late in this city could be worrisome. She watched the people pass by outside in their daily, calm manner. No one ran, or jogged. Business as usual. Vehicles passed on the street, mostly those appointed within the new government. The trains and busses were good enough for the Ordinary Citizen.

She brought the cup to her lips just as she caught sight of him across the street.

Relief washed over her and she felt her heart thunder against her chest. If they weren't in public she'd give the ex-infantryman a dressing down. But not here.

Not now.

She watched him as he waited for the light to change. Raven was still in awe of how someone who looked like Quinn could blend into the population so well. Average height—even short for a Capellan—Quinn had an almost androgynous quality. He was slim and wiry, lithe in many ways. A thin face, with a strong straight, nose and pointed chin. His hair was an odd balance of deep gray to almost blue, something very unique for someone so young. He insisted he never dyed it, but Raven often wondered. He kept it long about his face to mask his features.

And if there was one feature that stood out on the young man it was his eyes—which could be a detriment as well as a boon. Quinn

WITH CARRION MEN

had gold eyes that sometimes gleamed with a ferocious light when he was angry. Luckily he wore dark contacts while on this mission.

His unnerving talent with computers and networks made him a vital player in the group's charade, his knowledge of communication bordering on unnerving.

Quinn's unique talents had landed him a job in a vital part of the Citizens network, policing data packets and keeping an eye on all outgoing and incoming transmissions.

Raven had been suspicious when he'd gotten the job so easily. She was still suspicious. Not of Quinn, but of the system that hired him. After all, they were in the center of a Word of Blake stronghold.

Twice now he'd had to endure a group of recruiters at his doorstep, encouraging him to be tested for higher training. Raven could only assume that would mean teaching Quinn about the HPGs. She figured he already knew how they worked—he just wasn't letting anyone know.

He's upset, Raven pursed her lips as he kept his head down, his hands shoved into his pockets. The gray of his tunic and pants matched his hair. A nondescript Ordinary Citizen. A surveillance camera might pick him up on the screen, but the human eye would run over him like water over a fall. He could blend in.

And vanish from the mind.

He moved amongst a group of people, under an overcast sky. And then he was inside the cafe. Raven noticed a few of the younger girls looking at him, hoping to catch his eye. But Quinn kept his head down and gracefully slid into the chair opposite Raven.

Within minutes, the waitress was by his side, setting chai tea in front of him. That bothered Raven. Usually if the waitress remembered what Quinn ordered, it meant they'd remained too long in one place. But in this situation, the smoother the acclimatization, the better. He looked up at her and smiled, and she smiled as well before leaving.

He didn't speak at first, only sipped his tea. When he did speak, it was in an ancient dialect of Mandarin, used by House Hiritsu operatives, his voice low, "I got confirmation today."

Quinn's voice was strong for his size. A conflicting tone that spoke of experience and youth. He finally looked at Raven. His eyes were fierce beneath the gray of his hair. "Positive identification. It was Aris' *Wraith*."

Raven closed her eyes. Four months. Since the disastrous landing near Jakarta it had taken four months working with small pockets of resistance among the citizens to get confirmation that the destroyed 'Mech near the old city ruins had indeed been Aris' 'Mech.

The wobbies had been quick to clean up the mess. And since Ordinary Citizens weren't allowed outside the city without valid papers—which were becoming harder to come by—validation of the 'Mech's identity had been slow.

She looked at Quinn. He didn't look away. "And Aris?"

His eyes unfocused, as if he were looking at something only he could see. "There was nothing written in the reports about the pilot of that 'Mech, or the 'Mech that was destroyed six kilometers away. But Danton, over in research and development," Quinn refocused on her. "He came across some interesting files on a research subject that was," he held up the index and middle fingers of each hand and made a quotes gesture, "*Misplaced.*"

Raven leaned in close, but not close enough to cause any suspicion of conspiracy from any would-be loyalist in the cafe. "Research subject? Misplaced?"

Quinn's eyes flashed for a second as he sat up and sipped his chai. "Sounds interesting, eh? I thought so too. Apparently the subject went missing. And the data compiled from whatever research came from that subject was locked away. Renamed under an encrypted password."

"What are you thinking, Quinn?" Raven put her hands on her cup, keeping her voice low. "You think that subject was Aris?"

"Yeah, I do. And I think he escaped—which would explain their more than toned down reports of a research subject gone missing."

The excitement in his tone was evident, though he kept his expression even. It sounded almost too good to be true—to find any word or sign on this planet that Aris Sung or even Mikhail Chess was alive. She understood Quinn's excitement.

"There's no evidence that a research experiment was a man—"

But Quinn wasn't going to be deterred. "Do you know of any other research experiment that included a sword?"

That intel set Raven back. She didn't suppress her smile. "A sword?"

"Yeah, catalogued as a Capellan *jian*." He sat back and folded his arms over his chest. "I monitor communications. Which means I also snoop. And I retraced any communiques in and out two days before and after the subject's disappearance."

"You need to be careful doing that," Raven said as she sipped her coffee. It was cold. "You're going to get caught."

"Maybe, but we need to find him, Raven." His gaze intensified and she could have sworn his eyes glowed. "My guess is he made it outside."

"Why do you think that?"

"Because there's nothing else in the files about him."

"Aren't they locked?"

Quinn shook his head. "No, only any research pertaining to the subject is locked." He frowned. "It's almost as if there was something they did or found or were going to do and then, when the subject went missing, they covered it up."

"Sounds like another day in governmental bureaucracy if you ask me," Raven sat back and sighed. "So you believe if Aris made it out, he would try and complete his mission."

"Yes, which would be to lay low and find us or Trahn's team."

"And you want to find him first?" Raven believed if anyone could find Aris it would be Quinn. He'd already completed several covert operations on his own since the Word of Blake war began, all concerning the acquisition of precious objects, mostly technology.

"Yes. We need to get outside the city, preferably on the other side of the Jakarta ruins. I've already rigged a pulse beacon, set up to broadcast during one of the more popular shows."

"And you think he'll find it?"

A smile. "Oh, Aris will find it. His duty is to make contact with the resistance cell. If he can't find us, he'll do it himself. And I don't plan on letting him take all the glory."

"But the coordinates you have for the cell's whereabouts are speculative."

"I have a hunch."

Raven shook her head. "Hunches can get you killed."

"They can protect you. Intuition," he pointed to his temple with the index finger of his right hand.

She considered the idea. Four months and this was the first lead they'd had that maybe Aris had survived. There had been no more communications from Ty Wu Non, and it was doubtful Sun-Tzu would continue this fool's mission, and convince the Magestrix that it was hopeless to find any living resistance cell near Canopus.

If they didn't make some kind of move, it was theoretical that if they didn't extract themselves from Farandir, no one else would. She suspected Lynn knew as much, as did Yu and Rosenberg. But Quinn was still naïve to believe their existence here was important.

Without any solid evidence of a cell—their very lives were forfeit.

"I'll contact Trahn—tell her what you've found. If they can arrange it from where they are, I can get you traveling papers and then use my business license to get myself transported out—at least to the space-port. We can disappear from there."

Quinn could hardly contain his excitement. "Just send me a signal and I can start the broadcast."

"Wait for me to contact you," Raven said as she pulled a few C-bills out of her jacket and placed them on the table. "Wait for me, Quinn. I can't afford to have you shot. Or worse."

He shivered, having seen what worse could mean.

Re-education camps.

As she stood, he reached out for her hand. Raven looked down at him and his eyes. "We'll find him."

Raven nodded. Or he would find them first.

Unknown
Farandir
Magistracy of Canopus
30 May 3072

November and her assistant, Ensign Kachi Hutchinson, oversaw his recovery. Once his body adjusted to the physical exertion and his heart didn't put him on his back for a day, and he could grip a ball, a pipe and a pen with his reattached right hand, Aris was allowed out of the infirmary and able to interact inside the cell's facility as well as its personnel.

There were more members of the cell than he'd hoped, or the Magestrix could have imagined, and they were very well organized. Though their living conditions were less than perfect—with temper-atures sometimes dropping dangerously during the night or when Word of Blake patrols were near and the power output had to be low-ered in order to escape detection—it appeared they put a great deal of their supplies and funds into the infirmary as well as small intel gathering missions with dual purposes in retrieving medical supplies.

His contacts here were always on his mind, but he never spoke of them aloud to November, or any of her people. He needed to make con-tact with them—let them know he was alive and that he was with the cell.

"It means we've kept our heads down," November told him dur-ing one of their practice/briefing sessions in the bunker's training room. Aris understood her need to call the exercises practice, but he knew they were rehabilitation sessions, specifically to test out his new heart and to build strength in his right hand.

It was the largest room in the complex from what Aris had seen, and could hold the entire force, which November claimed was close to forty strong. What impressed him most was that half of her forces lived on Farandir in their own homes, using a facade of supporting Word of Blake. Working in key positions.

Aris was sure the Magistrix would be overjoyed to receive this intel—it was the reason he was sent there. But November had been very reluctant to allow him access to any communication equipment.

"It's not that we don't trust you," she'd said during dinner in her quarters one night after their first few strength training sessions. "It's that we don't trust anyone at this moment. We've worked hard to build what we have—we can't risk exposure."

"But the Magistrix could help you—you could work on getting the sick and injured, old and young, off of this world. She could smuggle in supplies."

"You mean the way you were smuggled in?" Her tone wasn't angry—not even condescending.

But Aris understood the warning in her voice. His and Mikhail's arrival had been less than clandestine. It was an error in planning that still plagued him. The loss of his partner—the swift way he had been nearly dispatched by Setiwah.

The name—even when whispered inside his mind—sent a shiver down his spine and he closed his eyes.

November paused in her meal. "Are you all right? Do you feel ill?"

"No, no," he shook his head and took several deep gulps of water, ignoring the abrupt sweat covering his body. He'd seen her face in his nightmares. The silver gleam in her inhuman eyes. The supple curve of her chin, her ruby red lips.

And then he would feel the cold metal as it sliced through his heart. He felt an ache in his hand and brought it up to look at it. It still looked like his hand—all the old scars were there. He flexed his fingers, the pinky still not moving as well as it had before. The cuff of his long-sleeved shirt hid the fusing line where the flesh had been grafted back in place. From a distance no one would know—but up close it was evident that the hand wasn't what it once was.

"You're thinking of the Manei Domini that attacked you."

"I—I keep seeing her face. Over and over again. I—I keep reliving the moment she—killed me—" he'd briefed November and her team on his initial landing and what had happened after escaping his *Wraith*.

"Aris," November's voice was soft and the gentle tone caused him to look from his hand to her face. "Had you seen a Manei Domini before then?" She nodded to his hand. "Before it took your hand?"

He looked back at the hand. He had also noticed the way November refused to use pronouns when referring to the MD, as she called them. Naming them she or he apparently made them too human for her liking.

He shook his head. "I'd never seen one. No. I mean," he flexed his fingers. "There is always a disconnect, between imagination and reality. I think—I believe the reality wasn't as vastly absurd as I'd convinced myself it would be."

November nodded. "The Manei Domini—the MD—aren't physical monstrosities. There are a few that look completely human. But they are cybernetic atrocities that rival any genetic aberrations the Clans could come up with." She set down her fork and leaned back in her chair. "It only confirms the stories we'd all suspected—that the Word of Blake was even more twisted than we feared. Many of our people here suspect the being they refer to as The Master is little more than a mainframe AI housed on Terra somewhere, and not a real person at all."

Mention of the Master brought Aris' mind back to the moment of his death again. Something Setiwah had said—about—

"I—I believe the Master is a real human being." He said in a very quiet voice. "She—she told me—she called me the Warrior. A prince." He looked at November, his dark eyebrows knitted together. "Said that I had protected the Master's progeny."

"Progeny?" November's expression was one of genuine surprise. "You're telling me that wacko has a kid running around the Inner Sphere?" Her face broke into a wide smile. "And you defended it?"

He looked away, almost afraid she would see the answer in his eyes. He had defended so many and so much, his entire race at times, but narrowing down the playing field left only one place where he protected anyone in particular, on the very planet he had seen Setiwah before.

Hustaing.

Thomas Marik—whom everyone, including Isis, believed was her father—had been proven a fake. He was presently leading a quasi-exiled government on Oriente, rather then from the FWL throneworld of Atreus.

Yet—Setiwah had indicated Isis was the master's daughter.

I've seen you fight before...

Had it been—had there been a Manei Domini trailing him the en-

tire time on Hustaing? He'd always sensed something in the background, behind him, above him, in front of him, but had assumed it was Robert Cheng.

Aris' head ached when he tried to understand what it all meant—that Thomas Marik—the fake one—wasn't Isis' father at all. And if The Master is her father—then who the hell is he? And why would he leave his own flesh and blood to believe her father to be someone else entirely?

He frowned. Did others know of this? Was he purposefully kept in the dark about Isis' true lineage? Had Sun-Tzu known?

"Aris?"

He looked at November. "I'm sorry."

"It will pass," she said in a said voice. "The shock. And the fear. And eventually you will adjust to it."

"To what?"

"To your hand." She took up her cup of steaming tea. "And your heart."

He watched her sip the tea and replace it in its saucer. He didn't want to her know what he'd really been thinking—about Isis or about the master's identity. "I'm not sure I'll ever—fit in again. When I return."

"To the Confederation?" November shrugged. "Implants aren't a bane, Aris. There are some I'm sure in the CCAF who possess such enhancements."

"Yes," he thought of Talon Zahn's enhanced implants, including his myomer muscles. It had been a stupid smokescreen to divert her from his real thoughts.

"But to be safe, I would keep the knowledge of any of it being Word of Blake to yourself, Aris Sung. Always claim they are wholly Ebon-made."

She held her hands out, palms up. "Eighty percent of the occupants of this place have some sort of implant. Something that sets them apart. Before this war, we openly used implants on our Ebon operatives. But with the appearance of the MD—" She gave him a half-smile. "—we make sure others know where the implants come from."

"We," Aris tilted his head to one side. "You were originally part of Ebon?"

"After Elan Karagin died in the first blow stuck at us on Canopus, I took over as the CO for the Ebon Magistrate." And to his surprise she pulled at the fingers of her left hand with her right and removed a form-fitting glove much like the one he wore and exposed a thin, streamlined forearm and hand.

But then she removed a cover from the right hand as well and exposed a second mechanical arm.

He held his expression but finally understood November's caution. As well as her resolve in protecting her cell's anonymity. "You realize that if the Magistrix knew you were here, that the Magistrate survived in some form on Farandir," he said with growing understanding. "She would jump at the chance to send reinforcements in to help."

"And possibly get us killed," November picked up her gloved skins and pushed her chair from the table. "Which is precisely why I wish to proceed with caution. I have operatives living under the noses of the Blakist supporters in the new capitol, Aris. I can't endanger them with any show of force."

She stood. "I didn't want to retrieve you from the lab. I wanted no part of something that would cast attention on me or mine. But in you I sense a strong determination to do what's right. And I have a soft spot for those the Blakists have destroyed."

She nodded to him and left.

Aris sat back in his chair, unsure of what had just happened. And wondering if November was a friend.

Or foe.

New Serang
Blakist Stronghold
Farandir
Magistracy of Canopus
10 June 3072

They came during the night—that much Quinn discovered later, during his clandestine monitoring of the Blakist network. Somehow they'd gotten her name—seized her papers, her identity and taken her from her home.

Raven.

He was to meet her at the cafe at 1000 hours. But he'd spotted the dark-suited men inside and had continued on down the street, keeping his gait and countenance calm and easy. But inside he was in full panic. He'd ducked out of sight, aware of where all the cameras were on the streets and took an indirect route to Raven's apartment.

WITH CARRION MEN

He'd been in a few dangerous situations before and survived, claiming a calm and cool mind as he moved through the motions. But nothing had prepared him for the way his brain numbed this time.

His *Sifu* was in trouble. Possibly dead. Tortured.

And from everything he could see, there wasn't a damned thing he could do about it.

It was the same there—though he knew better than to go into the building. Raven's window was visible from the street below, and as a code she'd always put a Word of Blake decal in the window when it was a bad time to come by.

The decal was there. And the curtains were pulled back.

This wasn't a good sign.

They had already come here, and could still be around. Luckily he'd kept his head down and out of sight. He needed to think. Raven had already signaled for him to start the broadcasts. He doubted anyone had noticed the signal—it was still broadcasting—a piggyback on one of his favorite holo-shows.

If they found Raven—it could be for a number of reasons not necessarily because she was there under Sun-Tzu's orders. Anything could have made them suspicious. And Quinn couldn't take the chance that they hadn't noticed him with her.

Going to work was a bad idea, as was going home. Luckily he'd made plans for this, stashing money, identification, and clothing in different locations all over New Serang.

Keeping his head down, he walked west along the street to the bus station, where he had a cache in a locker. But before he touched it, he took up a position to watch the area, in case any of the Blakist forces were there.

After an hour of nothing unusual, Quinn opened his locker and removed his satchel. Once in the bathroom he changed clothes in the farthest stall, careful not to make too much noise. He also slipped in a pair of blue contact lenses, making his eyes lighter, and combed his hair back from his face.

Replacing his clothes in the bag and removing his ID, Quinn dropped the satchel into a nearby incinerator and walked back into the street.

He walked for several blocks, running over in his mind why they would have taken Raven. He had no idea how to retrieve her—and having worked for the Blakist regime for the past five months— Quinn knew taking on the whole of them was a bad idea.

No—he had to find Trahn, Yu and Rosenberg. But he didn't know their contact information. The three of them hadn't been informed of Quinn's existence—making his presence a mystery except to Raven and Aris.

Coming to a decision, Quinn turned left down the main street and headed to the next train station. He needed to get to the spaceport. He had the papers—Raven had already issued them to him.

But would they work? Or would he be picked up at the spaceport?

Either way, he had to try and find Aris. Quinn had to get to the coordinates he'd given out in the broadcast, outside the Jakarta ruins. Even if it meant getting there on his own.

Trying hard to keep a level head, Quinn entered the main train station. The center globe decoration had been replaced with a large, terrifying statue of the Blake Sword. Quinn stood in front of the statue, looking up at it.

He'd been in this station only a month ago and hadn't seen this monolith before. Its presence was something more than daunting. It made him forget his surroundings and realize where he was. And how much danger he was in.

Someone tapped his shoulder. "Excuse me?"

Keeping his reaction calm he turned slowly, masking his face in a soft smile, and faced a matronly woman. Her gray and white hair was tucked neatly into a bun. She wore a slimming white suit, cut perfectly to her body-type. A cosmetic enhancement used by most of the Wobby operatives to infuse a sense of peace and justice.

The ones they called ROM. Out of the hundreds of people inside the train station, there were few that would recognize this woman for who or what she was.

But letting her know he knew wasn't the way to handle this situation. Wait and see what she wanted. "Yes?" He managed a smile.

"Aren't you Alec Mensa?"

His cover name. "Yes. I'm sorry—did I bump you or something?" *Take the offensive out of the situation,* came Raven's voice in his head. *Put any possible assailant at ease if you are unarmed or not in a position to defend yourself.*

She smiled. "No, no. We've been looking for you. Are you familiar with a woman by the name of Devon Sid?"

Raven's cover identity. Denying this would only make him look suspicious. She wouldn't be asking him if she didn't already know the answer. "Yes. I do. Is there something wrong? Did something happen to Miss Sid?"

WITH CARRION MEN

The woman actually looked concerned. "It's okay, son," she put her hand on his shoulder. It was a firm pressure, but not too harsh. Calling him son told him that she believed him younger than he was. They always did. "May we talk in private?"

He glanced at the chronometer on the wall. Twenty minutes before his train boarded.

"Are you going somewhere, dear?" she asked.

He decided to lie. "No ma'am. I'm meeting some friends. They're coming in from the south end and we were supposed to catch the New World Order movie over at the Ritz."

He watched her carefully. His words seemed to confuse her, but she quickly regained her composure. "I won't keep you long. Can we talk over there?"

He looked to where she pointed. It was near the doors marked "Word Of Blake Loyalists Only."

He didn't have a weapon, or even a knife. He was unarmed.

But he wasn't helpless.

Raven had made sure of that.

With a nod and a half smile he moved side-by-side with her, pacing himself so that she never got behind him. He kept her in sight as they neared the door.

"So what's happened to Miss Sid?" he started in first before they arrived, turning slightly to keep her in sight. "Why do you need to talk to me?"

She made a mistake then, believing him easily compliant, and had pulled out her surprise weapon too soon.

A needle in her right hand.

The doors opened and two large men in black suits stepped out.

A collapsing student being taken to the offices by big, burly men could be easily explained as an illness by the ROM operative in her simple white suit and soothing voice.

But he was going to use that to his advantage.

Stepping back a bit, he widened his eyes and held out his hands. The two men hung back in the shadows to keep from being conspicuous. "What—what is that for? Is she contagious? Does she have a disease and you think I'm infected?"

The ploy worked and the woman looked confused again. She no longer tried to hide the needle. "No, son. We just need to ask you some questions."

"So you need *that*?" He pointed to the needle, raising his voice just enough to catch some passerby's attention. "Just ask me."

He saw one of the men move quickly—

Quinn knew his reflexes were too quick for the average person—his emotions had heightened his reaction time. Seconds slowed as he crouched and sprinted forward, throwing his weight into the woman's solar plexus and moving her backwards into the two men.

They weren't prepared.

Quinn was. He rolled and came up on his feet, then took off at a dead run through the train terminal. He'd be stupid to think those were the only ones looking for him. There would be others at the exits and entrance, at the gates for arrivals and departures.

But he couldn't stay in here. He needed to get out into the city—the trains would be delayed because of him so even that escape would be denied.

Think, think, think. He sprinted along the side and into a door that still had "Employees Only" across the midpoint. Before him stretched a corridor, only half lit. Was this the abandoned train office? If so—there could be a door to the outside.

An exit. And maybe one that wouldn't be guarded.

With a quick glance into each room he found one office that still had a computer terminal in it. And the computer was on. He typed in one of his co-worker's passwords to check the communications network and found where his own identity had been erased.

Shit.

He checked in the files he'd hidden in several packets and found them still there. They hadn't found his alternate identities. Keeping one eye on the door, he quickly activated the older of the identities, turning himself into Tseng Addison, a student from Davis Community College.

He kept in his contacts but mussed his hair once again. He didn't have the needed coloring to make himself a blonde—so he pulled a baseball cap from the deep pocket of his tunic. Retrieving a small drive from his shoe, Quinn uploaded a virus into the train mainframe—within seconds he heard a klaxon sounding outside.

Was it for him, or for the miss-opening of six gates? He then uploaded a new ticket for Tseng Addison to the spaceport—transfer of credits for a "summer" job in transportation efficiency.

Right. Sounded bogus to him. But these Word of Blake idiot loyalists would buy anything that sounded like it conformed to mind control.

Removing that drive, he plugged in the back of the drive and shorted out the CPU of the machine he was on. Once out of that of-

fice he turned left, cursing himself for not looking up the old maps for the building and finding the right exit.

After several wrong turns he found a door clearly marked "Exit." With a glance out through a wired glass window, he didn't see anyone. No guards. No one. He eased himself out and stood there a few seconds before walking calmly in the direction of the train station entrance.

Guards rushed out and past him, not even questioning that a criminal would be moving toward them. Once inside, huddled in the center of a group of students, Quinn moved with them to the counter. He showed them his ID, and he was searched and shown through to the waiting area.

The train was waiting; indeed delayed because of the chaos his virus had wrought on the scheduling system. He was just to the closest door when a hand grabbed his arm. He turned, ready to deliver a punch, and was surprised to see Shindo Rosenberg standing beside him.

"Damned punk," the Hiritsu Warrior growled.

Quinn was too stunned to react as Rosenberg's hand crashed into his chest, knocking the air out of his lungs. Hazy from the pain as he doubled over, he realized Shindo didn't recognize him. They had only met a few times, and Quinn was now in disguise.

Rosenberg delivered a well-aimed kick into Quinn's side, lifting him a few centimeters as he flipped over onto his back. He couldn't pull air into his chest—

"You think you can sabotage the trains and get away with it, you punk?" Rosenberg loomed over him again.

Quinn tried to speak, but couldn't pull air in. He needed to tell Shindo who he was—but he couldn't with his voice. So he used the only other thing he had available.

His feet.

Pulling his legs up, Quinn caught Rosenberg behind his knees. The Warrior came down as Quinn groaned out of the way, spun up into a crouch and delivered a well-aimed blow to the back of Shindo's head.

Citizens ignored the two of them. Seeing only an unruly student and a Blakist loyalist, they didn't want to get involved. Couldn't get involved. Wanted nothing that would destroy or interfere with their small, comfortable lives.

The doors were closing. Quinn ran to them.

The sting in his back was real, and sudden. He hissed as he fell into the train, aware there was now a knife sticking out of his back.

Rosenberg was good at his job—even if it was a fake job. He was a hothead, which worked well as security.

Pulling himself up by the silver poles, Quinn faced Rosenberg, who was stalking toward the train.

Finally he pulled air into his lungs, and winced at the pain in his back. "Shindo!" he managed to bark. "They have her!"

And it was enough. Enough of a warning that Rosenberg recognized him and realized what he'd done. *Who* he'd attacked. Shindo's expression went from rage to panic and he tried run to the closing doors.

But the train was already moving.

"I have to find... Aris," Quinn said through the window. He put his hand to the glass before the train lurched and pulled out of the station.

Unknown
Farandir
Magistracy of Canopus
16 June 3072

Aris worked hard rebuilding his body, growing more accustomed to the new changes in his heartbeat, working strength in his hand.

The most annoying adjustment was the inability to feel hot or cold in his fingertips. Nerve damage. Non-repairable.

He could rub his hands along the carved, rock walls. There was no sensation of sharp edges or of gritty sand.

Holding the practice sword was the same. There was no sensation of the hilt in his hand, only the sensation of something solid and the weight on his wrist. He was relearning how to fight from his arm, not his hand and wrist.

He watched teams come and go, but wasn't allowed to join, or train with them. He did help where he could, teaching young men and women how to use a sword, as well as techniques for keeping invisible in the dark. And with each successful student he gained a bit more confidence in his own abilities once again.

He helped with the wounded when they were brought in, and he wept along with the others for the dead. Several of which died before his eyes.

They all sacrificed so much for the sake of freedom. He wanted to help.

He felt ready.

And useless.

And nothing could stop the nightmares, the voice of Setiwah in his mind, whispering to him in his dreams, caressing his cheek in his waking moments, or dispelling the smell of plum blossoms when he opened his eyes.

It was as if she was still there.

"Aris Sung," November came to him one night before dinner.

He was in his small quarters, not far from the infirmary. Marina liked to keep him close, very proud of her work on him and his subsequent adjustment.

Standing, he faced her. "November—what is it?"

She looked torn, and he realized she was pulled apart inside. She wanted to trust him—wanted to bring him into her circle. But she was also cautious.

"We've received a transmission. Evidence of what we believe might be another cell operating here on Farandir."

What? He took a step closer, his heart beating quicker. "Are you sure? Could it be a trap?"

"That's why I need you, Aris Sung," she stepped back to the door. "Because the message is directed at you personally."

▲▼▲

Aris was brought into the command and control center of the cell—an oval area deep in the ground. November claimed it had once been a waste disposal station before the planet's environmental reforms over a hundred years ago.

It was all but forgotten, but the structure was still there. As was the technological links that once connected this command center to others all over the planet.

He recognized a few faces as he walked into the room, dressed in Magistracy black and turquoise. A top, pants, boots and turquoise body-suit beneath.

November gestured for him to join the small group gathered around what he recognized as a holo-HUD, an antiquated but precise piece of equipment that pulled from planetary defense satellites and gave back a three-dimensional image projected into the air above the domed table.

He saw a landscape of snow, mountains, trees, but to his right he saw the ruins of Jakarta City, and then the new Blakist stronghold within New Serang. A small dot pulsed nearest the mountains, and another one close to the ruins.

Very close.

The three individuals, two females and one male, looked up from the table. Each of them was dressed semi-formally. The male had a silver left eye.

Another cybernetic enhancement? Or a replacement?

"Mr. Sung," the man said and his voice was reedy, as if he were speaking through bamboo. Aris noticed a small piece of metal protruding from his throat, nearly hidden by the high collar. "I am Colonel Robert Holden, in charge of base security. The communique in question wasn't directed at this facility, but was more of a layered broadcast."

Aris frowned. "Layered?"

"Force Major Daria Martin," the taller of the two women said and Aris looked at her. "We monitor all broadcasts to and from Canopus—"

"But that's impossible," Aris interrupted. "You'd have to pinpoint the exact time for burst transmissions, as well as monitor hand-carried radio traffic to JumpShips," he looked at each of them. "You're capable of doing all of that—from here?"

Holden nodded. "The Ebon Magistrate has been working at surveillance a long time. We have a network but not nearly enough people to monitor every communiquÉ that comes in or goes out. Even though most of the capital city was destroyed—the lower west side, near the spaceport—the intact areas, and the occupied ones—still operate on an all-is-well basis. Though many of the supporters are visible with their Word of Blake pins. There is still limited commerce, and the citizens are encouraged to continue their lives as relatively normal."

"Normal?" Aris looked at each of them, even at the woman he'd not been introduced to. She was shorter than the others, but carried a much stronger presence. She radiated authority and seemed to be simply—watching. "How can any of this be normal with these Manei Domini moving about? They're nightmares."

"Yes," Colonel Holden nodded and took in a wheezing breath. "But most of the forces aren't the MD. There are only perhaps four Manei Domini on Farandir, with the host of them centered on Canopus. At least none of the angel-demon-named."

"Angel-demon-named?"

"The MD believe themselves to be the messengers of Blake, Mr. Sung," the shorter woman spoke, and her voice held as much authori-

ty as her presence. "Their hierarchy is determined by their devotion to the Master, who delivers the word of Blake. They rename their most devout after angels or demons from different Terran pantheons. Their leader—a terrifying creature that refers to himself as Apollyon—is at the very heart of the invasion. And he is the only one I am aware of that speaks directly to the Master."

Aris kept his features as unreadable as possible as he looked this woman. He again thought of Setiwah. Angel and demon. "I'm sorry—but we've not been introduced."

"I am acting General Erzulie March," she said and gave him a curt bow.

"General," Aris returned the bow. "Your intelligence operatives are indeed well trained to have garnered this information."

"This doesn't come from operatives," March said. "This comes from personal experience. I spent the first year of this war in one of their re-educations camps, Mr. Sung. I know first hand what it is to have one's mind—" she pursed her lips. "Altered."

"But you escaped?"

"I slipped my handler," she nodded. "I managed to keep a part of myself free from their brainwashing techniques, but I also remember everything. Which has proven a boon to this operation."

"It's kept us off the radar," Holden said. He wheezed. "Until this message," he pushed several buttons on the console. The image shifted closer, giving a detailed terrain map of the city and the mountains on the left, but then opening a rectangular inset of sound waves on the right. "The upper bars represent a commercial—broadcast on the holovids. It ran three times during a four-hour span, and each time something in the broadcast tripped this."

One of the aides stepped forward with a small, black square the size of a juniper berry. Aris recognized it as a Capellan sub-dermal communication device. He and Mikhail had been implanted with them specifically for the mission. All of them had. "Where did you get that?"

"From the lab where we found you," Holden said as he retrieved the small device from the aide's hand. "I can only assume the Blakists removed it."

He handed it to Aris.

Aris stared at it—remembering the slight surgery needed to embed it into his wrist.

Something ached behind his eyes and he closed them.

"Mr. Sung?"

He opened them and handed the device back to Holden. "It's nothing. You said there was a message?"

He nodded. "It makes no sense to us—none of the translators we use can decipher it. Therefore we can't even authenticate it. But because it came through this," he set the device on the dome. Its presence didn't interrupt the image above. "We hoped you could."

Holden depressed a button.

The sound bars expanded and contracted as a voice came through. It was choppy, distorted.

It was Quinn Tudor, Raven's student.

Aris listened once, motioned for Holden to play it again. He listened a third time and finally smiled. "It's authentic."

"What is it?" March asked. "Some language?"

"It's a southern dialect of Mandarin—something long forgotten—but taught to the members of House Hiritsu. It's only used when one believes their communications are being monitored."

"What does it say?" November said from where she remained standing near the door.

He turned to look at November and hesitated. He trusted her. And the message itself would hold no meaning to anyone but himself or Raven Clearwater.

It said, "I do not understand."

The declaration for the beginning of wisdom.

November shook her head. "I'm asking you what the message said."

He smiled. "I know." He looked at Holden. "How long has this been broadcasting?"

"For a couple of weeks," he gave a breathy response. "We weren't sure what it was at first—only an echo. And it wasn't until it continued to play on the same show, same episode, that we started to look into it."

"What's the show?" Aris said.

March gave a half-smile. "*The Immortal Warrior.*"

▲▼▲

Later that evening, November brought Aris back into the command and control center. There were fewer people this time. March was missing, but Holden was there, as well as Daria Martin. The center holo-dome was in operation, displaying the same landscape as before. And with the same blinking dots.

"What are those?" Aris asked no one in particular.

"This is our location," Martin pointed to pulsing circle near the ruined city. "That's a place we sometimes detect activities. Magnetic fields that come and go."

Aris looked at their present location. "We're this close to the ruined capital." He looked at Holden and then to Martin. "Is that wise?"

"This location has proven the best place of operation," Martin said. "It's why we were able to find you and act quickly when you were being moved. The same went for the day we discovered Erzulie March was still alive."

Aris watched her for a few seconds, studying her face, her body movement. "I suspect her retrieval from the Word of Blake was not easy?"

Holden chuckled. It was a raspy, eerie sound. "Not at all. But if she hadn't destroyed Liwet, then there would have been no return to us."

"Liwet?"

"Her Manei Domini handler," Martin said. "Erzulie was badly injured to the point of death when her offices were stormed during the initial coup—one of the quiet raids that took the city by surprise. Much like you, Mr. Sung, she was preserved and taken to one of the infirmary facilities and implanted with cyberware. Liwet was there to train her to become an operative."

Thoughts of Setiwah returned to Aris. A flash of her lips. The touch of her fingers. Always the memories were at the surface. Would they ever disappear?

He also remembered her strength. Her inhuman reflexes. "How—how was she able to remove herself from something—" he looked at Martin. "How?"

"She paid attention, Aris. Erzulie was—and is—Ebon. Heart and soul." She narrowed her eyes at him, and he was almost sure there was something unspoken in her gaze. "Never forget who—or what—you were trained to be."

"We have it," Holden said from the other side of the dome. The image shifted and the pulse began again, with the voice tracks displayed. Aris listened to the message—repeated again in the exact tone and cadence as before.

I do not understand.

There could be only one response. He closed his eyes and took in several deep breaths, calling forth his *chi*, rolling it over the valleys of his mind, to a place where memory slept.

Once his eyes opened, he stared at the pulsing track and repeated the response in the precise tonal manner he'd been taught since joining House Hiritsu.

He watched his voice pattern reflect that of the message. *The declaration for the beginning of wisdom.*

"Okay," Holden said. "We have the recording. You may go."

"Go?" Aris straightened up. "I want to wait for the response."

"Aris," November finally stepped out of the shadows. "The response may not come tonight, or tomorrow. It may be next week, or next month. But when we hear it, we will let you know."

▲▼▲

The response came in less than twenty-four hours. November woke Aris, who'd just turned in after a grueling day of teaching combat to a small group of trainees. He threw on a pair of pants and a t-shirt and followed her to command and control.

Everyone was there, including March.

"Ah, Aris," Martin said. "Please, listen to this."

They replayed the message back.

Aris kept his features passive.

Quinn's words were clear. *There is a cell, Ebon Magistrate, possible first assault survivors. Rendezvous at preset destination. They have clear water.*

"What is it?" Holden reached out and grabbed Aris' upper arm. "What did they say?"

Aris stood his ground and waited until Holden pulled his hand away. Once everyone had stopped what they were doing and looked at him, Aris spoke. "Have you pinpointed where the message is coming from? Can you find him?"

"Find who?" Martin said.

Holden stepped forward. "Is your contact in trouble?"

Aris turned to him. "I don't know. I just know the news—I have to see him. I have to see his face. I have to go to him."

"That's impossible," March said.

Aris turned to her. "I'm going."

March stood her ground and narrowed her eyes at Aris. He matched her gaze. "That message contained coordinates—as well as some sort of missive." March lowered her chin. "One you do not wish to share with us."

Aris gave her a shallow bow. She was right, on every count. A very smart woman, intelligent, and one to watch. Looking at her, he could not tell what parts of her the Blakists had reconstructed.

WITH CARRION MEN

Senior General March paused only for a second when Aris didn't answer. "You realize I can't let you go. You can't leave here."

Aris arched his eyebrows. "Am I a prisoner?"

"I can't risk you being captured again and compromising this cell."

"I will not be captured again," Aris said as he stood firmly on both of his feet. He felt he'd been patient, for months, and tolerant, mainly because he'd had no choice. He'd lost weeks, months since that moment at death's door in the city. He wasn't even sure exactly how long he'd been on Farandir. Or what was happening outside of this place. In the Confederation.

Anywhere.

"General," Aris said with as much respect as he could muster in his tone. "You want to help any who oppose the Blakists and their regime of terror. You fought nobly to extricate yourself from their presence. Would you turn back now when there are those out there who would welcome your assistance?"

She stared at him for several minutes before giving only a slight nod. "The origination point of the transmission is on the outskirts of the Jakarta ruins—near where your 'Mech was destroyed. You will take a small team of my choosing."

Aris nodded as well. "Only if I am allowed November to accompany me."

"Agreed."

Jakarta Ruins
Farandir
Magistracy of Canopus
17 June 3072

The house in the ruins was easy enough to find—what caused the small group of four trouble were the constant patrols of the area by Blakists forces. They were able to evade detection, however, and November led the way, using a small GPS device in her left hand.

The two soldiers flanking them took up position on either side of the house's destroyed front door. Aris had his pistol drawn, trusting his damaged hand's reflexes more in pulling a trigger than swinging a blade. Stepping inside he crouched and looked around the room. He gave the silent signal for all-clear, and the two soldiers stepped in and took up positions.

November came in and held the device in her hand. It had stopped snowing and the sun was high in the sky outside, casting the interior in deep shadows. "The signal's here," she looked around. "But I don't see anything."

"Might be in a basement," one of the men said, his weapon at the ready.

Aris nodded and started examining the floor for anything that would resemble a cellar door. He spotted something near a stack of boxes. After re-holstering his pistol, Aris held out his hands and pointed at the snow accumulated on the area, blown into the house through the broken windows by the wind.

"What is it?"

Aris said, "They were here. See their tracks?"

November looked carefully. "No, I can't make out anything."

"Stay back," he hooked a finger around a small latch and pulled the trap door back. The two soldiers were there in an instant, their weapons on their shoulders, their sights aimed into the hole.

But no one came out.

Aris caught the smell first.

Death.

"Oh no," November said.

Panic gnawing at the back of his mind Aris went down first, praying with each step he wouldn't find what he feared he would.

The room was dark and he pulled out a light from the parka's many pockets and held it high.

Bodies—both Blakist Loyalists and his own people. He could make out Trahn's body to his right, as well as Rosenberg's. There were three other bodies, all wearing Word of Blake battle-gear.

Where were Tudor and Yu?

He knelt beside his people. Dead. As he feared. The cavities in their chests revealed how they died. And the smell told him it'd been several days ago.

"Were—" November said from behind him. He whirled to face her, not realizing she'd followed him down. Her eyes were wide. "Were these your people?"

"Two of them," he said in a quiet voice. "Two are missing." He moved through the lower rooms. In the back he found a smaller area, more of a storage nook, where a bed and table were.

On the bed lay Quinn Tudor.

Aris raced to the bedside and set the lamp on the table. He removed the glove from his left hand and checked for a pulse.

WITH CARRION MEN

Quinn opened his amber eyes. "*Lien-Zhang—*"

"Shhh," Aris said. "Don't talk." He started to stand and call for help.

But Quinn's hand was on his arm. "They took her, *Lien-Zhang*," he said.

Aris nodded. "I know. I got your message."

"And I—" he smiled at Aris. "I have the contact information—" he winced as pain washed over him.

Aris leaned in close. "For?"

"Mikhail," Quinn said in a rush. "Mikhail Chess is with the cell." And with that the young man closed his eyes and went still. Aris checked his pulse. Still there. He was only unconscious. He glanced at the wound burned deep into Quinn's chest.

He turned and yelled out. "We need to get out of here—*now!*"

▲▼▲

Aris heard November's approach as he stood beside Quinn's bed—the same one he had occupied for several months.

The young man was still very pale, but his vitals were good. Marina estimated he'd been in that basement a good two days with the other dead bodies. Either by luck or by fate Quinn's wounds had been enough to incapacitate, but not kill him. Another day, and things could have turned out different.

"Marina found a knife wound beneath his left shoulder blade," November said in a quiet voice. "Appears he was stabbed some time ago. It was infected."

"That might explain why he was in the bed," Aris said, never taking his gaze from Quinn's face. "The Blakists who came in to destroy them might have mistook him for wounded. Figured one shot would kill him. Lucky they didn't check to see if he was dead."

He felt a pressure on his shoulder and looked to see November's hand. "He's going to sleep for a while, Aris. You should eat, and rest."

"I can't," he looked back at the young man. A thought occurred to him. "November, Marina didn't have to give Quinn any implants, did she?" He looked at her.

Reading his expression she shook her head. "No—the damage didn't extend to his heart. Only to the tissue and beneath. It was almost superficial—as if the one who shot him did it from the doorway." She moved past him and leaned over the bed, gently moving a wisp of gray hair from the young man's forehead. "He's so young."

"Twenty-eight."

She glanced back at him. "I would ask if he were your son—but there isn't much of a resemblance."

"I—" Aris pondered explaining his relationship with Quinn to her, and considered such knowledge wasn't to be shared. That way it couldn't be used against him later. "He's the student of one of my friends."

"One of the missing people?"

Aris nodded.

November stood and faced Aris. Her demeanor changed and she was now all business. "One of my men said he spoke to you before he passed out. They couldn't understand him."

"Your men have good hearing," Aris said. "He spoke in the same language he used to send me the missive."

"Are you going to tell me what it was he said?"

He looked directly at her. "What he said is the reason I'm standing by his bedside. I have to know what it meant." He swallowed. "He said—" he hesitated again. Why was it he felt both comfortable as well as wary around November? Was it because she reminded him so much of Raven? He took in a deep breath. "Mikhail Chess was alive and with the resistance cell."

Her eyes widened. "That's not possible. We have positive confirmation that he died with his 'Mech."

"Exactly. I have to talk to him—I have to know where Quinn got the intel. As well as a few other matters."

November pursed her lips and put her hands on her hips. "This information has to be a trap. There aren't any other cells. Don't you think we've looked?"

"I don't know," Aris snapped, and instantly regretted his anger. But he was tired, and his chest and hand ached such a way that made his head ache as well. He sighed. "I'm sorry—it's just that—"

"You're worried about him. And you lost people in that basement. I understand."

"There are still two missing. Two females."

"One is his teacher? Your friend."

He wanted to lie. "Yes. We've been through a lot together. She was—" he reached up with his left hand and pulled down on the back of his neck, stretching the muscles. "One of them was captured by Blake."

November didn't reply. She didn't need too. They both knew what that could mean. Neither spoke for a while.

Until, "This young man—he's good with intel?"

"Quinn's gifted in communications. He's got a knack for systems, networks," he glanced at November. "I'd almost say he could take an HPG apart and put it back together."

"Oh I doubt that," November said. Then she narrowed her eyes at him. "Could he really?"

"Given enough time, I'm sure he could." Aris rubbed his eyes with his left hand. He was still having tactile issues, as well as a few tendon twitches, with his right hand. He'd dropped a glass earlier that day—his hand just spasmed open. No control. Marina had assured him it was just nerves firing.

Aris wasn't so sure. His right hand didn't feel—right.

"How do you know him? Are you sure he's not a Blake Loyalist?"

"I'm sure. Quinn is Hiritsu born and bred. He was infantry—until about nine years ago. I took a small interest in him—and noticed how he was always late to drills because others always asked him to fix things and Quinn could never say no. Computer terminals mostly—and then I found him inside the network system of one of the Drop-Ships—and I mean literally inside of it, beneath the communications console. There'd been a glitch that canceled lift off."

"And he fixed it?"

Aris nodded. "I checked his record, mentioned him to the House Master, and much to my amusement, he assigned Quinn as my friend's student. I had assumed he'd give him to me. But apparently he has something else in mind. But Quinn's good. If he has information about a resistance cell, then I'd say he got through underhanded or back door channels. And it's legit—" he looked at her. "As long as it's not planted."

But she only shook her head. "I don't know, Aris. March and Holden are skeptical. It was one issue to see you fall from the sky—but this man was deep in occupied territory, working for the wobbies. How are you so sure he wasn't compromised?"

"I'm not," Aris said and turned his attention back to Quinn. "But I'm ready to wait as long as it takes, and if Mikhail is with another cell, then we have to find them, November." He set his jaw. "And we have to contact Sun-Tzu and let him and all of Sian know that there are those loyal to the Magistracy of Canopus still alive here. And they're willing and ready to fight."

Forgive me, Raven. But we have a job to do before I can look for you. If at all.

New Serang
Blakist Stronghold
Farandir
Magistracy of Canopus
28 July 3072

She had no idea how many days or nights she'd lain on the floor of her cell. The same two woman and men had entered every morning and asked her the same questions. Who are you? Who do you work for? Who do you serve?

Who are you here for?

And every day she would give them the same answers. *I am Devon Sid. I work for the Hauss Beill Trading Company. I serve their customer service department. I am here for my boss, Alvin Sylvester.*

Over and over and over, until Raven started having dreams of living this other life. Of being Devon Sid. Of living the life of a normal customer service executive.

And through it all there was the same sound inside her cell. The same soft, monotonous female voice telling her how great Blake was. How good it would be to serve The Master.

Schlock, schlock, schlock.

To her amazement they had never given her drugs. Not once. Or even tried to inflict physical harm.

So why am I here? And what happened to Quinn? Or Yu, Rosenberg or even Trahn? Where are they? Did they find Aris?

She hoped as much. And if that damned voice kept whispering through the speakers set too high for her to pummel in the ceiling, she was going to hope for a short sword and commit seppuku.

Raven ignored the stench of her own body—wearing the same clothes with no shower or bath for—how many days? She was fed. There was a toilet in the corner with no privacy. No shower. Her skin itched. And her nails were—well—dirty.

I've never been a girlie girl. Not like that Princess was. *But I could sure use some soap right now.*

And a sword. Any sword. A pipe? Where were those damned speakers?

She heard the shush of the door opening, felt the slight change in air pressure. And she started to say something—a greeting to the two men and two women as they came in again.

Only—it wasn't them this time.

No—there was something different about the room. Something... Cold.

Maleficent.

"Rested, no?"

It was a female's voice, with a strange accent. Languid vowels. Rich tone. Raven pushed herself up into a sitting position and looked at the door.

Nothing could have stopped the gasp that escaped her.

Standing close to two meters tall, the woman was larger than life. Dressed scantily in a white dress and matching pants beneath, her collar was in a Mandarin-style, much like the tops Raven enjoyed wearing when not in uniform. Her arms were bare—and the left one was human—olive skin.

But the right—

It gleamed a polished silver, and though it mimicked the lithe, slender left arm, it wasn't anything living, but made of metal parts.

Dark, close-cropped black hair framed high cheekbones, a small, pointed chin, and full, red lips. Even her silver eyes looked perfect for her face.

She glided toward Raven, who scrambled up onto her feet and backed away. She didn't know what the hell this was—but it wasn't getting too close.

The woman/machine stopped and stared at her with those blinding silver eyes. "Raven Clearwater... " came the voice as smooth as Sian silk.

"How—" she blinked. "How did you—" not once in all the days had she spoken that name. Not once! How did this—this—this thing know that!

"You were with the prince, no? The Warrior."

Raven pressed herself into the corner of the room, but she felt her expression give again. Prince? Warrior? She looked at the silver eyes and shook her head. "I don't understand—"

"Ah," the woman was instantly beside her. No more than a flash of time and her human hand was caressing Raven's chin. Raven shuddered and closed her eyes, not wanting to see into those metallic eyes. "Very Pre-tea. Warrior woman. You saved the princess, no? And now you are here. Did you come with the prince? Or did you come to find him?"

Raven had no idea what it was she was talking about. All she could do was avoid the stare. The woman moved away and went to the door. It opened and a box was pushed inside. It was perhaps a meter squared—large enough to store something small.

The women gave Raven a dazzling smile. "Your prince is mine.

You should look inside the box." And then she was gone.

Several minutes passed before Raven moved from the corner, al-most afraid the woman would step back inside. It'd been years since Raven had feared anything. But there was something—wrong—about that woman. Besides the fact she was put together with 'Mech parts.

Finally she knelt beside the box. There were no markings on it. Just a plain silver box. She found a small button on one side and pushed it.

A soft hiss expelled a small blast of cold air and Raven nearly yelled aloud. She pulled back but once the lid was raised she tenta-tively looked inside.

Nausea pulled bile as well as her day's meal to the tip of her throat as she stared down at the half of a human heart nestled inside a human hand.

A human heart.

Half of a heart.

She recognized the hand, and the ring of silver on its thumb.

Raven scrambled back, pressing her hands to her mouth. The woman had said the prince was now hers. *I saved a princess.* Raven sat in the corner trying hard not to throw up.

Princess. Princess. Yes, she'd helped save a princess once. But that was a long time ago—twelve years? Thirteen? And she had been with Aris—

The prince.

Are you here with him, or to find him?

She was here to find one man.

Oh god. No.

Aris... *this was Aris' heart!*

ARIS!!!

She never made it to the toilet.

Jakarta Ruins
Farandir
Magistracy of Canopus
3 August 3072

Aris could just make out the top of Quinn's hair in the clump of a patch of wild winter flowers. It was something close to spring now on Farandir. The warmest the planet ever became on this hemisphere.

With temperatures close to eighteen degrees Celsius, it was hard for November and her superiors to keep the residents of the under-

ground cell confined inside. Everyone wanted to feel the sun on their faces, their arms. They wanted to know warmth.

And Quinn was no exception.

He'd been sullen since his recovery—distancing himself from everyone—angry at the world. More at Aris because the young man had not wanted to disclose the information he'd learned to March or Holden or November.

In fact he'd been certain he'd seen November's face before. Somewhere, and she'd assured him that if he'd been privy to the Blakest network then he'd seen her face several times.

But mostly he was angry at Aris because he refused to allow the young man to rescue his *Sifu*.

"We have a job to do, Tudor," Aris had said in the privacy of the infirmary. Marina had allowed them some time together. "We all knew the risks when we took this job. Rescuing Raven is the lowest priority."

"And finding Mikhail is the highest? Because he knew your dead student?" Quinn had said.

Aris hadn't meant to strike out at Quinn. Yes, both of them had high emotions. And Quinn knew where to punch. But Aris had turned his hand backward on Quinn before he realized it. The impact had sent the younger man down, slicing his lip against his teeth.

Quinn had given little argument after that, and done as Aris asked, offering assistance in the communications room. But Holden had refused and ordered Quinn to keep a healthy distance from the command center.

And now Aris had news and needed to find him. As he made his way over the rubble, noticing the sprouts of grass whose life span lasted no more than five months on this world, his right hand twinged again, refusing to grip a particular rock.

He paused and looked at it, pulling the black glove off and holding it up in the light. He made a fist. Released it. Everything worked—

"That's not your hand," Quinn said from his left.

Aris had heard him, but kept to himself. "It's my hand. I recognize the scars."

"It's only my opinion, *sir*."

Aris lowered his hand and looked a Quinn. He still chose to dress in grays and subdued silvers, blending into the sides of a picture. He stood just to Aris' right, his hands thrust deep into the pockets of his camouflage pants.

"I have news."

Quinn nodded. "Mikhail answered."

A sigh escaped Aris as he crossed his arms over his chest. "You already knew?"

"Why else come out here to find me?" He looked around, and a small breeze ruffled the hair around his face. His eyes were shadowed and unreadable. "I come out here a lot."

"You can't keep blaming yourself—"

"Yes I can," the man snapped. He looked away. "Raven warned me about poking around those networks. And I knew they'd found several of my aliases already. But I kept using that last one, thinking it was somehow safe."

Aris knew the rest. That was how the wobbies had found them, found the house in the ruins, on the other side of the city. He'd taken ill, not letting Yu or Rosenberg tend to the stab wound as he should. He'd developed a high fever and Yu had gone out to find medicine and antibiotics when they were attacked.

No one had seen or heard from her since that day.

And Quinn blamed himself.

"We all make mistakes. I've made many greater than that one."

"I know, Aris," Quinn said, dropping the honorific. Aris knew he did this when he was unsure of himself and the situation. "It's just that—I can help these people with their network, but they won't let me." He pointed at the cell's opening. "Do you realize they're running off of unsecured networks in there? That's what I was doing when I was caught, Aris. Anyone can see their traffic."

"I'm sure there's some sort of security, Quinn. They wouldn't do that."

He didn't push the argument. Quinn only shrugged. "I know I've seen November, Aris. And I remember it—because it's important. There's something wrong about her."

"She was left for dead," Aris said. "She was held in Blakist custody, Quinn. Her name and face will show up on a manifest of some sort if you look for it. November has been more than an ally to me while I've been here," he nodded. "She's even offered to help go after Raven."

Quinn snorted. "You think she's still alive?"

"We can hope."

He shook his head. "I'm losing my hope, *sir*, and my confidence." He moved past a large chunk of building. "So where is Mikhail?"

"We have the location," he set his lips thin, knowing this wasn't going to be easy. "But you're not coming."

The young man reacted nothing like Aris thought he would. Quinn nodded. "I thought as much. November said no."

There was an awkward pause. And then Quinn abruptly moved closer and switched to Mandarin. "Then agree, but give me the space to act on my own."

He narrowed his eyes at Quinn and answered in Mandarin as well. "Act on your own?"

"I'll sneak out and follow you. I can keep back—"

"No."

"But—"

"No. And if you talk about this again I'll have you confined to your room, do you understand?"

But it was obvious by his expression that Quinn didn't understand. He shook his head slowly. "What's wrong with you, Aris? It's like the fight's been somehow beat out of you."

"That's not true—"

"Yes, it is. You've given over your trust in these people one hundred percent. You refuse to go after Raven, saying it's our duty to contact Chess. We're here to reassure the Chancellor that a resistance cell exists. And it does. This one. And there are two once you see Chess. We could have already taken Raven back and gotten off this planet in the time it's taken you to act."

"That's enough, Quinn."

"No, it's not." Quinn backed up. "You trust her. You trust all of them. You don't know them."

"I know they rescued me from the Wobbies. I know they gave me life again when a Manei Domini would have taken it. I know that November and Holden, March—all of them have taken a chance on me. They've taken me into their confidence and I—"

His hand spasmed. He hissed and held out to his side, amazed at how the fingers of his right hand could spread so far apart. The movement was painful.

Quinn came forward and watched, though he kept a distance. "Beware the hand that might betray you."

Jakarta Ruins
Farandir
Magistracy of Canopus
5 August 3072

The snow along the mountain range was hip deep in places as they traveled to the coordinates given to Quinn. Aris traveled light—keeping only his *jian* with him, a pistol and utility belt. He'd dressed in white as had the other five of March's team, so they would blend into the surrounding areas, into the mountains where the snow was still thick.

The snow started to fall more heavily, and it was getting harder to see. Aris put on his goggles as did November. She touched his hand then and pointed behind them.

There was no sign of the others.

With only a slight bit of panic Aris turned back and climbed onto the nearest bank to take a look at a higher elevation. He could just see the others, nearly a half kilometer back.

How had they gotten so far behind?

The snow thickened as he walked down to November. He told her how far back they were. She wanted to stay and wait.

"We should have brought Quinn," he said finally.

"He was better off staying in the bunker, Aris."

He looked at her. "Better off locked in the infirmary?"

She put her hand on his arm. "He'll be fine, Aris. Like you said, Quinn's a big boy, and he can take care of himself."

Several more minutes passed, and Aris felt it was finally time to execute the plan he and Quinn had worked out. He looked at November. "I can't stay and wait. There's only a small window of time," he said. "I have to fulfill my mission."

"What is your mission, Aris Sung?" she said, reaching out to grab his left wrist.

He didn't look away. His dark eyes locked with her lighter ones. "I'm here to find out whether a resistance cell exists and offer assistance from the Magistrix. I've done that. But now I have to return to my commander and report."

"Now? You have to tell them now?"

"You've refused to allow me to contact the Chancellor of the Cappellan Confederation. You have refused to let me offer up help from both he and the Magestrix. Mikhail has arranged for me to have that communication. Please... "

He removed his goggles and looked at her, taking in every nuance of her face. Aris hadn't made the decision to do what he was about to—until that moment.

"Thank you, November. For everything you've done." He put his hand on her shoulder.

She tensed seconds before he struck, pressing down on the nerves along her neck, recalling the muscles he'd memorized during their training. He could incapacitate her blindfolded.

November fell forward into his arms. He carefully wrapped her in his outer coat, set up a small red flag visible to the others' snow goggles and quietly retreated into the nearby woods.

▲▼▲

Aris moved with precision as he double-checked the real coordinates Quinn gave him as opposed to the ones he'd given November. He looked at his pedometer, counting the meters, sun position and mountain range. Luckily the secondary cell's position was in the rockier terrain—not as easy to track his passage as he searched the forests.

And he knew he'd reached his destination when he found a single man sitting on a tree stump. He was cloaked in a white coat with a fur-lined hood.

And he was eating an apple.

Aris moved along the trees, keeping to the forest as he watched the man. Watched him cut a piece of apple with a knife and pull it up into the dark recess of the hood.

The movements were—familiar.

"I know you're there," came a male voice. "This area's heavily guarded and patrolled. They saw you coming a mile away. And I have to thank you for leaving your new friends behind."

Aris couldn't suppress the smile that played on his lips. He kept his pistol out as he stepped into view, a white, shadowy silhouette between two trees. "I was surprised to hear your message."

"Well," Mikhail stood, still holding the apple. "I was surprised you answered it. Quinn was the only one that thought you were still alive—so I had to see you for myself. I had to know it was you."

"And?"

Aris heard their footsteps, slight indentations in the snow. There were perhaps seven—all dressed in white camouflage and all of them heavily armed.

It was so quiet, save for the clicking of snow on the leaves. "There is no need for this," Aris re-holstered his pistol and held up his hands. And he gave Mikhail his identification in his native tongue.

Mikhail gave the proper response, but his body movements told a different story. He seemed tenser than when last he'd seen him, on board the *Midnight Caller*. He pocketed the apple before taking several steps toward Aris until the two faced one another.

Aris slowly reached up and removed his goggles, setting them on his forehead as his hood fell back.

Mikhail did the same.

"Aiya—" Aris took a step back as he concentrated on the black eye that peered out at him from a nearly ruined face. A black eye with a red, pinpoint center.

The men and women nearest him moved quickly, grabbing his arms on either side as he tried to go for his sword strapped to his back.

He'd only seen one eye like that before, seconds before he died— Setiwah.

And now Mikhail looked at him with the same eye and smiled. "Relax, Aris. I'm not the enemy." His smile faded. "Are you?"

And to Aris' surprise, his subordinate reared back and brought his right hand up and across Aris' face. The impact wasn't as final as Setiwah's had been, but it carried with it an anger, and a resentment Aris had never known before.

The strike left him a bit dazed and he was hit again from underneath, one of his guards striking him in the gut.

Winded, Aris would have fell forward if he'd not been held upright.

Mikhail bent down to look at him, and his eye turned Aris' stomach. "Quinn sent me a new message, Aris. I have to make sure... " and his friend nodded.

Something struck him from behind and Aris slumped forward.

▲▼▲

He wasn't tortured, as he believed he would be. Instead he was questioned repeatedly, kept awake for several days, and made to retell his story again and again. He had to give the names of the leaders of the Ebon resistance cell several times, describe them.

Until finally he was injected with something that made him sick. He lost nearly a day and woke to find himself cleaned and naked on a mattress beneath several blankets in the corner of a room. He

was shivering, and pulled the stacked blankets close to him. They smelled of oil and grease.

"I'm sorry," came a voice from the dark.

Aris expected to hear Mikhail—he'd already noted his breathing as he woke. "I commend you on your... tactics." His teeth rattled. "Th-though I'm sure you found I am telling the t-truth."

"Yes," Mikhail moved in the farthest corner, and a light brightened the room. Aris took in as much detail as he could from where he lay. A few shelves full of old books, hooks along the wall near a door where several pieces of clothing hung.

Where Mikhail had been there was a metal table and two chairs. On the table sat a small heating unit—the sort Aris had used when on wilderness training missions. Mikhail moved his chair closer to the mattress and sat down. His eyes once more covered in sunglasses. He leaned forward and rested his elbows on his knees. "Yeah—every test checked out. You're telling the "truth." And as far as we can tell, the identities of those you met all check out as well. This Erzulie March—she did escape and is wanted in connection for the destruction of a Manei Domini named Liwet."

Aris nodded. "Her handler. She was being trained as an operative."

"I'd say she was too well trained."

Aris stared at Mikhail, and then shivered.

"Oh, sorry about the reaction," Mikhail nodded to him. "You're going to go through some tremors as the serum works its way through your system. The truth box here is a bit antiquated and needs the juice to help it work. We don't have all the amenities your last stay had. We're not... funded."

Aris nodded, again taken back by the changes in Mikhail. Even his speech pattern was different. More native rather than natural.

"But other than that," Mikhail sat back. "You're in damn fine health, *Lien-Zhang*." He nodded to him. "Care to tell me where the arm came from? Manei Domini?"

The arm? Aris looked down at his right hand. "No, I lost my hand during a battle with a Manei Domini—but not my arm. The Ebon cell I was with reattached it."

Mikhail stared at Aris. "That's what they told you."

Fighting a relatively harsh tremor, Aris pushed himself up until he was sitting and wrapped the blankets around him. "Could I have some clothes?"

"Not the ones you had—they were redistributed. I have extras over by the bed."

Aris rubbed at his arms. The shaking was subsiding, but he was still nauseated. He narrowed his eyes at Mikhail. "What happened to you? The last I saw—I thought you had died."

"So did I." Mikhail shrugged. "I was thrown from the cockpit when the reactor imploded—luckily somehow the eject lever was triggered. I ended up several floors up in a building, covered in rubble, and pretty much dying.

"Half my face was gone, my side, as well as my left foot. I was found by this cell, probably seconds before it was too late." He pursed his lips and sat back. Most of his face was still in shadow, and the ruined part of it, the area around his eyes, was hidden by the shades.

"They patched me up—using what little Ebon technology they possessed. Not as pretty as yours."

Mikhail shook his head. "A month before I was found, before we landed and created such a spectacular event—this cell lost their leader in an intel mission.

"Apparently one of those Manei Domini was scheduled to arrive, and they gathered information on its identity. What they were after was why it was coming in. There's already one heading up the main operations in the new capitol. Unfortunately the mission lost six out of eight people. They never did learn why it was arriving—and we're still not sure where it was positioned."

Aris took in several deep breaths. He was going to need food soon. He also needed to bring up the subject of contacting Ty Wu Non. "What was the name?"

"Setiwah."

Aris couldn't stop the abrupt revulsion that twisted his stomach. He steadied himself where he sat.

Mikhail noticed his reaction as well. "She was the one that took your hand?"

Aris took in several deep breaths before answering. "Yes. But you never discovered why she arrived?"

Mikhail shrugged. "Only that something had to be in the works for a Precentor Delta to be arriving clandestinely."

Aris narrowed his eyes. "Why so?"

"Well because they always seem to make a big deal when another one of those robots sets down on the planet. Big fanfare. Huge party, the whole works. You'd believe Buddha had returned." He shook his head. "But not with this one. Which is why everyone was so nervous. This one—this intel came with a price. They didn't want anyone to know about this Setiwah coming in."

It was like her arrival to the planet was the same as it had been on Hustaing. As it was when she'd suddenly appeared behind him in the ruins.

"She arrived a month before you and I?"

He nodded.

A very deep pit formed in the center of Aris' stomach. Overwhelming dread.

Mikhail sighed as he stood and went to the row of shirts. He dug deep into the pocket of one of the shirts and pulled out a small roll of paper. He tossed it to Aris. "Quinn wanted you to read that. I haven't heard from him since you left."

The paper was handwritten—Mikhail's writing.

The attack came before you were even a kilometer up the road—but I was prepared for it. If you don't hear from me—then I died, sir. And I failed. Just know that November Talliard was, and is, a high ranking Blakist. Not a loyalist, Aris, but a person born to her station. She was never interned in a camp because her father runs camps. She's trained in deep infiltration. Programmed and designed to look normal in every way.

Manei Domini, Aris. That's where I saw her face—when I was digging through classified files in connection to a research subject that went missing in a lab. A test subject they called the Prince.

A realization born of the ultimate betrayal pulled at Aris' stomach.

Manei Domini. Quinn was accusing November of being—

"I checked out everything Quinn wrote, Aris. She is what he learned she is. Quinn disappeared just after that last transmission. My guess is he snuck into their communications room and sent it before either being killed or taken. Either way, it's only a matter of time now."

Aris sat with his mouth half parted as his mind worked on ahead. A subject they called *prince*.

Setiwah had been watching Isis on Hustaing to make sure she wasn't harmed. And she'd helped Aris when it looked as if he might fail—though in truth the MD could have allowed Richardson to kill him and then simply dispatched him as easily as the others.

But she'd saved—

Me.

And here she just happened to be on Farandir on the very day, in the very hour he and Mikhail arrived. And she's there, watching him, taunting him, ready to kill him.

But I'm not dead.

Aris began breathing heavily as he started putting the pieces together.

And now November was—

He was on his feet in less than a second.

But it was too late.

Thunder shook the floor beneath them. Mikhail was on his feet, his eyes wide as he materialized a pistol from the folds of his clothing. Aris became dizzy for only a few seconds before he stood up straight. "What was that?"

"Sounds like they're here," he pointed at Aris. "Stay put."

"No, I can't do that. Mikhail, that sounded like an explosive, and it felt much worse. Either there's been an accident somewhere in your facility—"

"Or we've been compromised." Mikhail's expression was unreadable, his dark eyes fixing on Aris. "Which is all the more reason you should stay here."

He reached out and touched Aris' shoulder before turning and running out the door.

There was no way Aris was going to stay put. Voices now echoed from above and below as another explosion that rocked the foundation again.

With a glance at the door he went to a small chest of drawers and yanked out clothes. A black turtleneck, utility pants, socks and pulled them all on. He then spied boots in the corner and realized they were his own. He pulled them on and saw his sword and holster hanging on the wall, along with a rifle and set of pistols.

He grabbed all of them and outfitted himself. Someone ran past the room, and Aris heard them stop. He had the rifle up and resting on the crook of his arm, the barrel aimed at the door before the person peered inside.

It was a young man, his face still bearing the scars of adolescence. He was wild-eyed and his cheeks smudged. "Mister—you'd better get out of here! The wobbies have found us."

The wobbies have—

Aris felt his heart skip. And there it was—the dread that had been building inside of him since the moment Mikhail mentioned Setiwah's name.

We were set up...

He swallowed as he clutched the weapon in his hand. *I was set up.* November was a Manei Domini...

The kid vanished, his footsteps sounding down the hall. Aris listened carefully again, and heard screams above him. There were more explosions, closer to his position.

More vibrations from above and below. Precision hits. Screams. It had to be Setiwah. Her arrival was secret.

Aris paused.

He recalled his conversation with November, telling her about Setiwah, even though he'd already briefed her months earlier. Never had she mentioned not knowing the name, or even wondering where this new MD had come from. This cell had gone as far as losing lives to discover the identity and purpose for her being here.

But not November's group.

Not. One. Word.

Oh... no...

Peering around the corner of the room, Aris looked from left to right. He had no idea which way was out or which way lead deeper in. The kid had run to the right, after telling Aris to get out, so he could safely assume he was trying to find his own way out.

Rifle poised, barrel up, finger on trigger, Aris started out to the right. Smoke filled the corridor the further he went and he could smell the oxidation of metal, the burnt odor of flesh.

They were indeed under attack.

Aris thought of a few choice words before moving ahead quickly. He needed to find Mikhail and those in charge of this cell—he needed to offer his help for evacuation. Fighting a might as strong as the Word of Blake in close quarters like this was a fool's mission.

And if they had Manei Domini with them—

An explosion of red and orange followed by a rain of shrapnel and rock caused Aris to hit the floor as sharp stones pelted him and the walls around him. The smoke was choking, but it was clearer closer to the floor. He looked up in time to see a figure stagger toward him.

Aris crouched low and pushed himself to the side, ignoring the ache in his left shoulder where he was sure something from the explosion had lodged.

The figure became clearer and he recognized Mikhail—

Or what was left of him.

He knew the clothes, the boots, the jacket, the man's long fingered hands.

But Mikhail no longer had the top part of his head. His skull, just above his eyebrows, was cleaved off, and his brain was visible, a glistening mass of—

"Everyone get out!" came a voice behind Aris.

He turned to see a man in black beckoning to him to follow him. "You—they're coming in! You have to—"

But he was cut down by a laser blast that issued from Aris' left. He spun, going down on his left knee, bringing the rifle up into his site.

Coming through the smoke and fire were soldiers, dressed in winter camouflage with full helmets and faceplates, the only evidence of their identity was the all too familiar sword emblem on the arms of their uniforms.

More than a dozen streamed into the corridor, several running past Aris before he had time to react. He got a few in his sight and started to fire at them as they came at him—

But they all moved past him, as if he weren't even there.

None of them seemed to notice him. And when he did try to fire, his hand spasmed again. He couldn't pull the trigger with his right hand.

"Aris."

The voice came through even, clear, soft in his ears. He felt his spine stiffen, straighten, as his arms automatically lowered the rifle. He turned back to the left. The Blake soldiers were gone, leaving only a single, black-cloaked figure, flanked by two familiar faces, dressed in ablative and practical uniforms, their faceplates open.

March, Setiwah, and November.

Setiwah straightened, and the hood of the black robe fell back, revealing a smaller, thinner helmet. She raised her arms and removed it, revealing her beautiful face, not accentuated in shadows and smoke. He could see her lips from where he stood, helplessly rooted to the spot where he stood.

Setiwah.

She came slowly toward him, each movement a precise decision, each undulation a ploy for attention. His attention. And he felt himself reacting—automatically turning to face her as he lowered his weapon.

She stood in front of him, her lips playing into a smile. "Very good, my prince. You have played your part well."

He blinked. "My part?"

"Yes. As your handler, the Master will be very happy with me," she smiled even wider as she reached out with her metallic hand and with an uncanny speed, grabbed him by the neck.

Aris brought the rifle up in reaction—but Setiwah reached over with her other hand and tapped something on her metallic arm.

His chest seized—tightening from the inside. His vision blurred as the pain shot down his left arm. He dropped the rifle and groaned aloud. What—what was happening to him?

"Your implants have a transponder that's linked to me," she smiled at him. "As your handler, I have the codes that will effective-

ly shut you down. You have exposed the last of the resistance cells on Farandir, Aris Sung. The reason you were sent here," she blinked slowly. "By us."

The pain intensified and he clutched at his left side with his right arm. Shut him down? His implants... had a transponder?

"By... you" he tried to pull air into his lungs, but it was hard as she held his neck. He couldn't fall, and he couldn't escape. But he knew she spoke the truth. Had realized it in Mikhail's quarters, but didn't want to believe it was true.

No... he'd been sent by the Chancellor. For the Magestrix.

"We knew there was a single cell left, but hadn't been able to find it—so it was my job to feed rumors into the communications of the Capellan Confederation of a possible cell on Farandir. And of course, we knew the Chancellor would send his people to appease his whore." She smiled. "I hoped they would send you."

Aris felt his heart lurch again—but this time not from anything Setiwah did physically, but because of the realization of how they'd all been played.

It made sense—the swiftness of their being made before entering Farandir space—the odd greeting once on the surface. They'd been split up—and he'd been—

"You were my target, Aris Sung. The one I watched on Hustaing. And I chose you to be mine one day. I saw you as beautiful and skilled. And I have been in control of this mission since the moment you left alive off of Hustaing."

No.

But yet he knew it was true. She had been the shimmer, as he'd seen in the ruins of the capitol. He hadn't wanted to think of it. To understand it.

"The Ebon cell that rescued you is one we set up a year ago. We suspected there was a true cell here... but we couldn't find them. It was with luck your companion survived—and was left in a position so that anyone watching might take him.

"But you... " She almost glowed with pride. "You were to be mine. I knew your people here would try to find you once they were fed hope that you lived. Their indecision gave us time to improve your body. And we waited. And I was right." Setiwah sighed. "And now it's done, Aris Sung. The last of the resistance forces are destroyed."

He reached up with his right hand and grabbed at her metallic one, his gaze repeatedly looking over at November, at March, at the serene expressions on their faces.

No... November, March, Martin... it had all been a lie. Everything. And Quinn? Where was he? Had they killed him? Was it like Mikhail feared, that he'd never made it out of the cell alive?

"Aris—they all were at one time very loyal to the Magistracy. But now they serve the Master. And they were sincere in their jobs, and did their parts. And now they are here, destroying their former friends and family, and bringing victory to me."

He struggled to pull free, but it was no use. It was like being held in a steel vise. He was manacled. Fixed in time.

She squeezed harder. He gasped for breath.

"And I wanted you to know who you served, Aris Sung. Of who you gave your information too. The Master—" she pulled him closer and kissed him, pressing her cold lips to his again. "Will be so pleased."

She pressed the button again.

The trigger in his artificial heart was enough to cause the beating to stop. He gasped once as his blood ceased to pump.

And slumped forward onto her arm, exhaling his last breath.

Setiwah smiled and ran her human fingers through his thick, dark hair. "Goodnight, sweet prince. And flights of angels sing thee to thy rest."

FIRST ACQUISITION

JOHN HELFERS

Lothario
Marian Hegemony
Periphery
0238 Hours, 17 May 3059

Kithain Valas heard the 'Mech before he saw it and ducked behind a pile of half-frozen garbage just in time.

The *Hunchback* materialized out of the cold rain, each step of the fifty-ton armored colossus reverberating off the buildings around it. One second the avenue was empty, the next the 'Mech's distinctive silhouette broke through sheets of slanted raindrops, its signature huge, blocky autocannon jutting from its right shoulder.

The 'Mech paused at the narrow, refuse-choked alley, its menacing presence scattering a pack of feral rats into the night. Kithain pressed against the mound of slop, causing a cascade of filth to rain down on him. After scanning for a few seconds, the MechWarrior turned his machine away and continued down the street.

Half-buried in the pile of rotting refuse, Kithain poked his head out, trying not to breathe through his nose. Hearing the *Hunchback* move on, he sighed with relief. *Too close.*

Straightening, he peered after the receding 'Mech, listening to its footfalls echo off the buildings of the run-down section of town. *Subtle as usual, like piloting an* Atlas *to the corner store for a jug of milk. They know no one can even come close to taking them on. Damn Caesar O'Reilly and his blasted Hegemony!*

But at the same time he cursed the planet's overseers, he also tried to push away that stab of jealousy he felt whenever he saw a 'Mech nowadays, remembering all too well the invincible feeling that could only be had in the cockpit of one of the armored juggernauts.

Once he too had been among those elite warriors, with a 'Mech of his own...

But that was a long time ago. Shaking his head, Kithain tried to brush the muck and slime off his battered *zysle*skin jacket, but gave up after a half-hearted swipe. *Doubt I could make a worse impression right now, being as cold, filthy, and miserable as possible,* he thought.

Something skittered nearby, making him cock his head. His wrist flexed once, and in a single smooth motion, he whirled around and flicked his right hand out, rewarded by a startled squeal a few meters away.

Kithain walked to the six-legged, cat-sized rat, a stainless-steel throwing spike protruding from its right eye. Withdrawing the weapon, he replaced it in the sheath at his wrist, then picked up the carcass by the tail.

What the Khas am I doing here at this hour? This guy ain't gonna show. I'll have a little chat with Joz about running me out here at this time of night on a fool's errand. At least the trip wasn't a total waste; after all, I caught dinner. Six months ago the thought of eating rat would have made him retch, but tonight it was a feast. *Five more minutes, then I'm outta he–*

The heavy hand on his shoulder made Kithain react instinctively. The fist holding the rat came up and around, throwing the slimy body at his assailant as he tried to leap forward, tearing himself from the other man's grasp. While not the best plan, it should have worked well enough to allow him to escape and face his foe.

But the fingers on his jacket clamped down with relentless force, preventing him from accomplishing anything more than an off-balance hop. The flying rat was batted onto the garbage heap, and he found himself shoved against a grimy building wall, his free arm twisted up between his shoulder blades. He tried to wriggle free, but the hands on his shoulder and wrist were as inflexible as titanium.

"You got reflexes, kid, I'll give you that," an electronically-modulated voice said in his ear. "That distraction with the rat was a nice move, too. On someone else."

The crushing pressures on his shoulder and arm relaxed, and Kithain pushed himself off the slick wall, ready to whirl around and let this thug have it—.

"I like your caution too, scoping out the meeting place early, but I didn't think you'd be this jumpy. Turn around and let's have a look at you."

This is my meet? Kithain complied, and beheld a man who topped

his own one-hundred eighty-two centimeters by another ten, give or take, and clad in a full suit of light powered armor. A smooth, featureless mask helmet hid his face, with a dim red light from inside telling Kithain he was probably being scanned for weapons. His suit—*what is that?*—was patterned in urban camouflage, streaks of gray, blue, and black that matched his surroundings perfectly. If the man had stood perfectly still on a night like this, Kithain would have walked right by him. In fact, he just might have.

The barrel of a light assault rifle/grenade launcher combo jutted up behind one shoulder, and the deadliest-looking machine pistol Kithain had ever seen was clipped to a magnetic holster on his left leg. His fingers twitched, but he stilled the impulse to drop a spike, knowing it would be much like attacking that *Hunchback* in the street—completely pointless. The other man inclined his head a bit, as if he had read Kithain's thoughts and approved of the final decision.

Straightening, Kithain adjusted his jacket and said, "I just don't like anyone sneaking up on me. Who're you?"

The man shook his head. "Uh-uh. Who sent you?"

Kithain squinted, trying to see past the reflective faceplate, but got nothing. *Hell, in for a kilo, in for a kiloton.* "Joz flashed me on the wire that I could find employment here at 0300."

The taller man nodded. "You must be Valas."

Kithain nodded.

"Call me Armitage." The man gave him a closer once-over. "Street punk? That toss with the spike was straight-up milspec, not to mention an—exotic weapon, shall we say?"

Kithain shrugged. "It suits me."

"Apparently. Who trained you?"

"My father."

The helmet drew back in surprise. "Come again?"

"My father was Raist Valas, graduated from the Taurian *Ecole Militaire* '24, served with them for ten years before settling here and starting a family. He taught me everything I know, including piloting."

"See any action?"

"I wasn't part of the planetary forces here, but when our government surrendered—" Kithain spit the word out like rotten meat, "—to the Hegemony, some of the militia went guerilla. We held out for nine months, but never had a real chance. That's when I lost my family—and my 'Mech." He clamped down on the bitter tide of memories that rose unbidden in his mind—the hopeless skirmishes, always outnumbered, always outgunned, the comrades that had fallen during the months of slaughter—and punching out of his *Grasshopper* that fateful morning as it had exploded underneath him...

"Okay," Armitage mused. "Still, a trained boy like yourself should have been able to find work around here...."

"Doing what? Joining the military—what there is of it—would be too much like working for the enemy. I can run a jacklift or grappler in a warehouse, or I can oversee assembly lines in any one of light industrial factories around the city. Not my style." Kithain felt his hand shaking as he recounted the jobs he 'qualified for,' and tucked it behind his back, curling his fingers into a tight fist.

If Armitage noticed, he gave no sign. "According to what I heard, you already tried a few of those, and each one ended in your termination."

"Let's just say I don't take orders from bureaucrats very well."

"That explains your current situation. Ever think of striking out off-planet?"

"Hard to get ship clearance when the local overseers label you a troublemaker. When the Hegemony took over, my name was mentioned as being associated with certain...circles that opposed them. Nothing proven, but they'd love to make something stick. That was fourteen months ago. I lost everything, career, standing—my family. I have to eat."

The armored man cocked his head, and Kithain swore he was smiling behind his mask. "I think you and I will get along just fine, Valas. So, you're looking for work."

"Isn't that why we're both standing here?"

"Yup. You just passed the first test. Anyone brave enough to come to this part of town and survive, alone, and relatively unarmed, must want whatever's being offered pretty badly."

Kithain looked away. "Something like that."

Armitage chuckled, a low buzz emanating from his faceplate. "Something like that, indeed. Well, tonight's your lucky night, 'cause I got a job you're perfectly suited for, and it's just up the street. Pays five hundred C-bills, and no questions asked. Interested?"

"Joz said you weren't into anything illegal," Kithain said, his eyes narrowing.

Armitage clucked in disapproval. "Didn't he tell you what this was about? I'm after a criminal, and if you assist me on this job, there could be more work down the line. You interested?"

"Maybe," Although this guy sounded on the level, Kithain knew there just might be some two-legged rat that would try to bait a sucker

play for an unsuspecting local. *Although if he can afford powered armor, he wouldn't be doing small-time back-alley scams in the first place.*

"You aren't—the Hunter, are you?"

Armitage threw back his head and laughed. "If I was, do you think I'd be wasting my time in this dump?"

"Okay, why me? I'm just a pilot with nothing to my name."

"First, you're honest, and I appreciate that. I'm looking to expand my operation, branch out to take on bigger quarry, including 'Mechs. For that I'll need a partner to start, and I prefer breaking one in from the beginning. Fewer bad habits that way. I also want someone who's hungry, and from the fringe, not tied down by Inner Sphere history. After all, who knows who we might be going after in time. When I asked Joz if there were any potential candidates out here, he mentioned you. 'Kid knows how to handle himself, and he's got at least as much scruples as brains, which are considerable.' His exact words, as I recall."

Kithain's mouth crooked in a wry smile. *That figures.* He wasn't a criminal, and had no desire to become one, despite the numerous opportunities that appeared in this part of town. *Hunting them, however... maybe someday I could get enough juice to take on the Hegemony on my own terms someday.*

He nodded. "Let's say I'm interested—for now. Take me to the job, and you can fill me in as we go."

Armitage led the way to the far end of the alley, where the 'Mech had passed a few minutes ago. He scanned the street, then pointed to a large, run-down warehouse across the way. "Your acquisition's inside. An accountant, wanted for embezzling from the Lyrans," Armitage said. "You go in, take him into custody—alive, mind you—and deliver him to me."

"Why aren't you handling this?" Kithain asked.

"It's actually a pick-up job, since I've already busted my main quarry here. When I found out about this target, I decided to subcontract. This is small fry for me. So I thought I'd give the local talent a shot, see what you can do. Besides, can you see me bracing an accountant? He'd probably keel over and die of fright."

Kithain rubbed a hand over his stubbled chin as he scoped the building. The set-up sounded decent, if a bit too easy. "My father had a saying about any job: Never trust your intel."

Armitage chuckled again. "Your father was a smart man. He also teach you that no plan ever survives contact with the enemy?"

"Till I was saying it in my sleep." Kithain grinned, instinctively liking the other man. He also trusted Joz, and if he said this Armitage was on the level... "All right, I'm in."

"Excellent. Take these," Armitage held out a compact laser pistol and a magcard.

Kithain accepted the gun and checked its load, then tucked it into his waistband at the small of his back. The card he kept out as he measured the distance between him and the building, then checked both ways on the deserted street.

"The magcard will get you into the building, and anywhere else you might need to go inside. One more thing—lose the jacket, or you'll alert him before you even get inside." Armitage waved a gloved hand in front of his helmet. "Even *I* can smell you."

"That bad?" Kithain shrugged out of his battered duster and was instantly soaked. "Hold this for me." He slipped out of the alley and zigzagged across the street to the recessed doorway. He fiddled with it for a second, then the door whisked open, and Kithain disappeared into the darkness inside.

▲▼▲

Stepping to one side of the entryway, Kithain waited for his eyes to adjust to the gloom as the door closed behind him with a soft hiss. He scanned the area as soon as he could see, making sure he hadn't attracted any undue attention. The pistol he'd drawn just before entering comfortable in his hand.

He stood on a loading dock, with several huge cargo doors used by the tractor trains that brought supplies and trade goods from outlying provinces into the city in a row next to him. Liftcrates and jackpallets of just about everything one could imagine were stacked around him in long tall rows that stretched up into the darkness. At the far end of the cavernous room, Kithain saw a glimmer of light coming from a window set in the wall about ten meters off the ground. He began threading his way through the maze-like corridors of crates and pallets.

After several minutes and three wrong turns, he stood at the foot of the staircase leading to the upper levels. *So far, so good. Practically done, and no one knows I'm here.* He climbed the steel-grid stairs, careful to step near the outer edge to prevent creaks. Two flights later, he stood to one side of the office suite door. There was a similar magcard lock on it. Holding his breath, Kithain swiped his card through. The door light changed from red to green, and it slid open with a small click. *Nothing to it*, he thought. Taking one last look around, he slipped inside.

FIRST ACQUISITION

This long room was the heart of the operation. Everywhere Kithain saw computer screens and databanks, all powered down, that tracked the vast inventory moving in and out of the warehouse every day. He also saw several control stations for the overhead mechanical grapplers mounted on a rail grid near the ceiling, used to move the enormous pallets of boxes.

The room continued beyond the control area, and the light Kithain had seen came from the other side of a row of computers. *Perfect*, he thought, *I'll use those as cover, sneak over, and get the drop on him.*

No sooner had he come up with this plan then he was in motion, gliding without a sound over to the far end of the control area. He paused there, fingers tense on the laser, listening for any noise on the other side. Only silence greeted him.

Probably napping. Even easier than I thought. Kithain took a deep breath, steadied his gun hand, and stepped around the corner.

"Don't—move?" he said, sweeping the half of the room before him.

The area contained everything expected of a normal office, a large faux-wood desk with a computer monitor and the remains of a large meal on it, a tall, leather chair pushed back against the far wall next to another door, a gently waving *ithril* plant hanging from the ceiling. It had everything, in fact, except one thing—Kithain's quarry.

Hmm, I didn't think accountants had such huge appetites, he thought. *He's probably through that door–*

Before he could move, there came the distinct sound of a toilet cycling, and the far door opened.

The figure that ducked to enter the office was easily a half-meter taller than Kithain. But where he was lean and sinewy, this guy was massive, with thick slabs of muscle slowly turning to fat under his stained vest and button-down, collarless shirt. His face was wide, with porcine, squinting eyes stuffed between fleshy cheeks and a bulbous nose. When he saw Kithain he froze, a frown creasing his sweating forehead.

Crap, security, he thought. *Clanner? No way, not out here. Just really big.* "Stop where you are and raise your hands. I'm looking for the accountant that's supposed to be here."

The man didn't reply, but stepped further into the room, his muddy-brown eyes staying on Kithain, who aimed his pistol at the middle point of the man's heavy brow, right above his nose.

"Don't come any closer, or I will shoot."

The man's answer was to take another ponderous step, moving to the middle of the room. Shaking his head, Kithain shifted his aim to the guy's right kneecap and squeezed the trigger.

The laser clicked in his hand, but no brilliant ray of focused light flashed out to cripple his target.

The two men stared at each other for a moment. Kithain pressed the firing stud of his weapon again, and was rewarded with the same result. The huge man smiled, exposing large, sharp, yellow teeth. Before Kithain could regroup or move, the huge man moved.

With a grace that belied his size, the man charged, his massive arm swinging towards Kithain's head. Trying to deflect the blow, Kithain partially succeeded.

The guard's club-like fist slammed into his upraised arms, sending him flying across the room. He skidded to a stop under the large row of windows. The pistol popped out of his grasp and slid under a row of computers. Shaking his head, Kithain pushed himself up against the wall in time to see the thug striding over, his other fist cocked and ready.

There was no time to think, only move. Despite his screaming instincts, Kithain waited until his opponent committed to his attack.

The man reached him and swung again, intending to punch Kithain through the wall. At the last second, he rolled to one side, ducking the blow that whistled over his head and slammed into the wall with enough force to shake the entire side of the room. His enemy grunted, although Kithain couldn't tell if the sound was from pain or anger.

Standing up, Kithain swung with all his might, burying his fist in the man's abdomen. The huge guy grunted again, but didn't seem fazed at all. Cocking his other arm, Kithain let go with a left hook that snapped the behemoth's head back, but it only seemed to make him madder. The man grabbed him by the scruff of his shirt and hurled him over the nearest bank of computers. Kithain crashed onto a wheeled chair, its back stabbing into his ribcage, and slammed to the ground, holding his side. He heard the guy's footsteps as he approached, the heavy thuds reminding him of the *Hunchback* outside.

Kithain crawled around the corner of the computer wall and scrambled to his feet, scurrying for the entry door. Another rush of air swept over him, and he felt something brush the back of his shirt as he ran across the room. Slamming the card on the door lock, he risked a glance over his shoulder while praying for the door to open *right now*.

The man lumbered toward him, only a few meters away. Kithain looked around, but there was nowhere to go in here that the guy couldn't get to him eventually. If the door didn't open—

With a slight hiss, the doors slid apart, and Kithain scraped through as soon as the hole was large enough. He slapped at the closing mechanism on the other side, but didn't wait for it to work. Instead,

he took the stairs four at a time and ran for the exit the moment he hit the ground. Behind him, he heard the staircase clang and groan as a massive weight descended on them.

Screw the money, no one said anything about this man-mountain being here, he thought. *Besides, I don't have a working weapon, and I sure as hell am not going to face him hand-to-hand again, or whatever the hell he was trying to pulp me with.*

Quickened by equal parts fear and adrenaline, Kithain retraced his path through the maze of stacked crates, finding the door just where he remembered. Breathing a sigh of relief, he fumbled the magcard out of his pocket and ran it through the sec slot.

The door didn't move. Kithain stared at it, then ran it through again. The door's sec light remained an obstinate red. *Hell and damnation*, he swore, *now what?*

A low, rumbling growl from behind him alerted Kithain that he had company. Whirling, he saw the huge man running at him, working up a good head of steam, obviously intending to smear him into the door.

Oh shit, Kithain thought. There was only one way to go.

He leaped for the nearest tier of jackpallets, grabbing the edge of one and pulling himself up to where he could get a foothold, then began climbing as fast as he dared. A crash shook the tower he was climbing, almost shaking Kithain loose as he was reaching for another handhold. The impact spurred him toward the top of the stack, now only a meter away. With a final burst of energy, he crested the top and rolled over on his back, panting with the effort.

He couldn't savor his victory, however, as a loud thud echoed through the warehouse, then another. Kithain crawled to the edge and looked over, his eyes widening in disbelief.

Using two portable electro-magnetic crate handles, the man levered himself up after Kithain, teeth bared in a savage smile. *Screw not taking anyone out.* Kithain scooted to the next vertical stack of crates, wedged his feet between the first and second rows, and waited.

The thuds grew louder, and before long a meaty hand slammed an electro-handle down on the top of the box. As soon as he saw it, Kithain pushed at the crate the guard was climbing onto with all his might. Already unbalanced by 200 kilos of furious human and Kithain's shove, the large box toppled over. Realizing what was happening, his opponent tried to leap free, but with a shriek of metal, the overbalanced crate tumbled off the pile, taking the silent psycho with it. Kithain cocked his head, enjoying the earth-shaking crash that came a second later.

Wiping his sweating forehead, he leaned back against the liftcrate and caught his breath for a moment. *Time to get out of here,* he thought, *and then I'm going to have a few words with that Armitage falafe. No one uses me.*

Scooting to the edge of the pile and peering over, Kithain expected to see a bloody lump of meat underneath the spilled remains of whatever had been in the box. But he only saw the smashed liftcrate on the floor. There was no trace of the guy anywhere.

Did I miss? Kithain thought in disbelief, then spun around, looking for that massive shape to come hurtling at him from somewhere else. But nothing happened. The warehouse was eerily quiet. *How hard is it to take this guy down?* He thought. *And where the hell is he?*

The answer to his second question came seconds later. Rows of huge floodlights burst into life on both sides of the warehouse section, illuminating the entire area. Kithain heard the hum of power generators whirring to life, and kept looking around, trying to figure out where the next attack would come from. *A diversion,* he thought. *But where'd he'd go?*

Kithain heard the whine of servomotors above his head, and looked up just in time to see one of the grapplers plummet towards him, its pincers ready to bite into whatever they touched. He dove out of the way, but felt one of the grapplers graze his leg, pinning him to the crate he was lying on.

Gritting his teeth, Kithain tore his pants and wrenched his leg free, stifling the cry of pain that rose in his throat. The grappler rose again, and moved over him. With his injured leg, Kithain couldn't move out of the way fast enough. He saw the machine descend again, and, unable to dodge without getting impaled, curled up in the center of the crate he lay on and closed his eyes, waiting for the central mechanism to crush him—

—There was a loud bang as the arms slammed into the crate, and Kithain opened his eyes to see the bottom of the grappler mechanism just a few centimeters away from his chest. Its curved arms had hit the sides of the crate first, forming a four-armed cage around Kithain, but stopping short of touching him. The breath he had been holding whooshed out, but his relief was short-lived.

The grappler whined again, and the crate he was on rose into the air. *Great, now he's gonna drop me,* he thought. Inspiration hit. *Maybe I can use this against him....*

Scooting over to the grappler's main joint, Kithain popped the maintenance access panel open. Inside were basic button controls to

test and control the device when a servicer was working on it. One of them would lock the arms in place, and it couldn't be overridden, even from the ground. Kithain stabbed it just as the grappler ground to a halt, far above the warehouse floor.

Ok, let's see how you like this, he thought. Peeking out around the control stem of the machine, he saw the guy shoving levers with all his considerable strength. A savage grin curling his lips, Kithain overrode all the grappler's safety programs, including the one that would automatically stop the machine if it was headed directly for a wall or other obstacle. Using the touchpad arrows, he lined up the grappler with its cargo so it was parallel with the workstation the man was still abusing. Noting the nearest pile of crates, Kithain stabbed the forward button and hit full power.

The grappler picked up speed as it approached the row of windows. The man pounded at the workstation, oblivious to what was coming at him. Just before Kithain leaped to the last stack of crates the grappler passed, he decided to be polite.

"Hey!" he shouted as he jumped off, rewarded by seeing his enemy look up and realize what was about to happen. Kithain hit the crates hard, agony flaring in his injured leg and side even as he tucked into a sloppy shoulder roll. Skidding to a stop on the far edge, he rolled over on his back and looked up just in time.

Although the windows were impact resistant, they weren't tough enough to withstand five tons of cargo moving at top speed. With a splinter of plastic shards and scream of overstressed metal, the grappler and crate burst through the offices, smashing a huge hole in the warehouse wall. The collision buried the huge man in an avalanche of debris, smaller boxes, and the remains of the grappler itself. Fragments of the broken crate and windows sprayed across the warehouse floor. The grappler's overstressed servomotors strained against what was left of the wall, then shrieked in one last burst of energy, burning out with a wisp of smoke and shower of sparks. Silence descended over the warehouse, broken only by Kithain's rapid panting.

He didn't relax, but watched the pile of debris for several long minutes while his pulse returned to normal, half-expecting the man to push aside the barrels and grapple arms he was buried under and come after him again. Only after he was sure the guy wasn't getting up again did he rise to his feet, gingerly testing his hurt leg and finding it able to support his weight. Wincing, he limped towards the stairway that led up to the offices.

▲▼▲

A half-hour later, Armitage crossed the street. Punching a code into the red-lighted sec lock that slid the door open, he stepped through, activated the sensor suite in his helmet and looked around, spotting his quarry at the foot of the stairs.

As he walked, Armitage thought about what he was going to say. *Assuming he's still alive, the kid's going to be steamed, I can't blame him, but that's the way this game is played; only the strongest survive, and I can't take on someone who's not up to it.*

Kithain sat on the bottom rung of the staircase, a huge body, its chest rising and falling in slow, even breaths, lying in front of him. Armitage walked over to him and checked the man's vitals.

"Still alive, good," he said. "Looks like you ran into a bit of trouble."

"You set me up," was Kithain's toneless response.

"I gave you a test," Armitage said. "And you came through like a pro." He nudged the unconscious man-mountain with his foot. "This is your target, by the way He's just a bit bigger that you expected, I'll wager. Sending you in with a bum laser and no way out was my way of making sure you have the balls big enough to handle whatever we might run across."

Kithain snorted and shook his head.

Armitage walked over until he was standing in front of the smaller man. "Your father had the right idea when he taught you that lesson. There are four cardinal rules to this job. You can never trust your information. You can never trust your equipment. You can never fully trust your allies. The only one you can trust is yourself, your skills, your abilities. Those are the only sure things you have."

"If that's true, then I shouldn't even trust you, especially after what you just pulled," Kithain said, his eyes narrowing.

"Now you're thinking like a hunter, but this was the first—and last—time I'll ever do that to you." Armitage slipped a C-card out of his sleeve pocket and flipped it to the other man. "Your share of the bounty on Jonas here." He knelt down and opened the unconscious man's mouth. "One of his former employers actually cut out his tongue a few years back—it's why he's so quiet. It was actually four thousand for the capture, however, since there's going to be a bill from the warehouse for the damages, I've had to subtract a few deductions."

"Really." Kithain said as he hit the total button on the card. "Two hundred C-bills? That's all?"

"Hey, I didn't wreck a wall and a grappler taking out whatever it

was you ran into, did I? Well, get him on a pallet or something, and let's go." Armitage spun on his heel and headed towards the exit.

"Hey, Armitage. When you took this job, it was under your name, right?"

The question brought the bounty hunter up short. He paused and started to turn around. "Yeah?"

"Good, then I won't feel so bad about this." The bounty hunter's instincts shrieked a warning, but before he could react, he felt a sharp pain in his elbow, followed by what felt like a plasma grenade going off right next to him. He collapsed, his numb limbs suddenly unable to support his weight. The armor's power subroutines, temporarily disrupted by the massive burst of energy, came back online. Armitage felt himself being rolled over and saw Kithain bending over him, the other man's nimble fingers rifling his pockets.

"I fixed my pistol's energy pack while waiting for you," Kithain said, slipping the assault rifle from his shoulder. "Just so you don't get any ideas." He fiddled with the slim pistol at Armitage's side, but couldn't unlock the mag-holster. He did, however, remove the pistol's magazine. "I figured your suit was insulated, so I reconfigured the power setting to release the entire charge in one huge shock. Sorry about the stab, but I had to make sure I touched skin."

He stared into Armitage's faceplace. "Let's get two things straight. *If* I decide to work with you, it'll be as your partner—not an apprentice, not a lackey, and definitely not as a porter. And don't *ever* cross me like that again."

Kithain snatched the rifle up. "I'll keep this for now. Don't worry, I'm not stealing it, just-borrowing it. And if there are any bills resulting from this job, I expect you to handle them."

"You'll be up and around in a few minutes, just long enough for me to leave. Don't come looking for me. I'll get in touch with you after you've settled things with the company and collected *our* bounty. Thanks for the interview, by the way." With that, Kithain stepped around the fallen man and limped towards the outer door. His steps faded away, leaving the bounty hunter surrounded by silence.

After a few minutes, Armitage rolled over and got on his hands and knees, resisting the strong urge to vomit. He flexed a finger inside his glove, activating a small neuroinjection to clear away the lingering effects of the shock, and reared back until he was kneeling on the floor.

I can't believe it. Maybe I am getting to old for this. Taken down like a rookie on his first acquisition. He looked towards the door with a nod and a smile. *I know one thing, though. He'll make a hell of a partner.* He looked around, eyeing the unconscious accountant.

Better arrange to get Jonas picked up and get out of here. Armitage got to his feet and walked to the door. He hit the open button, but nothing happened. He hit it again, with the same effect.

Great, now what? he thought. *This night can't get any worse.*

A low growl rumbled behind him. Armitage slowly turned around, already knowing what he was going to see.

Jonas rose to his feet, staring holes through Armitage. The hunter looked at the useless pistol at his side. He looked back up in time to see the huge accountant walking towards him, a feral grin on his broad face.

I stand corrected, he thought.

HIGH-VALUE TARGET

PHILIP A. LEE

Orloff Grenadiers Command Post
Sophia, Vanra
Duchy of Orloff, Free Worlds League
9 April 2996

"All senior First Battalion staff," the CO's voice echoed from the barracks' PA system, "my office, fifteen minutes."

Captain Cyril De Milo snapped his book closed and sat up straight in his bunk. He knew it wouldn't take fifteen minutes to get to Major Duarte's office, but he was a Grenadier. Officers and grunts from other regiments would probably read a few more pages before thinking about *maybe* making themselves presentable for a staff meeting with their commanding officer. Not him: he'd throw himself before a firing squad before letting himself being late for any official meeting.

Plus, Cyril knew that tone. Duarte had at least three ways of calling line-officer meetings. This one meant deployment. Anyone late for a deployment meeting would find themselves reassigned to some backwater post in the worst Marik Militia unit Colonel Polzin could find for them.

Cyril shrugged on his white, purple-piped service jacket. He scabbarded his saber, donned his burgundy Grenadiers beret, and checked himself in the mirror. With a brush he smoothed away all of the wrinkles and dust he could see, then stood up straight. Took a deep breath. Puffed out his chest.

His silhouette cut the profile of a damn good serviceman, he thought. And not just *any* serviceman: an *Orloff Grenadier*. One of the best-trained, best-disciplined soldiers in the entire Free Worlds League.

Best of the best—except, he'd never fought in a war before. Sure, he'd repelled a few pirate raids here and there, but all the good parts of the Third Succession War seemed to have happened long before he was even old enough to see over a 'Mech's instrument panel. Shooting pirates and running drills did not a real war make. At military academy, all he and his classmates had dreamed about was repelling an invasion from the duchy's Capellan neighbors. During every 'Mech simulation, he imagined a tide of Confederation 'Mechs, armor, and infantry closing on his position, he alone standing between the collapse of the Duchy of Orloff or the Free Worlds League itself.

Cyril and his classmates graduated, got assigned to Grenadiers regiments or other prestigious Free Worlds League Military units, and slowly climbed up the ranks. In all those years, that dreamed-of invasion never became reality. The Capellan military was simply too exhausted defending itself against Federated Suns incursion to worry about waging war against the League, and the League focused its rancor against the Lyran Commonwealth.

For the hundredth time, Cyril silently asked his reflection if he should request reassignment to some FWLM outfit fighting along the Lyran front. At least then he'd get his war. But he never followed through on the idea. Deep down he knew that few Free Worlds Guards or Marik Militia regiments cared for the dog-and-pony show of Orloff military tradition. Those units failed to realize that lax traditions meant low morale, and low morale lost battles, lives, worlds. Nations.

Cyril straightened his beret, exhaled with satisfaction, and stepped into the hallway.

▲▼▲

"Atten-*hut*!"

Every First Battalion captain stood at rail-straight attention in front of their CO's desk, waiting for the major to acknowledge them. Cyril knew he could hold this position for hours if he needed to. In some ways, parade rest felt downright lazy, and he found himself standing at attention even in casual situations, even when out of uniform. No one would ever accuse him of tarnishing the Grenadiers' reputation by accident.

Over the top of a file folder, the middle-aged Major Vítor Duarte glared up at Cyril and his fellow captains standing in a perfect line.

"At ease," Duarte said, leaning back in his chair. A simmering frown melted the sides of his face as he snapped the folder closed and nonchalantly frisbeed it onto the desktop. Some of the folder's contents peeked out from the manila cardboard, but Cyril couldn't

HIGH-VALUE TARGET

read anything from where he stood. "Our new orders just came in. We're, ah, being deployed."

Cyril bit his lower lip to hide a budding smile.

"Within fifteen hours, we'll be shipping out to Tsinghai A-S-A-P."

"Trouble along the Capellan border, sir?" Cyril wondered.

Duarte's frown deepened. His salt-and-pepper crewcut shook. "Not yet there isn't." He sighed. "This is diplomatic support, first and foremost. Duke Orloff is trying to woo Tsinghai into joining the duchy, and he's sending a delegation to meet with Prime Minister Jain. Our role is to accompany this delegation and perform readiness drills for the benefit of the prime minister, her cabinet, and the planetary media. Duke Orloff hopes our presence will show Prime Minister Jain firsthand the military benefits of throwing her lot in with the duchy. It's one thing to see pictures of the best damn brigade in the Free Worlds League, but seeing us in action will be something else. The captain-general himself also believes our presence in the system will deter any Capellan attempts to misbehave."

Cyril let his stiff parade rest slacken in surprise. What madness was this? Diplomatic support was a job for the *Fifth* Orloff Grenadiers, not the First. "So this isn't a combat deployment, sir," he said.

"No. This is a 'wearing the purple' mission, plain and simple. The captain-general and Duke Orloff want us solely for our reputation. We're to go make some noise, not start any fights."

Duarte thumbed the file folder open just enough to withdraw a single sheet and display it to his captains. Cyril recognized the black-and-white portrait immediately.

Son of a bitch, Cyril thought.

A soft, rounded face stared back at him from the photo: lanky black hair, deep-set eyes, a knowing smirk. Cyril *almost* swore out loud. He almost let his anger shine through his façade, but in the name of decorum, he bit his lower lip even harder to keep his focus.

"Our guest of honor for this trip is Ambassador Skylar Orloff," Duarte said. "At his father's behest, he'll be heading up the Tsinghai delegation in his father's name. In addition to redeployment, our orders are also to provide him with an honor guard while he meets with Prime Minister Jain." His lower lip protruded with disappointment as he afforded each of his captains a look of commiseration. "I know you boys want some action, and I hate to disappoint. But these orders come straight from the top. I know we're better than glorified babysitters for nobility. Duke Orloff knows it. Even the captain-general knows it. But we've got a job to do, and by God, we're going to get it done, and in Grenadier fashion."

"Better to have a well-trained army and not need it than to need one and not have it," Cyril said, swallowing down his regret.

"That's the spirit, De Milo. Any questions?"

Cyril wasn't quite so sure about anything. He held his tongue and shook his head along with his fellow company commanders. Worse things could happen, he supposed. If the Capellans ever decided to mount a full-scale invasion of Orloff territory—or the neighboring Duchy of Oriente—the Grenadiers would be horrendously outnumbered, and the Free Worlds' Parliament would probably deadlock over whether to give aid to the duchy or just let the Capellans claim it. Better to avoid war altogether than to never have a chance of winning in the first place.

"All right," the major said. "Wheels-up at 0600 sharp. Dis-*missed!*"

Command Post, Fifth Confederation Reserve Cavalry
Ingersoll
Capella Commonality, Capellan Confederation
9 April 2996

Lin Wei Jiang inhaled behind closed eyes and silenced the entire universe beyond herself as she sat upon a mat in her office. All within was void and empty, a formless mass of clay ready to take shape. The clay, her future; she, the potter. Even her name was gone. In this state, she needed no name. She would remain nameless until her name was required once more.

Exhale.

Inhale.

Sandalwood incense filled her lungs, and she grasped onto the sensation of noiseless calm the scent brought her, clutching it to her like it were a phantom that could slip away at any time. These precious few moments of serenity were perhaps the last she would know for quite some time.

The superior man seeks what lies in himself, she recited. *The small man seeks what lies in others.* No matter what happened over the next few years, months, days—she would find her answer only through quiet reflection. She alone was the master of her own fate. The universe could throw anything at her, and she would refuse to budge.

Inhale.

Exhale.

Out with the bad. In with the good. Every little bit helped. Or so she told herself.

Her inner void slipped for only an instant, but an instant was all it needed. The errant thought took shape as a seed of doubt that barged into her tranquility like an *Atlas* smashing its way through a corrugated-metal warehouse.

That doubt made her consider—not for the first time—retiring. Hanging up her uniform. Finding another, simpler vocation. She was certainly old enough to be eligible for retirement if she wanted it. She'd put in enough years of service and saved up a decent nest egg that would let her live comfortably for the rest of her days—however long that would be. But a good invasion from one or more of the Capellan Confederation's neighbors could send that security toppling down on her head at any moment.

That calm surety she had first felt vanished like so much mist in Ingersoll's morning sun. Her entire life was in tailspin, spiraling toward the ground, and she did not know if she would be able to pull up in time ...

Through heady tendrils of sandalwood smoke, she descended back into herself in search of answers, delving into the darkness behind her eyes. No name. No form.

Inhale.

Exhale.

"Captain?"

The sound intruded on her silent world, shattering it into a thousand pieces, and Lin Wei gasped in surprise. Her eyes popped open to see her executive officer standing in the doorway to her office. Commander Myeong Park deflected her gaze with downcast eyes, and Lin saw him subtly cringing beneath his CCAF duty uniform, as if he knew exactly the kind of reception to expect from her.

"I *said* I was not to be disturbed, Commander," she snapped, far more harshly than she intended. That *Atlas*-shaped seed of doubt still ran amok in the back of her thoughts, more so now that her name had returned to her so prematurely.

"Forgive me, Captain," Park said, bowing his shoulders in deference, "but we have received orders."

Lin sighed and shook her head. "Whatever Colonel Romanov wants, I'm sure it can wait."

Park swallowed and held out a file folder marked EYES ONLY. "Uh, according to Romanov, his orders came from Maximilian Liao himself."

The *chancellor?* Lin leapt to her feet and snatched the folder from her XO. She scanned the outside; the seal said the file contents came from the CCAF High Command, but most Capellan officers knew the Strategios was merely a rubber stamp for the Chancellor's military whims. She flipped through the folder contents. Some of the orders did not make sense to her, but that was of little consequence. As a soldier of the Capellan state, she had a duty to follow those orders regardless of whether she understood them or not.

One thing made perfect sense, however: Lin Wei Jiang was going home. Perhaps there she would finally be able to lose her own name until she needed it again.

Wasn't time to hang up the uniform just yet.

Orloff Grenadiers Command Post
Sophia, Vanra
Duchy of Orloff, Free Worlds League
9 April 2996

While waiting in the 'Mech hangar for First Battalion's techs to finish prepping for departure, Cyril sat on the foot of his *Trebuchet,* Peacemaker, and reviewed his orders with a grimace. He'd met Duke Reinhard Orloff a grand total of once, back when the duke pinned the Distinguished Service Award on his uniform and formally inducted him into the Orloff Grenadiers. In newscasts, Reinhard always struck Cyril as a genial and magnanimous individual truly committed to governing his duchy with fairness, and the moment Reinhard shook his hand at the ceremony, Cyril knew all of this was true. Reinhard's only claim to infamy was his adamant usage of the title "duke," even though he could only legally lay claim to the title of earl or banneret within the League's nobility. Cyril thought Reinhard did that just to poke at Parliament, which made him like the duke even more.

Reinhard Orloff's son, however—that was a different story altogether. Skylar Orloff was always showing up in some tabloid or other, parading around with more mistresses than SAFE probably even knew about and engaging in other vices Cyril didn't even want to consider. The ducal heir was a piece of work, no doubts about it. Just looking at the presumptuous smirk in Skylar's photo made Cyril want to slug the condescension right off his bastard face.

No, no, he reminded himself. *Calling him a bastard only insults his father—who is without a doubt the far better man.*

He should've looked forward to hobnobbing with royalty, even if Skylar was only the firstborn of a lesser noble in the League, but Cyril found no joy in the prospect. If it came down to the choice between drinking expensive wine with Skylar Orloff and Tsinghai's prime minister or throwing back a cheap beer with his lancemates, he'd choose his lancemates any day of the week.

Cyril looked up from the folder to see a gaggle of snappily dressed men and women wandering through the 'Mech hangar as though it were a shopping boutique. *Speak of the devil.* The fat slob himself and his retinue were laughing to themselves over some private joke when they reached Cyril's 'Mech.

"Excuse me—Captain, is it?" Skylar said in a patronizing lilt that set Cyril skin crawling. "I was told someone here might help me with my 'Mech?"

Cyril's eyebrows rose. Most scions of the Orloff family served at least a tour or two of duty in the duchy's military. Reinhard had served in the Fifth Grenadiers back when his mother ruled the duchy, but somehow Skylar had found some way to worm himself out of proper military service. In fact, Cyril was surprised Skylar even *had* a BattleMech.

Cyril bit the inside of his cheek to bury all the potential insults running through his head before he could voice them and be accused of treason. *Maintain decorum, Cyril. It's just for a few months.* "Lead Tech Huerta's over yonder," he said, pointing in the general direction of the technician's office. "She can take care of anything you need."

Skylar frowned. "Captain, do you know who I am? I am Ambassador Orloff, heir to this duchy. I was told you would be taking care of me personally."

Cyril's stomach lurched. This was a trap; he just knew it. If he brushed off the heir, he'd land in hot water with Major Duarte or Colonel Polzin—or *worse*—but if he waited on Skylar like an obedient lapdog, the Grenadiers' wheels would likely not be going up at 0600 sharp as planned.

The faux smile Cyril flashed nearly caused him physical pain. "Certainly," he said, immediately regretting the words. "I just never knew you were a MechWarrior."

Skylar hooked his thumb towards the hangar entrance, where a freight train had just arrived with last-minute supplies. "Wicked Witch is just outside. Treat her gently for me, Captain." And just like that, he and his entourage wandered down the walkway, laughing at another private joke Cyril couldn't hear.

"Of all the ..." Cyril muttered on his way to the freight train, shaking his head.

If he passed this off to one of his subordinates after Skylar was out of earshot, he knew the ambassador would find out somehow, and the decision would ultimately come back to haunt him.

In all honesty, Cyril expected a training platform or a some light 'Mech secured in the train's freight car—some piece of hardware a fool like Skylar Orloff could easily pilot without getting himself in too much trouble. Instead, the freight handlers directed him to a BattleMech that dwarfed everything else in the entire hold.

All eighty tons of AWS-8Q *Awesome* loomed above him—a brick house bristling with a trio of particle projection cannon. Even more surprising than the assault 'Mech's presence was that Cyril found not a single spot of rust, wear, or carbon scoring across the entire 'Mech. Each armor panel looked like a factory job rather than field patches or refits. The metal beast's paint scheme—lime-green torso with olive-drab legs—literally *glistened* in the overhead lighting, and the only indication of personalization was the hand-painted image to the left of the 'Mech's cockpit: a beautiful, long-legged, green-skinned witch riding a broom in the moonlight. Cyril had never before seen such a pristine BattleMech outside of a Technicron Manufacturing catalog.

It was, in a word, *gorgeous*.

The green Orloff Grenadiers parade scheme immediately reflected the green monster in his chest. The Orloff family was rich, yes, but some lazy pretender like Skylar Orloff didn't deserve a BattleMech of this caliber, especially not a 'Mech in such good repair. With the bulk of the FWLM focused on the Lyran Commonwealth border, Capellan border units—even prestigious brigades like the Grenadiers—received whatever leftovers remained, so the Orloff Grenadiers had to subsist on whatever the Quartermaster General provided them. Not even Colonel Polzin's command staff could claim a working *Awesome* among its ranks.

Cyril sighed. *Such a waste.*

Scaling the cockpit ladder, he inhaled fresh-paint fumes and some other sharp scent he couldn't quite place. It reminded him of the last new car he'd bought. "New 'Mech smell"? That was it. While the rest of the Inner Sphere sometimes had to field repair 'Mechs with chewing gum, baling wire, and duct tape, this rich bastard had a *brand-spanking-new* assault-class BattleMech that had never once seen combat and probably never would.

Unbe-*liev*-able. It was like putting lipstick on a pig. Watering a tree with a bottle of Timbiqui Dark.

Cyril slid into the open cockpit hatch to discover Wicked Witch's interior was just as impressive as he had expected. It smelled factory-floor new, and only a few parts of the cockpit console—mostly expensive computer readouts that were difficult to come by—looked refurbished. He wanted to admire every little detail about this new war machine, but there was no time to waste. When he started the fusion reactor in maintenance mode, the huge machine thrumming beneath him sent chills down his spine. Never in a thousand years would he get the chance to pilot a 'Mech like this in the field.

Heaving a heavy sigh, he began walking the *Awesome* out of the freight car like he was nothing but a common technician.

DropShip **Divine Thunder**
Zenith jump point, Ingersoll system
Capella Commonality, Capellan Confederation
22 April 2996

Lin Wei and Commander Park crowded around the holotank with the rest of the Fifth Cavalry's senior staff. Bad enough that they all had to cram into such an uncomfortably small space, but Lin's nerves were shot through like wires melted in an electrical surge. For the past nine days of transit to the jump point and four additional days of waiting in a holding pattern, she had been unable to burn incense in her DropShip berth—safety regulations, the skipper claimed—so she was forced to meditate without it. The nameless serenity still came, but each time she spent longer and longer trying to find it.

The cautious seldom err, she quoted to herself and took a deep breath.

Colonel Romanov was running this show. Had this meeting taken place on the ground, Romanov would've paced in front of the holotank, arms folded at the small of his back. Here in microgravity, he couldn't pace, and Lin saw the frustration on his face that every other officer in the Fifth Cavalry mirrored.

"You're all probably wondering why we're still in a holding pattern," the colonel said at length. "I am not at liberty to divulge that information. Suffice it to say that phase one of the operation has run into some snags, so we're basically stuck here until I either receive positive word to continue or someone sends the abort code.

"That said, I have full authorization to go over the mission plans. Since we've got nothing but time waiting out here, we're going to review it, poke holes in it until it leaks like a sieve, then patch up the holes as best we can. Because goddammit, we're the Fifth Confederation Reserve Cavalry, and patching holes is what we do best. Am I right?"

Lin joined in the resounding chorus of "Sir yes sir!" that echoed throughout the cabin.

"That's what I like to hear. Now, here's a flyover of our target." The holotank lit up, displaying the topographical terrain near the planned LZs. "We're the cleanup crew, so we're landing last. Our LZs are here, here, and here, site Gamma being our fallback in the event of ..."

Lin watched the holotank with interest, but she found herself tuning Romanov out. Wasn't that she didn't *want* to focus on the briefing. Something distracted her. Something internal. She could feel it creeping up inside, threatening to drag her away. She needed to find her center again, needed to find some source of inner peace. A sudden lightheadedness washed over her, and nausea twisted her insides into knots.

Before she could throw up, she silently excused herself and floated into the corridor outside the meeting room to fight down her last meal. The sensation subsided, but she still felt too weak to present a strong face to the rest of the senior staff.

Half an hour later, a loud, fearsome fist pounded on Lin's stateroom door before her CO, Major Petrowski, let himself in. The frown in his piercing, ice-blue eyes wasn't quite angry, but it certainly didn't look pleased, and his head of close-cropped gray hair shook with disappointment.

"What the hell happened back there, Jiang?" he demanded. "Looked like you'd seen a ghost. Some of the crew are a little spooked."

Lin closed her eyes for a moment. The nauseous, peaky sensation hadn't returned, yet all her attempts to relocate her fragile center since had met with futility. "Just a bit of space sickness, sir," she said. "Not used to being stuck in zero-gee for this long. Starting to drive me batty."

"And why haven't you been using the *Silk Road*'s perfectly functional grav deck?"

"No time," she said, shaking her head, "especially considering we might get the call to jump at any moment."

HIGH-VALUE TARGET

"I don't give a damn about that. Go spend a couple hours on the grav deck. That's an order. If you're not 100 percent, maybe you should sit this one out."

"No, I'll be fine." Lin swallowed and looked away. "To be honest, sir, I'd probably feel better if I could just burn some incense. It helps me meditate."

Petrowski crossed his arms. "You know that's against safety regulations."

Lin twisted her expression to show what she thought of that.

Petrowski's frown lightened on one side of his mouth. "Tell you what," he said. "Go down to the cargo bay and look for freight container 31C. It's a sealed freight container that's not completely full, due to cutbacks and all. Me and the boys've been using to have a smoke now and then. You burn *anything* outside of that container, it'll be your ass, all right?"

"*Xie xie*," Lin said. She wasn't sure whether meditating would help anymore, but it couldn't hurt.

"Don't mention it. Seriously, *don't mention it.* I don't want the skipper yelling at us. Just make sure you're in good form for this mission, all right?"

"Sir, yes, sir."

Downtown
Kokonor, Tsinghai
Free Worlds League
25 April 2996

On the main drag through Tsinghai's capital, three infantry companies from the Fourteenth Orloff Irregulars marched down the empty boulevard in perfect lockstep formation, rifles on shoulders, their white-and-purple dress uniforms immaculate. Every few dozen yards, the infantry battalion would halt on a ten-cent piece, turn to the side, do amazing rifle tricks without missing a beat, and then continue down the street without a single infantryman knocking into his or her mates. Three platoons of Vedette tanks crawled in a precisely arranged box behind the infantry, and a lance of freshly painted 'Mechs from Able Company—a *Stinger, Spider, Hermes II,* and *Phoenix Hawk*—followed behind them with a practiced gait.

As the cherry on top of the already impressive parade, a quartet each of olive-drab F-10 *Cheetahs* and F-90 *Stingrays* from the First

Orloff Aerospace Wing rocketed through the sky, leaving perfectly parallel contrails in their wake before veering apart and swooping back around again to follow Kokonor's main traffic vein in the opposite direction.

Cyril, seated on a raised platform at the end of the parade route, would've been amazed had he not seen this exact spectacle repeated countless dozens of times throughout his military career with the Grenadiers. Still, this dog-and-pony show put a smile on his face, for it reminded him of the illustrious military tradition that his brigade upheld for centuries.

"As you can see, Madam Prime Minister," Skylar Orloff said with a confident smile from the parade box, "the Duchy of Orloff maintains the most professional soldiery brigade in the Free Worlds League Military. Any soldier who fails to meet the Orloff Grenadiers' impeccable standards of martial excellence gets drummed out to a lesser League military formation."

"I can see that," middle-aged Prime Minister Jain said with a cautious smile. Cyril noted how mesmerized her eyes grew as she continued watching the soldiery with rapt attention. "Remarkable. Nothing at all like our planetary militia."

"Now, Prime Minister," Skylar continued, "if you do decide to join the Duchy of Orloff, no longer will you be at the mercy of relying on your understaffed, undertrained, and lackluster militia. If you cast your lot with me, your membership in the duchy will furnish you with a degree of military security in addition to affording you economic and political protections. Should the need arise, my well-trained, well-disciplined soldiers you see arrayed here today will be your most immediate line of defense against pirate and Capellan predation."

Cyril fought down the urge to visibly cringe upon hearing Skylar make yet another one of his blowhard speeches. The words the ambassador said made a lot of sense, but over the past month Cyril had grown increasingly tired of the perpetually self-important way Skylar spoke, even when addressing everyday concerns—and *especially* on occasions when he addressed Cyril directly. Every sentence out of Skylar's mouth sounded to Cyril like *Be careful: these shoes are worth 2,500 eagles,* or *Did you know Carbonis Jewelers only made twelve exclusive pairs of these platinum-sapphire cufflinks?* or *Only the son of esteemed Free Worlds royalty deserves to pilot an assault 'Mech like Wicked Witch in battle.* In all honesty, Cyril *did* want to witness this merger take place. He just preferred to see history in the making without its facilitator dripping condescension over everything.

"I see, Ambassador," Jain said, nodding cautiously. Her aging smile struck Cyril as guarded and perfunctory. A politician through and through, this prime minister was.

Cyril glanced from the rocketing *Cheetah*s overhead to Skylar's far-too-rich profile. The man had an almost predatory look about him, a shark sniffing just-dumped chum in the water. Had Jain detected some veiled ultimatum? Cyril glanced at the impressive military parade again, with a different lens this time, and suddenly he saw his fellow Grenadiers as a fearsome occupying force capable of taking the planet without much bloodshed should the prime minister refuse Skylar's overtures.

Blood drained from Cyril's face. Had Skylar come here under the guise of diplomacy merely to cow Tsinghai's government into joining the duchy by force? No. Couldn't be. Cyril sucked in a breath and blinked, but he could not shake the idea. From that moment on, everything Skylar said—regardless of the actual words—sounded to Cyril like *I'm making you an offer you can't refuse* or *This deal really only benefits my eventual inheritance* or *Beware this knife I am holding at your throat.*

He thought he was going to be sick. At that moment, he had half a mind to snatch the Grenadiers beret from his head just to show the prime minister's entourage that he didn't belong with Skylar's people.

Before Cyril could do anything rash, one of Jain's aides worked his way through the assembly of Grenadiers officers in the box and touched the shoulder of Skylar's maddeningly expensive suit. The aide handed the ambassador something—a slip of paper with an official ComStar seal—then spoke some quiet words before withdrawing.

Skylar looked like a *Banshee* had punched him in the solar plexus as he tore open the message. Color drained from his face, and he held a fist over his mouth as though fighting the urge to throw up.

Jain touched him lightly on the arm. "Is everything all right, Ambassador?"

The haughty, spoiled mask Skylar Orloff always wore in public shattered as the ghosts of tears rimmed his eyes. "My father ..." His voice hitched. "My father's been *killed.*"

Cyril blinked. With no small amount of horror, he realized he was sitting mere meters from the new Duke Orloff.

Before that could sink in, Cyril caught sight of commotion further down the box. Colonel Polzin raised a buzzing comm unit to his ear. Cyril couldn't make out what he said to the caller, but the uncomfortable bob of Polzin's Adam's apple—a noticeable dry swallow—could only signal bad news.

"Madam Prime Minister," the colonel said, his mouth a grim line, "we've got Capellans in our skies. If Tsinghai wants the duchy's protection, then you had better decide where you stand *right now*."

"Colonel—"

"We don't have orders to protect your planet, ma'am," Polzin countered. "Not unless Tsinghai is a member of the duchy or we get orders from the captain-general himself." It was heartless to say, but Cyril knew the regiment's CO spoke the truth.

The marching Fourteenth Irregulars kept right on performing rifle tricks, completely oblivious to the assassination and the incoming foreign troops. Then, without warning, the quartet of *Cheetah*s and *Stingray*s tore across the afternoon towards the nearest airbase, and the parade's three jump-capable recon 'Mechs took to the air on superheated vents of plasma.

DropShip Divine Thunder
Zenith jump point, Ingersoll system
Capella Commonality, Capellan Confederation
25 April 2996

Lin Wei was sitting in place yet running in a nocturnal forest built in her imagination, imagining the cool night air, the pine needles grazing the sides of her face, the earthy smell of nature surrounding her. Then something tore her away from the fantasy and replaced pines with stark corrugated-metal walls and earthy scents with the burnt smell of an abused DropShip cargo bay.

It took her several seconds to realize Commander Park was shaking her by the shoulders inside freight container 31C. He was kitted out in his MechWarrior togs—boots, shorts, and a cooling vest.

"Captain!" Park called, seemingly kilometers away. "Didn't you hear the jump alarms?"

Lin tore away at the cobwebs, but some still remained. "Alarms ...?"

"The balloon is up!" Park insisted. "We jump for Tsinghai in ten minutes! The rest of the men are already assembled. Now come on!"

She slapped at her cheeks, snatched up her nearby incense paraphernalia, and stuffed it into a utility pocket. "Right behind you."

The pair dashed out into the 'Mech bay, where jump klaxons pummeled Lin's eardrums. Once they reached the 'Mech cubicles, she wasted no time scaling the ladder up her green-camo *Vindicator*. As she slid inside and dogged the exterior hatch closed, her training kicked into full

gear. She sloughed off her pants, shrugged off her shirt, tugged on a spare set of shorts she kept in a side compartment, buckled on her cooling vest, and connected all of the necessary biosensor leads in record time. When the two-minute jump warning resounded over the *Divine Thunder*'s PA system, Lin only needed to secure her neurohelmet.

During those two minutes of anticipation, she pulled herself into the present, tried to shift her focus on the mission. The incense, her thoughts about retiring—that all dwelled on the future, none of which would happen should she fail here today.

The jump alarm sounded, and the *Silk Road*'s Kearny-Fuchida drive wrenched the *Divine Thunder*—and all of her other attached DropShips—through hyperspace. Reality *bent* around Lin's consciousness, until she felt herself slipping sideways, as though she was trying to run up the side of a building ...

... Pine boughs smacked her cheeks and stung her arms as she ran through the darkness. Something was after her, something snarling, vicious, and fast. She couldn't outrun it, but she was unarmed, sprinting naked and barefoot away from it as fast as her legs could carry her. She had no name here, and soon her true name wouldn't even matter—not if her hunter caught her. Her only recourse was to turn and face the beast, to show her that even in death she was unafraid, that she would wrestle it barehanded to the carpet of evergreen needles and choke the life out of it, if need be.

She turned, faced the pale light of the moons, and waited, breathless and filled with fear and bloodlust.

The forest was empty. Only the wind chased her. She stared out into an endless blackness, pine needles like fangs waiting to suck the lifeblood from her.

The massive viper pounced from above—a blinding blur of electric green scales streaked with darker green. It went straight to her neck, bit down deep on her carotid artery, and she felt life leave her as blood pulsed from the wound ...

... "—ttention! Attention!" The resounding words set hooks in her brain and pulled. "Jump complete. All *Divine Thunder* crew, prepare for detachment in thirty seconds!"

Lin found herself panting, almost to the point of hyperventilation. Sweat bathed every centimeter of her exposed skin, and she shook her head to dispel what she'd just experienced. The jump was supposed to be instantaneous, but she felt *exhausted*, as though she'd just come off participating in one of the regiment's yearly marathons. She'd had strange hallucinations during hyperspace jumps before—

who *hadn't*, really?—but never anything this disturbing.

Her arms shook with a meat-locker chill; only squeezing gloved fingers around the control sticks seemed to steady her torso. Then, distant metal groaned. Her insides shifted, and her inner ear could no longer tell up from down.

Her neurohelmet radio crackled to life. "All units, this is First Battalion actual," Major Petrowski said. "We are go for descent. ETA until combat drop, thirty-five minutes."

A private channel lit up on Lin's communication board—battalion command. Her forearm shuddered when she keyed it up. "Jiang," she radioed.

"You sure you're okay, Captain?" Petrowski said.

"I'm fine, sir," she insisted.

"Flight surgeons tell me your vitals are spiking. It's not too late to sit this one out. I'll brevet Park to captain if need be."

An image of the viper flashed in her head. "Just ... got spooked by the jump is all. No need to worry about me."

The major chuckled. "We've all got jump stories," he said. "Tell me about it over a beer later, all right? Petrowski out."

Over the next half hour, Lin came to terms with the realization that she had made a terrible mistake. Not even venting waste heat from her 'Mech's fusion reactor could stop herself from shivering.

I should have retired, she told herself over and over again. So why hadn't she? Park could easily have taken her place on this mission; even Petrowski confirmed that. But Park had his whole career ahead of him; Lin's was on the wane. And though she had earned her Capellan citizenship decades ago, she still felt she owed the Capellan Confederation at least one more successful mission.

Her radio clicked back to life. "All units," Major Petrowski announced, "prepare for combat drop in five minutes."

Lin squeezed her control sticks in a white-knuckled death grip. *One more mission*, she told herself.

Orloff Grenadiers Temporary Command Post
Outside Kokonor, Tsinghai
Free Worlds League
25 April 2996

Cyril threw open the armored car's passenger door and stuck a leg out before the vehicle had come to a complete stop in front of the

hangar housing most of the First Grenadiers' 'Mechs. The thunderclap of distant explosions greeted him as he and his lancemates stepped out of the vehicle.

The battle wasn't here yet, but it would be soon. There was no time to waste. Rather than wait for the new Duke Orloff to extricate his considerable girth from the armored car, Cyril grabbed him by the hand and wrenched him out onto the tarmac.

"Unhand me, ruffian!" Skylar shrieked. "I am the duke!"

After nearly a month of this nonsense, Cyril had reached the end of his patience. "Shove it," he snapped. "If you want to stay alive, *Your Grace,* you'll shut your mouth and stop announcing to the whole god-damned *planet* that you're here!"

Another distant string of explosions—short-range missiles, from the sound of it—reinforced his need for urgency. He and the rest of his men hurried into the hangar just as the armored car drove off with the rest of the retreating Tsinghai dignitaries, but Cyril brought up the rear of the pack to keep an eye on his duke. The rest of his lance—Carlson, Kramer, and Harrelson—had already reached their 'Mechs and climbed into their cockpits by the time Cyril escorted Skylar to the foot of the Wicked Witch.

Skylar considered the rope ladder and craned his fat neck upward. His trembling jowls and reddened eyes told Cyril everything he needed to know: the ducal heir had never actually piloted this towering machine of death in combat before.

"I—I can't do this," Skylar said.

The diamond-plate floor shook beneath Cyril's feet. Probably a long-range missile salvo, from the sustained reverberation. "*Get in,*" he demanded. "Colonel Polzin ordered me to ensure your safety, and I can't keep you safe if you're standing on the ground."

Tears welled up in the duke's eyes. His shoulders shuddered, shaking his entire frame. "I ... I *can't.*"

Cyril heaved a sigh heavy enough to pulverize a boulder and advanced on Skylar just enough to make him backpedal toward Wicked Witch's leg. "I don't *like* you. Never have. I think you're a goddamn disgrace to the Orloff line. But your father is *dead.* If you die, the duchy dies with you, the Grenadiers lose their funding and disband, and the whole spinward flank of the Free Worlds League crumbles under a Capellan onslaught. Do you want that on your conscience?"

Skylar backed into the *Awesome*'s leg and stopped cold when his spine struck armor plating. His eyes radiated black pits of terror despair.

"You are a high value target, do you understand?" Cyril said. "We need to get you off-planet before any of those Capellan devils realize you are literally right under their noses."

The duke nodded solemnly and sniffed. "Then take my 'Mech," he said. "If the Capellans recognize it, they will come after you instead."

Cyril nodded. "My *Trebuchet* is much faster than this tub here, so you stand a better chance of escaping pursuers if things really go south."

Skylar hesitated.

"You *do* know how to keep a 'Mech at a steady run, don't you?" Cyril said,

"I ... *think* so," Skylar said, nodding slowly. "The ... uh ... passcode for Wicked Witch is 'Follow the yellow brick road.' Just ... promise me you'll take good care of her."

Cyril grabbed the first rung of the *Awesome's* ladder and began climbing. "I can't promise that," he said, sparing a glance down at his duke. "The only thing I *can* promise is that I'll uphold the oath I took when I first put on this uniform. Now get moving! My 'Mech's security override is 'Long live the duchy.'"

"See you on the other side, Captain," Skylar said. From the grave look on his face, it seemed he meant it.

Instinct kicked in the moment Cyril slid into Wicked Witch's cockpit. With a shake of his head hard enough to rattle his brain, he dogged the hatch, shed his uniform jacket, and pulled on the coolant vest tucked behind the ejection seat. The neurohelmet was sized for someone much larger than himself, but there was no time to dwell on it.

A burst of dizziness flooded his senses when he toggled the 'Mech out of maintenance mode. He felt like he'd gone one too many rounds with a shot glass and a bottle of tequila, but there was nothing for it but to push through and focus. No time to properly calibrate the neurohelmet. He had a job to do.

After quickly memorizing the layout of all vital functions inside the cockpit, he flicked on all necessary systems. Out of the corner of his eye he saw the weighty duke struggle up Peacemaker's last few ladder rungs and slide into the 'Mech's cockpit. Moments later, the *Trebuchet* powered up and showed as a friendly contact in Cyril's HUD. With Skylar at the controls, Cyril's family 'Mech tottered from side to side like a punched-up pugilist about to go down to the canvas.

This was a bad idea, he thought.

Without wasting another moment, he ordered the rest of his lance to move out. Lieutenant Carlson's *Griffin*, Harrelson's *Wolverine*,

and Kramer's *Shadow Hawk* stomped out of the hangar ahead of him at a brisk pace, and the punch-drunk *Trebuchet* staggered out after them. Cyril lumbered the *Awesome* out of the hangar fast enough to get a sense for how it handled before opening up the throttle. It was a much heavier 'Mech than he was used to—much slower, too—but he would make do. He'd trained on all BattleMech weight classes in the simulator; this time would just be the real thing.

The moment Wicked Witch left the safety of the ⊠Mech hangar, large-bore autocannon fire punched dozens of holes in the nearest building⊠s façade, just a few meters above the *Awesome*'s head. A cascade of cement hail clattered across Cyril's canopy as a *Transit* in green Capellan camo banked off at a steep angle and rocketed away to safety before Cyril could consider lining up a retaliatory shot.

He kept his *Trebuchet*—Skylar—firmly in his sights and keyed the radio to broadcast on the battalion-wide channel. "This is Baker Company actual," he transmitted. "I've secured the package and we're in a hot zone. What's your status?"

The line stayed silent for several tense moments, but Cyril kept moving, kept redlining the throttle to try keeping pace behind his much faster lancemates.

"Duarte here," Cyril's CO replied. "Head to these coordinates I'm sending. We're going to try a hot retrieval and evac. Copy?"

Cyril studied his tactical map while kicking Wicked Witch up to a full run to keep pace with Skylar and the rest of his lance. The spot was a mere ten kilometers away from their current position.

A lot could happen in ten klicks.

"Good copy, Major," he said. "The Wicked Witch is secured and moving out for evac. Over."

"Keep watch on your flanks, De Milo. Cappies are throwing a *lot* of hardware at us."

"We've already hit aerospace cover. What kind of opposition are we facing out here, sir? How many 'Mech companies are in this raid?"

"*Companies*, Captain?" Duarte forced a dismal laugh. "The colonel's estimating two full 'Mech battalions—maybe more. We've got combat drops all over the place. This is an *invasion*. Our best hope is to hold them off until you can evacuate the duke, then we'll fall back to Hassad to reassess the situation."

A grim smile pained Cyril's face as he scanned for more aerofighters. "No pressure, sir."

"We're boxed in over here. I might be able to spare some armor to cover your retreat, but beyond that, you're on your own for now.

I'm trying to get you some air support, but that might take some doing.

"Make us proud, Captain. Duarte out."

The line went to static.

Kokonor Foothills
Tsinghai
Free Worlds League
25 April 2996

Across the rolling fields, Lin Wei sat in her jostling cockpit and watched the prairie and forests burn as she and her lance's 'Mechs traversed the field. Errant missile salvos had blown a few nearby farmhouses into scattered matchsticks and ashes. Smoke from the fires and downed 'Mechs blew into the sky, reminding her of the smoldering incense stick situated atop her dash.

Lin's family had always considered Tsinghai home. She had never lived here, of course—Tsinghai had not been a part of the Capellan Confederation since the latter years of the First Succession War—but her family could trace its ancestry here. All throughout her military career she held romantic notions of someday setting foot on the planet along with her CCAF brothers- and sisters-in-arms and reclaiming it in the name of the Confederation. Chancellor Tormax Liao never had any illusions of conquest, but his son and successor Maximilian wanted to try taking this planet to remind his people that the Capellan Confederation could still reclaim a small portion its lost glory.

Never had Lin expected to return home only to find it in flames. The Prefectorate Guard and Warrior House Hiritsu battalions had performed efficiently before the Fifth Cavalry had even made landfall, but Reserve Cavalry units were meant to patch holes in the battle lines, not create them.

Lin's company frequency chirped on. "Three-One," said Commander Huang from Recon Lance, "this is Three-Niner. Over."

"Copy, Three-Niner. Go ahead."

"Sir, we've got some strange 'Mech activity out here on the MSR out of Kokonor, away from the action. Thought we should call it in."

"Define 'strange,' Commander."

"Reinforced lance of mediums. Only, the extra 'Mech is an assault. Its parade scheme matches the other Grenadiers 'Mechs, but it's got no visible unit insignias, no official markings whatsoever."

No unit markings? That was odd.

"Looks like a VIP if I ever saw one," Huang added. "They're high-tailing it down the MSR like they stole something. Should we engage, sir?"

"That's a negative, Three-Niner," she replied. "Keep an eye on them but do not engage until I give the order." She switched the channel to battalion command. "First Battalion actual, this is Three-One. I've got eyes on a potential Hotel-Victor-Tango following MSR One south out of Kokonor. Permission to advance and engage. Over."

"Three-One, this is First Battalion," Major Petrowski replied a few seconds later. "Permission denied. Continue on your present course. A Grenadiers lance managed to poke through a Prefectorate Guard picket, and I need those holes patched ASAP. Sending you the coordinates now."

Lin's eyes flicked to her tactical map to assess the situation. According to intel, the First Orloff Grenadiers only had one 'Mech battalion on the planet. Their armor and infantry forces were harrying House Hiritsu along the western flank, while most of two Grenadiers 'Mech companies gave the Prefectorate Guard something to chase across the Kokonor Foothills. Only a few Capellan aerospace lances were covering the southern reaches. If the Grenadiers managed to evacuate an important dignitary, like the planet's prime minister or some other sympathetic political figure, the Capellan garrison could face decades of riots and uprisings.

Plus, if Lin could snag a VIP, that would make her career, and she could finally retire with accolades and a clear conscience.

"Sir, we have the enemy on the run. It's only a matter of time until they capitulate. If that HVT escapes ..."

"Leave it, Captain. If—*if*—you've got eyes on an HVT, they're not going anywhere. First Battalion out."

An icy sensation of lightheadedness washed over her, but she pushed through it, breaking through the surface of dizziness. Now wasn't the time to dwell on what was *wrong*—there'd be plenty of time for that later. Right now she had to do what she knew was *right*.

Lin took a moment to light another incense stick—one of her last few, she noted—and set it in the dashboard receptacle. Thick sandalwood smoke filled her lungs before her cockpit's air filtration system sucked it into the vents. Her eyes closed long enough for her to imagine a calm forest at night. The sun setting. A cool breeze rippling over the water. For a moment she forgot her name and basked in the liberating sensation of buoyancy that her 'Mech's steadily advancing pace afforded her.

Who contains himself seldom goes wrong, she recited.

Her eyes snapped open, and she toggled the company channel. "Three-Niner," she said, "this is Three-One. Hold position on the Hotel-Victor-Tango. We're coming to you."

Main Supply Route One
South of Kokonor, Tsinghai
Free Worlds League
25 April 2996

With a string of every expletive he could think of, Cyril cursed this infernal 'Mech he'd been stuck with. If it could go any slower, he felt he'd be going backward along this road cutting through the forest. Skylar probably liked this cumbersome beast because an *Awesome* did cut an impressive silhouette on a parade ground, but out here on the battlefield that bulk was going to cost them. Cyril forever brought up the rear of the group, always twelve steps or more behind Peacemaker, which lagged from the inexperienced duke at the controls. Harrelson's *Wolverine* was ranging as far ahead as she could get away with, but at least Carlson and Kramer stuck around to ensure no one got too far behind.

And that confounded buzz in his head from the uncalibrated neurohelmet was slowly driving him insane.

A quick glance at his radar and MAD sensor readout confirmed Cyril's fear: the quartet of trailing radar contacts at the edge of his range were steadily gaining. Before long they'd overtake him and Skylar, and this whole plan would be for nothing.

If only Skylar had had the good sense to own something faster. Even a cobbled-together *Orion* or *BattleMaster*—both slower than Peacemaker—would've outrun this brand-new assault 'Mech.

"I have visual on the rendezvous point," Harrelson radioed from a few kilometers downrange. "Hangar and runway look intact. I don't think the Cappies know this is a functioning airfield."

Cyril glanced at his tactical display. The contacts were drawing closer by the moment. "They're going to find out pretty soon. Radio ahead and tell the ground crew that we might be coming in hot, and get back here ASAP."

Just as the transmission cut out, Wicked Witch jostled to one side beneath him as though struck by a bullet train, and a pair of hollow *pangs* resounded throughout his cockpit. Missile impacts, from the sounds of it.

A series of small explosions—more LRM fire—fell short right at Peacemaker's feet. Under Skylar's untrained control, the *Trebuchet* wobbled to one side but thankfully remained upright.

Cyril shook his head hard enough to feel his brain rattle around, and he fought to push his focus through the baseline neurohelmet hum. The sensation was starting to make him feel sick to his stomach.

"I've got contact!" Lieutenant Carlson radioed. "Returning fire!" Her *Griffin's* torso turned, and the 'Mech's shoulder-mounted launcher loosed a flight of missiles at a target outside Cyril's field of view.

"Four more radar contacts coming in from the northeast!" Kramer reported.

"Keep moving!" Cyril shouted. "Protect the duke at all costs!"

He pivoted Wicked Witch to get a better look at the incoming threats. A *Valkyrie* in green-and-brown jungle camo sprinted out from behind a nearby ravine and fired another LRM salvo. A matching *Javelin*, *Firestarter*, and *Clint* followed right on its heels in perfect formation, each one opening fire almost in unison.

Sergeant Kramer's *Shadow Hawk* took the brunt of the fusillade. Armor plates melted, exploded, and chipped away beneath the onslaught of missile, laser, and autocannon. Kramer answered, but none of his shots connected: while he was at full throttle, his intended targets were just moving too fast.

Carlson's *Griffin* scored a few missiles on the *Javelin*, but she kept moving according to plan. Getting the duke to the airfield was priority, no matter how many Capellan 'Mechs were chasing them.

Cyril flipped up the safety cover on his weapon controls. All three of Wicked Witch's PPCs were charged and ready. *Time to see what this tub of lard can do*, he thought as he tried to get a bead on the *Clint* while maintaining as much of a full run as the assault 'Mech could muster. Even in Cyril's younger days his academy instructors declared him a fast shot, but the *Awesome's* targeting system moved the 'Mech's arm-mounted PPC like cold tar, and the lack of a twistable torso kept him from tracking the target as quickly as he was accustomed. He led the *Clint* anyway, tried to eyeball it with his reticule, and mashed the firing stud.

Three instantaneous bolts of charged particles struck the forested hill just behind the dashing 'Mech, and a wash of waste heat swept through the cockpit.

From the look of things, Kramer and Carlson were faring no better. The scout lance was moving too fast. A few shots connected—a missile here, a minor laser graze there—but by and large the Capellan quartet weathered the assault and continued to take potshots at Cyril's lance before withdrawing back into the ravine near the road.

Through the neurohelmet hum, Cyril kept Wicked Witch at a full run. Each eighty-ton step seemed like he was wading through a diving pool, trudging through a swamp of cold molasses.

At that moment, the *Javelin* and *Clint* barreled out of the ravine, shot to the sky on wings of vented plasma plumes, and laid into the *Trebuchet* with missiles, lasers, and autocannon shells. The pair worried armor plating all across Peacemaker's flank, but one of the *Javelin*'s SRMs burrowed through a chewed-up section of the *Treb*'s left elbow bend. Cyril winced as the explosive force detonated through exterior seams from *inside* the arm, blasting away the few armor plates like roof shingles shorn off in high winds. Smoke trailed from the busted seams, and a second later, the whole limb tore off in a sympathetic explosion as missiles in the arm's ammo feed mechanism ignited.

Color drained from Cyril's face: a prisoner of Wicked Witch, he would be forced to watch his family 'Mech's inevitable destruction.

"Urgh!" Duke Orloff's flustered voice crackled through the comms. "Keep 'em off me!"

In retaliation Cyril aimed all three PPCs at the *Javelin* and fired one after the other in hopes that at least one might connect and kneecap the Cappie bastard. But no: Wicked Witch was too slow. Each shot in the salvo missed by a whisper because the damned 'Mech's arm mass couldn't keep up with Cyril's honed reflexes.

"Con*found* this thing!" he shouted, slamming a fist on the dashboard.

His duke—the leader of the political institution he had sworn to defend to his last breath—was going to get killed, and the *Trebuchet* that had been in the De Milo family for more than three generations was going to get smashed to unrecognizable bits in the process. All because of this ridiculous, accursed BattleMech.

"Captain!" Carlson radioed. "We've got incoming!"

In the heat of battle, Cyril didn't need to check his instruments to know what his XO meant. Four more Fifth Confederation Reserve Cavalry 'Mechs done up in two-tone jungle camo crested the rise not far to the north.

He glanced down at his map readout. Five kilometers to the airfield.

Damn. Not near enough, not by a long shot.

While waiting for his PPCs to cycle, he switched to the battalion-command frequency. "This is Baker Company actual," he transmitted.

"We're five klicks from the pickup point and have two CRC lances in pursuit. How about those reinforcements, Major?"

No response.

"This is Baker Company. Please respond."

Empty static replied.

▲▼▲

"Captain Jiang!" Major Petrowski's transmission trumpeted in Lin Wei's ear. "Get your wángbadàn ass back here on the double, do you hear me?!"

Lin's vision blurred for a moment, as though a haze of tears obscured her view of the forested landscape ahead. But it wasn't tears. "If I am right," she said, "this may be the last good deed I ever do."

And with that she flicked off the channel. The incoming transmission light flashed, but she ignored it. What could Petrowski do to her now, anyway? Court-martial her? Drum her out of the service? None of that would matter after this battle.

She closed her eyes while her *Vindicator* kept right on jogging toward the road leading into the forest. *A sin against Heaven is past praying for*, she recited.

"Commander," she radioed on the company channel, "status report."

"Recon Lance has engaged the target, sir," Park replied from his nearby *Whitworth*. "The HVT's escort has taken some minor damage, but not enough to slow them down."

"Three-Niner here," Commander Huang radioed. "There's an airfield due south of our current position. It looks abandoned, but Massey thinks the Leaguers might have a DropShip stashed out there. We'll need to hurry."

Lin dialed up her magnification and zoomed in on the distant skirmish already taking place between the target lance and Recon Lance. Among the Grenadiers 'Mechs, a beat-up *Trebuchet* showed the most significant damage: oily black smoke trailed from the shoulder of its missing left arm. "Keep them busy," she said. "We're on our way."

Her lance approached through the forested foothills on an intercept course. The Grenadiers loosed a few salvos in their direction, but nothing found its mark: Recon Lance's hard-hitting distraction was working perfectly.

This close, Lin finally got a good look at the VIP. Amid the quartet of medium BattleMechs, the blocky, lime-green and olive-drab *Awe-*

some stuck out like a sore thumb. Huang had been right: there were no identifying markings on it whatsoever—no designation number, no company sigils, nothing.

And then the great 'Mech turned toward her. The noonday sun struck the torso near the cockpit, and she saw the horrid face of the green viper from her hyperspace vision. Skin the color of radioactive waste. A leering mouthful of fangs ready to sink into her neck and drain her blood. The crudely painted title next to the nose art said "The Wicked Witch," but Lin saw only the viper.

Her heart pulsed loud enough she could hear it over the rhythmic pumping of her 'Mech's legs running across the open ground.

While Lin remained zoomed in, the *Awesome* fired a scintillating pair of PPC bolts at Massey's *Javelin*. Both spears gouged the lighter 'Mech clean through. The *Javelin* stumbled in mid-stride, just before a blooming fireball from an ammo explosion tore the 'Mech in half.

Lin's throat went dry. The *Awesome* continued its ungainly jog into the forest until it vanished from her visual sensors. Somewhere in those woods, the viper was waiting for her.

"Concentrate on the lighter 'Mechs," she radioed to Park and Huang, "but leave that Hotel-Victor-Tango to me."

▲▼▲

"Off the road!" Cyril radioed to his lance. "Try to lose them in the forest!"

He knew it was a rout, plain and simple. Carlson, Kramer, and Harrelson had already taking a pounding; Peacemaker was down an arm and had an inept pilot at the controls; and the cumbersome Wicked Witch barely seemed capable of hitting anything. All of the Capellan light lance—except the *Javelin* Cyril had miraculously blasted apart—was still functional, and the incoming medium lance only made things worse. A Capellan *Griffin*, *Clint*, *Vindicator*, and *Whitworth* were barreling down the hills at a full run. Cyril's lance could use the forest to their advantage, but that was a risky proposition, considering Duke Orloff might accidentally trip Peacemaker on an overgrown root and fall face first to the forest floor.

Did Skylar even *know* how to get a 'Mech back on its feet, especially if it were already missing an arm?

"Keep moving!" Cyril radioed. "We're almost there!"

Almost being a relative term: his tactical computer showed three klicks to the airfield—as the crow flies, that was. Three goddamn

klicks. And that neurohelmet hum was on the verge of making him throw up all over his cooling vest.

Something slammed his right shoulder into the cockpit wall before he even registered the white-hot flash of a PPC discharge in his peripheral vision. Wicked Witch reeled to the side as though donkey-kicked—a hit to the left arm, damage readout showing yellow. Once Cyril balanced himself, he saw the *Vindicator* on approach; its right-arm particle cannon positively glowed on his infrared sensors.

So it seemed Wicked Witch was good for at least one thing: such a hit would've shredded the armor from Peacemaker's remaining arm. Assault 'Mechs had a lot of armor and armaments, which meant they drew a lot of fire on the battlefield. Cyril knew if he could keep the Cappies focused on the *Awesome*'s threat, perhaps it might buy his lancemates enough time to get the duke to safety. There was no way he could outrun these 'Mechs. That *Vindicator* and its *Whitworth* partner could clock over sixty kph in a dead run, but so far Wicked Witch only topped out at around fifty-two, and running the whole way would expose her less-than-impressive rear armor.

Assault 'Mechs could take a lot of punishment, but they certainly weren't invincible. And sooner or later, the *Awesome*'s armor would fail.

Missiles from the *Whitworth* and *Griffin* arced white contrails toward Peacemaker. A few of the warheads hit home—not enough to knock Skylar off balance—but the rest fell short and exploded around the *Treb*'s feet. The three remaining light 'Mechs swarmed Cyril's lancemates.

Two more klicks. Just two more ...

Before Cyril knew what was happening, the IFF transponder from Carlson's *Griffin* disappeared from his HUD. The 'Mech stopped moving in mid-stride and pitched forward just as explosive bolts fired and the lieutenant's ejection seat launched from the doomed 'Mech on a plume of hellfire. A guilty Capellan *Firestarter* ducked around the falling *Griffin* and vaulted up and over the road before Harrelson could successfully retaliate. A jellyfish of white silk ballooned in the sky above the treetops, and the emergency transponder from Carlson's command couch pinged on Cyril's HUD.

It was past time to even the odds. Cyril swallowed down his nausea and helped Harrelson pelt the *Firestarter* with enough PPC strikes and autocannon fire to shear off two different limbs and smash the Capellan 'Mech's torso to pieces before its pilot could even land the jump. The rest of the 'Mech nearly disintegrated when it crashed down onto its remaining leg and tumbled into the ravine beside the road.

Cyril knew that kill alone wouldn't be enough. The *Clint* and *Valkyrie* started bugging out at losing half of their lance, but the pursuing heavier 'Mechs were fast closing the gap.

The *Vindicator* fired its PPC again, this time adding the rest of its weapons into the mix. Cyril rocked with the blows; more of Wicked Witch's armor plates sailed out from the 'Mech's torso like a pack of playing cards thrown into the wind.

One and a half klicks. Cyril closed his eyes, felt hot tears form at the edge of his eyelashes. Not all of them were going to make it to the rendezvous point. Not all of them were going to make it off the planet. Every soldier in every single House, mercenary, or private army across the Inner Sphere had to accept in some capacity that he might not survive a combat op. But with four enemy 'Mechs converging near his location, Cyril De Milo knew he was probably staring his future in the face. And he would be less of a soldier if he did not confront it with every milliliter of blood, sweat, and tears he could muster.

He swallowed down the churning in his stomach, turned around, and walked the *Awesome* backwards through the trees, away from the pursuing *Vindicator* while keeping it in his sights. "Harrelson," he said as calmly as he could muster, "get the duke to the airfield, no matter what it takes."

"Sir," she replied, "what are you doing?"

"That's an order, soldier," Cyril shot back. "Get him out of here, now!"

Behind him in his 360-degree view, he watched Harrelson and Skylar disappear into the forest's shadows. Whether the duke made it back to Vanra was inconsequential: Cyril knew it was the last time he would ever see Peacemaker.

No time to dwell on it. The *Vindicator* was gaining on him fast, and its *Whitworth* companion trailed only a few steps behind. Cyril's already lethargic assault 'Mech slowed down even further while backpedaling away from the Capellans. In any kind of battle, speed meant life, but better to slow and face incoming fire than expose weaker rear armor while running away at a speed the Capellans could easily exceed to begin with. The Capellans would catch up with him no matter where he ran.

All that mattered was drawing as much Capellan fire as he could away from the fleeing duke. And he *would* do it, even if it meant his life. Because he was one of the best goddamned soldiers in the Free Worlds League.

HIGH-VALUE TARGET

He was an Orloff Grenadier.

The *Vindicator* was already following him; he just needed to catch the others' attention as well. At this speed, Wicked Witch's frozen-tar aiming system seemed to warm up noticeably. Before waiting for all off his weapons to finish cycling, he lined up his crosshairs on the *Whitworth*. Right when the ready tone chirped, he jammed the trigger. As if thrown from the arm of Zeus himself, the charged-particle bolt tore through the 'Mech's side torso, showering the forest floor with chipped and melting armor fragments.

Without wasting another second, he tracked a second shot on the *Clint* weaving its way through the largest trees. He fired, clipped the 'Mech in the leg, and fused some armor into slag around the ankle joint. His third shot tracked the distant *Griffin* he could still barely see at the edge of the forest. Again he fired, blasting an interposing evergreen into kindling instead. The smell of heat and ozone flushed through the cockpit.

"Come on, come on, come on," he whispered at the Capellan 'Mechs. "Look this way. Come after the big, scary Witch."

Cyril held his breath for five interminable seconds.

The *Whitworth*'s torso swiveled to face him. IR showed its lasers powering up, a score of long-range warheads loading into its paired missile launchers. A few seconds later, the *Clint* took the bait. The *Griffin*, however, continued on through the forest to chase after the rest of Cyril's lance.

And just like that, Cyril found himself facing three Capellan 'Mechs bearing down on him all at once—three Capellan 'Mechs that weren't chasing after his duke.

As the advancing 'Mech shadows spilled over his cockpit, he began rethinking the whole idea. He imagined Maskirovka interrogation rooms that never saw the light of day. Beatings. Torture. Privation. If even half of the rumors about the Capellan intelligence service were accurate, perhaps a quick battlefield death would be the better option ...

Biting his lip against the dizzying sickness from the neurohelmet hum, Cyril took a moment to remember why he was here. He pictured himself in the mirror back on Vanra, wearing his immaculate dress uniform—a model soldier in a model regiment. That image reminded him he had a duty to the duchy, to a duke he didn't fully respect, but the job had to be done, regardless of whether he liked it.

The Capellan trio closed in, weapons charged and preparing to fire.

COUNTERATTACK

And then Cyril waded Wicked Witch backwards into the thickest, tallest patch of trees in this part of the forest, until shadows enveloped him on all sides.

▲▼▲

Captain Lin Wei Jiang of C Company, First Battalion, Fifth Confederation Reserve Cavalry Regiment, stared into the forest's shadows long enough to permanently forget her own name. It was just as well. Whether her future invited a court-martial, revoked citizenship, retirement, or certain death, she knew this moment would be her last official act as a member of the Capellan Confederation Armed Forces.

Further into the forest the monstrous viper led her. Through a rippling haze of waste heat and the last, lingering traces of incense filling her cockpit, catching visual confirmation of the elusive high value target proved impossible through the dense arboreal growth. Here, the trees grew so tall and so close together that the upper branches latticed together with neighboring tree branches, casting the forest floor in a twilight shade. MAD sensors also proved useless: each of the thousands of nearby trees showed up as a metallic object, likely from their roots absorbing a high concentration of heavy metals from the soil. The *Awesome* had also gone dark on infrared. Its weapons had gone quiet, and it was moving slowly enough that she saw only an occasional, distant flicker of color between the army of boles.

Somewhere in this darkness, the snake lurked, waiting to pounce on her and sink its fangs into her neck ...

"Three-four here," Subcommander Ferro radioed from his *Clint*. "Can either of you get a lock on this thing?"

"Can't see it," Park remarked as his *Whitworth* ranged cautiously forward.

A deep breath filled her nameless lungs. Whoever this target was had to know he or she was outnumbered and alone. She keyed on the general broadcast frequency and spoke in as deep and authoritative a voice as she could summon: "Attention, pilot of the Free Worlds League *Awesome*: surrender, and your life will be spared. Resist, and that guarantee is rescinded."

Crackling white noise replied. Another warm flare of greenish color danced between the cool blue hues of the surrounding forest. She tried to line up a shot, but then the color vanished.

"Free Worlds pilot," she transmitted again, "this is your last chance. Stand down."

"Long live the Duchy of Orloff," came the distorted response.

Seemingly from nowhere, a vivid-green infrared silhouette darted into the open. A trio of PPC bolts flashed past her 'Mech, lighting up the interior of her cockpit before all three connected with Ferro's *Clint*. One tore off the already-damaged leg at the ankle, and the rest found enough holes in the torso to send wrecked gyroscope fragments spinning off into the underbrush. Unable to remain upright without a functioning gyro, the *Clint* crumpled under its own weight.

"No good, Captain," Ferro said with a pained grunt, his transmission weak. "Arm's broken, I think. Can't help you ..."

"Sit tight," she replied. "This won't take long."

Now the blocky viper glowed yellow-orange on her scopes amid the blue forest. An easy target.

"Aim for the legs," she told Park. "Take it down!"

Following her own advice proved more difficult than expected, despite the *Awesome*'s PPC waste heat lighting it up like a buoy in the vast sea of cooler temperatures. Her hands shook on the *Vindicator*'s controls. The reticule danced unbidden over the *Awesome*'s luminous shape. For a few seconds she lifted her right hand, drew the fingers into a fist, and squeezed. Released. Squeezed. Tried again.

This time her whole arm trembled. She braced it against the armrest, but the involuntary twitching persisted. Then her right eyelid fluttered—subtly at first, then it trembled hard and often enough to make her vision in that eye look like a projected film running slow enough to see the gutter flash between each frame.

She opened her radio channel, tried to call for Park, only what came out between her lips was nothing but a strained and desperate "*Paaaahh*," like the sound of some dying animal. Her mouth wouldn't work right, and the sound of her own voice horrified her. "*Paaaa-aaaah!*"

No use.

The viper sinking its teeth into her neck wasn't this bulky 'Mech heading straight for her. She had thought she had one good mission left in her, but she'd been mistaken. The incense was gone, her serenity was gone, and none of that would ever return.

Right before her, all three of the *Awesome*'s PPC barrels glowed whitish blue as they charged up to fire.

Every finger of her right hand convulsed like an angry spider around the control stick as she fought to center the *Vindicator*'s PPC's reticule somewhere—*anywhere*—on the 'Mech that was about to kill her. She fired anyway.

Her shot tagged the *Awesome* in the hip, rocked it just enough to make its own bolts miss her completely but not enough to slow it down. The 'Mech was a beast, even after all the damage it had already sustained in battle along the road ...

All the while, Park's *Whitworth* was circling the *Awesome* and pounding it with laser and missile fire at range. Park was a decent shot, but even he could only do so much against an ungainly monster twice his own mass.

The *Awesome* must've realized Park constituted the greater threat because it slowly turned to bring all of its weapons to bear on the *Whitworth*.

In an effort to ensnare the Leaguer's attention, she somehow managed to fire her *Vindicator's* PPC, this time missing entirely. The *Awesome* ignored her, rounded on Park, and slammed the *Whitworth* dead on across its midsection with three blinding bolts of charged particles. The whole left-hand side of Park's 'Mech exploded in a fiery ammo detonation. He ejected, but the tree cover was so dense his parachute lines tangled in the trees; his command couch dangled more than twenty meters above the forest floor. His radio was out. She had no way to tell whether her XO was alive or dead.

Now it was just her and the hideously scarred beast pacing around each other like a pair of Greco-Roman wrestlers looking for an opening. For several seconds she found herself unable to move her targeting controls. All of her training and discipline, all her decades of military experience, it all vanished like so much flash powder. She registered only the last vestiges of incense ashes smoldering on her dashboard.

The *Awesome's* right-arm PPC leveled in her direction. A crackling, whitish blue glow filled the cannon's barrel. Every hair on her arms and neck stood on end.

Wiping tears from her eyes with her left hand, she triggered her missiles and lasers in a last-ditch effort for redemption. At this range every laser beam struck, every missile found its mark. Holes erupted in the *Awesome's* armor as it staggered backwards.

The chirp indicated her PPC had recycled. With every last amount of fine motor control she could summon, she aimed and fired dead center on the melted hag's face.

Something burst deep inside the machine's bowels. The *Awesome* remained upright just a moment longer before all eighty tons of assault 'Mech suddenly fell to the side and struck one of the large tree trunks on its way down.

▲▼▲

Cyril awoke in darkness, surprised to still be alive. How long had he been out? All of his displays were dark.

Unaware of the situation outside the cockpit, he emerged from Wicked Witch's hatch slowly, his auto-pistol drawn, the safety off. The *Vindicator* that shot him down hovered above his prone 'Mech. He expected this enemy MechWarrior to vaporize him at any moment, but the Capellan 'Mech seemed unsteady on its feet, despite him seeing no external signs of gyroscopic or sensor damage. Something must've been wrong with the pilot.

Two more Fifth CRC 'Mechs, a *Thunderbolt* and *Catapult*, pulled up alongside the *Vindicator*, and an infantry-filled truck trailed right behind them.

"Identify yourself, pilot," the *Thunderbolt*'s external speakers boomed in Mandarin then again in English.

Cyril withdrew the burgundy beret from his pocket and situated it on his head. Then he stood up straight and proud to meet his fate like a Grenadier should. "I am Captain Cyril De Milo," he said with an authoritative air, "B Company, First Battalion, First Orloff Grenadiers."

"All right, men," the *Thunderbolt* speaker said, "take him in."

There seemed little point in resisting three 'Mechs and a mechanized infantry platoon with just a single auto-pistol, so Cyril went quietly. The infantry cuffed him and shoved him onto a bench at the back of the truck bed, right next to Carlson and Kramer. Both of his lancemates sported a fair share of bruises, but at least he knew they were alive.

"Kramer?" Cyril whispered as the truck jostled its way back onto the road. "The others—"

"Did they get out?" The sergeant's head drooped to his chest and shook slowly from side to side. "I don't know, sir. That Cappie *Griffin* shot me down before we could reach the rendezvous."

As the truck turned north on the road, a deep rumble shook the ground. Cyril looked up to see a *Leopard*-class DropShip in Orloff colors tearing across the afternoon. The contrail came from the south. From the airfield.

He couldn't help but smile.

MASH theater
Outskirts of Kokonor, Tsinghai
Sarna Commonality, Capellan Confederation
26 April 2996

Major Petrowski stomped his way through the cots of other wounded and stopped at her bedside. "Jiang, goddammit," he growled, "what the hell happened out there?"

Jiang ... that was her name. Lin Wei Jiang. She blinked and stared up at her commanding officer. Words formed in her head, but she had trouble forming them with her lips. Anything she tried to say came out as strangled, half-formed animal noises.

Instead, she fumbled around on her bedside stand to pick up the noteputer and clumsily used her left hand to type out a message.

Had to perform final service for Confederation.

"Refusing to follow orders isn't *service*, Captain," Petrowski said. "I should *court-martial* you for this."

Lin typed as furiously as she could. *Diagnosed with acute Huntington's disease four months ago. Neurodegenerative condition.* More typing. *Should've retired or gone on medical leave, but the Confederation deserved more from me.*

The major's scowl softened into a frown. "Huntington's, huh? Why didn't you tell me back on *Divine Thunder*?" He looked down, took off his cap, and fiddled with it in his hands as he sat at the edge of her cot. "You know, one of my distant relatives had that. It's a shame—doctors told him we used to have the technology to cure that, back in the Star League days." He sighed. "But it doesn't justify throwing two lances at capturing a Grenadiers captain. Commander Park nearly lost an arm when it got tangled in his parachute lines."

Must've been a decoy, Lin typed. *The real HVT must've been in one of the other 'Mechs. One of those that got away.*

Petrowski shook his head. "Doesn't matter. The Leaguers are bugging out. The planet's ours. The chancellor will be happy. First planet the Confederation has regained in a long time, but it'll probably the last one for a while."

Lin twisted the left side of her face into a weak smile. *At least now I'm home*, she typed. *At least now I can die in peace.* "To learn the truth at daybreak and die at eve were enough."

"Confucius, huh? I always figured you for a Daoist." Petrowski sighed and patted her on the shin. "You need anything—anything at all—you let me know, all right?"

Incense, she typed. *Some sandalwood incense would be nice.*

Petrowski's haunted smile met her eyes with sincerity. "I'll see what I can do."

TWISTING IN THE VACUUM

JASON M. HARDY

Above Tomans
Lyran Alliance
13 July 3069

Marcel Webb never ceased to be amazed that a person could be on the exterior of a vehicle hurtling through space at thousands of kilometers per hour and feel like they weren't even moving at all.

But that was one of the great secrets of zero-g operations. You could always tell the rookies by watching how tightly they clung to the hull of a ship when they were on the outside. They'd try to get their mission done, sure, but first and foremost in their minds was the worry that if they lost hold of their ship, they would drift into the endless, cold hostility of space. That fear was awfully tough to avoid.

Until you learned that you could let go. You could completely lose contact with the ship, and instead of being left behind, your inertia would carry you right along next to it. No air resistance to slow you down, nothing to keep you from maintaining your velocity.

Unless, of course, the ship was accelerating. Working outside an accelerating ship was generally something to be avoided.

This ship wasn't accelerating at the moment. Webb's helmet shut out any exterior noise, but the flashing red lights to his right made it clear the ship was on emergency alert, and that usually wasn't a good time to go for a quick speed burst.

He took one more look around. This was a sight he wouldn't ever want to forget. The Star Seeds' DropShip was trying to move backward, ripping apart pieces of an Overlord-*class DropShip, the* Silhouette, *as it did so. The Seeds' DropShip had just rammed the* Silhouette's *bay doors, forcing an opening. That was the cause of the emergency signals flaring all over the* Silhouette. *Soldiers swarmed over the* Silhouette *like ants,*

working their way toward the damaged bay doors, ready to jump in and invade the ship.

This would be a good story, *Webb thought. Even more than that— this is the type of thing that might be taught in military schools, had House militaries condescended to use the techniques of mere mercenaries. But, like so much more about Webb's unit, it was a story that never would be told accurately. It would be a legend, a growing myth that often couldn't be confirmed as fact.*

Triergart
Hamilton
Lyran Alliance
4 February 3072

In some ways this was the best part of being a mercenary—the negotiation, the conception of a job. When everything was possible and everything was perfect. You could imagine how the mission would proceed, and you could picture how everything would go right. Your troops would go where they were supposed to go, be where they were supposed to be, and they would move with grace, with skill, with cunning. The enemy would cooperate, being surprised when they were supposed to be surprised, dying when they were supposed to die. Like a holovid, only real.

Webb, though, had been at this long enough not to be swayed by the lovely visions that spun through his head. Reality was always messier, and reality was where the bullets would fly.

"We, ah, we, of course, do not imagine you operating on the frontline of the, ah, of this particular mission," Steuben said. He reached to his neck, scratched near his collar, then attempted to tuck some of the fleshy folds back under his tight shirt.

Webb let the Lyran administrator squirm a little bit before he answered. "I'm sure you're not saying that we won't be involved in combat operations," he said.

Steuben fidgeted even more, his stomach bumping repeatedly against his metal desk. "No, of course. Well, that is to say—there will, of course, be operations taking place, and should you wish to be involved in the combat—unless you don't want to be—not that I am saying you have complete control over the matter, of course. It will all be spelled out in the contract, which we will negotiate between all of us, and so forth."

There were, Webb knew, several competent individuals within the Lyran Alliance. The fact that he hadn't drawn a meeting with one of them didn't say a lot for his standing with the nation. Such was often the fate of a relatively untested mercenary company.

"And when did you think these negotiations were going to take place?" Webb asked.

Steuben blinked several times. "Well. Ah. Now. Right now. I, ah, I thought that's what we were doing right now. Negotiating."

Webb looked to his right at Geri Krantz, whose eyes had narrowed so much that Webb didn't think she could see anything anymore. He then looked back at Steuben.

"No," he said. "This isn't negotiating. If it was, you'd be actually proposing something instead of trying to back out of sentences two seconds after you start them. All we know right now is that you want us to go to Bountiful Harvest and do something that is in some way associated with the Jade Falcons. Based on your various vague descriptions, there may either be significant weapons fire involved, or we may spend our time sitting in our barracks and playing cards. Which means we're looking at a contract of anywhere from one hundred thousand to two million C-bills a month. If you want me to be more specific, I'm afraid I'll have to ask you to stop waffling and start throwing out some good, hard facts."

"Facts. Right. Of course. I have those." Steuben's fingers danced across the screen of his noteputer. "Right. Okay. Your mission." His eyes lit up. "A ship," he said. "A DropShip."

"What of it?"

"We need you to take it."

Webb leaned back in his chair and folded his hands on his stomach. "Ah," he said.

"Tomans," Steuben said. "Tomans was a, ah, impressive operation. The ship. The DropShip you took. People, people who watched were impressed. Or so we have heard. Accounts, there are different accounts, of course. But all good."

"So you want a repeat performance."

"Well, we, ah, of course we understand that, um, in extraordinary circumstances, difficult operations, cannot do everything the same, ah, we, well." He took a breath. "Yes."

Webb thought he heard Krantz's teeth grinding.

"Okay," he said before she could speak. "Now we know what you want. You have to understand that zero-g operations don't come cheap. I'll need to run this by my accounting and supply people, and

they'll be able to get you a specific proposal later tonight."

"That, that would be fine," Steuben said. "I need to make you understand, of course, that we appreciate the expertise and experience you could bring to this, ah, this thing, but we also are not going to, ah, provide unlimited funds. You are, ah, are not the only mercenaries in the Inner Sphere."

"So you're advising me not to gouge you. Thanks—that's good to know." Webb stood, and Krantz followed his lead. "You'll hear from us by the evening."

▲▼▲

He made Krantz keep herself contained until they were well away from the government building. When they had covered enough distance, all he had to do was turn to her and arc an eyebrow.

"He's an idiot!" she exclaimed. Her face was already red and moved toward purple. "That meeting could have been over in five minutes if he had any idea how to talk!"

"I'm pretty sure we'll be able to convince him to pay us quite well," Webb said calmly. "I think we can afford to let him babble a bit in exchange."

"I don't care what we can *afford*. He's damn annoying."

Webb watched her as they quickly strode across the wide sidewalks of downtown Triergart. She was still fuming, both fists clenched tight. Webb could've used Montague, his XO, right now. Montague had a temper, too, but he tended to act, to *do something* when he was mad, not just fume. But Montague was taking care of things back on the *Sisyphus*, so on the surface Webb was left with Krantz as his acting XO. She was good, of course, but sometimes he needed to be patient and wait for her helpful qualities to come out.

"What else is bothering you about this?" he said. "It must be more than just Steuben's inability to put two words together."

Krantz opened one of her hands. It clenched again almost immediately. "No," she said. "It's just him."

"No it's not," Webb said. He didn't like accusing his people of lying to him, but they usually weren't this obvious.

Krantz, though, didn't seem to mind. In fact, her face was slowly returning back to its normal color.

"There's nothing else," Krantz said. "I'm fine."

Webb was trying to decide if he should say more or let it drop when something hit his shoulder, spinning him a little. A short man, so stocky he was almost a cube, had walked into him. The man was wearing sunglasses and kept his head down.

"Many pardons, Sergeant Zhil," the man grunted as he walked by.

"Who?"

The man stopped but did not turn to face Webb. "Would you like me to say the name louder?"

Webb frowned. "I'm sure it doesn't matter to me."

"If you say so, Sergeant," the man said. He stood still for another moment, then moved on his way without another word.

Webb glanced over at Krantz as the short man walked away. If she had noticed the exchange or cared about it, she gave no sign.

There had been ample time, in the aftermath of it all, to analyze all of the things that could have gone wrong. The first fifty of them had to do with the collision. The collision never should have happened—DropShips were not built for sprinting or quick maneuvers, and any self-respecting pilot should have been able to avoid the whole thing. But there had been a series of circumstances—other craft here, comm calls there, distractions elsewhere—that left the Green Ghosts' ship sitting there, unable to get out of the way.

Then there was the fact that the Ghosts' DropShip—or at least, what was rumored to be the Ghosts' DropShip—was not alone. They had a Jump-Ship there, waiting. Webb and his troops had stayed out of sensor range as long as possible, but once they'd started their approach, there'd been no avoiding it. The JumpShip had a perfect view of them and should have fired whatever defensive weapons they had. But they didn't. The Seeds had managed to stay in the exact wrong position for the JumpShip—any shots they would have taken would have damaged their own DropShip more than the Seeds' ship. So the weapons never fired.

After that came the fact they attempted a ram in outer space. A ram. In outer space. *How could they try that? How could you guarantee who would come out better from that? It seemed all too likely that any ramming action that caused actual damage would result in both ships becoming outer space rubble while all hands were sucked into the blackness.*

But that hadn't happened. All of it, each improbable step, had worked. And Webb couldn't help but build a reputation on what they had done, to go on pretending that the whole thing had been due to skill. When you pulled off a one-in-a-million coup, how could you not take advantage of it?

"They want us to do it again. What we did at Tomans."

"Bloody *hell*." Eddie Bennett stood up and scowled. The expression made him look like a child who was told he couldn't go out for recess. "Anytime we go near a DropShip any more, people will be waiting for us. They'll be ready. Most of the reason we got away with it was they weren't expecting what we did. Without the advantage of surprise, we're dead."

Three of the Star Seeds—Krantz, Bennett, and Conrad Vrane— were crammed into a motel room barely big enough for two. Krantz and Bennett were next to a small plastic table with chips all around the edges. Vrane reclined on one of the narrow beds, legs stretched out, hands behind his head.

"You didn't object so much when we were doing about the same thing over Orestes," Krantz said.

"That was different," Bennett said. "That was, you know, fun!"

"Don't get carried away," Vrane said, speaking slowly. "Orestes was no picnic."

Bennett glared at him, his hands on his hips. "I didn't say it was easy. Just that it was, you know, a job worth doing. Isn't that—" he cut himself off abruptly, looked around the room, then lowered his voice. "Isn't that what we signed on for? Isn't that what we thought we should be doing?"

"Maybe," Vrane said. "But this job at Bountiful Harvest, it could pay more than any hunting party. That might make it worth the effort."

"We're in it for the money now?" Bennett said, forgetting to control his voice.

"We're mercenaries. It's what we do."

Bennett was working himself into a lather, but Krantz cut him off with a quick wave of her arm. She'd had time to collect herself.

"We need the money to pay our way, of course, but we're not in this for maximum profit," she said. The chin at the end of her crescent-moon face quivered as she spoke. "We all know what we're doing here. We're not looking to fight just anyone. We want to fight good fights, and the way things are going, we know who most of the good fights should be against."

"Exactly," Bennett said.

"I want that as much as any of you," Vrane said. "But if no one's offering us the right job..."

"I don't think there's any shortage of the right kind of missions out there," Krantz said. "If we hold out a little longer, we'll find one. It just takes a little effort."

"And not even much of that," Bennett said. "If you take what we know, we can anticipate where the need is going to be. We can be places a step ahead of the demand..." He trailed off when he saw the glares Vrane and Krantz were giving him. "What?"

"We don't know anything," Krantz said firmly.

"We don't?"

"No," Vrane said. "We cannot anticipate any strategies or tactics the BI—that anyone is going to employ. How could we?"

"We—" Then Bennett finally caught on. "Oh. Right."

"I'll talk to Marcel," Krantz said. "Maybe I can make him see sense and get this thing on the right track."

"The trouble is, his right track may not be the same as our right track," Vrane said.

▲▼▲

Over the past few hours, Webb had typed four letters into his terminal several times. Each time he'd deleted the letters before he did anything else.

He should at least do a check, see how much chatter might be out there about those letters, if any. He wanted to believe it had just been a coincidence. Or that he had misheard the name the short man had called him. He knew that wasn't true, but it wouldn't be the first time he allowed himself to believe a lie.

He tried to focus on the contract information for Steuben. The numbers had come together pretty easily, and he didn't think the negotiations would be difficult. Heaven knows the Lyrans had the money. He threw an extra ten percent on top of the estimate just to make sure they came out ahead.

He leaned back and rubbed his eyes. He hoped he could just send all the official documents to Steuben without having to actually talk to the man again. Maybe they could be on their way in a day or two—fast takeoffs were one of the benefits of owning your own transportation.

There was a knock at his door, a splintered plastic sound. Webb walked slowly to the door, his hand ready to grab the gun tucked near the small of his back. He opened the door, saw Krantz, then opened it the rest of the way. But he remained tense.

"What do you want?" he said.

Krantz looked less severe than she had earlier in the day. Her hair and eyes both sagged.

"Do you have a minute?"

"For what?"

"To talk."

"About?"

"About the Lyran job."

"That's business talk. It's not business hours right now."

"Good hell, Webb, does that stick in your ass *ever* budge?"

Webb didn't say anything.

"I know you were working on the contract, and that means it's business hours for you. So let me the hell in."

Webb stepped back, and Krantz quickly walked into the room. He closed the door behind her.

"You understand this room isn't secure," he said.

Krantz looked at the thin plaster walls. "You don't say?"

"People forget sometimes."

"Not when they're around you," Krantz said.

Webb tilted his head and decided to take the remark as a compliment. He made a vague gesture toward a plastic chair, then sat down on the edge of his bed. "What do you want?"

"I—we—want you to rethink this job at Bountiful Harvest."

"Who is 'we'?"

"A number of us."

"Uh-huh. What's the problem? Worried about the risk?"

"That's an insult," Krantz snapped.

"Then what is it?"

"The target," Krantz said. "We'd be wasting our time. We're not—this isn't—what we're doing isn't about the Jade Falcons."

When Webb spoke, he talked slowly, thinking carefully about each word. "I don't recall any conversations where it was agreed we had to focus on a single target."

Krantz slapped the table hard. "Don't play games with me!"

"I'm not playing anything. But you—you and your people—you sometimes act as though everyone here is like you. That we all share your agenda."

"Everyone *should* share our agenda," Krantz said, her face showing a little more life. "When you know what we know. When you understand—this isn't about personal agendas. This is about—this is about—"

"This is about *things we are not going to talk about here*!" Webb shouted. "Look, if you want to keep arguing about this, I'll make you a deal. You pick one of the other offers we have, any one of them, and convince me it's better than this one. Do that, and we won't have to take this contract."

"Other offers? There...there aren't any others. We don't..."

"*Exactly!*" Webb said. "It's do this or sit around in crummy motels for a while longer. Does that help any of us do what we want to do?"

Krantz's voice rose to match Webb's. "If we don't have any offers, it's because you haven't bothered to find any! Planets all over are *begging* for help. It's like you're *avoiding* the people we should be—"

There was a thumping on one wall, then joined by thumping on the other. The neighbors were upset.

When Webb spoke again, he managed to keep his voice level. "This job is right in front of us. It's not that far away, it'll pay us well, and we'll at least be out of these damn motels and fighting someone."

Krantz shook her head. "We've only been in this a few years, and you're already talking like some run-of-the-mill merc commander. Like this is just some ordinary unit."

"Did it ever occur to you that it might be better for us, safer for us, if we spent some time being ordinary? Being run-of-the-mill?"

Krantz's eyes narrowed, and their color seemed to drain away until there was no more blue in them, only grey.

"No," she said. Then she walked out without another word.

Webb stood by the door for a few moments, then walked slowly back to his battered little table. He sat down heavily and looked at his terminal screen, though he wasn't really focused on anything.

It took him a while to notice the gentle blinking in the screen's corner that told him a new message was waiting. He didn't really want to look at it—more than likely, Krantz had thought of a few more points to make and had decided not to deliver them in person. Or worse, it could be Steuben, electronically stammering to him.

He didn't want to look, but out of habit he called it up anyway. And when the message opened, he really, really wished he hadn't.

There was no sender listed, only a subject line, a line two words long. But that was enough to send Webb's stomach down to the floor.

It said *Frederick Zhil.*

He deleted it as fast as he could. As if that would change anything. It didn't stay gone long, though. Within a few seconds, another message appeared on his terminal. Same subject line, same lack of sender. Webb deleted that one quickly, too.

He spent the next few moments staring at the screen, gripping the edge of the table. He felt sweat collecting on his temples. He wanted to vomit. He waited for the screen to change, waited for another message to pop up. He felt a pain in his jaw, and only then realized how hard he was clenching his teeth.

Whoever was out there made him wait a good five minutes. Webb, though, never started to believe the next message wouldn't come. He did not for a moment take hope that the nameless messenger was going to forget him or leave him alone.

When the third message came, it was different. Again, there was no sender listed, but this time the subject line was four words instead of two.

We'll be in touch, it said.

Webb stood up, walked around the table, then sat back down. He drummed his fingers on the table, but the hollow sound only made him feel more nervous.

He struggled to breathe evenly. He had done this before. He had been chased for a long time, sometimes they had gotten close, but they'd never tracked him down. He could get away again.

His legs kept telling him to run out of the room, run as far as he could go. But there were better ways to run.

At least, he thought, *Krantz should be happy that we're not going to Bountiful Harvest after all.*

▲▼▲

It's only when you have something to exploit that you start to understand how many methods of exploitation are out there.

Vrane had wanted them to keep a low profile. "There's no point in advertising how we got this ship, or even that we have *another ship. Do any of us really want our names–or worse, our faces–out there? We keep it silent, we have a better chance of going where we want and keeping a low profile."*

Montague was exactly opposite. "Do you know how many people pull off what we did?" he said. "Look, we all know there's plenty of mercs out there. Okay, there's less than there used to be, but there's still plenty. Anything we can do to set us apart, anything that builds our reputation is good. This builds our reputation. We'd be foolish not to talk about it."

Webb was inclined to agree with Vrane. As mercenaries, their business was to take care of their business–nothing less, but also nothing more if he could avoid it.

But word had way of getting out. And since none of the Seeds openly talked about the assault, the words that emerged were half-truths and inaccuracies that all served to make the capture of the Silhouette *seem even more risky and daring than it really was. On the plus side, though, these distortions made the whole thing ring slightly false, and many who heard the story dismissed it outright.*

Maybe, Webb realized too late, that's how they should have exploited the capture. To build a mythology about themselves that made them seem unreal, phantasmal. A unit that was nothing more than a story or a delusion—like the Green Ghosts, according to some people. But he didn't come up with that idea until too many people were firmly convinced that the Star Seeds were quite real.

▲▼▲

The next morning Webb's eyes were dry and wouldn't focus. He rubbed them constantly as he walked along the nearly empty streets of Triergart. The rest of the city wouldn't think about getting to business for another hour or two, but Webb had gotten lucky. Extremely lucky. He hadn't slept during the night, but his efforts were going to pay off.

He walked into an office building, made it through security, rode an elevator to the eighth floor, and almost wept when the doors opened and he saw the familiar slanted, melded I and E. An organization he could trust, and an organization that could send him a long, long ways away.

He almost couldn't believe his luck in finding an IE office here. He'd learned never to underestimate Interstellar Expeditions' reach, but when he'd sent out his feelers and found out he could contact some IE officials within kilometers of his current location—it was almost too good to be true.

It was enough to make him think that maybe Krantz had been right. If there had been an IE office so close, with people who seemed happy to talk about possible work, maybe he really had been taking the easy way out with the Lyran offer. He had worked with IE long enough to know there was little chance they would offer any easy jobs—the jobs they had available always had two or three weird twists to them. But they also usually came with a fair amount of traveling, which was just what Webb wanted.

The office he walked into didn't seem fully settled yet. It looked as if they'd put a few desks in place, thrown the logo up on the wall, and then waited for the rest of their office supplies to arrive. Webb didn't think of Hamilton as a new frontier for the kind of things IE did, but he knew enough about them to understand that they had the resources to open an office wherever they wanted.

There was a glass door in front of a bland, sterile-looking reception area. The room was dark and empty. Webb reached hesitantly for the door and pulled. It was unlocked. He slowly walked into the room.

"Hello?" he said. He thought he heard a noise coming from the hallway leading out of the room.

He took a few steps forward. "Hello?" he said again.

This time the noise was clearer. It was a voice. "Come on back," it said. At least, that's what Webb thought he heard.

He reached around to the small of his back. His sidearm was where it was supposed to be. He patted it for reassurance, then walked down the hall.

It was a short corridor with only three doors off it. The farthest door, at the end of the hall, had light shining beneath it. Webb walked toward that. When he was in front of it he stopped. He listened for any sign of movement or life.

"It's open," a voice said, clear now, from inside.

Webb opened the door and found where all the missing office items where. They were in this room, packed in boxes stacked against every wall. There were two men in the room, one behind a large steel desk, the other sitting in a plastic chair wedged between stacks of boxes. The one behind the desk was younger, a friendly looking man with sandy hair and light freckles. He smiled and stood as Webb walked in.

"You must be Captain Webb," he said, extending his hand. "I can't tell you how glad I am that you could come by."

Webb shook his hand, then sat in a small, hard chair. "I'm happy to be here," he said. "You have no idea what a relief it is to find you."

The man across the desk smiled. "You're lucky to find us. As you may be able to tell, we haven't been here long. I'm surprised you managed to find us at all."

Webb waved a hand with feigned nonchalance. "I know a few people in your organization, and they're kind enough to point me where I need to go."

"You'll have to give me their names so I can properly thank them. But with all this mutual politeness, I'm afraid I've neglected to introduce myself. I'm Stephen Peterson, and over there is David Michaels."

"I'm happy to meet you both," Webb said. "And of course you already know who I am."

Peterson held Webb's gaze for a moment, then his eyes dropped. His finger traced a lazy circle on top of his desk, and an odd, mischievous smile curved his lips.

"Yes," he said. "Yes, we already know who you are."

Webb heard it. He heard it immediately. The note in Peterson's voice. He stood quickly, turned, ran for the door, waiting for guns to be pulled or alarms to sound or bars and locks to secure the only door he could see to the room.

None of that happened. The way out was clear.

The only thing that happened was that Peterson cleared his throat, then spoke.

"Sergeant Zhil," he said. "Where do you think you can go?"

Webb's hand was on the doorknob, but he didn't turn it. He didn't say anything. He didn't move.

"Let me be clear," Peterson said, his voice as personable and upbeat as it was when Webb walked into his office. "You could walk out of this office without us doing anything and return to your unit. You can keep trying to run. But what you should understand is, you won't succeed. You will be found."

Webb still didn't speak.

"Just think of the past day or so," Peterson said. "We managed to get one operative to greet you on the street. We managed to get messages through to your terminal. And now, here you are. We were able to get you to walk right to us. Can you really believe that you'll be able to run away?" He paused. "Did you ever really believe you'd get away?"

Webb didn't turn around. He didn't want to look at Peterson.

"What do you want?" he asked.

"Well, for you to ask that question, for starters. So I'd count that as progress. Now, what I want next is for you to come back and sit down so we can have a pleasant conversation."

"I'm not making any deals with you. You can arrest me, you can haul me wherever you want, but I'm not making any deals."

"I hope you don't find this too offensive, but it's a foolish man who makes such statements when he doesn't really know what's at stake."

Webb finally turned. Peterson was still at his desk, leaning forward, propping himself on his elbows, and smiling eagerly. Michaels still sat in his chair, implacable.

"So what's at stake?" Webb said.

▲▼▲

Krantz asked everyone in the unit where Webb was, and no one knew. As far as she could tell, she was the last one to see him when she had left his room the previous night.

"He probably went to finish up negotiations with Steuben," Bennett said over lunch. "And it's taking longer than he thought."

Krantz had to agree that any conversation with Steuben would likely take longer than expected, but she still didn't like that explanation. "Webb knows better than to go into a negotiation alone," she told Bennett. "You always need someone to watch your back."

"I'm sure he'll turn up sooner or later," Bennett said, and Krantz was forced to agree. She just couldn't be confident about his condition would be when he finally turned up.

She couldn't talk to Bennett about this. He was a good soldier, competent and quick to follow orders, but she didn't need a good soldier now. She needed someone who might understand some of the twisted paths Webb might have to follow that would take him away from his unit.

If there's one thing this unit knows about, it's twisted paths, she thought sourly, and the one person who seemed the most capable of perceiving life's twists and turns was Vrane. She excused herself from lunch as soon as practical and went to track him down.

She eventually found him in a coffee shop about half a kilometer from their motel. The décor of the place was plain and sparse, but most of the furniture was intact and there was no visible mildew, making it a step up from the motel.

He was browsing a screamsheet when she slid next to him.

"Webb's gone, and it's got something to do with something."

Vrane didn't look up. "No argument there," he said.

"What I mean is, there's a reason he's gone. It's not just random. Something's happening, and it would be good for us to know what it is."

"And how do you think we should do that?"

"I have no idea."

Vrane finally put his screamsheet down. "Let me ask this, then. Which 'something' do you think his disappearance is tied to?"

"I don't know," Krantz said. "We have so many somethings." She looked around the mostly empty room and suddenly felt nervous. "And we probably shouldn't talk about them here."

"Nonsense," Vrane said. "I'm sure we can be vague enough that no eavesdropper, assuming there is one, will actually learn anything of use."

Krantz frowned, but she didn't get up.

"The first question is this—did Webb vanish against his will or because of it?"

Krantz hesitated only slightly. "Against," she said. "He wouldn't just take off on us."

"Really?"

"Are you questioning his loyalty?"

Vrane laughed once, a short bark. "I think it's pretty fair to say that, as a unit, loyalty isn't our greatest strength."

"That's not fair," Krantz protested. "I mean, I know that we're all—well, you know what we are. But to hold that against us—we all had reasons, right? We all did what we did for a reason."

"I'm not arguing that. All I'm saying is that, for each of us, our reasons trumped loyalty. Who's to say that hasn't happened again to Webb?"

"Because this is different!" Krantz said. "This is *us*! He made this unit—*we* made this unit—so we'd have something we could depend on. Something we could be loyal to. He wouldn't just abandon us!"

"You know him so well?"

"Of course!" Krantz said. "I've been serving under him for four years!"

Vrane shook his head, then leaned forward, speaking in a low voice. "You know Marcel Webb," he said. "But you don't know anything about who he *really* is."

▲▼▲

The conversation left Krantz unsettled all afternoon. So when Webb returned that night, looking healthy and oddly nonchalant, she was considerably relieved. Then, almost immediately, she was pissed.

It had been a long afternoon. Steuben had been calling repeatedly, wanting to know the status of the pending contract, and Krantz had nothing to tell him because Webb hadn't bothered to let her know anything. She fended him off as long as she could, trying to invent plausible excuses for Webb's complete unavailability, but finally decided she'd had it with being left in the dark enough, so she decided to break into Webb's motel room.

When she got to the door, though, she hesitated. She was well acquainted with Webb's caution/paranoia, and she knew he'd add extra security to even the most dilapidated quarters.

The basic security he used in these situations included a motion sensor just inside the door that would scream like a banshee unless you punched in an override code within fifteen seconds of its activation. He'd let her see his motion detector plenty of times, but he'd damn sure never let her catch so much as a glimpse of his code.

She could always just shoot the thing. She knew where it was hanging in the room, and she could get a few rounds into it before it

started squawking. Even if it had some sort of failsafe that activated it when it was damaged, enough bullets would shut it up. The gunshots would make a fair amount of noise, of course, but since when where gunshots unusual at a seedy motel?

All of this thinking was rendered moot, though, when Webb sauntered by, nodded his head briefly at her, and walked into his room.

She was right on his heels as he turned off the motion detector. "Where the hell have you been?"

"Something came up," he said without turning around.

"What?"

He walked slowly toward the bed, unbuttoning the top of his dress uniform. He rolled onto the bed and lay on his back with his hands behind his head.

"An interesting offer."

"Another offer? That soon?"

He smiled, and it had a malicious edge to it. "Weren't you the one telling me there was plenty of work out there if I just looked for it?"

"Yes, but—well, I didn't expect you to dig something up so quickly."

He closed his eyes. "I'm resourceful."

"So what's the offer?"

"We're going to Arcturus."

"They're asking us to go to Arcturus?"

"That's not what I said. I said we're going to Arcturus. No asking left to do. It's all set."

"You accepted the mission?"

"Yes."

Krantz leaned forward to get a better look at Webb's face. It was completely impassive. "You accepted without consulting any of us?"

"Yes."

She tried to keep her breathing even. "All right. Well, it must be a good job. What's the mission?"

"That's kind of vague at the moment," Webb said.

"How vague? I mean, is it an escort mission? Defense? Offense? What?"

"I don't know."

Krantz walked over to him, standing over his prone form. "You accepted a job and you don't know what we're going to do?"

"That's right."

She looked down at him. He wasn't very tall, but his compact form looked dense, making the mattress sag beneath him. Or maybe it was just a bad mattress.

"Okay. So who's the employer?"

"That's also a little vague."

"What?"

Webb didn't say anything. He looked like he might be asleep.

"You don't know what we're doing, you don't know who we're working for, and you took the job?"

"That's right."

She was about to explode at him, screaming while pummeling his midsection, but the truth came to her like a jolt of electricity.

"Oh hell," she said.

Again, Webb didn't respond.

"Someone found us. Who?"

"I don't know."

"Damnit, Webb, you know *something*! If one of us, any of us has been exposed, we need to know who it is and what we can do about it. You can do better than just sitting there saying 'I don't know'!"

Webb finally opened his eyes. His face was impassive, but his eyes were hard and determined. He looked directly at Krantz. "No," he said. "I can't."

She sat in the chair next to the bed. "So it's you, then," she said. "Someone's found you."

Webb stayed silent.

"If I knew who was chasing you, that might help," she said. "We could make some guesses about what they want us to do on Arcturus. I'm not saying we can get out of whatever they want us to do, but we can at least go in there with our eyes open."

Webb stayed silent for a long time. His eyes stayed open, but Krantz couldn't tell if he ever blinked.

When he finally spoke, his voice was different. Slightly higher than normal, with an accent Krantz had never heard from him. The more he talked, the lighter he seemed to get. She thought she could see the mattress beneath him lift.

"My real name," he said, "is Frederick Zhil."

▲▼▲

The members of the Star Seeds, like members of almost any mercenary unit, liked to think that someday there would be a definitive history written about them, so that people across the Inner Sphere could learn more about this daring, glorious unit. They wanted their story to be told mainly because they firmly believed that, by the time it was over, it would be one hell of a story.

Each member of the Star Seeds could tell a different tale of how the disparate members of the unit came together, stories whose details differed because of various perspectives and because most of the tellers had no interest in telling the truth about their past. But each of them, when asked to point to the moment the Star Seeds went from a collection of individual mercenaries to a cohesive unit, they would point to the capture of the **Silhouette**.

The atmosphere aboard the DropShip after its capture was continually festive. As a rule, the more Star Seeds soldiers were together in one place, the quieter they became, since the easiest way to keep from saying anything untoward was not to say anything at all. On board the **Silhouette**, though, it was a different story. It was an outsider-free zone, one they had well and truly earned, and unlike their other craft, being on the **Silhouette** didn't feel like being on duty. The soldiers used it for R&R, for all-night bull sessions, and mercs who hadn't said more than ten words in the initial days and weeks of the Star Seeds' existence now talked a blue streak.

That didn't mean they threw caution to the wind. In fact, if anyone had planted a bug on the **Silhouette**, they'd hear a lot more chatter than normal from the Seeds, but they wouldn't necessarily get more information. There were certain topics that the group's members avoided by instinct, and the casual atmosphere of the DropShip wasn't enough to override that.

But there was one morning, after a long, rowdy night on the grav deck, that Krantz found herself talking to Betsy Poole and Vikram Apsara. They were basking in the reflective glow that comes from being the last ones standing after a strenuous party. The conversation didn't follow a clear path, making abrupt jumps and shifts whenever a stray notion popped into anyone's mind.

"This is what I'm telling you," Apsara said at one point. "None of us heard anything! We were all on the outside, clinging to the hull, surrounded by vacuum. Whatever stray air may have leaked from the ship certainly was not enough to carry sound to us. Those inside the bay already—they, possibly, may have heard a noise. Though even that I doubt. The air was leaving everywhere. There was no air, so there was no sound."

"If a DropShip hits a DropShip, and no air is around the crash, does it make a noise?" Poole said, attempting a philosophical tone.

"No. This is what I'm telling you," Apsara said.

"I don't care," Krantz said. "I heard the screech. The metal scraping metal. I heard it."

"You heard some feedback over the comm while you were looking at the wreckage, and your mind made a mistake and called the screech the sound of the metal," Apsara said. "But that's all it was. A mistake."

Poole raised a glass that only had a thin layer of tan liquid remaining. "To mistakes!" she said.

"To mistakes," Krantz said. "Without which we'd have no unit."

"Amen," Poole said and drank what she had left.

Apsara, however, did not drink. "Are you saying this unit is a mistake?"

"No," Krantz said. "I don't think so."

"Then what are you saying?"

"I'm saying mistakes brought us together. Our own mistakes, the things that made us ... eligible to join."

"I do not call what I did a mistake," Apsara said. He lowered his chin, and his eyes almost disappeared in the shadow of his brow.

"Then what do you call it?"

"Courage," he said. "The courage to do what was right when everyone around me was wrong. The courage to stand up for something."

"Well, that sounds all fine and good to me," Krantz said. "But here's the thing—when you're surrounded by people who are all doing wrong, there's a good chance you made a mistake in getting to that particular place."

"You make a rather broad assumption about people and the decisions they are able to make. We do not always have the options we want."

"I'm just calling it as I see it," Krantz said. "Look, don't take it personally. So maybe you made a mistake. We all make mistakes. It's not worth getting bothered over."

"You don't understand," Apsara said.

"What don't I understand?"

"Many things. You think that the way things were for you is the way they were for everyone else. You joined an organization of your own free will and choice, only to find that organization was involved in things of which you wanted no part. So you realized you made a mistake in joining, and so you left. What you do not understand is that many of us do not share your story. We did not choose the company that surrounded us. We did not choose the circumstances of our lives. In the end, the only thing we could do was flee, remove ourselves from those circumstances, and hope to find something better."

"If you want me to understand, you'll have to be more clear than that."

Apsara crossed his arms on the table and leaned forward. Behind him, a maintenance drone whirred as it mopped the floor.

"This is our DropShip, correct? Our new and private space?"

"Yeah, that's right," Krantz said.

"This is the place where we can be open with each other. Where we have built bonds with each other that were not possible in other quarters. Am I not correct?"

"You are right on the nose."

"Good. Then take it as a measure of the seriousness of these things when I tell you that even here, even now, I cannot tell you what you want to know."

He turned to Poole. "What was that you were drinking?" Apsara asked. "You look like you could use another." He took her glass and walked away.

Krantz watched him go. "Isn't he quite the man of mystery," she said.

"Of course he is," Poole said. "He's a Star Seed."

▲▼▲

The man who called himself Stephen Peterson never returned to the office that had briefly served as an Interstellar Expeditions branch. It had served its purpose. As far as he was concerned, the whole planet had done the same and he was finished with it, but he had neither the means nor the orders that would take him off it.

While he couldn't leave, he also couldn't do much work on Hamilton. His primary mission had been accomplished, and all that was left him was to see what he could of this dismal city.

There wasn't much to see. The city held some good restaurants, cultural institutions that didn't interest him, and a handful of parks that were sporadically cared for by slow-moving municipal employees. There were plenty of bars, though, and Peterson figured he could pass whatever time he had left on this planet by sampling each and every drink they had to offer.

He didn't bother trying to be inconspicuous. There was only one person on the planet who might come looking for him, and if Zhil found him, so what? He wouldn't try anything rash. Zhil was too smart to lash out with violence that would do him no good. The only precaution Peterson took was to make sure he never got too drunk. There were certain parts of his brain that should stay alert at all times, to make sure information that needed to be hidden remained that way.

As days passed, he spent more and more times in bars that had large holovid screens, watching more sports and melodramas than he had in years. He even became somewhat attached to a serial called '39 Days, a thriller about a young Combine intelligence officer trying to gather information about the Davion offensive against the Dragon in 3039 and rally the troops for Theodore Kurita's famed counterstrike. Peterson liked the protagonist—when he slipped up, it was out of dedication to his nation and to his House. He generally could only be faulted for overzealousness, and in Peterson's mind that barely counted as a fault at all.

Had Peterson watched the people around him as much as he watched the holovids, he would have noticed a few regulars at the bars he frequented. There was the middle-aged woman who liked floral prints and who drank furtively, her hands covering her glass while her eyes strayed toward the door. There was the rotund young man who glowered whenever anyone switched away from a sports program. And there was the thin, grey-faced man who never ate or drank much, but occasionally held up the small metal box in his hand and pointed it at Peterson.

▲▼▲

"He's O5P," Vrane said.

"Get the hell out of here," Krantz said.

This was a conversation that could not take place in public. Krantz didn't trust any of the unit's motel rooms, either, no matter how many of Webb's gadgets they placed around them. She'd driven Vrane out of town and kept them moving, rolling at 125 kph past the farms northwest of Triergart. There was no distracting scenery, and no one nearby who could conceivably be eavesdropping. Still, Krantz kept the radio loud just to be on the safe side.

"There's no doubt about it," Vrane said. "Order of the Five Pillars, through and through."

"Are you sure about the source?"

"Yeah. As sure as I can be. There's a guy here, Aziz Rakmani, who sees just about every piece of intelligence information that's available. He's got Peterson's face on file, and my snaps were a perfect match. He's clearly labeled as O5P."

"Will Rakmani find out you broke into his files?"

Vrane shot her a quick glare. "Of course not," he said. "If there's anything my past life taught me, it's how to find back doors to systems that their owners knew nothing about. Our former associates left entryways everywhere for us to exploit."

Krantz tapped the steering wheel of her car. "So O5P has something on Webb. He's Combine after all."

"That means at least one of the stories people tell about us is at least partially right," Vrane said. "I should've guessed, though—I always found Webb's liking for sushi suspicious."

Krantz didn't smile. "If they tracked him all the way here, he can't just be an ordinary grunt. He must've been someone important."

"Unless it's not just about him. Maybe it's about all of us."

"What do you mean?"

"I mean that, by himself, he's not important. But as the head of a crack mercenary unit..."

Krantz nodded. "That's why he's free. They want us at Arcturus. So what do we do about it?"

"Why not just go?" Vrane said. "Sure, they're strong-arming us, but it's a job, and given the location it's probably anti-Blake. Isn't that what we've been looking for?"

"Not with this amount of secrecy, it's not. I like to have some idea what the mission is before I go in."

"So how do we find that out? Webb doesn't know, and I'll bet this Peterson character doesn't know either."

"We don't," Vrane said.

"We don't? We go in blind?"

"We go in blind."

Krantz drove silently for a while, staring at the endless fields of dirt in front of her.

"That can't be all you're suggesting," she finally said.

"Not quite," Vrane said. "We need to remember the lessons of the *Silhouette*."

▲▼▲

Krantz stopped outside the door to Webb's room.

"Are we sure this is the approach we want?"

"Yes," said Vrane. The flashing red neon of the motel's sign made Vrane's pale skin look ghoulish.

"You don't think it's too blunt?"

"There's no such thing as too blunt," he said. "It's better than beating around the bush and making him guess what we're after."

"I'm just worried how he's going to react."

"Good. That will make you aware. Now knock on the door."

Krantz knocked.

Webb opened the door so quickly that Krantz worried he had been standing on the other side of it all along, listening to every word she said through the hollow plastic.

"What do you want?" he said.

"We need to talk," Krantz said. "And it needs to happen inside."

"Then I guess you should come in," he said, and let them in to the small room.

Webb sat in the room's only chair, and Krantz and Vrane remained standing.

"So?" Webb said. The close-cut hair on his head looked like sand-paper.

"You're a deserter of the Draconis Elite Strike Team," Vrane said flatly.

Krantz blinked. The individual words, taken by themselves, sounded oddly innocuous. Not the sort of thing that would turn someone into a wanted man.

"And?" Webb said.

Vrane started to talk, but Krantz cut him off. "That's it?" she said. "We throw that in front of you, and that's all you have to say? No denial? No explanation?"

"I haven't heard anything worth responding to yet," Webb said. "Just the repetition of a rumor that's been passed around by sleep-deprived conspiracy theorists."

"Except for that rumor is why we're going to Arcturus. Your contact, this Peterson guy, is a member of the Order of the Five Pillars, and he tracked you down for your extreme violation of correct thought. And he's forcing you into this Arcturus mission."

Webb leaned back a little. "I guess you two have been busy. So—what if that's true? What do you expect me, or you, or anyone else to do about it?"

"It's simple," Vrane said. "Come clean."

"Come again?"

"Come clean. Tell everyone in the unit what's going on and why."

"You want me to tell everyone I'm a fugitive from the Draconis Combine?"

"Yes."

"Are you at all familiar with Combine law enforcement?"

"Look," Vrane said, his voice straining to be patient. "What's the worst anyone is going to do? Expose you? Point Combine agents in your direction? You've already been found! The troops deserve to know what's going on."

"Remember the first days we had the *Silhouette*?" Krantz said. "We stopped being a bunch of people working to hide our past and became a *unit*. You tell everyone what's going on, that effect will come back. You don't have to be the only one watching your ass—we'll all know what to look out for. We'll help."

"You really think we can build that sort of loyalty?" Webb said.

"We were all out there on the *Silhouette* with you," Krantz said. "Wasn't that a big enough loyalty test?"

Webb sat still for a while, not doing anything besides breathing. When he finally spoke, his expression didn't change, but his voice sounded a bit lighter.

"Would I have to make a speech?" he said.

Above Orestes
Draconis Combine
22 September 3070

"We want you. We know who you are."

That's what the ComStar operative had said to Webb when he hired the Star Seeds to go to Orestes, and it nearly gave Webb a heart attack. But then the operative clarified herself.

"We know what your people did at Tomans. Show us that kind of skill and you will see how grateful we can be."

▲▼▲

The unity the Star Seeds had established after the capture of the Silhouette *was tested by the Orestes mission. Some of the soldiers were unabashedly positive–they couldn't leave soon enough. Others were more reluctant.*

"Do we really want to get in the middle of this?" Vrane asked. "I know how some people feel about this, and I understand. But if we plunge right back into that whole thing–I don't know. Maybe it's just too soon. Couldn't we think about it a little more?"

"No," Webb said, and left it at that. The number of offers the Star Seeds received since Tomans had significantly increased, but, for one reason or another, many of them were jobs the unit just couldn't accept. There were some hitches in this Orestes job, but compared to the complications some of the other efforts offered, the Orestes job was–well, possible.

There was no surprise in the kind of job the Seeds were hired to do, but that didn't mean everything went as planned. The trouble started when they approached the True Blood. *The DropShip had already been softened up, and the Seeds were in their suits, drifting through space. Webb still found this part a little nerve-wracking–the sheer size of the lasers flying through space made him feel like an ant, waiting for a giant magnifying glass to focus beams of sunlight on him. Logically, he knew it couldn't happen–they'd*

waited to move until they were out of the main weapons' firing arc. But logic didn't make the huge lights flashing in front of him go away.

But they made it to the hull of the ship, and all was well. The threats he was about to face would be just as deadly as the laser, of course, but smaller. He didn't know why that was comforting, but it was.

Now that they had survived the journey to the hull, the next trick was getting in. Unfortunately for Webb, his two best options weren't available. He couldn't use a ramming attack–they had done that on Tomans, the Blakists would be waiting for that. And he couldn't scare them into surrendering the ship by threatening to blow it up, since extremists were often unimpressed by extreme gestures from others.

That left the air locks. The Seeds divided into four teams, each hitting an air lock. They set explosives to blow at the same time, then moved back, floating in crack coordination. The explosives blew in beautiful synchronicity, and pieces of metal drifted away from the ship. There was no noise, but Webb imagined he could hear klaxons going off in the ship. Once the boarding officially started, the Blakist DropShip moved to a higher level of alert.

But the boarding didn't start where they thought it would be. Webb and the rest of the Star Seeds were already moving away from the blown air locks. If the Blakists had a vulnerability, it was that they didn't think enough about escape.

The Seeds moved as quickly as the slow-motion vacuum would let them, cutting a hole into the bay holding the escape pods, then breaking into one of the pods and using that as their entry into the ship.

It wasn't unguarded, of course, but it might have been the easiest way into the ship. And they moved fast, each person doing their part, cutting here, pulling there, then moving forward. The Blakists were waiting, filling hallways with frangible rounds and not giving a step unless they were dead.

But Webb had learned one more thing from Blakist thought: The side that takes the bigger chance can get the upper hand. The Seeds went into the DropShip with no specialist rounds. They fired lasers and bullets. They drifted through the halls, herding Blakist troops before them, taking shots only when they thought they would hit someone. The vast majority of the time they were right.

The corridors of the DropShip had been dark except for a dim red light. The Blakists wanted it dark, and Webb obliged them. If they shone lights, it would only let the defenders know where they were. The Blakists would have the advantage because they knew their ship, but Webb would give it to them. He had the advantage of his people, gliding through corridors in smooth uniformity.

The Blakists fell back and regrouped at the ship's critical locations, so the Seeds stayed away from those. They went to the forward crew areas, floating fast and slamming doors open, shaking out whatever troops they could and taking them down. The Blakists dug in to their positions, waiting for attacks that they thought would come soon.

It took a long time. There was a lingering worry that some outside Blakist help would come while the Seeds were whittling the inner defenses away, but DropShips didn't just appear out of nowhere. The Seeds had checked carefully, and they knew there wouldn't be a new arrival until long after the fight was over.

The whole thing took almost thirty hours. The Blakists weren't ready to wait that long, but the Seeds were–complete with IV nutrients that kept them well fed in their suits. The Blakists weren't exactly starving when the Seeds burst in on them, but they weren't at their peak, either. When they broke in the bridge, the Seeds actually waited before firing, absorbing the first wave of fire from the Blakists while still moving forward. They held formation and found targets, using lasers, picking targets and taking them down. The Blakists' shots grew increasingly wild, bullet fragments floated in the air, and more and more of them fell. They waited for help that didn't come–the Blakists had become so worried about their individual areas that they forgot to help each other out, and their defense wasn't as coordinated as it would have been if the attacks came a day earlier.

No ranking Blakist formally surrendered the ship to the Star Seeds, but eventually there weren't enough of them left to mount a credible defense. Webb had the survivors loaded into escape pods and shot out of the ship, which was far more generous than many of his crewmembers wanted. Webb watched as some of the prisoners were being led away, and he saw one of them looking around frantically, from Star Seed to Star Seed, his eyes growing wider.

"I know you!" he said. "I know who you are!"

One of Webb's troops–was it Krantz?–kicked the Blakists in the back, pushing him into an escape pod.

"No, you don't," Krantz said.

It made Webb remember how he had almost corrected the ComStar operative when she had briefly seemed to know more than she really did about his unit.

"You don't know who we are," he had been about to say. "All you know is what we can do."

▲▼▲

Afterward, when Webb had gathered everyone together and laid his cards on the table, Vrane and Krantz decided to use Bennett as their test case. He was young, impetuous, and headstrong. If Webb made an impact on him, there was a good chance he'd affect plenty of other troops too.

They were in Vrane's room, eating a pizza they'd picked up on the way back from Webb's meeting. Usually a laconic man, Webb had taken a while to get to the point of what he wanted to tell everyone, and the gathering of the Star Seeds had gone on for an unusually long time.

"The question I have," Vrane said between bites, "is why anyone would leave DEST in the first place. I mean, you don't get to join unless you're pretty committed to the Combine in the first place. And I know the jobs are tough, but it's big-time work—the stuff they make holovids about. Why leave?"

"Maybe it got to be too much for him," Krantz said. "Maybe the jobs were too big."

"Too big for Webb?" Bennett said. "I don't believe it. Have you guys ever seen him intimidated by anything?"

Vrane and Krantz both shook their heads.

"That's what I'm saying. If he was going to back down from things, he wouldn't be leading this unit. He wouldn't have led us onto the *Silhouette*. It has to be something else."

"What?" Vrane asked.

"I don't know," Bennett said. "Something about the lifestyle chafed him, maybe. Look, who was it that tracked him down? Order of the Five Pillars, right? With all their 'think this way, don't think that way' crap? It's bad for plenty of Combine citizens, but how much worse has it gotta be for DEST commandos? They've got all the abilities in the world, but they aren't allowed to think for themselves. What if it were you? Don't you think that might push you to the edge?"

"Maybe," Vrane said.

"That's right," Bennett said. "And that's probably what happened to Webb. Look what he's got now. His own command, where he can do crackerjack, DEST-type missions, but he can think for himself. Be his own man. How much better is that?"

"You sound like you've become pretty pro-Webb since we were talking about going to Bountiful Harvest," Krantz said.

"Why shouldn't I be? The man just stood in front of us and gave enough information to turn him in and probably collect a nice-sized reward. That's trust, isn't it? That's what this unit's been missing, and now Webb's given it to us in spades."

Vrane was nodding slowly. "You're right," he said. "And it can't stop here."

"What do you mean?" Krantz said.

"We may not know why we're going to Arcturus," Vrane said, "but we can guess. We at least know who the target's going to be. We're going to hit the Word. We all know it. I think that's one reason why we weren't that hard for Webb to convince. So what if we tell everyone who we are? Tell them about our past? Put it all out there and tell them just how much we want to hurt the Word of Blake, and why?"

Bennett was looking back and forth quickly, his movements rapid and jerky. "I don't think we can tell anyone everything."

"It's all about trust," Vrane said. "Just think if they knew why we're here. Why we want to fight. They've already fought beside us, they're comrades-in-arms. When we make it personal—and we all have stories that can make any fight against the Word look plenty personal—they'll hate the Word as much as we do. They'll hit them as hard as we want to."

"I don't know," Bennett said.

"What? What don't you know?"

"Telling stories to get people all angry—I don't know about that. Things could get ugly."

Vrane laughed. "Oh really? Then you've forgotten the absolute hell we came from. Things already *were* ugly, as ugly as they could get. Look, you know I haven't always wanted to get back in the middle of all of this, but how much longer can we wait? We have to do something, if only to pay them back. They have it coming. No matter how bad it might get when we strike back at the Word, no matter what we can do to them, it could never be as ugly as what they have done. Time and time again."

Bennett looked even more nervous now. His shoulders were hunched, and his hands were clenched, buried between his legs.

"All right, that's enough for tonight," Krantz said. "You're going to give the boy flashbacks."

Vrane blinked several times. "Right. Right. Sorry, I forgot myself. Got a little carried away."

"Don't worry about it," Krantz said. "We should all get some sleep. Come on, Eddie, get up."

Bennett stood, still looking everywhere, his head darting like a bird trying to keep its eyes on a predator.

"Sorry, Eddie," Vrane said. "Didn't mean to get you all keyed up."

"It's okay," Bennett said, but he didn't stop looking around.

COUNTERATTACK

▲▼▲

Bennett's jerky movements continued until Krantz and he left the room, turned a corner, and were out of sight of Vrane's doorway. As if a switch had been flipped, he walked smoothly and calmly next to her.

Neither spoke until they were in Krantz's car. As soon as they sat down, Krantz started the engine, then pushed a button. The car was filled with white noise.

"Do you understand now?" Krantz said.

Bennett nodded.

"I like Vrane. I understand how you feel. He was an asset, and I know you want him to be an asset again. But you saw how he spoke."

"He will never return," Bennett said, his voice barely above a whisper. "He will never return to the truth."

"Exactly. He is lost to us. And like so many apostates, he will fight against us to his dying breath. Even more strongly than someone who never was a part of us."

"He will need to be taken care of," Bennett said. "Should we do it here? Now?"

"No. Too many people know we were with him." She thought for a bit. "It should probably be on the battlefield. If he dies before then, too many suspicions may be raised. It could interfere with our work. Besides, he will likely be a good source of information. And the more information we learn and disseminate about this Arcturus mission, the better."

"So what do we do until we get to Arcturus?" Bennett asked.

Krantz smiled as she watched the road ahead. "We do what Vrane said," she said. "We work to get everyone in the unit to trust us."

GODFATHER

JASON SCHMETZER

Dunnin Badlands
Berenson
Free Worlds League
24 October 3014

Nathan White struggled to keep his *Rifleman* on its feet as the sixty-ton BattleMech rocked under the impacts of a quintet of long-range missiles. He gave up trying to keep a target lock on the rebel *Trebuchet* and concentrated on staying upright. The *Rifleman*'s broad feet crushed the soft earth to the bedrock with each step. The high-pitched whine of the gyro buried in the Mech's massive chest filled the cockpit as it compensated for the sudden imbalance, and the gentle vibration of a loose cooling fan in his neurohelmet kicked to a higher notch. The 'Mech's computers were feeding from Nathan's own sense of balance to keep the machine upright, and it was a losing battle.

"Get it in gear, White," Sergeant Ramirez said. The sergeant's blocky *Hunchback* stepped closer and grabbed the *Rifleman* by the shoulder. "You got to keep shooting, son. I can't reach the devil." The fifty-ton 'Mech moved back to cover as soon as the *Rifleman* was steady. Nathan took a deep breath to get his bearings before he brought the *Rifleman*'s cannon-barrel arms up again. The sergeant was right.

"On target," he murmured, watching his heads-up display. The *Trebuchet* was about four hundred meters away, edged around a bristly patch of briarwoods while its arm-mounted long-range missile batteries cycled. The medium support 'Mech massed fewer tons than Nathan's *Rifleman*, but just about matched him in armor. The Garret D2j targeting computer painted a red crosshair across the *Trebuchet*'s purple-highlighted frame and then shimmered it to gold. Nathan squeezed the triggers beneath his middle fingers.

On either arm, the lower of the paired weapons barrels exploded into three-meter gouts of flame as the sixty-millimeter autocannons spat depleted uranium slugs downrange. Both streams of high-velocity metal exploded against the *Trebuchet*'s torso armor, staggering the medium 'Mech. Nathan shouted in triumph as the insignia of the Third Marik Militia was erased by his fire, leaving only tattered armor and smoke behind.

"I've got him now," Gerhard called. The rookie MechWarrior brought his forty-ton *Whitworth* next to the *Rifleman* and took a settled stance. Panels on the *Whitworth*'s shoulders flipped open and a score of long-range missiles streaked across the field. One bunch missed to the left, annihilating the briarwood patch, but the other capitalized on the damage Nathan's fire had done, knocking the *Trebuchet* backward and out of sight behind the smoke from the briarwood pyre.

"Nice shooting, children," Sergeant Ramirez said. "Now if you're done using up all the ammunition, can we get out of here?" The *Hunchback* didn't wait for a reply, but instead stepped from cover and started down the well-worn path through the Badlands the rest of the Fifteenth had taken to withdraw from the engagement. They were the last, but the Third didn't seem eager to follow.

Nathan started the *Rifleman* walking backward, splitting his attention between the center and the edges of his 360 degree vision strip in the HUD—between the enemy in front of him and the terrain behind. There was no movement from where the *Trebuchet* had fallen. *Maybe it's down for the count.* Gerhard locked into step beside him. Nathan snorted. That kind of show of bravado after a single barrage was just what he expected from a Regulan.

"Nothing I can scan," the fourth member of Ramirez's lance radioed. Light flashed from the bluffs above them before Magdaleno's *Valkyrie* descended on silvery plasma thrusters. He'd been on overwatch, trying to keep track of the Third's advance while the rest of the lance held the ground. "And I can't locate the *Trebuchet* you guys put down." The *Valkyrie* fell into the reverse step with the other two support 'Mechs while Ramirez's *Hunchback*—and its big Tomodzuru autocannon—watched for trouble in front of them.

"I can't believe we're fighting the Third," Gerhard said.

"Believe it," Ramirez said. Nathan chanced a look at the *Hunchback*'s back in his HUD. The sergeant's voice was rougher than usual. "They're the reason I'm here playing nursemaid to you support troopies instead of in an assault lance where I belong." The *Hunchback*

twisted at the torso and burned at a briarwood copse with its medium laser. Nathan had never seen a 'Mech sulk before.

"The Duke of Procyon sure stepped in it this time," Nathan said.

"Little Anton!" Magdaleno spat.

"Anton Marik didn't kill my lancemates," Ramirez growled. "It was those devils across the way in the Third." The *Hunchback*'s torso swung back to true and the medium 'Mech stalked forward, kicking his speed up another notch. "Keep up, children," he said.

Nathan turned his reverse into an about face and brought the *Rifleman* up to speed, trailing the *Hunchback* by a hundred meters or so. He saw Magdaleno do the same but he was distracted by a short-lived flash of red on his HUD. Throttling back, Nathan began to key the Garret for a more detailed scan. He opened his mouth to call a warning, but Gerhard beat him to it.

"Sergeant?" Gerhard said. The doubt in his voice was palpable, even across the radio. "I had a contact for a moment, but it's gone now." Nathan understood his hesitation. No one wanted to be the one telling Old Man Ramirez he was seeing phantoms.

"The *Trebuchet*?"

"I don't think so," Gerhard said. The *Whitworth* was standing still, leaning forward, as if listening for something. "The MAD registered more than sixty tons, but just for a second."

Nathan chopped his throttle and let the *Rifleman* slow ever further. Sixty tons was more than a *Whitworth* could handle. He waited for the order to turn around, knowing Ramirez would tear him a new one if he did so without orders.

"All right," Ramirez began, when the *Whitworth* exploded.

"Jesus!" Magdaleno shouted. The *Valkyrie* danced away from the cloud of smoke and fire that had been Gerhard's 'Mech a moment earlier. Nathan blinked and saw a green tracery, an afterimage burned into his retina that from a shot he hadn't seen. "Contacts! Big ones!"

"White!"

"I got nothing, Sergeant," Nathan said. The *Rifleman* turned ponderously slow, too slow to bring Gerhard's death into the view out the narrow ferroglass canopy. Red icons were flickering to life on his HUD, relayed by the *Valkyrie*'s computers. Alphanumerics were flickering pasts too quickly for him to decipher as his computers labored to identify the attacking 'Mechs.

"You've got guns, damn it!" Ramirez said. The *Hunchback* started back toward them, closing the distance while the *Rifleman* was still turning. "Shoot something!"

"Mary, Mother of Christ," Magdaleno whispered.

Another explosion rocked the area, knocking several of the bulbous briarwoods loose from their roots. One of the spiky trees crashed into the *Rifleman*'s left leg, smearing foul-looking green sap across the knee actuator. The icon for the *Valkyrie* disappered from Nathan's HUD.

The red icons stayed. The Garret beeped a confirmation at him. Nathan spared a glance at the secondary console to see what his attackers looked like. He squinted, reading the letters from the tiny screen despite the crashing echoes of the *Valkyrie*'s engine cutting loose still ringing through the hollows.

AWS-8Q. Three of them.

"Sergeant—" Nathan began.

"I see them!" The *Hunchback* stopped as it came even with the *Rifleman*. Nathan cranked his torso around, bringing his arm-mounted weapons to bear before the legs and hips could get around to the correct alignment. The D2j was silent, having lost its lock on the Third Militia *Awesome*s.

"There were three of them," Nathan said.

"I know, God damn it!"

"They killed Gerhard and Magdaleno."

"White!"

"What do we do?"

The *Hunchback*'s pilot was silent for several seconds. The *Rifleman*'s MAD scanner pinged a few times but refused to lock on. *They're coming*, Nathan thought. *I'd be coming right now. They have to be coming, and we're all that stands between them and the rest of the regiment.* His hands slipped on the *Rifleman*'s yokes. He wiped the sweat against his shorts, then gripped the controls tighter.

The massive Tomodzuru-series 200 millimeter autocannon on the *Hunchback*'s shoulder—the gun that gave the squat 'Mech its name—ripped a long burst not six meters away from Nathan's cockpit. The *Rifleman* shook nearly as much as it did when he fired his own smaller cannons. He didn't understand how the smaller 'Mech's frame could handle that stress.

A portion of the rock face fell down and blocked the path. It wasn't enough to block it off, but it would slow any pursuers who didn't mount jump jets or climbing equipment. It would slow the *Awesome*s.

"We run," Ramirez said.

▲▼▲

Gerhard and Magdaleno's cots were not the only empty spaces Nathan saw when they reached the regimental bivouac later as night fell. Most of the assembled 'Mechs were beaten and scarred with weapons fire. The Fifteenth's techs had become experts over the last month at scrounging spare parts from the most unlikely places, but they didn't have the surplus to repair battle damage. A cluster of technicians studied Nathan's *Rifleman* as he climbed down the ladder. He saw that they were arguing, but he didn't catch anything but the final outburst.

"Okay, fine... you pull that actuator out of your ass, then!"

The few infantrymen who'd been able to keep up with Colonel Hawkins' command post had the Hawk's CP sewed up tightly. Nathan walked past the dun-colored tent on his way to his billet. He heard arguing from in there, too. Ramirez followed him to the tent, carrying his neurohelmet by one of the shoulder posts. Nathan didn't say anything. He knew they were supposed to be stored in the 'Mechs, but he wasn't going to say anything to the veteran.

Not after he'd lost most of two lances.

They'd barely gotten the flap closed behind them before the assembly horn went off. Nathan was in the middle of prying his sweat-caked cooling vest off. He grimaced as the sweat-glued hairs on his chest tugged as he pulled the heavy coils of tubing away from his body. "Not even a shower," he mumbled.

"Let's go, kid," Ramirez said. He left the tent, still carrying his neurohelmet.

"Look," Nathan said when they reached the cleared area in front of the CP. "It's the Colonel himself." He took a moment to look at the faces around him. There were too few, too few by a quarter at least. Nathan remembered being awed by the size of the capacity-filled auditorium the regiment had last assembled at.

Colonel Jake Hawkins looked tired. He was young for his command, barely into his late thirties, but he'd amassed a record that made his men fight for him. When Nathan had learned he'd been assigned to the Fifteenth, he'd been thrilled. They talked about the Hawk at Allison, and what they said made the cadets envious.

And now the Hawk looked like a man, and a tired one.

"At least it's not Bartlett," Ramirez muttered. Force Commander Bartlett, the regimental operations officer, could plan a campaign with finesse, but needed someone else to explain it to the troops. It was telling that the Colonel was doing the briefing.

"No speeches," the Hawk said. "Yesterday another rebel regiment landed on Berenson. One of Anton's Ducal Guard formations." He paused to let the susurrus of groans and mutters subside before he continued. "Scouts tell me they're already in the field."

"Great," Nathan grunted. Several of the older MechWarriors around him, men who'd normally have been giving him a hard time for being a rookie, just nodded in agreement.

"We're out here," Hawkins said, "because they can't catch us out here. And because the LCCC won't leave us to wither on the vine." A hint of the old fire came back into the Colonel's voice. "You all know we can't let Anton's festering treason grow. It's our job to hold these regiments here, until the Captain-General and his staff can get us reinforcements."

"How are we supposed to hold two regiments?" Nathan didn't see who shouted, but he'd been ready to ask the same question. He saw the same question, the same nodding head, on the men and women around him.

"They've already announced they're not leaving until they've destroyed us," Hawkins said. "They put it on the trivid as soon as they grounded and found us gone." He paused, looking around, as if trying to catch the eye of every warrior and technician present. "They want us to surrender."

Nathan snorted.

"You ask how we can hold two regiments here, when we're already out of supplies and beaten down?" He waited, nodding back to those brave enough to show fear or bravado to their colonel.

"We do it by not letting them catch us."

"If they can't leave," the Hawk said, "until they catch us, then we don't let them catch us. We make them chase us all across Berenson, if we have to, but we keep them here until the Captain-General can get us some support. We make them pay for every casualty they inflict, but we stay out of set-piece engagements. In short," he said, grinning, "we disappear."

Ramirez muttered something Nathan couldn't catch and turned away. He began shouldering his way through the crowd as the Colonel stepped down and Force Commander Bartlett stepped up. Nathan half-turned, looking between his retreating lance leader and the reed-thin operations officer. Bartlett cleared his throat and began pretty much repeating what the Colonel had already said.

Nathan followed Ramirez. He figured it was more important to know what his lance leader was doing than to hear the -3 talk about a

GODFATHER

plan that the captain would explain tomorrow anyway. It was halfway back to the tents when he caught up with Ramirez. He was hunched over, leaning against a trimmed briarwood bole, listening as another figure spoke quietly. Nathan frowned and stepped closer.

"Help you, trooper?" Colonel Hawkins asked.

"White," Ramirez said lowly, "take a hike, hey?"

Nathan froze from where he'd begun straightening to attention. He did an about-face and marched away, carefully keeping his mouth closed until he'd circled the square and made his way into his tent. He sat down on his cot next to the sweat-caked cooling vest and leaned forward, elbows on knees.

"The Colonel," he whispered.

"We got a history," Ramirez said from the doorway. Nathan started and jumped to his feet.

"What kind of history, Sergeant?"

Ramirez looked at him. "Kid, it ain't nothing you need to worry about now." He stepped past Nathan and dropped his neurohelmet on his own cot. He looked at himself in the small mirror tacked to the tent's central upright and pulled down at the bags beneath his red-rimmed eyes. "Me and the Colonel, we go back a ways. Back before the Fifteenth, anyway."

Nathan kept his mouth shut.

"You and me are going out before first light," Ramirez said. He moved his neurohelmet to the tent's floor and lay down. "Get some rest." He folded his hands across his chest and closed his eyes. Within seconds he was asleep.

Nathan just stared at him. After a few seconds he moved to his own cot and laid down, but sleep would not come. He heard the echoes of Magdaleno's engine exploding. His skin remembered the way his *Rifleman* shook when the shockwave of Gerhard's death washed over it. And, when he finally did fall asleep, he dreamed that he had fallen during that first exchange, and that the *Awesome*s had caught up with him.

He woke up before the great flat foot came down on his cockpit.

▲▼▲

Nathan guided the *Rifleman* down the narrow path the *Hunchback* was cutting through the briarwoods. He kept the 'Mech's arms elevated, trying to keep his cannons clear of the cloying sap as the thick spines on the trees bent and snapped and popped. He figured the lasers would just burn through it, but he didn't want anything slowing his rounds down before they got out of the barrel.

Ramirez just put the *Hunchback*'s shoulder down and bowled through. *I guess when you're shooting rounds that big you just don't care,* Nathan thought. Slowing to side-step the *Rifleman* around a clump of crushed spines, Nathan replayed the short briefing Ramirez had given him that morning before they climbed into their 'Mechs.

"Listen," the sergeant had said. "We're going back out where we were yesterday."

"We're what?" Nathan had blurted.

"The Colonel wants us to see if the Third is coming up fast or waiting to salvage."

"Isn't that a job for the recon boys?"

Ramirez had grinned. "It's heavy recon, White. If those rear-echelon pongos are there, you and me are going to shoot them up."

"And if those *Awesomes* are there?"

"Then we already know the way back, don't we?"

Nathan straightened the *Rifleman* and notched his throttle a littler higher to catch up with Ramirez. The briarwoods were thinning. In the deep of the forest they grew incredibly wide as the spines began to intertwine with the trees around them. Near the edges, where animals and men had infiltrated the forest, the spines were smaller from having been broken off. Nathan wondered briefly if the predator these plants had evolved a defense mechanism for had survived human colonization. Certainly nothing he'd seen on Berenson in the past six months warranted such huge spikes.

The *Hunchback* slowed and raised its right fist, the signal for halt. Nathan brought the *Rifleman* to a standstill and hovered his finger over the activate control for his targeting system. The D2j was one of the better BattleMech targeting computers, but operating cold with all the active scanners off was the only way to avoid detection.

Nathan chuckled. *As if you could sneak sixty tons of walking steel up on anyone.*

They proceeded slowly forward, near enough to the edge of the forest that Nathan saw the same slender hollow they'd fought in yesterday. The *Rifleman*'s foot clanged off of something metal. He stopped and hunched the sixty-ton 'Mech over.

It was the hand from Magdaleno's *Valkyrie.*

"No contacts I can see..." Nathan whispered to himself. *But that doesn't mean they're not there.* He waited, watching Ramirez take one hesitant step forward at a time. The *Hunchback*'s arms were leveled,

lasers ready. Ramirez had mentioned he'd not been able to replace the ammunition he spent yesterday. The techs had loaded Nathan's bins while he slept; the Fifteenth had lots of *Riflemen*, after all.

Ramirez lurched forward, pitching the *Hunchback* into a charging run. His lasers flashed, bright red light against something Nathan couldn't see. He jerked the *Rifleman* forward, toggling for his active scanners, swearing as the D2j cycled. There were no targets on his screen, but he was almost to Ramirez's position. He opened his mouth. The D2j pinged.

There were no targets.

Ramirez's gravelly chuckle came across Nathan's headphones, faint and low-powered. "Just seeing if I could flush them out." The *Hunchback* did a slow three-sixty, all scanners going. The *Rifleman's* warning indicators flashed as the *Hunchback's* targeting scanners washed over it and passed by. Nathan did the same, letting the slowly-rotating head of the D2j get a good look in each direction.

"They're not here."

Ramirez turned his 'Mech toward the wreckage of Gerhard's *Whitworth*. Nathan followed. The hulk had already been picked clean. There were shards of useless metal all around and what remained showed the bright marks of having been pried and worked on. "Came during the night, I expect."

Nathan grunted, looking down. Rebel technicians had field-stripped the mostly-intact ankle of the *Whitworth*. It looked as though someone had splayed the foot out, leaving bits of armor and myomer trimmings scattered across the ground. Normally the technicians would police up the scraps—even slag had value if you knew how to use it—but they must have been in a hurry.

"Let's see if we can spot their trail."

Nathan started rotating the *Rifleman's* torso, watching the briarwoods through his canopy. The three-sixty strip was good for spotting movement but not very good for details. He knew the paths around him were the same ones they'd split on their retreat yesterday. There were trundled black rings where the two 'Mechs had exploded and then been stripped, and the distinctive tracks of BattleMech recovery vehicles led back toward the capital.

"Back toward town," Nathan said.

"The haulers, yeah," Ramirez said. "But what about the 'Mechs?" The D2j pinged.

"Contact east, six hundred meters," Nathan shouted. He jerked the *Rifleman's* controls to the right to swing the heavy machine around. He'd let the arms fall after they cleared the briarwoods; now they came back up and locked into firing position, aimed at the contact's estimated location.

"What is it, White?" Ramirez asked. He was moving in a slow predatory circle behind the *Rifleman*, careful to keep out of its line of aim. Six hundred meters was well out of range for anything the *Hunchback* mounted—it was a hundred fifty meters outside of Nathan's effective range—but that didn't mean the contact was alone. *Hunchbacks* fought short-range; *Riflemen* fought long-range; they made a good pair.

"No ID," Nathan said. The computer was flashing schematics again, unable to define one way or another. He looked at the next display over. "The MAD calls it sixty-plus, Sergeant."

"A heavy," Ramirez said. "Or a couple of lights in close formation." The *Hunchback* stopped its circling and angled toward the contact. "Either way, we should be able to take it." Nathan frowned. "I thought this was a recon, Sergeant."

"Recon-by-force," Ramirez said. "Let's go."

Nathan followed Ramirez's lead, staying a little over sixty meters back, far enough that he could fire safely past the *Hunchback*. The sensors refused to lock on to the 'Mech. All he could get it to confirm was the MAD reading. *Sixty tons or more. Gerhard called sixty-plus*, Nathan thought, *before the first* Awesome *got him*. Nathan pre-heated his Magna Mk III lasers and checked that the Imperator-A cannons were loaded.

"I've got the contact," Ramirez said. "Confirm seventy-five tons."

"An *Orion*," Nathan said. "Or a *Marauder*." Both were fairly common heavy BattleMechs in the Free Worlds League, with the *Orion* slightly more so. Either of them would be a tough opponent for his *Rifleman* by itself, and would give the pair of them a run for their money.

"Probably so," said Ramirez. "Trail back a bit. I'm going to see if I can tease him out of the briarwoods."

They stepped out of the hollow and onto a smallish plain, maybe a kilometer square or a little less. Nathan knew he could get the exact area by bouncing a ranging laser across the far walls, but he didn't dare take his attention from his HUD. They'd closed to just over four hundred meters, just inside the outside envelope for his lasers and cannon.

"If he's in your range," Nathan whispered, "you're in his." An old axiom from Allison. He risked a glance away from the contact and through his canopy. The briarwoods were thin and sparse. This valley had been domesticated at one time, then. And then left to fallow.

And now it would host a battle.

"Got it," Ramirez said. The *Hunchback* broke into a trot. "An *Orion*, White."

The D2j hooked into the *Hunchback*'s computer for a moment and swiped some targeting data before it painted a wireframe schematic of the rebel *Orion* on his secondary screen. The schematic was in motion as the enemy moved toward them. The range was almost down to three hundred meters.

"We've got him," Ramirez growled. Anticipation filled his voice, and the *Hunchback* was running full-out to close the range to where he could reach the target with his Tomodzuru autocannon. Nathan nudged the *Rifleman* into a slow run, eager to keep up. *Payback time.*

The *Orion* broke from cover at just over two hundred and fifty meters. A block-shaped 'Mech, it was a common command 'Mech in the Free Worlds. Nathan knew it well from training. He'd piloted one in the simulator. A variety of missiles, medium lasers, and one big autocannon that threw a round as big as both of Nathan's put together. Tough armor. Decent ground speed.

But it was all alone.

Nathan brought his crosshairs over the *Orion* and waited for the golden tone. He prayed for it, and when it came, he squeezed all four of his triggers, index fingers first. The big focusing lenses of the Magna Mk III heavy laser flickered with coherent light for an infinitesimal time before snapping into the tough armor over the *Orion*'s left hip and right torso. The Imperators exploded to life, the muzzle flare igniting a briarwood that stood too close. One stream of high-explosives missed left, but the other dug into the softened armor over the *Orion*'s left leg. The *Orion* staggered under the blows.

"Hoo-ah!" he called.

"Keep it down, kid," Ramirez said. The *Hunchback* slowed for an instant and then disappeared behind a pall of gun smoke. As soon as the cloud appeared it distorted, carried downrange by the torrential passage of the massive rounds. The *Orion* staggered and fell, a massive rent torn in its torso armor. The desultory barrage of LRM's flew a dozen meters over Nathan's head.

"That's for Gerhard, you son of a bitch!" Nathan called. The temperature in his cockpit had just tripled, the air superheated by the waste heat generated by the firing of so many weapons. The cooling vest surged to life, shivering like a chilled lover, icy against his sweat-slicked skin. The edges of his neurohelmet faceplate fogged where he could never quite rub the defogger in all the way.

The *Orion* struggled to its feet while the Fifteenth 'Mechs' weapons cycled. The armor over its left torso was savaged, but beyond that it wasn't terribly hurt. The heavy torso tracked left, unmasking the muzzle of the big Kali Yama cannon. The barrel tracked left, then right, then an instant left, and then fired.

The *Rifleman* shook like a leaf in the wind. Damage alarms clanged to life in the hot air of the cockpit even as the 'Mech's heat sinks labored to vent the heat away. The status indicator changed the armor over the *Rifleman*'s heart from green to yellow. In a single strike the *Rifleman*'s center torso armor had been almost halved.

"Hit him again!" Ramirez shouted. The *Hunchback* broke left, trying to force the *Orion* to split his attention. Nathan recognized the tactic and went right, rotating the *Rifleman*'s torso to the left to keep the *Orion* in his sights. The *Orion* twisted to follow him. Nathan snarled.

The Magna lasers fired again, this time striking the armor over the *Orion*'s right arm and right leg. Nathan held back the Imperators, hoping to cut just a bit from his heat margin, but preheated the smaller lasers in the *Rifleman*'s torso. If the fight got much closer, he'd be too close for the Imperators to target accurately.

The *Orion* struck back with its cannon—which missed, thankfully—and a burst of short-range missiles. Laser light flashed as the pair of medium lasers in the *Orion*'s arms fired, digging into the armor over the *Rifleman*'s legs. Nathan rode it out, holding off returning fire again. He saw movement in his HUD, behind the *Orion*.

Ramirez cut loose, and the *Orion* collapsed like it had been turned off.

"Magdaleno, too," Nathan whispered.

"Hatton, Parker, and Khatib," said Ramirez.

The D2j pinged.

"I see them," Ramirez said when Nathan called the warning. Three contacts at the other end of the valley, just coming active. They'd been hidden while shut down, sheltered by the briarwoods and likely ores in the rock face behind them. The MAD scanner beeped a figure: 240 tons, give or take.

"The *Awesome*s."

"Right in one, kid," Ramirez said. "The *Orion* must have been patrolling while the assault were down. He bought them enough time to power up." The *Hunchback* looked at the other end of the valley for a long moment, then turned away. "Come on."

"We're leaving?" The *Orion* was still smoking on the ground, but the ammunition hadn't cooked off. While Nathan watched the pilot

climbed out of the downed 'Mech's cockpit and drew his sidearm. A flash an accompanying *ping* on the *Rifleman*'s shoulder told Nathan where he'd been shooting. It was a useless gesture, of course, but the intent was clear.

"We can't take those monsters," Ramirez said. "Our job is to get back to the regiment and tell the Colonel that the Third is still in the area. Then he can decide if he wants to poke them in the snout or not."

The *Rifleman* fell into step behind the *Hunchback*. They didn't hurry, knowing that they had greater speed and fewer trees to go through than the *Awesome*s. Unless they made a very grievous mistake, there was no way the assault 'Mechs could catch them. "Poke them?"

"Don't you know to lead something, White?" Ramirez swung the *Hunchback*'s left hand out and slapped a nearby briarwood, snapping several of the spines and splashing sap across the fifty-ton machine's hand actuators. "It's real simple," he said.

"You get in front of something, and you keep poking it with a stick until it chases you."

Nathan looked at the edge of this three-sixty where the *Orion*'s MechWarrior was reloading his pistol. The report of the light-caliber gun just barely crawled through the ferroglass and ceramic armor of the *Rifleman*'s cockpit.

"That's a pretty big poke," he murmured.

▲▼▲

Three days and four hundred kilometers later, they got a new lance-mate. Wallabi drove a big *Quickdraw*. Ramirez told Nathan that he'd been transferred after the rest of his company was sidelined—scrapped for parts, not destroyed by enemy fire—because the *Quickdraw* was fast and because it hadn't taken a single hit. The three of them were sent out along the regiment's backtrail again to try and stir up some attention. The last thing the Hawk wanted was the Third Militia turning away from the Fifteenth.

Wallabi was leading, with Ramirez following and Nathan bringing up the rear. Nathan admired the planning in the placement: Wallabi in front where his mobility would let him escape, with Ramirez and his big gun in the middle to support in either direction, and the *Rifleman* in the rear, able to fire all the way to the front if need be. If they were attacked on the march, they should be able to handle it.

Unless they were taken in one blast like Gerhard and Magdaleno.

The nightmares had been keeping him up. He kept hearing Magdaleno's final curse, imagining Gerhard's scream as his cockpit exploded around him. The instructors at Allison always said you'd go quickly if your 'Mech went up, but the cadets had never believed them. Horror stories filled the spaces between bunks after lights-out, and Nathan's subconscious remembered them all.

"What're we doing out here, Sergeant?" Wallabi asked.

"Poking the Third with a stick," Nathan put in.

"Quiet, kid," Ramirez said. "He's right, though."

"Poking," said Wallabi.

"Poking," said Ramirez.

"Right."

The next half-hour of the march went in comparative silence. They didn't travel in passive mode any longer. They weren't hiding from the Third. They wanted to be seen. They wanted the Third's ops officer to send a recon lance out to see what the noise was.

They wanted to shoot that recon lance up.

Wallabi got the signal first, a pair of 'Mechs at long range. They broke to cover, Wallabi and Ramirez to the briarwoods off the path and Nathan to a high scrub-encrusted rise a couple hundred meters back, taking overwatch. With any luck they'd see the lone *Rifleman* and charge in, trying to get under the Imperators' range.

And then Ramirez and Wallabi would spring the ambush. Nathan and Ramirez had done it several times over the last few days. They had it down, but they'd never worked with Wallabi before.

"Come on in," Nathan whispered. He was careful to keep his voice low enough that the sound didn't activate his microphone. Broadcasting an intercom-strength radio signal would be a sure sign of ambush for the approaching Third. A man talking on his intercoms had someone close enough to talk to. *There's no one here, you murdering devils*, Nathan thought.

The computer identified the 'Mechs, both of them mediums. The trailing 'Mech was another common one, a fifty-ton *Centurion*. The leader was less common in the Free Worlds but found everywhere just across the border in Capellan space: a *Vindicator*. Nathan squirmed in his command couch a little. Both of those 'Mechs mounted weapons that outreached his, and the *Vindicator*'s big PPC was a powerful weapon.

The pair passed the arbitrary boundary the *Rifleman*'s HUD had displayed at four-hundred fifty meters. They were within range of Nathan's guns. And yet they hadn't fired. He zoomed his optics in, trying to find an identifying mark. The paint scheme was unfamiliar in the

details: the colors were right, purple and white with some blue and black, but they weren't the Third's colors.

They were Ducal Guards.

"Zero," Ramirez whispered. Nathan fired, all four barrels, at the *Vindicator*.

One of his lasers missed low, turning a patch of scrub and sand into a steaming plate of glass. The other bit into the thick armor over the *Vindicator*'s right arm. Nathan had just opened his mouth to voice the satisfaction in his chest when his cannon shells all missed. His shout turned to a curse as his cockpit heat soared again, and fresh sweat broke out to wet the dried-salt cake of old sweat on his cooling vest.

The *Hunchback* stepped clear of the briarwoods and leveled his arms. Two ruby lancets of laser light dug at the *Centurion*'s arm and torso, but it shrugged that damage off. The Romanesque head swiveled and the torso began to follow. The right arm with its powerful Luxor autocannon rose toward the *Hunchback*.

Ramirez squeezed his other trigger. The *Centurion*'s leg disappeared beneath the knee.

As the *Centurion* fell, the *Vindicator* was just reacting to the loss of armor from Nathan's solitary hit when the *Quickdraw* erupted out of the woods on silver plasma-flaming jump jets. LRM and lasers snapped down at the *Vindicator*, hurting its armor but not slowing it down. The right-arm-mounted PPC tracked the *Quickdraw* through the air, waiting.

"Watch it!" Nathan called.

The PPC took the *Quickdraw* in the right ankle just as the 'Mech's sixty-ton mass came down on it. The impact threw the limb backwards and out to the side, sprawling Wallabi's 'Mech across ten meters of scrub. Nathan pushed his throttles forward, desperate to get to a range where he could support the fallen MechWarrior.

The *Rifleman*'s autocannons cycled as he negotiated the steep slope. Nathan looked away from the rough terrain for an instant, triggering a long, rolling burst of fire from each Imperator at the *Vindicator*. He watched his rounds track true, tearing at the armor over the *Vindicator*'s right arm and right chest.

And then the *Rifleman*'s left foot crushed a loose rock and the sixty-ton BattleMech fell down. Nathan didn't have time to brace himself, or do more than just squeeze his yokes and his teeth and close his eyes. His head hit something hard when the *Rifleman* landed, and he saw a pinprick of light and then darkness.

He came to when the *Rifleman* rocked under a heavy impact. He shook his head as much as the neurohelmet's restraints would allow. Alarms blared at him from a dozen consoles. Nathan frowned and worked his jaw. All of his teeth felt solid and in place. There was blood in his mouth, but he swallowed it rather than chance opening his faceplate.

"Get up, White!" Ramirez screamed.

It took time to work a sixty-ton BattleMech with no hands to its feet. By the time he did so the battle had moved much closer than he realized. *Maybe I was out longer than I thought.* He searched his damage schematic—battered, but not broken—and then his HUD. Both Ducal 'Mechs were still active, but the *Centurion* was just sitting up, stump of a leg out before it, firing LRMs at anything it could see. Nathan grimaced and worked his controls. It was almost a stationary target.

Cannon rounds blew great divots from the *Centurion*'s chest, knocking it backward to lie flat. Because he had pressed his triggers backwards, the lasers flashed by over the supine *Centurion*'s form, harmlessly turning air molecules to ions. The *Vindicator*, missing its right arm, was running. Wallabi fired a spread of LRMs at the retreating 'Mech, but they missed.

"What'd I miss?" Nathan asked.

"Nothing much," Ramirez said. The *Hunchback* walked over to the fallen *Centurion* and leaned down until the Tomodzuru's barrel was just meters away from the cockpit. "Except a captive."

Wallabi's laughter echoed across the com lines as he loosed another spread of missiles at the fleeing Vindicator. Nathan let the *Rifleman*'s arms fall and began to shake. He'd never been knocked unconscious before. *Did I dream?*

They waited for the salvage crews before returning to base.

And a security team.

▲▼▲

The Hawk was out in front of the tent. It was cooler this time. All the MechWarriors kept their cooling vests on, and the techs wore jackets. The crowd had thinned even more but there was still a great mass of unwashed bodies in a small area. Nathan very consciously didn't consider what he was adding to that amalgam of scents.

"It's working, troopers," the Colonel said. Hawkins had never been a tall man, but his red-hair was particularly wild today and, like everyone else's, matted where sweat had stuck it to his head beneath a neurohelmet. "The Fourth Ducal is down and in the field, yes, but they're spread all to hell and gone."

"So are we!" Wallabi called. Ramirez, next to Nathan, turned and frowned at the man. The *Quickdraw* pilot seemed not to notice. Nathan kept his mouth even and watched the Colonel. They didn't call the man the Hawk just because of his name.

"Horseshit, Wallabi," he said. "We're right here, way the hell out on the sharp end, but all together." He looked around, making each trooper and techie feel like he was talking to them individually. Nathan stood a little straighter when the Hawk looked his way.

"All that's left," someone nearby muttered.

Hawkins clapped his hands and rubbed them together. "Okay, troopers. Only one more bit of news before we all get out of this ridiculous weather. Our canary sang a little more, and we've managed to corroborate it." He paused, grinning from ear to ear. "DropShips burning inbound," the Hawk said.

"And the rebels have no idea who they are."

Nathan cheered as loudly as the rest, but he held his doubts behind his lips. How many DropShips, and did the captured MechWarrior not know, or did no one know? It could just as easily be some rebels coming in dark as reinforcements.

The Colonel thought reinforcements, though. And that was good enough for Nathan.

It was good enough for the regiment.

Ramirez didn't head back toward the tent as the regiment dispersed. Nathan looked toward the tent—toward the cot in the tent, to be honest—and then followed his sergeant toward the 'Mech park. Wallabi went his own way, which suited Nathan just fine. The man was a capable MechWarrior, to be sure, but he was bit of a prick to be around. He'd never last in the lance outside of combat.

"Get some rack time, kid," Ramirez said at the gate.

"What's up, Sergeant?" Nathan nodded to the infantryman at the gate. The Colonel kept a tight guard on duty, and he knew the infantrymen weren't getting much more rest than the MechWarriors.

"It's going to be big one tomorrow," Ramirez said. "I just want to make sure the old girl is ready."

Nathan walked beside him as they moved toward their laager. "Why tomorrow?" He looked at the other 'Mechs as they passed, noting the varying levels of damage. None of them were untouched, not even the Colonel's *Orion*. Henderson's lance, the heavies of the regiment, were well-beaten. Henderson's *Awesome* was missing its left arm and most of the rest of its armor, and what remained was patchwork, but Nathan knew the MechWarrior would be in it come first light, no matter what. It was his duty.

Just as it was Nathan's duty to follow his sergeant.

"They'll know we know about the DropShips now," Ramirez said. "They won't know if we got that rebel jock back in one piece, but if their -2's any good he'll make the assumption. They'll be pushing hard and fast. Mediums and lights out front, trying to tie us up long enough for their heavies to close and smash us."

Ramirez's *Hunchback* stood at the rear of the assembly area, flanked by the *Rifleman* and the *Quickdraw*. There hadn't been armor to replace the nasty PPC scar across the *Hunchback*'s front torso, and the last of the ammunition had been loaded to replace what he'd expended. Nathan eyed the details he could see and grunted under his breath.

There was no more Imperator ammunition for his *Rifleman*. He had half a load, and then he was out.

"What'll we do?"

Ramirez leaned forward and rubbed his hand against the Hunchback's blocky foot. "We'll fight, kid."

"No more running?" If the reinforcements were on the way it would be the smart move, Nathan figured. *If they can't catch us they can't kill us*, the Colonel had said. *Why not just stay away?*

"We're not fast enough anymore. Henderson and his boys, the Colonel. You and me. We can't get away from their faster machines and they won't pull back like they usually do. They'll want to pin us down, and they'll pay whatever price they have to." Ramirez sighed and stepped back. "We should get some rack time," he said.

"How do you know?" Nathan asked, rookie to sergeant.

"It's what I would do," the veteran told him.

▲▼▲

"On the right, White! God damn it, hit that bastard!"

Nathan swallowed his protestations and cranked the *Rifleman*'s torso over. The *Hermes II* Ramirez was screaming about sprinted past, smoke trailing from the horrendous glowing holes Henderson had put in its torso. Nathan swung the *Rifleman*'s right arm out and squeezed his triggers, praying.

The precious autocannon burst chewed the gray-green landscape behind the *Hermes* to craters but the Magna large laser connected, fusing molten armor across the *Hermes*' right knee. The limb locked in midstride and sent the fast medium to the ground, gimped but not crippled.

"Back!" Henderson called.

"Not yet!" Ramirez said. "We need to take that other devil down, too!"

Nathan searched his HUD, ignoring the fresh heat in his cockpit. He had two ready-rounds of Imperator ammunition left and the armor over his left leg was in tatters from a run-in with a *Centurion*'s Luxor cannon. That same *Centurion*, a twin to the one they'd taken down yesterday, was hiding amongst the thin briarwoods and cleft valleys of the gully floor.

"You find him," Henderson said. The one-armed *Awesome* started shuffling backward.

"Dammit, Henderson," Ramirez growled.

"Lieutenant Henderson," the *Awesome's* pilot corrected. "I don't care if you're the Colonel's godfather, I'm getting out of here."

"Fine. White!" The *Hunchback* stalked forward, arms leveled. Its right ankle dragged where a rebel *Griffin* had fused the joint with its Fusigon PPC, but Ramirez didn't let that stop him. He had a target, and a big bullet to shoot it with. "Back me up!"

"On your six," Nathan said. He brought the *Rifleman* out of the stand of briarwoods he'd been using for cover and followed, arms leveled. The ready-lights on both of the Magna Mk IIIs glowed green. He'd husband the autocannon ammunition until he needed it and chance the heat curve.

The *Hunchback* had barely marched a hundred meters before the *Centurion* popped up from a slit valley and loosed a flight of long-range missiles. Ramirez kept walking, accepting the damage to his armor to get in close. The *Hunchback*'s arm-mounted lasers flashed, boiling moisture from the ground to either side of the *Centurion*. Nathan worked his yokes but couldn't get a lock-on. His heat was still too high for chancy shots.

"You're the back door, Sergeant," Henderson sent as the *Awesome* disappeared around the cliff walls. "Don't dawdle."

"Almost done," Ramirez muttered. Nathan pushed his throttle forward and edged to the side, trying for a clear shot. He'd heard the sergeant's voice like that often enough to know what was coming. His left finger reengaged the autocannon loaders.

"On your mark, Sergeant," Nathan said. He brought the *Rifleman's* arms on-target.

The *Hunchback* fired, both lasers again.

Again they missed, flash-heating the ground.

Again the *Centurion* popped up, missiles flying.

Ramirez fired.

Nathan fired.

The *Centurion* died.

"Let's go," Ramirez said. He spun the *Hunchback* in place and lurched into a hobbled run. Nathan grimaced in sympathy as he let the *Rifleman's* arms fall. That much speed would seriously strain the busted ankle actuator. The *Hunchback* passed him, edging just over fifty kph, and kept going. Nathan wiggled himself in his command couch to reseat his rear end, then slammed the *Rifleman's* throttle forward.

Missiles struck his rear armor, rocking him forward.

A rebel *Jenner* stood in the gap where the *Centurion* had died. Nathan swore and jerked at his controls, sending the *Rifleman's* arms traversing up, straight up, and over backward. The HUD shimmered and reformed to focus on his rear quarters. The crosshairs burned blessed gold over the *Jenner's* dome-shaped cockpit. Nathan took up the slack on his triggers.

"I'm bingo," Ramirez said.

"I've got him," Nathan said. The *Jenner* crouched and lurched into motion, but it was too late. The Imperators spat their last rounds downrange and buried themselves in the laser-scarred armor over the *Jenner's* heart. There they exploded, and then exploded again. And again, as the Thunderstoke SRM's ammunition locker exploded into sympathetic detonations.

The *Jenner* came apart in smoke and flame.

The *Rifleman* shut down.

"Damn it!" Nathan shouted to the now-silent cockpit. He began his emergency startup checklist when movement through his canopy caught his attention. A pair of rebel *Stingers* stood there, lasers leveled. "Oh, shit," Nathan whispered. He stabbed the restart button. Nothing.

He stabbed it again.

The left *Stinger* moved, taking a step closer.

The right *Stinger* crashed to the ground, torso armor crushed where Ramirez had put the *Hunchback's* shoulder into it. Ruby-red lasers flashed, cutting at the downed's *Stinger's* armor, and Nathan could imagine Ramirez's swearing without needing to hear it. A lift of the *Hunchback's* left foot and the downed *Stinger* was a salvage item.

"Hoo-ah!" Nathan shouted. Lights blinked in his cockpit as the reactor restarted.

"—stupid son of a bitch!" Ramirez was shouting.

"Sarge!"

"Get moving, kid," Ramirez said. He tried to twist the *Hunchback*

out of the way, but the other *Stinger* caught him with a cutting laser shot. The *Hunchback*'s right arm fell limp, the myomers severed at the shoulder. Nathan slammed his yokes to the side and screamed as the *Rifleman*'s still-sluggish controls responded. His arm came up, the laser charged. He watched the HUD, saw gold. He fired, saw armor run like water.

The *Stinger* crouched and leapt, climbing through the air and escaping over the escarpment. Nathan watched it go and then let the *Rifleman*'s arms come back around to their true facing. He pushed the throttle forward and started moving, still slow but increasing speed. Ramirez limped around to follow, then stopped.

"Sergeant?"

"Keep going, White," Ramirez said. He turned back to the gap, stepped once that way.

"Come on!" Nathan called. "We can make it back to the regiment."

"You go," Ramirez said. He crossed his functional arm across the *Hunchback*'s chest. Just as he finished the motion a brilliant blue-white streamer of charged particles struck the *Hunchback*, knocking it back a step. Then another, knocking it back a step further. Nathan heard Ramirez grunt.

The third PPC bolt knocked the *Hunchback* flat.

A rebel *Awesome* stepped through the gap, painted in the same Third Marik Militia colors as the phantoms from their previous engagements. Nathan felt his stomach tighten like someone had turned it in a vise. He staggered the *Rifleman* to a halt, turning as he did so.

"Not today," he whispered. The *Rifleman*'s arms began to rise. The lasers were already hot. Nathan brought the crosshairs over the *Awesome*'s massive bulk and held them there, waiting for the arm servos to catch up with the HUD. He started the *Rifleman* forward, toward the fallen *Hunchback*.

"Don't be stupid, Nathan," Ramirez said. The *Hunchback* stirred, raising itself on one arm. "Get back to the Colonel."

"He's already here," a new voice said. The D2j pinged and painted a cluster of green icons on the field behind the *Rifleman*. The lead *Orion* was tagged fifteen-six. It was the Colonel.

"Jake," Ramirez said. "For the love of Christ, get out of here."

"We're done running," the Hawk said.

The rebel *Awesome* twisted slightly to view the new arrivals, and then set itself. The PPC barrels traversed as far as their mounts would allow and aligned on the Colonel's *Orion*. Nathan saw the motion, judged the angle.

"Not today," he said again, and fired, both lasers. Heat soared into his cockpit, more heat than his already-taxed cooling vest could keep up with. He blinked, trying to see through the sudden haze on his canopy to see the *Awesome*.

The eighty-ton BattleMech's titanic armor drank in the Magna's energy and held it. The assault 'Mech rocked gently as the gyro compensated for the lost armor mass and twisted slightly on its torso ring.

"Uh-oh."

Three PPCs fired as one, not the one-two-three sequence Ramirez had felt. All three took the *Rifleman* in the torso, a trio of self-contained explosions that drank his remaining armor like and addict takes his hit. Nathan clutched in his controls, fighting for balance. He swore as the *Rifleman*'s left arm tore free with a wrenching scream of tortured metal. Half his firepower, gone. The *Rifleman* staggered, fell.

"Hit him," Hawkins said.

The *Rifleman* had fallen on its back, and without an arm Nathan had a difficult time rocking the sixty-ton BattleMech to its feet. He saw the whisper-thin afterimages of lasers and the whip-*crack* of PPCs through his canopy, but he didn't spare any attention to his secondary monitors to see how the fight was progressing. His only concern was getting his 'Mech back up and in position to cover Ramirez.

A distant motion caught his eye. Sparkles in the daylight sky, trailing smoke. He stopped moving for a moment and stared, trying to understand what he was seeing. He squinted, and then something clicked in his mind.

"The DropShips!" he called, and jerked the *Rifleman* upright. Once there Nathan took a moment to survey the field.

The Colonel's *Orion* was down but moving, its armor carbon-scored from repeated PPC strikes. The SRM launcher on one hand was a ruin. The rest of the supporting 'Mechs were down, most of them smoking. Henderson's *Awesome* was missing its cockpit. Nathan looked the other way.

The *Awesome* had exploded, but a second had taken its place. That 'Mech was busy kicking Ramirez's *Hunchback*. Laser scarring covered most of its armor surfaces, and it looked like someone had put an SRM into its canopy. The sergeant must have dragged his gyro-shot 'Mech hand over fist with one working arm and then grappled the *Awesome*'s leg.

"Sarge!" Nathan called. He charged the *Rifleman* toward the pair of struggling 'Mechs, remaining arm raised.

"White—" Ramirez began, but that was as far as he got. The *Awe-*

some reared back and released a kick that tore the *Hunchback*'s remaining arm free of the shoulder and sent the fifty-ton 'Mech sliding across the rough terrain. Nathan half-jumped the *Hunchback*'s leg as it whipped past and then stopped, arm leveled, laser pointing.

Exactly one and a half meters from the *Awesome*'s cracked canopy glass. Both 'Mechs froze, and Nathan saw through the polarized ferroglass the rebel MechWarrior freeze and then lift his hands from the controls.

Nathan exhaled a breath he hadn't realize he was holding and then drew a ragged replacement. Fire filled his throat, his chest, his soul. He felt his upper lip twitch, draw back into a snarl. His finger tensed.

"Gerhard," he whispered.

He fired. The *Awesome* collapsed.

"Magdaleno," he said, a few moments later. He lowered the *Rifleman*'s arm and fired again. The heat of repeated firings was bad, but with half his armament gone and no cannon ammunition, it was manageable. The cooling vest was still capable of taking care of that much.

The *Hunchback* didn't move.

"Ramirez," Nathan shouted. He fired again, screamed. He drew the *Rifleman*'s leg back and slammed it forward. He shattered armor, and structure beneath. Still-warm heat sinks exploded like green-goo-filled bombs under the impacts.

"Kid," a voice whispered. Nathan looked to his HUD. A figure waived from the *Hunchback*'s cockpit, still wearing its helmet.

"Ramirez!" Nathan turned his 'Mech away from the fallen *Awesome*. Across the field, the Colonel's *Orion* climbed to its feet.

"Let it go, White," Ramirez said. "It's over."

"But—"

Ramirez's figure collapsed across the *Hunchback*'s battered head.

▲▼▲

Nathan didn't look up when the Colonel excused himself from the field medic and came to stand behind him at Ramirez's cot. He didn't move when Hawk laid a hand on his shoulder, either.

"He'll pull through," Hawkins said.

Nathan grunted. "I heard he was your godfather."

Hawkins laughed. "That'd be Henderson, right? No, he's not a godparent. He was my first sergeant way back when I had my first lance out of Princefield." He stepped to the side and looked down at the craggy face. "Took care of me like a son, though."

Nathan smiled. "Me, too."

Hawkins chuckled again. "It'd piss him off to hear us talk about him like that, you know." When Nathan didn't reply he tapped the MechWarrior's shoulder again. "Take good care of him, Lieutenant."

Nathan looked up. "What?"

The Hawk smiled, the same irascible smile that had gotten him his nickname and his command. "Lots of slots open, White. You're an academy grad. It'll work out." He chuckled again and pointed. "I've given you the best lance sergeant in the regiment, after all." He slapped the new officer's shoulder one last time and walked away, still chuckling. Other wounded smiled when he went past, some of them trying to sit up.

Lieutenant. Nathan sat back on the campstool and tried to imagine it. He wasn't a leader. His leader was lying on the cot in front of him. He stared at that man for a long time, thinking. When he finally left, he knew he'd be watching him still for a while to come.

His sergeant. His teacher.

His godfather.

BLUE WATERS

STEVEN MOHAN, JR.

PART ONE

Monitor-Class Gunboat Orca
21 Kilometers SSW of Target Buoy, Off the Coast of Isla Uno
"Blue Water" (Monthey), Periphery, Two Jumps Anti-Spinward of
New India
30 June 3069

Colonel Janice Annapoulis leaned against the railing of the port bridge wing, feeling the deep *thrum* of the vessel's engines in her bones. She watched the low-slung hull knife through the ocean, churning cobalt water into ribbons of white foam.

They had a two-thirds bell on, making turns for fourteen knots.

Knots. An anachronistic term.

For an anachronistic branch of warfare.

She closed her eyes, enjoying the warmth of the sun on her face, the taste of brine on the air.

She didn't know what alerted her: the near-silent scuff of a shoe against decking, the faint mélange of soap and aftershave and perspiration. Or maybe it was something else, some unnamed sense honed by too many hours of combat.

Far too many.

"What can I do for you, Captain?" she asked without opening her eyes.

She heard the shrug in the boy's voice. *The boy.* "Just wondering if there was anything the Colonel needed?"

She opened her eyes and turned to look at him. Aaron Roche's employment record claimed he was twenty-six, but she didn't buy it for a second. Like her, he wore cotton khakis and a dark blue ball cap that said "ORCA" in yellow letters. But *unlike* her, he looked too young for the uniform.

He was bent over, arms resting on the railing, mischief in his pale green eyes, a spray of freckles across the bridge of his nose, his ball cap pulled low, like a kid who'd just come in from a sandlot game.

This *kid* was a captain?

"Just taking a moment," she said, "since there's nothing going on."

"Same mistake you groundpounders always make. Just because it's quiet doesn't mean there's nothing going on." He flashed her a lopsided grin. "Ma'am."

She laughed and shook her head. The smile took another few years off his face, if that was possible.

The rating standing the navigation watch stuck her head out of the bridge hatch. "Just took a visual fix, Captain. Crag bears one-nine-two, two four klicks."

"Very well," said Roche smoothly. He glanced at Janice. "Shall we see if we can find something noisy to entertain you, Colonel?"

She followed him through the hatch, dogging it behind her.

The gunboat's bridge was cramped, smaller than a *Union*'s bridge, *much* smaller than the command centers of the blue-water vessels that had once plied the ancient seas of Terra. To the right (*starboard*, Janice reminded herself) was a chart table manned by the navigator. Aft and port was the helm/lee-helm station from where a junior seaman controlled the gunboat's movement. In the center was the captain's station, which was laid out a little like a 'Mech cockpit: displays everywhere, a comms headset, a joystick within easy reach.

But Roche didn't go to his chair right away. Instead, he stepped toward one of the two-meter-square ferroglass ports that looked out on the sea and pressed a pair of binoculars to his face. Janice saw nothing but blue horizon and the tip of Crag, the volcano that was the island's highest point.

Roche must have seemed something more significant because he turned and snapped, "Right full rudder, steady on new course zero five six. All ahead flank."

"Right full rudder, steady on zero five six, all ahead flank, aye, aye, sir," repeated the young man at helm.

The pitch of the engines changed, from low growl to freight train. The boat started to shake. The vibration was suddenly punctuated by a shrill buzz.

"Maneuvering answers all ahead flank," said the seaman.

"Very well, helm."

The sailor's eyes flickered up to the compass repeater mounted above the windscreen. "Passing one-two-zero to the right."

"Belay your headings," said Roche, still scanning the sea.

"Belay my headings, aye, aye, sir."

"What do you see?" Janice asked in a low voice.

Roche smiled but didn't put the binos down. "I see where the enemy is *not*."

Janice wasn't sure what to say to *that*. She tried another tack. "Commodore Kennedy has a funny sense of humor. Anchor the hydrofoils to a defensive position and force the lumbering Monitor to execute a strike."

"She's trying to teach us flexibility," said Roche. "And guile. You never know what you'll find in combat."

You never know what you'll find in combat. Janice said nothing. It was a lesson that Poulsbo and Khon Kaen had taught her well.

Roche was still studying the sea. "Oh, and the hydrofoils won't be anchored."

"Where will they be?"

"One will be orbiting the buoy."

"And the other?"

He flashed an irreverent smile. "Freelancing."

"Six minutes to horizon," called out the rating.

"Very well, navigator," said Roche.

It was one of the few concepts of naval warfare that Janice understood. Right now the Monitor was using the curvature of the planet to hide, but in less than six minutes they were going to pop over the horizon and the radar of the hydrofoil near the buoy was going to paint them.

"Surface contact," sang out the rating. "Desig Sierra-One. Two-eight-four at eight thousand meters. Combat makes it the Skimmer."

Roche glanced back at Janice. "Know where she is?"

Janice lined up the boats in her mind. "Off our port quarter."

"Very good," said Roche happily. "Now here's a harder one. What do we do about her?"

Janice thought. The Skimmer gave up fifty tons and two AC/20s to the Monitor. "Close and kill her," said Janice. It's what she would have done in an assault 'Mech paired against a light machine.

"Hmmm," said Roche. "OK."

Janice waited for him to order the course change. For a full thirty seconds.

She sighed. "OK," she said, "why not?"

"Charging isn't a bad tactic on land, where the terrain might slow a fast 'Mech. But there's no terrain out here—just easy, blue water. And that Skimmer can do nearly 200 kph—that's a lot faster than most light 'Mechs. If we go at her, she'll run circles around us."

"So what are you...?"

He nodded at the chart table.

She glanced at the chart of the island. The buoy was a circled "X" hand-drawn in red pencil. It was located at the mouth of a protected harbor. The float was supposed to represent a command-and-control target. If Roche took it out, Blue Team won the exercise regardless of what happened to his Monitor.

And *Orca* was tracking right in.

Janice nodded, finally understanding. "You're going to let her come to you."

"Bingo," said Roche, finally settling into his chair. "Nice job, Colonel. We'll make a mariner out of you yet."

"Sir, steady on new course zero five six," intoned the helmsman.

"Very well, helm," said Roche.

Janice thought for a moment and then undogged the port hatch, pushing out onto the bridge wing. She saw the Skimmer in a high-power turn, kicking up a long rooster-tail of white water.

Her bow arcing toward the bigger ship.

The Monitor gave up 140 kph to the little hydrofoil. Which meant running flat out the little ship would close to firing range in... three, four minutes.

If Roche didn't turn and fight, the Skimmer was going to hang out in their rear, hitting them with SRMs and raking their fantail with machine gun fire. The lighter craft had the speed to evade the Monitor's return missile fire.

After awhile that was going to get irritating.

What was she missing?

Janice stepped back onto the bridge. The second hydrofoil, a Silverfin, was racing straight for them, closing at nearly 180 kph. She had to. Roche was running flat out for the big prize.

The second hydrofoil's angry white wake pointed back toward the island, rocking the red buoy that was the stand-in for the high-value target. The white light atop the buoy winked on and off as the float rode violent swells.

A computerized voice emerged from a speaker. "Three SRM strikes to Blue One. Starboard quarter. Light damage to armor. Mechanical shock produces light damage to Number One Main Engine.

Reduce maximum speed to five zero kph."

A change in pitch signaled the Monitor's drop in speed. Janice glanced at Roche's wireframe schematic. A section of armor flickered from green to yellow.

"Right hard rudder," Roche ordered.

"Right hard rudder," the helmsman sang out, his voice tight with tension. He spun the wheel all the way around, slamming the rudder against the stops. "Sir, my rudder is right full."

Roche didn't acknowledge the sailor's report. He was glancing between the spinning compass and his tactical display. Until he saw the attack vector he wanted.

"Meet her," Roche roared.

"Meet her, aye, aye," called the helmsman, swinging his rudder left to arrest the boat's turn.

Roche's finger tightened around his trigger and suddenly the turret forward of the bridge turned, its twin AC/20s elevating. And then the world was filled with the angry rattle of 185-millimeter shells.

Even through the sound-deadened bridge, Janice's ears rang. She glanced at the tactical display in time to see the hydrofoil skip away.

"Glancing blow to Red One," announced the computerized voice. "Starboard quarter. Light damage to armor."

Roche frowned.

"Torpedo detonation proximate to Blue One," said the mechanical voice. "Port quarter. Light damage to armor."

Red Two had rushed in to hit Roche while he was trying to bring his main battery to bear against Red One. Janice glanced at the tactical display. The second hydrofoil had already darted away, clearing *Orca's* guns.

Like a wounded lion beset by hyenas, *Orca* was in trouble.

One good salvo from Roche's autocannons would end the contest, but the Skimmer captains were too cagey to let that happen. They were going to dash in, worrying the greater beast with shallow bites, and then dash out again before the great cat could crush their skulls in its terrible jaws.

Orca would die from a thousand cuts.

And they were still a good five, six klicks from the buoy.

"Launch jump troops?" she asked.

Roche shook his head. "Those hydrofoils are too nimble. I doubt we could successfully board even one. And every armored trooper that hits the water will sink like a stone. I wouldn't risk drowning my marines even if those were real pirates."

Janice shook her head. "Then what's your plan?"

He jerked his head in the direction of the buoy. "Watch."

Janice frowned and raised a pair of binoculars to her face. A trio of white wakes streaked through the water.

Straight for the buoy.

"Torpedoes," she whispered.

The hydrofoils abruptly broke off, racing for the buoy.

But it was already too late.

She dropped the binos and glared at Roche. "You teamed up with *Dolphin*?" She shook her head. Her naval arm had picked up one of the new Leopard Seal-class submarines. "The sub wasn't assigned to this exercise. I read the deployment order myself."

"Commodore Kennedy is teaching us flexibility," he said. "And *guile*."

Janice raised the binoculars again. In time to see the first of the tracks intersect the buoy.

"Blue Two has destroyed the Red High Value Unit," announced the automated voice. "Exercise is awarded to Blue Team."

"It was all a feint," said Janice, "you decoyed the hydrofoils so the Leopard Seal could work her way in."

Roche didn't answer, he just smiled. And not the cute little-boy smile either.

This smile was tight and predatory.

And just like that Janice saw the captain in the boy.

▲▼▲

Janice spent most of the run back on the port bridge wing thinking. When the IE team first discovered this planet they nicknamed it "Blue Water" believing it to be a virgin world, untouched by human hands. But careful analysis of satellite images suggested the presence of ruins on the small continent on the other side of the world. It was beginning to look like this was the lost Rim Worlds planet Monthey, though everyone still called it Blue Water.

Janice used the discovery of the ruins as an opportunity to dispatch her 'Mechs to the small continent to train under the guise of providing "security" for the new dig location.

She hadn't gone with them. Janice was a MechWarrior by training, but if the Periphery Star Guard was going to avoid the kind of beatings it had taken on Poulsbo and Khon Kaen, its people would have to learn new ways.

And so here she was, trying to learn something about naval warfare, while her XO was on the other side of the world trying to meld a heartbreakingly small cadre of veteran MechWarriors and a gaggle of raw recruits into a disciplined unit without her looking over his shoulder.

The Star Guard needed a deeper bench and the only way to get it was to move people out of their comfort zones.

The Guard had been chopped apart during its garrison duty on Poulsbo, and the thrashing hadn't ended there. The Sixth Orloff Grenadiers had hit them again on Khon Kaen where Janice had lost still more equipment. More *people*.

Even a year later, it still hurt to think about.

Which was why she was here in the Periphery, supporting an Interstellar Expeditions dig.

It was familiar work, and it gave her troops enough room to train.

And if the news reports were to be believed she was happy to be tucked away in a boring corner of the Periphery. She didn't want to be anywhere near the Inner Sphere right now.

Not at *all*.

Dockworks, Treasure Cove, Isla Dos

The cove was shallow, five or six meters at its deepest sounding, and filled with water as clear and colorless as fine vodka. Peering into the water was like staring into a tropical aquarium.

Rubbery brown seaweed swayed in the light current, kept afloat by translucent bulbs. A round, ray-like creature rose from the bottom, scattering white sand in a milky cloud. A school of rainbow pseudofish drifted through crystal—until a rugged gray rock *moved*, revealing itself to be a nightmare with a thousand skittering legs. The ambush predator was big, as long as her arm shoulder to wrist, and *fast*. It shot some kind of tethered dart, spearing one of the beautiful pseudofish. All at once the rest of the school was *gone*.

It had all happened in the blink of an eye.

The cove"s waters were beautiful and eerie and strange and wondrous. No Terran transplants here.

And then Janice saw a black shape, jagged and broken, the kind of the shape that could never be mistaken for something natural no matter how thoroughly it was encrusted with barnacle-like creatures.

It was the mangled remnant of a DropShip, a *Union*, that had met her untimely end on this empty, beautiful world.

It was the reason they were all here.

Debris from the *Union* was scattered across the island and the surrounding waters, fragments sunk into white sand like blades buried in flesh. Since the island's foliage showed no signs of damage from the DropShip's traumatic passage the crash had to have happened some time ago. Maybe a century before.

Maybe longer.

The cove closest to the shore was crisscrossed with a network of wooden docks, giving the IE archaeologists access to the underwater debris field. As they recovered artifacts, the dockworks moved farther and farther out into the cove. Before the day was out the piece Janice spotted would be recovered, weighed, measured, photographed, X-rayed, and cataloged.

Orca tied up alongside one of the docks. As Janice stepped off the ship's quarterdeck and made her way down the brow, she realized their employer was waiting for her. Whatever peace Janice had found out on the strange, alien ocean vanished in an instant.

Dr. Richard Wallace, Ph.D. was a tall, humorless man, dressed in coal black coveralls much too warm for the tropical heat, trading practicality for a prissy authority. An aide stood behind Wallace and to his left, obviously there only to underline the doctor's importance.

Wallace's lips were turned down in an expression of disapproval. The scuttlebutt was that *Orca*'s crew had a pool going as to whether Wallace knew how to smile. Janice had it on good authority the odds were running three-to-one against.

Janice was almost tempted to sign up for some of that action herself.

She drew a deep breath and offered up her most professional smile. "Good afternoon, Dr. Wallace. What can I do for you today?"

"You can start by fulfilling your contract," said Wallace coldly.

Behind her, the rating standing quarterdeck watch gasped.

That's just what she needed, rumors of problems with IE spreading through her command. "Perhaps we could take a little walk along the dock," said Janice in a low voice, hoping Wallace would take the hint, "and we can discuss the problem."

Apparently the doctor wasn't good at taking hints. Wallace planted both his feet and snapped: "You left the dig defenseless during your little war games."

Wallace's aide, who'd been watching him with a faint smile, turned to look at Janice. He was Polynesian with copper skin, a broad, handsome face, wavy black hair just long enough to brush the white collar of his white cotton shirt. (Unlike Wallace, he *was* dressed for the tropics. He wore khaki shorts in addition to the shirt.) His brown eyes twinkled with amusement.

"No, sir," she said evenly. "I left *Sei* and *Narwhal* here to defend the crash site. And the remaining naval units were only eighty minutes away, a margin I judged to be adequate since the nearest pirate point is six hours out at a two-gee burn."

The aide looked back at the doctor as if he were curious to see what his boss would say to *that.*

"Still," said Wallace darkly, "something could have happened."

"I seriously doubt it, sir. We've spotted no JumpShips or droppers in-system other than scheduled IE cargo runs. There has been no trouble."

For a moment Wallace looked flummoxed by her argument.

The aide stepped forward. "Surely, Colonel Annapoulis, you must know that the total absence of security problems doesn't prove you're doing an adequate job of providing security," he said in perfect seriousness.

Wallace glanced back at the aide as if he wasn't sure if he were being mocked.

Janice *was* sure. She bit the insides of her cheeks to keep from laughing.

Wallace turned back to Janice. "Ye-es," said Wallace slowly. "I see what Maka means. Your security preparations might be flawed, but if we're unlucky enough to avoid an attack, we'd never know."

Janice blinked. "You're worried about *not* being attacked?"

"It's a question of getting good value for our money," said the aide with a straight face.

"Exactly," said Wallace triumphantly. "We're paying good money for protection and if we're never attacked how will we know you're providing the contracted services?"

Janice could do nothing but stare at the man.

He took her momentary silence as a sign that she'd ceded the conversational initiative. He stepped forward and finally, *finally* lowered his voice. "I believe this wreckage is the most important find of the 31st Century. I am certain that this DropShip once belonged to—"" he paused dramatically, "—the Minnesota Tribe."

"Then you've found the ship's memory core?" she asked.

"No, but—"

Janice couldn't resist needling him. "But I thought the last known sighting of the Tribe was a thousand light years from Blue Water."

"Which is why it will be such an astounding find," said Wallace smugly.

"All excellent points, sir," said the aide smoothly. "If you'd like, I will resolve all your security concerns with the Colonel so you can return to more important work."

"Thank you, Maka." Wallace glared at Janice. "It's good to see *someone* knows their business around here." And then he stalked off.

They watched him go for a moment, and then the aide sighed. "Sorry about that. Apparently when Dr. Wallace was a small child he was dropped on the head. Repeatedly."

"Even a mother can only take so much," Janice murmured.

The aide laughed heartily and reached out to shake her hand. "My name is Maka Launa. It means 'friendly' in Hawaiian."

"And are you?"

"Yes. *And* smart."

She laughed. "Well, that will be a welcome change. If you really are friendly and smart, how did you end up working for Wallace?"

"That's the funny thing." He leaned forward and whispered, "I *don't* work for Dr. Wallace. He's just so obtuse he hasn't realized it yet."

They both laughed.

Maka Launa's smile faded. "Look, I understand why the drills are so important to you. Between Poulsbo and Khon Kaen you lost, what, two-thirds of your 'Mechs? Heavy casualties among infantry, engineers, and naval support. And your armor. . ."

Janice felt her guts twist. Her entire armor battalion had been wiped out. Her mouth tasted dry. *All those people . . .* She swallowed. "You seem to know a lot about my command."

Maka Launa favored her with an easy smile. "I think you'll find that I'm exceptionally well informed. But there *is* one thing I would like to know."

Janice frowned. "What's that?"

"I'd like to know why you're working so hard to rebuild your unit. What's it really for, Colonel? Surely not to serve the next moron with a map of Atlantis?"

Janice opened her mouth, bewildered at the man's sudden hostility. "I don't—"

He snorted. "Is that really how you hold back entropy?" Then he turned and walked away, shaking his head.

Janice found that her hands were clenched into fists. She would have shouted at the man's retreating back.

But she didn't know what to say.

Dig Warehouse, Isla Dos
1 July 3069

Janice's boots clicked on the ferrocrete floor as she strode through

the warehouse. It was a measure of how upset Maka Launa had made her yesterday that she hadn't realized they'd failed to resolve the exercise issue until after he was gone.

Some time during her attempts to sleep the night before she'd decided she was done. Done trying to learn a new warfare discipline, done putting up with Wallace, done dealing with Maka Launa's inexplicable contempt.

She'd been surprised to find that it was the last that really stung.

She shook her head. No more. There was an IE *Mule* touching down on the 3rd to deliver supplies. She would catch a hop to the island where her BattleMechs were exercising. But she couldn't stick Allie Kennedy with the problem of naval drills.

Which meant she'd have to meet again with Wallace. So here she was in the warehouse.

Janice's engineers had put the building up to support the IE dig. It wasn't sophisticated, just a slab of ferrocrete ringed with corrugated aluminum hung off a skeleton of steel I-beams and topped off by a sheet metal roof, but they'd got it up fast. And most importantly, it was *big*.

Big enough to hold *three* DropShips.

Which was good, because the building had to house all the parts of the lost *Union*. Many of the components were immense. Janice walked past a twenty-meter shell of armor that might've come from a gargantuan egg, an engine nozzle scorched black, the mangled barrel of an autocannon. The dropper had been carrying BattleMechs and their severed mechanical limbs littered the ferrocrete floor, each one carefully marked with a card that told where the piece of debris had been collected.

There were smaller, more poignant artifacts, too. A golden locket; the fragment of a blue five-kroner note, a Steiner nose and chin just visible in profile; part of a family photograph showing the faded face of a smiling woman holding an infant in her arms. Janice stopped and picked up the photo.

She swallowed past a lump in her throat.

Real people had died on this DropShip. Including a man who would never return to the smiling woman and the child she cradled in her arms.

"Colonel Annapoulis," shouted Wallace.

She jumped.

"Please do not handle the artifacts."

Janice knelt down and gently placed the photo on the floor. She stood and faced the man. "My apologies," she said stiffly. She drew a deep breath. "I was just...interested in your work."

Wallace scowled. "Well, the *work* will go better if you didn't damage or misplace any of the artifacts."

Janice knew there was little chance of that, but she let it pass. "I *am* sorry, sir. Any luck on locating the memory core?"

"Indeed," said Wallace smugly. "Based on the location of other artifacts, we've been able to project an approximate impact zone. I'm confidant we'll have it in the next day or so."

"Excellent," said Janice. "Sir, I just came by to inform you that we intend to suspend drills at your request." She held out a data cube. "I've put together a schedule of our patrols."

"Yes, yes, very good," said Wallace, who took the cube and shoved it absently in the pocket of another set of officious black coveralls.

Janice suppressed a smile. She seriously doubted whether the good doctor would read what was on the cube or understand it if he did. She and Kennedy had assigned various vessels to check out Isla Uno—where they might just get in a few drills.

But as far as Wallace would be concerned, they'd be on "patrol."

First up was the Monitor paired against the same two hydrofoils. Janice wanted to see how well the young Aaron Roche would do *without* a hidden ally. She'd scheduled the exercise to coincide with the *Mule*'s visit—the time of maximum distraction for the survey team.

She turned away and then stopped and turned back. "Oh, and I wonder if you could give me your aide's full name? He was so helpful in working out this issue." Janice had no intention of speaking with Mr. Friendly again, but if Wallace's aide was nursing some kind of grudge against the Guard, she ought to let Kennedy know about it.

Wallace frowned. "My aide?"

"Maka Launa."

Wallace snorted. "He's not my aide. He's just some damn dig-gypsy. I haven't even been able to find him since yesterday."

Suddenly Janice was very still, listening to the alarms going off in her head. What had the charming Maka Launa said? *I don't work for Dr. Wallace. He's just so obtuse he hasn't realized it yet.*

She'd thought he'd been joking.

Apparently Wallace wasn't the only one who was obtuse.

Dig-Gypsy Camp

Janice made her way through the camp. The camp was a conglomeration of tents that more-or-less ran along the beach, paralleling the cove. Janice guessed there were nearly two hundred. Scientists

probably occupied some of the tents, but the bulk of the camp belonged to the gypsies.

It wasn't unusual for people with a mild interest in archaeology and a major interest in having a good time to accompany Interstellar Expeditions teams. Derisively called dig-gypsies by the real scientists, they were hippies and dealers, grad students, kids on summer break, the bored wives of powerful but inattentive men, hopeless romantics and wild-eyed nuts spouting conspiracy theories. They all had one thing in common.

They were rich.

And willing to make a donation to IE. No one was turned away if their check cleared.

So it was no surprise that most of the tents were large and luxurious—synth leather stretched over steel frames, portable generators and AC units chugging noisily away to provide all the comforts of home while the tent's inhabitants were "roughing it." If Mr. Friendly were truly a dig-gypsy, Janice would have expected to find him in one of these tents.

But there was a darker interpretation of the facts.

Which was why Janice had changed into civies and dark sunglasses, a ball cap pulled down low over her face. A small needle gun tucked into waistband of her jeans, snuggled up against the small of her back, hidden beneath a loose cotton top the color of the sea.

The search was long, hot work carried out in an alien community. But after an hour she found what she was looking for: a small nylon tent spattered with mud, tucked up against a large bush. Even from the outside she heard the sound of unsteady laughter, smelled the sweet odor of marijuana.

It was a dump.

Janice silently slipped her needler free.

She crept up on the small tent and pushed the tent flap back a centimeter with the barrel of her weapon.

The tent's interior was dimly lit except for the sharp blade of light admitted by the shift in the flap's position. A bony young man naked to the waist threw his arm up in front of his face. "Dude. What are you doing?" He held a hand-rolled cigarette pinched between thumb and forefinger. A pretty young blond lay sleeping, her head resting in his lap. There was no one else in the tent. There couldn't be. It was too small.

"I'm sorry," muttered Janice. "I was looking for someone. Must have gotten the wrong tent."

She was already stepping back, when the kid said, "Are you Annapoulis?"

She froze.

"Guy stopped by here. Said you'd be looking for him." The kid held out his hand. At first she thought he was offering her a hit, but then she realized he was holding a data cube. "He said you'd want this."

Mauna Kea-Class Command Vessel Sei
Dockworks, Treasure Cove, Isla Dos
2 July 3069

The *Sei* was a larger and more versatile vessel than *Orca*. The class had been named for a volcano in the Hawaiian island chain back on Terra. Mauna Kea commanded the northern approach to the island of Hawaii. A lookout posted on the mountain could warn of approaching danger.

And so it was true of the Mauna Kea-class command vessels. *Sei* was the flagship of the little Star Guard fleet. She had ten tons on Aaron Roche's Monitor and she bristled with five machine guns, an AC/10, and LRMs to give her some long-range punch. She also possessed all the amenities of a small flagship.

Janice hadn't shifted her command to the *Sei* because it was more comfortable. She had moved off Aaron Roche's little boat because something bad might be happening and she wanted to head it off.

After returning from the gypsy camp, Janice had immediately gone to her stateroom and began reading.

The file stored on the data cube turned out to be profoundly disturbing.

It had been labeled "Jihad Hot Spots" and it seemed to be an INN collection of clippings related to the terrible conflict tearing apart humanity. Two things separated this summary from the others Janice had read. One was that it pulled from news services across the Inner Sphere and even the Periphery. Not a single great house was neglected and many of the Clans and minor houses were included as well.

But even more interesting was the material that *hadn't* come from a recognized news service: the text of an unaired telecast of a Blakist blood match on Solaris VII, a meeting of something called the Council of Gems that seemed to be concerned with a very dark branch of Combine politics, the text of a desperate message from Archon Peter Steiner.

Janice shook her head. It was an extraordinary document. What was it all supposed to mean? Who would want her reading about "Jihad Hot Spots?" She had begun to think of Mr. Friendly as a potential pirate.

Now she wondered if he was something bigger.

But what? She couldn't believe he was a Blakist—why would the Robes tell on themselves? ComStar? LIC? A Federation agent? Nothing seemed to fit.

And how was she to judge the message itself? The material was chilling: Alarion falling silent. A garbled transmission of the nuclear attack on Kathil with a Blakist's ghostly voice rising triumphantly out of the static. Freighter crews begging for their lives as cold-hearted Snow Ravens turned their guns on civilians.

Considering Maka Launa's obvious contempt for the Guard, was this file some kind of elaborate threat? Maybe Mr. Friendly was a Blakist after all.

No matter how she parsed it, Janice couldn't make herself believe that the message was benign.

Her chest tight with tension, she reached for the sound-powered phone by her rack. She wedged the handset between her shoulder and head, clicked the rotary selector to "one," and turned the small handle. The growler emitted the strange whoop that gave it its name.

The person on the other end picked up immediately. "Commodore Kennedy."

"Allie, Janice. Could you come to my stateroom, please?" She drew a deep breath. "I think we need to talk."

Mauna Kea-Class Command Vessel Sei
Dockworks, Treasure Cove, Isla Dos
3 July 3069

Black water lapped gently against the *Sei*'s hull. The beach was dark and quiet, the dig-gypsy camp completely hidden by night. Sodium lights spaced every ten meters feebly illuminated the dockworks with their dirty, orange light.

It turned out that Zero Five Hundred came cold and early even on a tropical island. That was too bad, but then it wasn't Janice who had set the timing for this little dance. She glanced up; saw the white flare of a DropShip diamond bright in the purple sky, five, maybe ten minutes from atmospheric insertion.

COUNTERATTACK

Janice sipped the horrible coffee cradled in her hands and thought darkly of war crimes tribunals. Navy coffee really ought to be against the Ares Convention. She stood on the *Sei*'s port bridge wing, watching the deck crew take up slack in the lines as the vessel pushed hesitantly away from the dock. From the open hatch, she heard Kennedy issuing line and engine commands, trailing a screw to put a side force on the ship that would push her clear of the dock.

Janice watched *Sei*'s line handlers strain under the mild acceleration of the naval vessel. The nylon lines they used to hold their vessel in place wept seawater as the tension wrung them dry. Angry white water churned at the boat's stern

"Cast off all lines," called Kennedy. And then: "All back, one-third. Rudder amidships." The *Sei* swung smoothly out and away from the dock. Kennedy clearly knew what she was doing.

Though there really wasn't much to be worried about. There was a large floating crane moored to the next dock over, and if Janice turned completely around, she could see *Narwhal*'s port running light gleaming like a little ruby chip out beyond the cove's mouth. But other than that there were no navigation hazards. Still, it paid to be careful. Her eyes flickered skyward.

Always.

An angry buzz cut through the early morning darkness. Janice glanced back toward the shore and saw a small skiff skipping over black waves, racing for the *Sei*. She didn't recognize the coxswain, but it wasn't possible to mistake his passenger.

She knew him by his tall, thin frame. By the way he crossed his arms peevishly across his chest. But the biggest give away was the fact that he was *standing* in the small boat, in a position where he could easily capsize the little skiff.

Only one man on the entire planet could be so stupid.

Janice heaved a long-suffering sigh and went down to the quarterdeck to meet her guest.

▲▼▲

Wallace had to climb a Jacob's ladder dropped over the side to come aboard the command ship. Even in the cove's calm waters the ship's rocking threw him against the hull a few times, which was sure to do nothing to improve his mood.

While she waited, Janice watched the IE supply ship come down. It was a *Mule*, round and small in a sky painted lavender by the prom-

ise of day. Friction colored the DropShip orange as it fought the sky, its coppery glow transforming it into a one-pfennig coin.

And then Wallace made it over the side, angry and red-faced.

"I am extremely pressed for time, just now, Dr. Wallace," she said evenly. "But if you'd like to come forward to the wardroom, I can spare a few—"

"You are some piece of work, Annapoulis," he snapped.

Janice nodded at the sailor who'd helped Wallace aboard. The young rating wasted no time in disappearing. The ensign wearing sound powered phones remained at her side, silent and discreet.

Wallace jerked something out of his pocket. "You must think I'm some kind of idiot," Wallace snarled. "Did you think I wouldn't read it? Did you think I wouldn't *understand* it?"

Janice recognized a rhetorical question when she heard it. Plus she didn't think an honest answer would help move the conversation along, so she said nothing.

"You sent the Monitor and the hydrofoils away," Wallace bellowed, so angry that his face had graduated from red to *purple*. "When I gave you explicit orders—"

Mercifully, whatever he was about to say was cut off by the loud rumble of the *Mule* dropping below the sound barrier.

Wallace's mouth sagged into a shocked "oh."

"Your DropShip," Janice shouted over the sudden roar of the vessel's descent. The sky had faded to a slate gray in the east where the *Mule* was coming down. Still, Janice raised a pair of night-vision binoculars to her face, transforming the DropShip into a green sphere, supported by the emerald fire of its exhaust. She only studied the roll-up doors set into the dropper's flanks for a moment.

That was all she needed.

The DropShip was coming down fast. No longer a mere rumble, the *Mule* spoke to the world with the voice of God.

She turned away from Wallace and grabbed the ensign's collar. Pulled his face close to hers, touching her lips to his ear. *"Sound General Quarters,"* she shouted. *"All hands to battle stations."*

▲▼▲

Janice raced down the small ship's port side, nearly flying up the ladder that led to the port bridge wing. At the top, she glanced back. The ensign had raced off to his own battle station. An indignant Wallace was charging for the ladder.

Janice didn't wait for him.

She stepped into the pilot house, where she could just about hear above the roar of the *Mule*'s descent. Allie Kennedy sat in the ship's command chair. She wore a headset, the mic centered over her lips. Kennedy was a small, fiftyish woman with flaming red hair and piercing blue eyes. "Aerospace en route," she said sharply. "Tee minus 17."

Damn. Not fast enough to oppose the *Mule*'s landing. Janice thought pirates might have used the DropShip's arrival as cover to attack either the dig or her BattleMechs on the other side of the planet. She didn't know the supply ship itself was going to be the problem. If she had, she would have tasked her aerospace forces to fight the *Mule* all the way down.

"Alf?" she asked, referring to Captain Alfred Young-Davion, the XO of her BattleMech forces.

"He's combat loading," report Kennedy. "He'll lift in 35 minutes."

Which left her 'Mechs out of the action—unless company was planning to stay for awhile. Janice chewed on her lip for a moment, thinking. If she split her BattleMechs she might be in for a nasty surprise if this was only the first blow of a one-two punch. But there was no evidence of a second attack. She had to deal with the sure threat. "Concentrate on loading one DropShip," she said. "Tell Alf to get me a lance as fast as he can."

Kennedy nodded and touched a button on her comms panel. "Bravo Mike Two, this is November Sierra Actual."

The rest of Kennedy's words were cut off by Wallace's bellow, as he pushed through the closed hatch. *"Colonel Annapoulis I demand to know—"*

She dragged him forward and pointed up at the DropShip dropping out of the blue-gray sky. *"Mules* are cargo ships, doctor. Would you mind telling me why this one has cargo doors sized for BattleMechs?"

"That's ridiculous," Wallace snarled. "That's one of *ours.*"

The *Mule* was dropping slowly now, her engines flaring blue-white as she fought Blue Water's gravity. The vessel was maybe twenty or thirty meters above the ferrocrete landing pad on the east side of the island, showing a bottom-side aspect. She was painted white with a stylized blue "IE" on her underbelly and on each of the cargo doors. "I know it *looks* like yours," snapped Janice. "The pirates probably captured the real supply ship and substituted—"

Wallace jerked his arm free of her grip. "You are *mad,* woman." He was practically frothing at the mouth. "I will see your contract voided. You will find—"

And then at the very moment, one of the *Mule*'s roll-up doors opened and a portly *Javelin* painted in jungle camo came drifting down on a column of golden plasma. The light machine's pilots fired a double flight of SRMs.

Janice counted, one-two, and then explosions rippled through the air, a line of magma-orange fire rose along the main road that joined the landing pad to the warehouse. Dig-gypsies on the beach ran in circles like ants who'd just had their anthill kicked over.

The *Mule*'s guns joined in. Keeping everyone's heads downs, Janice thought.

She turned on Wallace who was staring at the DropShip, his eyes wide and his skin the color of chalk. "But, but—" he gibbered.

She grabbed his shirt front. "*Listen.* Have you found the memory core?"

Wallace blinked like she was speaking Swahili. "T-the memor—W-what?"

She slapped him. Hard. "Tell me where it is. *Now.*"

Wallace gasped. "The cove's m-mouth. We found it early this morning. There's a buoy—" He was pointing.

Janice's gaze followed the line of his arm. *There.* A small, red buoy topped with a white pennant. So she'd be fighting for a buoy again.

Only this time for real.

Janice pushed Wallace away and wheeled to face Kennedy. "Behind the cove, just beyond the mouth," she said. The cove was cee-shaped, with the bowl of the cee pointing east. The beach and the dig-gypsy camp hugged the rounded arc of that cee and the dockworks grew out of it. Beyond the cee's bowl to the east lay the jungle and the landing pad, which made it the threat axis. Janice was proposing they move to just beyond the cee's arms.

Kennedy nodded. "It's a good idea. We can take cover behind the jungle growing along the headlands and still guard the entrance to the cove. They'll have to come to us."

"Do it," Janice snapped.

Kennedy turned to her helm and snapped, "Left full rudder, steady on new course two six four. All ahead flank." Before the helmsman was even finished with his repeat backs, she was talking into her mic, repositioning her other assets.

Wallace looked lost. "I don't—"

Janice drew herself up. "Doctor," she said sternly. "You have belittled me and my command, threatened us with breach of contact, and questioned our competence and integrity." She took a step toward him.

He flinched.

"Nevertheless," she hissed. "My people are going to hold this island for you. All we ask from you is that you *stay out of our way.*"

Wallace shrank back from her tirade, which was exactly what she'd wanted.

Janice turned toward the forward ports, but the *Sei* was turning toward the cove's mouth, *away* from the threat vector. She crossed the bridge, pushed open the hatch, and stood straddling the combing looking out over the starboard bridge wing.

The *Mule* was down and motion in the trees told her that more enemy 'Mechs were coming. Janice swallowed. Even a single BattleMech would be hard for her handful of small naval vessels to handle. It wouldn't take too much firepower before they were overmatched.

Just had to hold on until reinforcements arrived.

She watched as the *Javelin* put a flight of missiles into the warehouse and then turn toward the beach.

Even holding was going to be hard.

The *Javelin* reached the edge of the beach and stopped. Of course. It could slog through the sand, wade through the shallow cove without covering up the SRMs in its torso, but why throw away the light machine's principal advantage: its tremendous mobility.

Not when the big boys were coming.

The *Javelin*'s task was obvious—put the fear of God into the island's defenders while the assault's real muscle safely disembarked. Janice saw a mix of hovercraft and bigger, uglier 'Mechs in her future. The only critical question left unanswered was whether or not the attackers knew where they were going. If they didn't they still had a chance.

But if they knew where the memory core was...

She considered sinking Wallace's buoy, but if the pirates *didn't* already know the memory core's location, turning her guns on the marker would certainly draw their attention.

She glanced left and saw jungle as the *Sei* passed between the two headlands that formed the cove's passage to the sea.

"Colonel."

She glanced back at Kennedy, strapped into her command chair. The commodore nodded at the lone BattleMech standing like a monument at the beach's edge. "What do you want to do about the *Javelin*, boss?"

Janice shook her head. "As long as he's willing to just watch, let's give him a hell of a show."

Kennedy nodded like she'd expected that answer.

"We're overmatched, Allie," said Janice grimly. "They're going to come in hard and fast."

"So we have to keep them off balance," said Kennedy.

"That's affirm." Janice flashed her commodore a wicked grin. "Well, we have a few tricks up our sleeves. Maybe we can give them something to think about."

And right then a Fulcrum hovertank burst from the jungle and raced across the beach, barely slowing when it hit the water.

Its hull pointed straight for Wallace's red buoy.

▲▼▲

The *Sei* shook as Kennedy loosed a flight of fifteen LRMs, followed rapidly by a second. The first wave hit the ocean just forward of the Fulcrum, sending great pillars of water geysering into the air.

The second flight smashed into the tank, shattering armor.

The Fulcrum answered back with its own flight of LRMs, but the *Sei* pulled back behind the headlands and most of the tank's Delta Darts lost acquisition among the intervening trees and exploded harmlessly in the jungle. The others swept past at incredible speed, arced back and impacted the command ship dead astern.

The 85-ton vessel rocked under the impact.

Wallace whimpered, his body pressed up against the bridge's aft bulkhead.

Kennedy nosed her vessel just beyond the arm of land. Janice put a pair of binoculars to her face and watched a Blizzard hover transport emerge from the jungle and skid to a halt next to the *Javelin*.

"They must have divers in the Blizzard," Janice shouted. "They're not going to risk their recovery team until they secure the objective. If we can take it out—"

Kennedy nodded. "Let's push the Fulcrum back and then go get the Blizzard before their big boys take the field."

"Go get the Blizzard?" asked Wallace. "We're not . . . not going into the cove?"

Kennedy hesitated, glancing back at their employer.

"Shut up," snapped Janice.

"But—"

Kennedy leaned forward in her chair toggling a switch on her comms board. "*Dolphin*, torpedoes," she shouted. Multiple tracks streaked through the cove's mouth headed straight toward the hovertank. Like the *Sei* and *Narwhal*, the Star Guard's Leopard Seal was stationed at the cove's mouth.

"I demand you let me off, *now*," Wallace snapped.

"Are you a good swimmer, Dr. Wallace?" Janice pointed at the starboard hatch. "The ocean's that way."

Several Sea Devastator torpedoes streaked past the hovercraft, but at least one detonated directly in front of the tank, punching a hole in the sea. The Fulcrum rocked violently and slid sideways.

Kennedy hit it again with another flight of LRMs.

He shook his head. "I *order* you to send someone else."

"That's great," muttered Janice. "Lead from the rear. Look our contract is very clear. You specify the objective and I determine how to defend it. We *are* going forward—unless you are ordering me not to defend the memory core."

Wallace's mouth worked, but no sound came out.

"That's what I thought," Janice sneered. She turned to Kennedy. "Go."

"All ahead flank," she shouted. "Let's go get that troop carrier." She touched a button on her comms board. "*Narwhal*, give the Fulcrum something to think about."

The little Waterspout-class strike hydrofoil darted into the cove at better than 180 kph and arced toward the hovertank, hitting it amidships with multiple SRM strikes.

It was a dangerous maneuver for the little 25-ton vessel, but the *Narwhal*'s captain, Brian Caster, didn't flinch. He kept on the attack even when the Fulcrum's turret swiveled and ruby light played across the *Narwhal*'s hull, melting armor and slicing into the boat's fragile forward foil strut.

The *Sei* lumbered toward the Blizzard. The little transport was armed with a LongFire V five-pack, but she gave up ten missiles per flight and 60 tons to the Mauna Kea. The Blizzard would lose a long-range duel to *Sei*, and as long the SRM-armed *Javelin* didn't stagger forward into the surf there was nothing it could do to defend its small charge.

And once they had destroyed the pirate's recovery team, this might all be over.

An explosion jerked Janice's attention to the right. A pair of short-range missiles ripped into the Fulcrum's lift skirt. Suddenly the tank was going down on its side, sinking fast, rapidly spinning fans shattering as they sliced into the water. Little *Narwhal* arced sharply away from the Fulcrum, cutting away from sudden burst of shrapnel.

It was a deadly mistake.

Under the titanic stresses of that tight turn, the damaged forward strut tore free. The suddenly unstable *Narwhal* flipped at 180 kph, skipping across the water like a flat stone, tumbling viciously. The hydrofoil smashed itself apart, leaving a long line of debris behind it before the battered hulk finally sank beneath the waves.

Suddenly Janice couldn't breathe.

From the moment the Fulcrum had gone down to the *Narwhal*'s death had taken less than 20 seconds.

There was a horrible crunching noise as *Sei* rode up and over the scattered and broken remains of the *Narwhal* and then the bigger ship was through.

And launching missiles at the Blizzard.

The little hovercraft darted right and returned fire, but the Blizzard was no match for the *Sei*. Janice watched fire ripple along the hovercraft's top and shatter armor along the turret that housed its LongFires.

The *Sei* shook violently as two of the Blizzard's missiles hit home. The blow knocked Janice to the deck; she heard Wallace cry out in pain. The impact had smashed Kennedy against the right side of her chair.

But it didn't stop the commodore from reaching down and firing another flight of missiles and unlimbering her autocannon just for good measure.

Janice pulled herself up.

The *Javelin* moved left, shadowing the Blizzard, but unable to help. The humanoid machine's posture mirrored its pilot's helplessness, as if the 'Mech were a person who could not swim standing at the edge of the pool while his best friend drowned.

Missiles rained down on the Blizzard, again smashing the missile box launcher.

A single second passed.

And then the turret erupted into an orange fireball.

Secondary explosion.

At 151 kph, the Blizzard was fast, but this one time where the machine's speed wouldn't save it. It could juke and run, but it couldn't outrun the *Sei*'s missiles. And if the naval vessel pounded the transport from range, there was nothing the *Javelin* could do.

A feral smile curled across Janice's face. The fight was over.

And then she saw something move out of the corner of her eye. She looked right and her blood suddenly ran cold.

A *Hammer* plunged out of the forest, but unlike the *Javelin*, it didn't stop. It stepped onto the beach, crashing through the dig-gypsy camp.

Wallace drifted up to the forward ports, his mouth sagging in terror.

The *Hammer* plunged into the sea, striking with its LRMs. The light machine was equipped with Artemis IV.

All her missiles ran straight and true.

A terrible rippling concussion shook the *Sei*.

And then a third 'Mech pushed out of the trees. A brawler.

A *JagerMech*.

"Fall back," Wallace shrieked. "For God's sake, *fall back.*"

"No, doctor" Janice snapped. "If we kill their recovery team, they're done. Hit the Blizzard and this can all be over."

But Wallace was shaking his head, his eyes glued to the monster striding out of the jungle. The *JagerMech*'s cockpit sat *below* its massive shoulders, making it look like a Neanderthal. Its broad feet carried it across the sand.

Toward the sea.

"Allie," Janice snapped. *"Fire."*

But at that moment something in Wallace snapped. He lunged at Kennedy, trying to wrestle her out of the chair. "We can't stand up to that kind of firepower," he said. "We *can't.*"

She hit Wallace from behind, trying to pull the scientist off her commodore. But Wallace was big and he fought with a desperate strength. "Just need a few seconds," she said between clenched teeth. "We get the Blizzard and they can't take the core."

It was the *Hammer* that ended the argument. Another round of missiles smashed into *Sei,* this time ripping across the bridge and the forward turret. The ferroglass ports cracked and starred under the missile impacts.

Janice suddenly tasted the sweet-bitter odor of exploded ordinance, heard the grim rattle of the *JagerMech*'s autocannons. The water twenty meters forward of the *Sei*'s bow erupted. The heavy 'Mech was missing, but its pilot was dialing in his range.

And he was moving forward.

Kennedy glanced down at her board and paled. "I have damage to the main turret," Kennedy sang out. "Missile fire control is out."

"How long?" asked Janice as she finally managed to jerk the crazed Wallace off Kennedy and ride him to the deck.

"Five minutes," said Kennedy. She hesitated. "Maybe ten."

Janice closed her eyes. *"Withdraw,"* she barked. She shook her head and said, "Withdraw."

"Withdraw, aye, aye," said Kennedy crisply. "Helm, right full rudder, steady up on new course two eight one, all ahead flank."

Sei heeled as she turned at speed. Janice saw the cove's mouth and the promise of safety drifting into the starboard port. And then the world was suddenly filled with thunder and the deck came up to meet her.

For a second the world went gray. And then the salty taste of blood brought her back.

She staggered to her feet. *"Report,"* she barked.

"Rudder's jammed," shouted Kennedy. "I can compensate with the mains but it'll cost us speed." She hesitated. "I can bring up the reserves."

"You don't have any reserves," Wallace sneered. "You sent them out on exercises."

"No we didn't," snapped Kennedy.

The rattle of an autocannon filtered into the bridge along with the whine of lasers.

Janice wiped her mouth, leaving a bright smear of scarlet on the back of her hand. "Someone on your staff is a traitor, Dr. Wallace," she said coldly. "We thought it best the pirates not know our force strength."

Wallace opened his mouth, but Kennedy cut him off. "Just shut up, doctor." She sought Janice's eyes. "Ma'am?"

There was no way that *Orca* and the two little hydrofoils could stand up to the *Hammer* and the *JagerMech*. She couldn't stop the pirates from recovering the core. They had lost. She wasn't going to throw away the lives of her people just to save face.

"Abandon ship," she said tightly. "Transfer operational command to *Orca*."

Kennedy sucked in a startled breath. "If we can make the cove—"

"Odds?" asked Janice.

"Fifty-fifty," said Kennedy. She swallowed. "M-maybe fifty-fifty."

Which meant a lot worse than fifty-fifty.

"Look," said Kennedy desperately, "Engines and rudder control could be routed to the command chair. One person could stay with the *Sei*. Steer her clear."

"Very well," said Janice.

Kennedy smiled.

Janice put her hands on her hips. "*I* will be that person."

Red roses bloomed on Kennedy's cheeks. "I will not abandon my post," she said fiercely.

"No," said Janice. "You will not. I am making it your personal responsibility to get Dr. Wallace here off this ship."

"But—"

"Go, Allie." Janice shook her head. "I'm done. And you are *not* going to be the last person I send to her death."

Kennedy scowled, but she punched something into her panel and then she grabbed Wallace and shoved him out the hatch.

Hell raging all around her, Janice settled into the command chair to see how much she'd really learned about naval warfare.

▲▼▲

Janice stared at the blue sea between the cove's arms. Maybe two, three hundred meters to safety.

Too far.

Her armor schematic was a fiery patchwork of reds and yellows, both bridge wings had been torn away, and she was down by the starboard quarter where she was taking on water.

She sat in the chair, her back straight.

She only hoped her flight had given Kennedy and the *Sei*'s crew the cover they needed to make it to shore.

Because she was running out of time.

An amplified voice carried into her damaged bridge. "You in the naval vessel, come to a stop or you will be destroyed. You have three seconds to comply."

She glanced down. The *Hammer* filled the center of her rear-view strip. One shot, that's all it would take to end her life. One shot.

But she was not about to surrender the Star Guard's secrets to pirates.

Her hand tightened around her joystick, urging her ship, *her ship,* onward.

"Naval vessel," warned the booming voice of the Hammer pilot.

Janice closed her eyes, her whole existence centered on the feel of the joystick under her hand. How strange to think she wasn't going to die in her 'Mech.

And then she heard something in.

The thrum of naval diesels, the deadly rattle of AC/20s.

She opened her eyes and was shocked to see the *Orca* charging the *Hammer.*

"NO," she cried as the Monitor steamed past her, weapons blazing. The *Hammer* staggered backward under the gunboat's furious assault, jerking left to clear the twin stream of heavy metal abrading its chest armor at a furious pace. Buying time for it to answer with its

trio of Martell medium lasers, spraying ruby fire across the gunboat's bridge.

The lasters left a horrible blackened scar across the *Orca*'s bridge. Unfortunately for the pirate it wasn't enough to put the gunboat down. For a moment the boat's guns tore into the BattleMech and then Janice blinked and the *Hammer* was just *gone*, angry white water rising from the place where the sea had swallowed the pirate machine.

Janice slapped a button on the comms board. "*Orca* Actual, this is *Sei* Actual. Fall back. You are ordered to fall back."

"You can't order me to fall back, Colonel," answered Roche. "You gave me operational command."

"Captain. *Aaron*. Don't do this."

"Don't worry, Colonel," he said, the *boy* said. "We've got you covered."

For just an instant, Janice thought the *Orca* might stand up to the pirate attack.

And then *JagerMech* brought its weapons to bear, cutting into Aaron Roche's little gunboat with its quartet of autocannons and adding its lasers.

The already damaged Monitor bucked and twisted under punishment she had never been designed to withstand.

And as the crippled *Sei* sailed into the safety of the open sea, Janice thought bitterly that she had been right, after all. Allie Kennedy had not been the last person she had sent to her death.

▲▼▲

They had held the island for less than forty minutes, but even in that short time the pirates had managed to stamp their nasty signature on this world.

Stray laser fire had started the jungle burning. At first the Star Guard engineers had tried to put the fire out, but it grew too quickly. Too dangerously.

So they let it burn.

Until trees were black shadows writhing in a raging sea of incandescent orange flame. Until a column of greasy, black smoke stabbed a thousand meters into the cobalt sky. Until the roar of inferno filled Janice's senses, punctuated by the terrified shrieks of trapped animals and the dirty smell of burning flesh.

Janice watched her people move frantically through the dig-gypsy camp, following the terrible path blazed by the pirate *Hammer*, her corpsmen treating those people who could be saved, her infantry bagging those people who could not.

She studied the north side of the dockworks where the Fulcrum had smashed the structure all to hell and where an indifferent sea was now carrying away broken timbers.

But nothing was as terrible as what she sought out in the cove.

A dark shadow in crystalline water.

"Colonel Annapoulis."

Janice closed her eyes and drew a deep breath. She consciously fitted her right hand inside her left at the small of her back. So it wouldn't drift down to her side arm.

"My dig has been disrupted," Wallace snarled, his narrow face turning crimson. "You allowed the memory core to be *stolen*."

"Dig...disrupted?" echoed Janice, clenching her left hand around her right.

"Yes. And I promise. Your incompetence won't go unnoticed."

Janice blinked. "The pirates knocked off your *Mule* and came in broadcasting an IE code. And you interfered with a naval operation. We could've stopped—"

Wallace wagged an index finger in her face. "Don't try to lay this off on me." I knew as soon as you started playing your little war games that you weren't serious about—"

"War games?" said Janice savagely. "All my vessels were in position when the attack came. Some of them," she said between clenched teeth, "still are."

"Yes," Wallace sneered. "And we know whose fault *that* is."

Right then something in Janice broke. She took a step toward and Wallace, ready to hurt him just as deeply as she could. "I've seen exactly what you've recovered, *doctor*. Rotting *kroner* bills," she said in a low, hard voice. "Copper *pfennigs* covered with verdigris. The smashed pieces of an *Atlas*. A *Flashman*. A *Zeus*. All designs built on Hesperus II. Repair hatches labeled in German. Taken one by one, each little piece means nothing. Any of these artifacts could be captured treasure. But all of them?" She shook her head and the sweep of her hand took in the cove and the scarred beach. "This isn't the remains of a Minnesota Tribe vessel. This *Union* belonged to the *Lyran Commonwealth*."

"No," Wallace whispered.

"I wondered what your supervisors at IE will say about *that*," she said, taking the knife she'd plunged into his psyche and *twisting* it.

The blood drained from Wallace's face. *"You,"* he said, his voice shaking with hatred. "You will never work for IE again."

"I might say the same to you," she shot back.

Wallace straightened to his full height, his face twisted with impotent rage. He turned and walked away, and stumbled, telling Janice just how deeply she'd struck him.

For a moment, Janice enjoyed a vindictive glee.

Until a too familiar voice said, "Congratulations. A most impressive victory."

She wheeled, jerking her weapon free of its holster and centering it on Maka Launa's bare chest.

He held her gaze, his eyes not flickering down to the weapon even once.

"You did this," she snarled.

Maka Launa snorted. "If you truly believe that, then my master's interest in you is misplaced."

Janice set her trembling finger on her trigger.

Maka Launa shook his head, still refusing to acknowledge the presence of his death clasped between her hands. "The fact that you don't like me—that I made you see certain things you did not wish to see—none of that makes me your enemy."

Janice swallowed hard. She did not lower the weapon, but she pointed it slightly away from Mr. Friendly.

The placid smile on his lips did not twitch a millimeter.

"If you were one of the pirates," she said, "you would've evaced when they lifted."

Maka Launa shrugged.

"Who were they?" she asked.

"Someone foolish enough to believe Wallace's ridiculous claims. Someone invested in secrets." He flashed her a grim smile. "Sound like anyone you might know?"

"Word of Blake," she whispered, guessing.

Again he shrugged. "Maybe. Who can say for sure? The universe is a confusing place."

She looked at him and he looked at her.

"You weren't one of them." Her voice tightened. "But you knew they were going to attack. You *knew*."

"Not with certainty," said Maka Launa.

"Don't play games with me," she snarled.

"Hai," he said. "We knew."

"And you did nothing," she said bitterly. She waved her weapon at the ruined, bloody beach framed by fire. "All the destruction. All the death."

"And what have you done to stop the destruction and death in the Inner Sphere?" asked Maka Launa softly. "Would you ask my master to treat you with more courtesy than you've seen fit to show the rest of humanity?"

Janice opened her mouth and closed it again. "But I can't—I mean. We're just a small unit. There's nothing we can do."

"And what if that were not true?" asked Maka Launa. "What if you could serve in a massive task force that could take the fight to the kind of people you fought today. That could end the madness in the report I shared with you yesterday? What then, Colonel Annapoulis?"

Janice dropped her weapon and turned away from this devil sent to torment her. Without a word, she walked to the very edge of the dockworks. The shattered hulk that had once been the *Orca* was clearly visible not five meters away, half-buried in the white sand. *Orca*. Lost with all hands. Sinuous black shapes swarmed over the gunboat's bridge, wriggling and fighting for position.

As they fed.

On her people.

She felt the presence of Maka Launa behind her. He had followed her. "I'm not in the mood," she said, her throat closing painfully around the words.

"It doesn't matter whether or not you're in the mood," he said softly. "The atrocities will continue. Until someone has the courage to stop them."

She looked down at the little boat in the crystalline water and thought of her young captain. Her too young captain. She turned to look at him, more because she couldn't bear to look at the *Orca* anymore than because she wanted to continue the conversation. "I can't," she whispered. "I can't throw the lives of my people away."

"Your people are warriors. Death is their business. They can either die for the ridiculous," Maka Launa nodded at the remnants of the dig-gypsy camp. "Or they can die for something noble."

He reached into the pocket of his khaki shorts and pulled out a data cube. Held it out to her.

"So what will it be, Colonel? Are you going to stay out here and play in the shallows. Or will you set sail for the deep ocean, where the water is dark and blue?"

Janice said nothing, but after a moment she reached out and snatched the cube out of his hand.

OFFICE POLITICS

BEN ROME

Sam Houston Plaza, Houston
North America
Terra
13 March 3068

Bowie Industries' Director of Transportation Sebastian Reginald rubbed his eyes once more and stifled another yawn. Giving up, he pushed his chair away from the desk and stood, arching his back and hearing several satisfying pops.

The office was stuffy, thanks to another cooling unit on the fritz. The Texan heat was beginning early this year—one glance at his desk unit told him the temperature was already at 27 degrees Centigrade in the office.

Sebastian opened his office door and walked to the end of the hall, grabbed a paper cup and filled it from the water dispenser.

"Director! Have you heard?"

Startled, Sebastian spilled some water on his hand as he jerked the cup away. Straightening slowly, he quelled his desire to hyperventilate and then turned to face the newcomer. It was Sandra Yemeni, one of his departmental accountants. "No, Yemeni, I've not heard anything. I've been analyzing next year's flight trial budgets."

The excitement on her face was obvious. "Bryant down in Security told us—the EASA mirror's picked up a battle in orbit!"

He felt his stomach drop. "Really now? Who is it? More Dragoon nonsense?"

"Better! It's ComStar! We're heading down to the main command center on Level Four. Director Carr is splicing a feed from the Euro-Asian Space Agency network and putting it up for us to watch. They're already throwing a party down there!"

"By all means, then. Pass the word: all departmental employees may take an extended lunch break to watch the festivities. I'll join you all shortly," he replied, forcing a smile to his face. Inside, his guts roiled. *Is this it at long last?*

He watched one of his best accountants excitedly flit from one cubicle to another, spreading the news. Like a wave of bees en route to a new flower patch, the employees got up and hurried to the elevator bank. Probably as many welcoming the change from monotony and a chance for air conditioning as those who truly wanted to see some space combat. *Though I doubt they'll see much of anything.*

Sebastian hurried back to his office and locked the door. He couldn't trust that everyone had left the floor—if someone walked in on him now he'd have a hard time explaining it. Pulling his personal datapad from his jacket pocket, he flipped through the addresses and tapped one with his stylus. Once the small screen opened, he began typing furiously on the small fold-out keyboard.

Using a secret code given to him several years ago—it was still valid as far as he knew—he entered a back door program built into the EASA mainframe. Careful to not trip any virtual alarms, he scanned several reports and video feeds. He was astonished at what he pulled up.

A massive fleet of Com Guard WarShips and attendant vessels had made it into Terran space, near the Moon. And they began to die...

The sheer amount of firepower the Word had brought to bear was astounding. Yet the EASA mirror did pick up something: several Drop-Ships had managed to run the deadly blockade and were on a high-G descent towards Terra.

Sebastian backed out of the system the same way he'd gone in and directed his powerful palmtop to another site. He had to check. Logging into the Interplanetary Comms System, he switched to the frequency he had memorized during his training.

It was there. Everything, just as they had said it would be. The code phrase was correct...they were coming, all right. The only thing Sebastian needed to do was get the viral code from another agent in the company.

He logged into the Bowie server's automated help desk with a question; innocuous to anyone else, but phrased in such a way to elicit a particular response—the reply would direct him to the agent who would give him the viral code he needed to continue his mission.

He had his answer less than five minutes later. A small file blinked slowly on his datapad. He glanced at the response, sighing. He knew his partner didn't take things as seriously as he did. *How was it that*

OFFICE POLITICS

Brent happened to be a highly-placed ComStar mole, unless it's all an act? And a good one at that... Sebastian shook his head. *No time to ponder it now.* He had to get that code.

Snapping closed his palmtop, he ejected the small datachip from the side port and pocketed it. As he stood up, the enormity of the situation suddenly pressed down on him.

They were coming.

They were coming!

The end was finally near!

Sebastian took one last look around his office, grabbed his ID card, and ran to the elevator.

▲▼▲

Noreen McGrady idly tapped her desk with the pad's stylus. Her boss was supposedly in conference at the moment, but one glance at the corner of her monitor told her otherwise. The small program window showed Brent Rothschild engaged in less-than-acceptable activities with Betty from the secretarial pool. *Honestly, I don't even know why he bothers to hide it. It's not like everyone doesn't know already...* She suppressed a surge of jealousy, wishing but for a moment to be the one lying on the couch beneath him...

She growled savagely. *One does not succumb to the base desires of the heretic. Purity of thought, Noreen.* She clenched and unclenched her hands, forcing the debasing thoughts from her mind. Taking a deep breath, she returned to her task at hand.

Well, the fact was that everyone *did* know about Brent's playboy ways. Noreen smiled. *The bigger question is, does he know that I know about his other secret?*

She finished keying in her report and then encrypted it, swapping out another translation chip as she had been taught. It was all so easy, thanks to her superior's heads-up regarding the secret white noise generator Brent kept in his office. If he only knew it was really a transmitter...

That was the thing about corporate higher-ups: they thought since they had the money and the power, they could do anything, even play spy games, without being caught. Bitch of it was, ROM always knew. *Always.*

"Even in the quiet, do not mock, or you will be judged and your secrets revealed to all," Noreen whispered. It was a phrase she'd memorized during her training so many years ago.

She glanced up at the sound of the elevator doors opening and noted Director Reginald heading at a brisk pace down the hallway. His stride quick, stuttered; not his usual lackadaisical stroll. Something was up and it most likely had to do with the news she'd picked up an hour ago. Seeing her boss still otherwise occupied, she stood to intercept the Director, if only to throw him off-kilter. She did enjoy antagonizing him so.

▲▼▲

Sebastian quickened his pace, his soft-soled loafers snicking quietly along the polished marble floor. He barely stopped to gaze at the ancient statue that adorned the center of the covered courtyard of Five Bowie Place, which bespoke volumes of the urgency of his mission.

He fidgeted in the elevator, trying to suppress the tremors in his hands. He fairly leaped out of his skin when the elevator dinged his arrival. It was all he could do not to sprint to the double doors at the end.

He nodded curtly at Noreen, whose vampirish frame blocked the entrance to the suite of the Vice President of Logistics. "I need to see Brent, now."

She stood resolute. "Absolutely not. You don't have an appointment. And he's currently in conference."

He stared at her. "It's a matter of the future of this company!"

"No."

The issue was decided before Sebastian could work up the courage to shoulder his way past the thin, frail woman. The door to the suite opened and Brent Rothschild, VP of Logistics of Bowie, Interstellar stuck his head out. "Noreen, what in blazes..." He looked at Sebastian and threw the door open wide. "Basty! What a pleasant surprise! Come in! I was about finished anyway," he said, motioning his friend in.

Secretly relieved to have dodged the impending confrontation, Sebastian avoided Noreen's dagger-like stare as he stepped past her into Brent's inner sanctum. He was momentarily distracted, however, as a young lady scooped up her bag from the large oak desk. She hurriedly tucked her shirt into the back of her skirt as she exited, furtively glancing back at the two men. Though she missed the piercing glare of Brent's assistant, Sebastian caught it. He shivered at the brutality that momentarily passed over her face.

The vision was cut off as the door swung shut. Sebastian shook the image from his mind and focused on the task at hand.

"Conference, eh?" Sebastian shook his head as he moved to the large glass window overlooking the Bowie, Interstellar corporate facility.

"We were... doing some dictation. Nothing I can't get to later." he smiled. "Drink?" Brent offered, going to his private bar near the massive picture window.

Sebastian nodded, admiring the view of the distant megopolis that abutted Bowie's massive aerofighter plant. The darkening sky blazed a mixture of golds and oranges .

"Never gets old, does it?" Brent handed Sebastian a glass of something coppery. It smelled divine.

"No." Sebastian paused for a moment, savoring the distinct taste of Cormerac whiskey. He took the opportunity to calm his nerves and slow his breathing. It was all happening too fast. He drained the glass, then set it on the table. Turning to his friend, he whispered fiercely, "Brent! It's finally happening."

"What's that, Basty?"

"The answer to our prayers. You know, what we were trained for all those years ago?"

Brent stared at his friend in a mixture of wonder and elation. "You're sure? They transmitted the proper codes?"

Sebastian walked over to Brent's desk and snapped a small disc into the embedded player. "Listen for yourself."

The Bowie executive reached over and punched a button. "Wait a minute, first." He pressed another button. "Noreen? Would you go to the file room and get me the new transshipment logs for the last month? Thanks." He then stepped around to the credenza behind his desk and palmed a lockpad. A small drawer clicked open, from which Brent retrieved a tiny pyramid.

Sebastian looked on, curious. *Well now, maybe he really is competent enough to be a mole. They don't just give those out to anyone...*

Brent grinned at his friend and tapped one side of the pyramid, placing it on the desk. "Now, we can talk. I have my suspicions—best to be cautious."

Sebastian nodded, then tapped the desk player. A burst of static erupted from the desk's speakers, then a babble of voices that faded to leave one transmission.

"General Cipher 4-4-Mark. Gamma sequence. Code words: Jedburgh. Jedburgh. Jedburgh. Upsilon sequence. Code words: Jedburgh. Jedbur—"

Brent stood, staring out at the deepening sky. The sky had turned scarlet, with blood-red clouds streaming from the west. The distant buildings looked to be on fire. Of course, it was only a trick of light.

"That's it, then. When did this start?"

"When I heard of the battle, I pulled some data from the EASA satellite mirror station. Seems several DropShips made it through the Word's blockade up there. I then scanned the IPC channels and picked this up on the band I was briefed on."

"Trap?"

"No. Brent, this is real. We've waited nearly ten years for this."

"Indeed." He glanced at his wristwatch. "You should go. I've downloaded the program to your datachip. Send the signal and prepare to activate Plan Kappa."

"What about Noreen? You know she abhors any changes to your schedule."

Brent laughed. "I'll handle her. She's only a glorified secretary, after all. You go and get things rolling. I suspect it'll get hot fast."

"Most likely. Once they land, I'm sure we'll have our own problems here."

Rothschild nodded. "Go. I've got plans in place. I'll get things rolling for the facility. Bowie will welcome the Guards as the saviors they are."

Sebastian quickly turned and left the office, barely missing Brent's assistant with the door. Unperturbed, she stuck her head into the suite.

"Got those files, sir. Anything else?" She stepped into the room.

Brent stood by the window, staring thoughtfully into the darkening sky. Already Venus was out, a baleful eye over the city. He turned to Noreen. "No, thanks. You can take the rest of the..." His voice trailed away as he took in the needler in her delicate hands.

"Day off? On this glorious day? No, I think rather, it's time for you to retire."

"Really now."

"Yes." She stepped over to his credenza, palming open the secret drawer and pulling out the pyramid Brent had only recently put away.

"You knew?"

"You never know exactly where these toys come from. You see, that's actually my *recorder*."

He couldn't hide the shock from his face. "Recorder? You mean, all this..." With a sudden awareness, he realized all the activities he'd done with that device present. All the plans set up. Accounts settled. Meetings conducted...

He could barely whisper. "A mole. All along. Right here."

"Did you really think the board would give so much freedom to their underlings?"

Brent turned from the window and went to the bar. "Mind if I get you a drink?"

Noreen grinned. "Go ahead. The holdout pistol you keep there isn't loaded."

He forced a laugh, his hands dropping to his sides. "I guess you're smarter than I thought." He shook his head sadly, then stepped up to the bar and poured himself another slug of whiskey.

"True. After all, you are a heretic. Such obvious disdain for those of us of the faith is rather simple to manipulate. Shall I help you understand?"

He nodded, meekly. His eyes were on the floor and she saw the sweat break out on his forehead.

"Simpletons like you serve a function. For instance, we know you've diverted millions of C-bills of assets to resistance efforts in the Chaos March."

Brent's glass stopped halfway to his mouth.

"Oh yes. Clever, trying to hide small shipment diversions through misdirected shipping records and quintuple-blind accounts. We almost didn't catch it. You are to be commended for that. But alas, Blake willed us to find out, and we did. And we used that information to pinpoint activities of those who would oppose Blake's Light and had them...taken care of."

"You mean murdered them." Rothschild slammed back the rest of his whiskey. "So what now? You're holding all the cards. But we both know that the Word can't possibly hold back—"

The pistol coughed twice. The first shot punctured the front of Rothschild's designer suit, mixing expensive Parmi wool with flesh, blood, and bits of organs. The second shot hammered into the large picture window behind him, a myriad of spider webs emanating from a fist-sized hole where the bulk of the flechettes hit. The nighttime view of the distant city was transformed into a tormented landscape of jagged glass and angles.

"All we needed was the code name. We know Focht had several contingencies planned," she said to her dying victim. His hands went to his stomach, trying to stop the flow of blood. Noreen took three quick steps towards him, grabbing his head and pulling it towards her lips in a crushing kiss.

He coughed, blood wetting his lips. She pulled back, gazed into his horror-filled eyes. "It's too bad. I could've shown you the full delights of Blake's Will. Alas, you're just—" She grabbed him by the throat.

"—a stupid—"

She suddenly kissed him once again, savoring the taste of blood, sweat, and fear.

Then with sudden force, she threw him back into the fractured window behind him. The weakened glass gave way with the barest hesitation.

"—heretic," she finished, watching her former boss fall from his lofty perch.

Noreen stepped away from the view and pulled a small communicator from her skirt pocket. "Commence phase two. Coordinates inbound." She stepped behind Brent's desk, tapped in a series of keystrokes. Thanks to the watcher virus she'd installed months ago, she knew exactly where to look and pulled up an encrypted file marked JEDBURGH. Overriding his code with a viral key, she sent the file off, straightened her jacket, and left the office, locking it.

There was a party going on downstairs she had to get to.

▲▼▲

Sebastian hurried to the elevator, a cold sweat breaking out on his forehead. He felt nauseated and elated at the same time —*finally, free of the Blakists!* He stepped into the crowded car, trying desperately to keep from fidgeting.

So much to do, so little time! The code words used with the two sequences meant that both primary landing quadrants were still active—one located near the old Houston aerodrome, now Bowie's main test flight facility. The other was somewhere else, but that wasn't his concern.

What mattered was prepping the facility to receive their liberators.

It would be easy. The site had been selected over the last several years for its proximity to both the Houston and Dallas megopolises and its defensibility as a forward base. The base defenses only needed a certain viral code inserted to convert the incoming DropShip IFF codes to friendly and allow them to ground safely.

Sebastian pushed through the crowd in the main lobby, making quick progress toward the communications suite. There was an uplink system there he could insert the code chip ...

He slowed as he saw the lone TerraSec guard by the suite's door step towards him. "Afternoon, Director. You have business here today?"

Sebastian smiled, trying to appear relaxed. "That's right, Cody. Need the latest hockey scores from Asia. Gotta make sure my fantasy team's kicking butt."

The guard smiled. "Sure thing, sir. Of course, you know the drill."

"Of course." Sebastian held out his arms and allowed the guard to wave a small pad over his body. He stared absently at the man's TerraSec badge clipped to his chest pocket.

Cody keyed the palm lock. "Go ahead, sir." The officer smiled as he waved him through.

Sebastian nodded back, already focused on the task at hand. He made his way to a door labeled UPLINK 1A and entered. Seating himself at the first terminal under the larger wall monitor, he keyed in the commands for a remote vid feed to the company's facility and then brought up the uplink screen. He put the chip into the correct slot as he tapped into the system. He knew on the roof, the satellite dishes were orienting and establishing the link to the distant airbase.

The monitor beeped as the small room's door slid open. Sebastian didn't look up as he quickly tapped in several commands on the uplink keypad.

"That doesn't look like hockey to me." Cody's voice was soft, startling Sebastian.

"Uh, no. Yeah, trying to get this thing to cooperate, you know?" Sebastian's hand froze when the pistol's barrel pressed against his head.

"Try using the *Rites of Satellus* next time. Though I'm sorry to say, Director, there won't be one."

Sebastian looked at the monitor. Already, four small plumes of fire had appeared in the night sky above the facility. All he needed to do was push the ENTER button...

His neck twitched slightly just as the pistol discharged.

▲▼▲

Pulling the body off the console, Cody wiped the monitor of brain bits and studied both it and the uplink command window. Satisfied with what he saw, he turned his head slightly and spoke into his collar mic. "Gamma neutralized. Condition green."

He listened for a moment, then smiled. Tapping in a command on the gore-soaked keyboard, he stepped back to take in the whole feed on the monitor.

The four plumes continued plunging downward. Below them, the facility's air defense turrets came to life, rotating around and upward, the covers on the massive capital missile ripple launchers swinging open. Then, as one, they vomited dark lances on plumes of fire, arrowing up at breakneck speed toward the descending DropShips.

Blake provides everything, thought Cody as he admired the explosions on the screen. *Even fireworks for an impromptu holiday...*

GODT BYTTE

KEVIN KILLIANY

Botany Bay
Periphery
30 May 2972

Standing two paces behind and to the left of his father, Olaf Jespersen was distracted by the savage wind beyond the curved ferroglass. He could barely make out the clan totem emblazoned on the curved hull of his father's *landingsfartøy* through the blowing sand, though the vessel was less than three hundred meters from the observation lounge.

DropShip, Olaf self-corrected. To *tuskhandel* in Star League one must think in Star League.

Noting the haze of scratches etched into the ferroglass, Olaf surmised the blowing sand was a constant. He fought the reflex to draw his fur-trimmed cloak tighter. The wind-blown sand was outside and he was inside—ostensibly beginning his education in the *firmaet* by listening to his father broker new deals.

On any world he knew—on the four worlds he knew—a business transaction would have involved drinks and long discussions of individual health and family wellbeing. Here on Botany Bay his father was evidently required to conduct business in what looked to be no more than a semi-private waiting area in the DropPort's passenger concourse. However his father did not seem to be taking offense, so Olaf schooled his features into a mask of professional courtesy to hide his righteous indignation.

"Indeed, Goodman Giles," his father was saying, at his ease in the foreigner's presence. "There is much to be said for exploiting the resources of your own solar system. But until one can afford to build or buy the necessary deep space habitats and factories, that option must remain hypothetical."

"There's nothing hypothetical about it, mate," the planetary factor said. He was a small man, more narrowly built than Olaf's father—all sharp lines and angles. He wore a broad-brimmed hat with one side of the brim folded up and held to the crown by a shield-shaped pin, which Olaf did not doubt was a symbol of some importance. "It's our goal and our intent to become completely self-sufficient. Then all we'd need you lot for is trinkets and toys. No offense."

"There is no offense, Goodman," Olaf could tell from his voice his father was grinning. "There is far more profit in luxury items."

Olaf adjusted his broad leather gunbelt, trying not to be noticeable. He was careful to keep his hand far from the *enhjørning*-ivory grip of his grandfather's pistol, lest his movement be mistaken for a threat. Though its slide and frame were intricately carved, the twelve millimeter was a weapon meant for use, not show. Built heavy to absorb recoil and drop back on target with brisk efficiency, it was easily twice the mass of the seven millimeter Olaf habitually carried.

Any JarnFolk who saw the heavy pistol on his belt would know Olaf had not the years to have earned such a weapon, but they would also know the fact he carried it bespoke his heritage and his family's confidence in his future. A thousand generations ago their ancestors had carried carved battle axes and intricately adorned war hammers when they traveled from their fjords out into the wide world—a testimony to their station and prowess even the densest barbarian could understand. Today, the traders of the JarnFolk carried pistols, as engraved and decorated—and as deadly—as any chieftain's war axe.

"...building materials, of course," the Botany Bay factor was saying. "Nothing stands up to this weathering long. You can see even the ferroglass only lasts a year or so."

Olaf looked at the etched window with new eyes. A year? He knew from the text his father had required him to study that the black sand was pulverized volcanic glass, but he had not considered the implications of thousands—billions—of tiny obsidian missiles in constant motion. The ceaseless wind might make Botany Bay a good customer for the wind turbines used to generate power on his native Hofn. Particularly since the destructive sand would guarantee they would be a lucrative market for spare parts.

He smiled slightly at his own joke. Though with all the sand and dust, would not Botany Bay have a continuous need for petroleum products—lubricants and plastics for seals and gaskets? Olaf made a mental note to ask his father when they were alone.

"... but at the core water," the thin-edged man said. "Water until we have the means to harvest—and decontaminate—the ice asteroids of our own system."

"The decontamination being the key," Olaf's father agreed. "An expensive technology. This is not something we produce ourselves, but I will keep an eye open."

The discussion devolved into the nuts and bolts of barter as Olaf's father and his father's opposite number negotiated their way through exchanging of a half-dozen or so minor items of mutual interest they possessed. Olaf knew this was the meat of his education—that he should be hanging on every word the *handlende* uttered—but the sand whistling and sighing and rattling against the ferroglass kept drawing his attention.

He imagined he could see the blowing grit scouring its way through the ferroglass. How long would it take such a scourging wind to shred his flesh from his bones?

With an effort he reined in his imagination and struggled to focus on the debate over the true value of six hundred assorted bolts of Alborg's best wool.

Oberon VI
Oberon Confederation
11 July 2972

Olaf was very aware of Nils, Frieda and Alice moving in close formation—a three-sided box with his father and him at the center—as they exited the groundcar that had carried them to the edge of the DropShip field from the Jespersen *landingsfartøy* (*DropShip*, he corrected). His father's assassin guards did not normally accompany the trader when he called on familiar customers as "civilized" as the Oberons— but a JumpShip that did not acknowledge their Jarnskip's hail hung at Oberon VI's zenith jump point and a squat grey DropShip had already been berthed when they made planetfall.

"Hansa," his father had said. "Upstart shopkeepers who call themselves traders. They do not respect the codes of honor and surround themselves with armed thugs to intimidate the weak willed."

That the Hansa were on Oberon VI was something new and not expected, Olaf knew. The Jespersen family had stood by the Oberons over a century ago, bringing food at cost to the starving world after the colonists' early efforts at mining had poisoned the delicate water table and triggered an ecological disaster.

So now Olaf strode across the ferrocrete toward the broad building of pillars and arches beside his father, doing his adolescent best to mirror the same air of inevitable right. The elder Jespersen's personal guard framed them, providing a context for men who needed no protection. A show of force almost certain to be numerically smaller than whatever the Hansa felt would intimidate the JarnFolk, but more than enough to meet any threat the interlopers might hope to mount.

His grandfather's pistol rode prominently at Olaf's belt, its ivory grip angled to his right hand. Not so evident was his left hand, thrust casually into the deep pocket of his formal overcoat and wrapped around the butt of his own snub-nosed seven millimeter—a boy's gun, but deadly enough if and when.

The Oberons did not trade in passenger concourses, Olaf saw. His father was leading them toward a broad building of pillars and arches—a stone and glass structure evidently intended to suggest a village of great tents.

The air was warm—almost too warm to justify the greatcoat—and Olaf was glad when they passed through the double doors into the air-conditioned interior. Holding the doors open, and spaced evenly along the walls of a great central room clearly designed for gatherings and ceremonies of note, were liveried men evidently meant to indicate a guard of some sort. Olaf noted their ceremonial edge weapons were obviously not intended for actual combat.

Nils caught his eye, then glanced toward the top of the far wall. Three steps later Olaf looked in the indicated direction and spotted the gunport. It was reassuring to see the Oberons did not merely play at security.

Nils was the team's outrider—normally he would have circulated, assessing threats by moving through the crowd. But here, where there was no crowd. he stayed in close formation.

There were two groups waiting for them, both proximate to a central table of refreshments everyone seemed to be ignoring. The group to the right had perhaps a dozen men and women wearing clothes of fabrics more appropriate to the climate than Olaf's greatcoat and cut in a fashion that struck him as elegant. These, he surmised, were the Oberons.

Standing opposite them—so that the approaching JarnFolk made a triangle—were four men in heavy robes and broad hats in rich but somber colors. Forming a crescent moon behind them were a dozen men in grey jumpsuits and black vests with the unmistakable bulk of ballistic armor. They carried short carbines slung across their shoulders.

GODT BYTTE

Olaf almost let go of his pocket pistol. The supposed guards were so unready none would live to unlimber his weapon if and when. Then it occurred to him that such apparent laxness may be as much a ruse as his casually pocketed hand. He checked the safety with his thumb and flexed his fingers before giving his full attention to his father and the negotiation.

"Well met, Sir Bjørn," said the regal woman who evidently lead the Oberon contingent in oddly accented Star League.

"Lady Marsa, you know well we JarnFolk do not use your titles," Olaf's father said with the grin he was coming to realize was his elder's bargaining mode. "I am Bjørn Jepersen of the Jepersen clan. A simple trader, no more."

The woman—Lady Marsa—bobbed her head, acknowledging the correction. Olaf was certain she did not accept his father's self-evaluation as a simple trader, no doubt assuming the JarnFolk chose not to share some arcane social order similar to her own. Why would someone so evidently a woman need to identify herself as "Lady?"

"And this young man?" Lady Marsa asked, looking at Olaf. "Those are your eyes, if I am not mistaken."

"My son Olaf," his father admitted. "Come to learn the trade."

"A pity he should waste his journey on your last visit to Oberon VI." The gravelly words came from the fattest of the Hansa.

"Herr Frederich, that has not yet been decided," Lady Marsa said sharply. "There are many options to explore."

The fat man turned his shoulder toward the JarnFolk, obviously dismissing them from any discussion.

"You wish to industrialize your world," Frederich said. "Develop, exploit the natural resources of Oberon VI. The people of the ice moon cannot help you do that. The *simple* traders cannot help you do that. Only the Hansa can help you do that—we have the personnel and the materiel to offer a long-term and profitable relationship. Technical expertise *simple* traders lack."

Olaf bristled, but he did not need Frieda's warning glance to keep his peace. It would take far more than insults from a man so clearly unaware of whom he faced to provoke him to ill-considered action. Besides, the Hansa had merely echoed his father's words.

"Ah," said Olaf's father as though pleasantly surprised. "If Oberon is seeking a construction contractor, the Hansa is right. Our technicians and craftsmen cannot meet the prices offered by slave labor.

"Though if it is craftsmanship you seek, from the poor condition of their JumpShips and DropShips, it is evident the Hansa lack the Jarn-Folk's understanding of technology."

"Gentlemen," Lady Marsa said before Frederich could respond.

Olaf understood why everyone was ignoring the refreshments. They wanted to have their weapon hands free when the shooting started.

"What did you learn?" his father asked in the groundcar an hour later.

"That the Hansa are offering a labor force in addition to equipment, something we are not interested in doing," Olaf answered. "While Oberon VI may become a profitable market once they have completed their industrialization, there is no percentage in trying to break the Hansa demand of exclusivity while they are so essential to the Oberons attaining their goals."

His father nodded slowly.

"Good as far as you go," he said. "But you looked only at the here and the horizon. What of the past?"

"The past?"

His father did not answer, waiting for Olaf to puzzle out the meaning behind his words. The Oberons were determined to develop the gold and mineral resources of their world. Resources that had attracted the first settlers to the isolated world, but which could not be exploited because the world's ecology was so delicate the least pollutant caused massive vegetation die-offs. There had been a famine generations ago when—

"Water purification!" Olaf said, recalling the key sentence. "They have acquired water purifiers effective enough to remove all pollution generated by their mines and factories."

"Water purifiers and—more importantly—simple water purification technology they can replicate to meet any need," his father nodded. "Otherwise they would not dare expand as rapidly as they are proposing.

"Now: Why is that good news?"

"Because they acquired it," Olaf said. "And what they acquired, we can acquire. And sell. Our only task is discovering who sold them the purifiers."

His father sighed.

"You were not paying attention."

Sigurd
Oberon Confederation
22 July 2972

The striped sphere of the gas giant filled a third of the sky. Only a slender crescent of the globe was lit by the distant primary—an unblinking white point that burned with the intensity of an arc light in the deep blue sky. The shadowy portion not lit by the faraway sun glowed with its own sullen red, like an ember covered with a thin film of black ash.

Olaf had his cloak on over his greatcoat and was still cold. He doubted even frozen Hamar could match the bitter cold that soaked its way through layers of wool and leather.

The cold in partner with the oppressive weight of the huge planet above made him want to hunch his shoulders as he followed his father across the ice field. It took all of his discipline to walk like a man and not pull himself into a heat-conserving ball. So deadening was the moon, so oppressive the planet above, that despite weighing only two-thirds what he did on his native Hofn, Olaf could manage no more than a trudge through the powdery snow covering the ice.

Almost as disturbing as the world above him was the knowledge there was nothing but water below him. The ice on which he walked extended down—how many hundreds of meters he was not sure—until it reached a point where the pressure kept the water fluid despite the temperature. There was some debate whether there was anything other than water at the core. Depending on the assumptions one brought to the readings, there was either a ball of rock a hundred kilometers down, or the pressure became so great that the liquid water was indistinguishable from stone.

Olaf found the core of rock theory more palatable. The thought that there was something solid beneath his feet was comforting.

Glancing back—and the hood of his cloak required he turn completely around—Olaf thought the brightly-colored landing shuttle looked forlorn on the icy field of whites and greys. The crew was already out, chipping away at the ice that had refrozen around the hot landing gear as it cooled. His father—and the ship's captain and Frieda—had explained that even a DropShip was in no danger of melting all the way through Sigurd's icy shell, but Olaf was still glad his father had chosen the smaller craft for this visit.

Directly ahead a glacial cliff rose from the plain—patterns of darker grey against the grey-white revealing windows and entrances. No trading pavilions or passenger concourses here. The moon's two thousand natives—fewer than found in many family enclaves on Hofn—lived in caves carved from the living ice.

The ground—ice—rose beneath their feet. The even gradient and raised edges convinced Olaf they were ascending a man-made ramp. Evidently leading to the entrance of the colony. Looking ahead, he found a wide archway in the cliff face to confirm his theory.

Olaf was startled by the sight of a carpet woven in an intricate pattern of greens and pinks that rose from the floor of the corridor ahead of them to cover the walls, framing the broad entrance. As he and his father passed the carpet revealed itself to be a brightly colored lichen, any pattern to its clashing hues an illusion.

The oppressive cold lost its bite the moment Olaf and his father stepped across the threshold into the lichen-lined tunnel and out of the wind. A dozen paces carried them around a sharp turn and the temperature rose a dozen degrees.

A party of natives—Sigurders?—waited for them in a circular chamber from which four other tunnels radiated. Glancing up, Olaf noted the light came from low-energy neon fixtures of ancient design—and that the carpet of lichen extended to cover every square centimeter of wall and ceiling.

There was a pungent scent to the air, like a baking spice he could not quite place, and a faint mustiness. A *godt bytte*—good exchange—for natural insulation he decided.

Copying his father's example, he opened his cloak and removed his gloves as they approached the welcoming committee. The Sigunders were a uniformly dark people, a phenotype that did not exist among the JarnFolk, but which Olaf recognized as African. They wore no-nonsense jumpsuits of bright safety orange with thick hoods, now thrown back in the cavern's relative warmth, and bulges at each cuff which no doubt held gloves.

There was no indication of rank, but the Sigurders' positioning made it clear a stout man with bars of grey through his densely curled hair and beard was their leader.

"Greetings," Olaf's father said in Star League. "I am Bjørn Jespersen and this is my son Olaf. We are simple traders of the JarnFolk come to see if there may be some means by which both you and we can profit."

"Tomas," the heavyset man answered in the same language. "We know the JarnFolk. Lars Heyerdahl and his son Liam traded here in my great-grandfather's time. After so many years we thought you had died out or forgotten us."

"I cannot speak for the Heyerdahls," Olaf's father said. "Except to say they valued you enough as trading partners to have never mentioned dealing with you. One does not broadcast such things. Why they have not visited in so long, I have no idea."

Tomas seemed to consider the words for a long moment.

"Come," he said at last. "Eat."

Without another word, he turned toward one of the tunnels that led deeper into the ice. The other Sigurders followed without a glance toward Olaf or his father.

"They do not get much company," Olaf said to his father in Norse.

"To offer food on a world as tightly rationed as this must be?" the elder Jespersen asked sharply. "You will seldom see a more hospitable act."

Chastised, Olaf fell in step behind his father.

▲▼▲

"Comets," Tomas was saying. "Meteors. For millions of years Odin has pulled them into orbit and Sigurd has swept the orbit clean."

Olaf nodded, though the headman was speaking to his father.

Expecting a stew of lichens, he had been pleasantly surprised by a vegetarian feast of unexpected variety. After the meal the Sigurds had taken their guests on a tour of the underground—underice?—farm: acres of rich topsoil imported from Oberon VI and warmed by banks of ultraviolet lights.

Sigurd's agriculture was not self-supporting, however. Lacking a complete ecology, the soil's nutrients had to be replenished regularly. The fertilizer—like the fabric for the Sigurders' clothes, and all of the raw materials for their limited manufacturing—was imported from Oberon VI. The Sigurders were aware the fertile planet claimed their world as part of the "Oberon Confederation," but as they saw their supposed rulers only for brief trading exchanges twice a year they paid no attention to their supposedly vassal status.

It was what the citizens of Sigurd traded for their fertilizer and building materials that interested the Jespersens. Olaf knew his father had expected to be shown a sophisticated manufacturing facility and suspected he was as bemused as Olaf at their tour through a wandering network of tunnels.

Here the insulating lichen was not so prevalent. The Sigurders had raised their hoods and pulled the mittens—not gloves—from their sleeve pouches. Olaf once again had his cloak firmly laced over his greatcoat, the fur-lined hood framing his view of the tunnels. Light was still provided by the ancient neon fixtures—suspended from wires so the minimal heat of their battery packs did not come in direct contact with the ice.

"Using sensors we are able to trace the densest veins of ore through the ice," Tomas pointed to something in the translucent wall that meant nothing to Olaf. "Then it's only a question of grinding it out."

"Grinding it out?" Olaf's father asked. "I thought lasers were used in mining ice."

"On worlds where you have ground to stand on," Tomas turned so his guests could see his grin. "Here we move much slower and are careful not to raise the temperature so much."

"So you have been trading heavy metals to Oberon VI in exchange for your basic needs," Olaf's father said. "How does their planned mining and industrialization affect that balance?"

Tomas's grin disappeared.

"It is not a good thing," he said flatly.

Turning abruptly, he resumed the tour of the ice mines.

"We drill or grind, depending on the ice and the sort of ore," he said, his voice echoing back off the walls of the tunnel. "Impact hammers and lasers both carry too much danger of fractures. Concussive or thermal, a sheer in the wall ice could crush a crew between ceiling and floor before anyone realized the danger."

"Coming down from the top is not an option?"

"More difficult to trace the veins and a much greater volume of ice must be shifted. That alone increases the danger far more than following the minerals through the strata."

"Way!" called a voice behind them.

Olaf and his father pressed themselves to the wall as a half dozen men and women pushed rectangular skids past them.

"Belts carry the shards of ore ice to the extractors along the main lines," Tomas explained. "But in these smaller tunnels we use hand sleds."

"Extractors?" Olaf glanced a belated apology to his father for blurting out of turn and was glad to receive an approving nod in return. "Are those a new development?"

"No," Tomas answered. "And yes. We have always used extractors—how else to separate the valuable metals from the ice? But until Alma's invention we had to transport the ice rubble to the surface because the heat of the process posed a danger to the tunnels."

"And what did Alma invent?" Olaf's father asked, only casual curiosity in his voice.

"I do not pretend to understand the science," Tomas answered. "But it is a method for pulling the metal from the dross with little energy."

"And it's simple," Olaf's father said, his eyes on his son rather than the back of their guide, "because Alma developed it using only basic materials imported from Oberon."

Olaf missed whatever Tomas answered.

The Sigurders had not developed a water purification system; they had developed a method of extracting comet dust from ice. For them the purified water was "dross." How long had it taken the Oberons to figure out what their poor *fetterne* had created?

"Here is the heart of what we do," Tomas said, standing aside. "This is a soft ice strata, so we are scraping our way forward."

The tunnel ended in an open room, well lit by neon lights on stands. Olaf saw a large device, looking very much like a small cannon with three meters of spiral bottle brush projecting from its barrel, mounted on a heavy tripod facing the far wall. Three men—a pair of those who had brought the sleds and one he had not seen before—pushed the tripod forward until the outsized bottle brush was pressed against the wall. Once they had secured it in position, two other sled-haulers joined them, adding their weight to brace the tripod as the brush began to spin.

Skipping and whining across the face of the ice, the wildly gyrating brush stripped away layers of ice, throwing chips in all directions. Most, however, slumped down from the wall to spread across the floor.

The two sled pushers not bracing the scraper used broad shovels as paddles to separate the flow. One shoveled dirty ice into the waiting sleds with practiced efficiency while the other slapped shovelfuls of clear ice against the wall around the tunnel. Olaf realized this transfer from the far wall to the entrance of the tunnel allowed the drilling room to move forward while leaving a narrower, more stable tunnel behind.

In a matter of minutes, the six skids were full. The brush operator shut down his machine. As the sled pullers left the chamber he began disassembling the brush, using what looked like a giant comb to clean the bristles.

Tomas gestured after the departing sleds, evidently indicating he intended to lead his guests to the extractors.

"Father."

Bjørn Jespersen stopped at his son's quiet word. He cast a quick glance after Tomas, then turned sharp eyes on Olaf.

"How much heat," Olaf asked in Norse, "is generated by a sand blaster?"

Botany Bay
Periphery
12 October 2972

"Damnedest thing," the trader Giles said for what Olaf believed was the thousandth time as he watched the giant skip loader fill another container. "All they want is bloody sand?"

Olaf nodded, aware of his father standing to one side. He did not glance toward the elder Jespersen.

This was his *handelen*; his first. True, his father had suggested including equipment for molding insulating building materials from sand in their presentation to the Sigurders—a practical safeguard against development of a recycling system, but the original idea had been Olaf's. And as the originator of the deal, the *forhandler*—the negotiating to bring it all together—was his to complete.

Fortunately the Sigurders and Botany Bayers both believed they were getting the best of the bargain.

Efficient water purification technology for sand was how the Botany Bay Factor saw it. Self-sufficiency in exchange for providing a constant supply of the sand that made his people's lives miserable was the focus of his attention.

For their part the Sigurders were developing the most efficient and profitable mining operation in their history in exchange for easily-produced dross extractors. And new trading partners in the Jespersens—now that both of them had been left out by the marriage of Oberon VI to the Hansa.

Olaf had offered the Sigurders far more in wool and topsoil and the luxuries of survival than they had ever commanded from the rulers of their so-called confederation, in exchange for heavy elements of the purest quality at a fraction of their value on the open market.

Some day the ice-moon miners would discover the value of their ore and demand full price. And on that day Olaf—or his son or his grandson—would shrug and smile and pay top coin for all new deliveries. Perhaps even a cut above. It would be a small price when balanced against decades of dirt cheap profits.

Godt bytte was good business.

THE SMALLER SACRIFICE

CHRISTIAN GRAINGER

Alpine, Texas
Terra
Word of Blake Protectorate
15 March 3068

William Fence looked out the picture window of the fourth floor apartment and shook with rage. "The warehouses on East Holland must have all collapsed; I can see the smoke cloud from here. It's not enough they destroy my business, now they have to attack our home. Lee, you should see this. It looks like the 'Mechs from last night are gone."

William's fists clenched as he watched the gray smoke billow into the deep blue sky. "It looks like they hit the fuel depot down where the university used to be." He looked around. "Lee, are you listening to me?" He turned from the large window and opened his mouth to yell for his wife just as she came into the living room from the hall.

She knew he been about to yell and raised an eyebrow at him. "I can hear you, Bill," she said quietly.

His anger faded almost instantly and he smiled sheepishly. She always had that effect on him.

She went on. "I was trying to get something on the vid. It's just static now. The comm is out too. The whole city must be cut off. It must be the attack." Lee nodded in the direction of the window. "The last thing on the news was that Terran Security forces were victorious in France and the Brewster County TerraSec Department wants any unusual activity reported. They don't know where the units are that attacked the depot last night."

"Anything else?"

Lee knew exactly what he meant. She went on even though she didn't want to. "All civilian airspace and sub-orbital traffic patterns are to remain closed until further notice. I'm so sorry, Bill."

He slowly turned away from her and walked back over to the window.

"I put everything into the business," Bill said softly. "All our savings, a second mortgage on this place. It was the only way to avoid bankruptcy." His head sagged.

He knew she hated to see him like this, to see him so pushed to the end.

"I know, baby," Lee said as she moved into the kitchen.

William listened for a moment as his wife began breakfast.

"I have over forty transports, all fully loaded, waiting to make deliveries and not a single one of them can get off the ground because of this attack." There was no sign of the enemy 'Mechs. The smoke and dust had cleared somewhat from the east edge of town. William looked up into the blue sky and laughed bitterly.

"Even the weather is perfect. Right now all of my transports would be delivering my customers' cargo and returning. All I needed was a week. Just a week and the company, us and everything would have been all set."

Lee stopped mixing eggs for a moment and looked up at her husband. "Bill," she said. "I know you feel bad about this and I know what it means to you. But honey, everything important is all right. We are healthy and we have a nice place to live. It could be a lot worse. Besides, maybe it's not such a bad thing, this attack, as long as we stay safe. You know how I feel about the Word of Blake, about what they did to my brother. I don't want you to have anything to do with those people. Leave it alone." Her face took on a blank, angry look that William hated to see. It seemed all the joy drained out of her when she looked that way.

William crossed the room and stood next to his wife.

"I know you're right," he said. "But it hurts to have tried so hard and then have this happen. There must be a way to make it work. If only this battle could end more quickly." William covered his eyes with his right hand and reached toward her with the other. "Just take my hand, honey, and tell me everything's going to be all right. If you hold my hand, everything will be all right."

Lee sighed then took his hand.

"Everything will be all right. I promise."

William peeked out between his fingers and smiled. "You're not supposed to promise. It doesn't work then. Remember? You promised me that time at the poker tournament and..."

Lee's tone turned mock serious, but her brown eyes twinkled. She

let go of his hand and turned back to the mixing bowl. "William Robert Fence, if you mention poker one more time in this house, I won't be held responsible."

William held up his hand in defense.

"If you want to make yourself useful, go down to Carters and get me some thyme. I think they still have some left. The ration book's in my bag."

"Keeping me busy? I'll figure this out, Lee. I'll make it work, I always have. We've been poor for so long. And I wanted to change that."

Lee looked up for a second and then went back to working on the breakfast.

"Just get me the thyme and don't forget your jacket."

"The zipper's broken."

"Don't make excuses, it's still cold out. Be quick."

"I will. I've got my shortcut."

▲▼▲

Ten minutes later, as William headed home down the narrow Seventh Street alley next to the old Stratham factory; he couldn't get the thought out of his mind that there must be some way to resolve his problem. The more he tried to forget about the fact that his entire shipping fleet was grounded the more it invaded his thoughts. The only way his business would survive was if the current unpleasantness was finished within the week.

That didn't seem likely. Even the Brewster County TerraSec units that had been moving down the street when William left the house seemed to be searching more in a random fashion than with any purpose. The two white and blue 'Mechs—*Sentinels* from the news vids, the TS3 troops—had moved down the street with two tracked tanks and two transports. The 'Mechs would move and then the tanks would move with the transports always following behind.

They must be looking for the guys that attacked us last night, William had thought to himself. *They're never going to find them and this is going to go on forever.*

William stopped and pulled his leather jacket tighter around him against the chill. He stood for a moment and then realized he was being silly and Lee was right. It came to him in a flash.

"There is nothing I can do about this," he said. "I've got to let it go. I did the best I could. And it nearly worked." It seemed as if a huge weight had been lifted.

"I've been such a fool." With a big smile on his face he started down the alley again. The old factory hadn't been used in years and was condemned. But one of the side doors was off its hinges and you could walk through to the assembly floor and out the gaping hole in the far side. The brick wall on that side had partially collapsed years ago. William had used the shortcut when he went to school as a child. He loved the fact that he could still use it now. Other kids in the neighborhood used the shortcut too.

He got to the broken door and went to push it aside as he always did. But the door was already partially open. "Stupid kids," William said, shaking his head. "One of these days the cops will find out and board the place up."

He walked through the abandoned offices on the first floor and then turned to cross the huge factory floor.

He stopped dead in his tracks.

Parked on the old factory floor was a 'Mech. It was crouched low to the ground, facing away from him. He didn't recognize it, but it was the same size as the *Sentinel*s he'd seen earlier. A small group of men stood talking near the open hatch of a tracked tank. The men's uniforms looked dirty and both the 'Mech and the tank had carbon scoring. The solders looked tired.

They were Com Guard.

Williams's blood froze as one of the enemy soldiers looked right at him. William couldn't move. He knew he should run but his legs wouldn't move. Then he realized he was still in the shadows and the soldiers were standing in the direct sunlight coming in through the hole in the wall. The soldier couldn't see him. The man turned away and continued talking to the others. William almost collapsed with relief.

That's why the TerraSec patrol couldn't find them, he thought. *They're hiding in the city*. Then the thought occurred to him. Maybe this was what he'd been looking for. If he turned these guys in, he'd be a hero and he'd bring the crisis one step closer to being finished. He'd get special permission to run his flights.

As William backed further into the shadows, he knew just what he had to do.

▲▼▲

William burst into the apartment a short while later. "Lee, guess what happened? I think I've found away to solve everything."

Lee came into the living room from the bedroom with a concerned

look on her face. "Where have you been? The vid's back on. The news is advising everyone who lives south of the tracks to stay inside."

"I found them. I found the guys who attacked the fuel depot last night."

Lee stood very still in the center of the living room. "What did you do?" she said is a small, quiet voice.

"They were hiding in my shortcut, the old factory on 7th Street. I almost didn't make it." His words came out in a rush and Lee just listened. "I had to run very fast but I caught up with the TerraSec guys just as they finished. They were getting ready to move on up towards Fort Davis. I almost missed them."

The life seemed to drain out of Lee's face. "You told them? You told them where they were?"

William was puzzled for a second. "Of course I did. I..." he stopped when he saw the look on his wife's face. She looked very angry and very scared.

"My God, Bill. That's only four blocks away. And why would you help those animals anyway. Those are the guys that took my brother away in the middle of the night. I never saw him again. You know what that means to me. I know you're upset about your business, but is it so important that you put our lives in jeopardy? And how do you expect to stop this attack all by yourself. What were you thinking?"

William had never seen his wife so upset. Suddenly the whole thing didn't seem like such a good idea.

"Listen," he said. "It's going to be all right. The sergeant took my name and said they could handle it. Look, they only had one 'Mech. The patrol I saw had two."

"So now you're a military expert?"

"No, but I think your overreacting. So we're afraid for a few hours. Our peace of mind is a small sacrifice in the grand scheme of things. The sergeant seemed to know what he was doing."

A sound like thunder came from the direction of the old factory. William and Lee turned as one and rushed over to the window. They watched as the entire building collapsed. Smoke and ash flew hundreds of meters into the sky. Emerald laser fire lanced into the rubble from the two *Sentinels*. Then one of the 'Mechs raised its cannon and fired point-blank into the mass of bricks and steel. An eerie quiet followed.

William looked over at his wife. She was terrified. He started to open his mouth to tell her it was going to be all right but never got the chance.

The entire apartment shook so hard they were knocked to the floor and the glass window exploded inward. William helped his wife up and they peered out the window just in time to see two missiles fly from one of the Word of Blake *Sentinels*. The pilot was firing blind at the fleeing target. It was the 'Mech from the factory, and it had survived the first onslaught. It was limping away from its pursuers, its right foot dragging. The 'Mech walked like a wounded bird and William felt an odd impulse to laugh. Then he realized it was heading for them. The first missile missed its target and hit the building next door. The second missile hit the fleeing 'Mech just above the damaged foot. The pilot tried to keep his balance but failed and slammed into the five-story apartment building two blocks down the street. Fire and smoke poured from the crushed side of the building. What looked like burning rags fell to the street. But William knew what they were. As the enemy 'Mech stood up the rest of the building collapsed. The 'Mech continued right at them as it tried to get away.

William turned to his wife, tears in his eyes.

"I'm sorry."

The 'Mech was almost on them.

"Never mind," she said. "We have to get to the basement. Take my hand."

William reached for his wife's hand as they stood to run for the door.

The entire apartment exploded around them as the fifty-ton enemy 'Mech was hit again from behind and slammed into their building.William spun in the air with debris and dirt and smoke and then everything went black.

▲▼▲

William woke up and felt a huge pressure on his chest. He couldn't see. He choked on the dust and coughed. He didn't know how long he'd been unconscious.

"Lee?" he called. "Lee? Are you there?"

Silence.

He reached out, moving his hand around. "Lee, I can't see anything. If you can hear me, take my hand." His hand was wet but he didn't want to think about that.

He felt her hand.

"Oh thank God. Baby, just hang on. I can't see. Just hold my hand. Everything's going to be all right."

He would never put the business before his wife again. He would never put anything before her again. Then William realized something was wrong.

Lee's hand was limp.

He reached up her arm. And then felt chunks of concrete. She was completely buried. He held her hand as he heard voices coming nearer.

"Sarge. I've got a live one over here. Hey, it's the guy who tipped us off."

William felt a hand on his shoulder.

"Don't worry, buddy, just hang on, we'll get you out."

▲▼▲

The next day William lay in the hospital bed numb. The pain drugs helped to dull his mind. He didn't want to think. Two men in TerraSec uniforms came in to his room with his doctor; one tall, the other short. Their white and blue uniforms seemed to fit into the sterile environment of the hospital.

The doctor seemed worried. "He's not strong enough to see anyone."

"We'll just be a moment, Doctor. Please wait outside," the short one said. He sounded to William like he was always used to getting his way.

"Mr. Fence. We just want to thank you for what you did."

He looked at the agents blankly.

"If you hadn't tipped us off, we never would have found them. And because of your heroism, we wish to help you."

The tall agent looked down at his data pad. "By special exemption Order 1138, the grounding of all civilian traffic for the duration of the crisis shall not apply to Striker Shipping or any Striker vehicles. Also, any losses incurred during the conflict shall be reimbursed by Word of Blake."

"Congratulations Mr. Fence. And thank you."

As William heard these words he felt his mind slipping into a dark cold place. A place alone and far away. He'd been right to do what he did.

"We are sorry for your loss." Something pulled at him for a moment. A memory. And then it faded away. William looked up at the men.

"It was a smaller sacrifice."

FERAL

JASON SCHMETZER

Wolfnet Safehouse
New Canton
The Chaos March
29 October 3067

Lieutenant Peter Whitehorse was thinking of the great Charles Bear, warrior of the Gray Death Legion and hero of the Delaware people. He had counted coup against the Jade Falcons. He had fought to save his chief's tribe from destruction on Helm, Sudeten, and Pandora. In the traditions of Peter's ancestors, Charles Bear was the pinnacle of aspiration. He faced his foes in open combat, 'Mech to 'Mech, on the field of battle.

Peter shook his head to clear the nagging memories from his mind. He wiped pollen from his nose and leaned over, trying to adjust the left gauntlet of his Nighthawk XXI powered armor suit. The tribal elders had probably been talking about Bear when Hasegawa and his *Lancelot* killed them in May 3052. Operation Scorpion and a little individual initiative had removed a thorn from ComStar's Blake-ridden back for good, slaughtering the stubborn tribal leaders.

But Bear hadn't been there. No one had stopped the local precentor's attack on the Delaware people. Bear hadn't come after the ComStar 'Mechs and tanks had left. Mercenaries had come, yes. But not the camouflaged 'Mechs of the Gray Death Legion. It had been black 'Mechs bearing a snarling wolf's head on a red field. The same snarling wolf he wore on the shoulder of his blue jumpsuit.

Wolf's Dragoons.

"How long until we deploy, LT?" Sergeant Dominguez asked. The hulking sibkid stood behind Peter's Nighthawk, looking down at him over the armor's right shoulder.

"Unity, Dom," Peter said, banishing the memories again. "This isn't a family trip. We'll go when we go." He raised the flat-head screwdriver like a knife and pointed over Dom's head. "Go and help Tara with her suit, would you?"

"Sure thing, LT," Dominguez said. He turned and sauntered toward the Nova Cat adoptee, calling a greeting full of contractions sure to tick the Clanner off.

Peter shook his head. Top of his ageframe, first in his sibko, and winner of the Dominguez Honorname. For all that he was still a child. A rookie. A combat virgin looking to pop his cherry. He'd come to this Wolfnet safehouse ten days ago with orders to lead the second Point in Peter's command. His codex was impressive enough—he was impressive enough—but he was still a rookie.

Peter went back to his suit, poking at the recalcitrant actuator until it gave. He made sure the suit's shoulder was locked before fitting the weapon to the armored glove. The rifle was on safe and disconnected from the power pack, but he checked again to make sure before he squeezed the trigger. There was no catch this time, nothing to stop his finger from applying the one-kilogram of pressure to fire the laser.

There was nothing to keep him from killing Robes, killing as many he could until their Blessed Blake took them all into his arms again.

▲▼▲

The deployment was more a sergeant's business than a lieutenant's, but Peter had volunteered and then called in a few favors. Two Points of light powered armor were tasked to sneak into the Blakist compound while the Dragoon 'Mechs made a fracas outside. Two Points—ten troopers— of Nighthawk armor, more than half the total number the Dragoons possessed. All of them had been stolen from the Blakists themselves, all across their damnable Protectorate. Peter smiled as he settled the helmet over his head, squinting his eyes against the dry hiss of the suit's air. Wolfnet stole them, Wolf Pack used them. He made sure his amusement didn't show before he raised the visor on his helmet.

"Two minutes to tone," Peter whispered. The other members of his Point clustered around him with their helmet visors raised. "No speeches, no warnings. You know the job."

"No prayer, LT?" Tara asked. There were quiet laughs, light chuckling designed to loosen tension.

"If you want to tempt Blake," Peter said, "you go right ahead. My ancestors are already watching."

A red LED flashed inside his visor. He frowned at it for a moment, and then inhaled when he remembered what it was for. "Delta call," he said to his Point before slapping his visor closed.

The senior Dragoon officer on-world appeared on the tiny screen on the inside of his visor. Peter had worked with Major Kormenski for two years, including six months Allied Mercenary Command duty here on New Canton. He'd never seen the look of pure fury on Kormenski's face before.

"The Wolf is dead," he said.

Peter blinked.

"We just got the news, Pete. Spread the word to your boys and girls: The Wolf is dead, and it looks like the Robes had something to do with it."

Peter had been on New Earth fifteen years ago. He saw the Com-Star 'Mechs, bright sun shining off of the white paint, as they razed the Delaware people's town hall. He felt the old pain in his chest, the white-hot emptiness that burned at his soul. He saw red.

"They got the Wacko Ranger to lead the dregs out of TempTown," Kormenski said. "I don't know how it happened. The Wolf is down, the Hall is down. It's bad, Pete. We're at Feral."

The first Dragoon 'Mech Peter had seen had been an *Archer*. Not The Wolf's *Archer*, but another just like it. The Dragoons had taken him in, put him with a sibko class, trained him as one of their own. The Wolf was his family.

"The plan stays in effect," Kormenski said. "But tell your people, Pete. Tell them to burn any Robes they see. Burn them all."

"*Aff*," Peter ground out. The tiny pixellated image blurred from the first tears he'd shed in fifteen years.

"You okay, Pete?"

"Yes, sir," he said.

"You heard me about the plan?"

"Yes, sir."

"You sure you're all right?"

"Unity, Major!" Peter swore. "Twenty seconds to tone!" He cut the radio image. The plan was still in effect. He took a deep breath and motioned to his Point to seal up.

"Fifteen to tone," he said on the Point channel. "Listen up." How to tell them? "New rules. If it wears white, kill it. If it shoots, kill it. If it moves, kill it."

"What did you hear, LT?" Tara asked.

Peter ignored her and repeated his instructions to Dominguez

and the other Point. He left the channel open as the incandescent timer slowly counted down on his faceplate.

"We're at Feral," he said, as the timer came to zero. "The Wolf is dead, and these bastards killed him."

▲▼▲

The Word of Blake operation on New Canton was innocuous to untrained eyes. They administered the HPG and kept to their compounds, coming out only to aid the civilians or quash the anti-Blakist demonstrations that popped up. The local precentor was a model citizen, always waiting to donate the Word's time, money, or 'Mechs to whatever cause came up. Peter had been watching him for the entire six months his Point had been on the ground. His name was Hasagawa, and this day Peter watched for him.

The 'Mech diversion started right on schedule. Peter waited half a heartbeat before he left his position. He didn't doubt Major Kormenski's abilities—no one became a major of Dragoons without the skills,—but he wanted to give the Robes all the time they needed to get it stuck in.

"Spirits of my fathers," he whispered, careful to disengage his microphone, "hear my call. I go to battle to slay my enemies. I go to battle with your breath in my ears. I go to battle with your honor in my blade." He closed his eyes and leapt up. "I think only of victory, until my enemies are dead or I am at my place at your sides." He toggled the mike back on and followed his Point over the berm.

The Word of Blake compound on New Canton was laid out much like the ComStar facilities on worlds across the Inner Sphere. A central cathedral-esque tower housed the hyperpulse generator machinery and hid the transmission dish from public view, while the supporting outbuildings held the more mundane tasks of a compound: barracks, housing, mess, and hospitals. Peter had been in any number of ComStar and Word of Blake facilities all through the Chaos March, but this one was special. Under Feral, this one was his.

The berm they hid behind was a hundred meters from the northern gate to the compound. A squad of Blakist infantry occupied the small alcove beside the 'Mech-scale gates. Only the small personnel portal inset in the armored gate was open. There were no customers. The ten Nighthawk troopers would cross that distance in a matter of seconds, and the Robe infantry weren't armed to stop them.

Not that the diversionary force would let them.

A glance at the ten-square-centimeter screen that showed the landscape behind him revealed the single Dragoon BattleMech detailed to the actual raid. Peter raised an eyebrow in surprise—the Major's own *Black Hawk* erupted from a drainage canal on fiery jump jets, all ten lasers flashing overhead and into the compound. The Robe infantry didn't even notice the charging battlesuits. They just raised their rifles and fired at the 'Mech. Peter blinked for his point commander's channel.

"Dom."

There were six Word of Blake sentries at the gate. Each of them was armed with what Peter recognized from the muzzle flash as an AX-22 assault rifle. At his command Dominguez's Point opened fire with their blazer rifles. At the run five lasers flashed at five targets; Dom's laser flashed again before his first target had collapsed, bringing the sixth guard down with his combat blouse smoking. The Point commander's voice whispered across the open channel.

"Gate. Now."

Two of the Nighthawk troopers released their blazers. Recoil slings drew the heavy lasers against their armored breastplates as the troopers reached behind them to pull around square brown satchels. The satchels went to each corner of the gate. A jerk ignited friction fuses that hissed and smoked as the Nighthawk troops hit their jets and hurtled away.

"Fire in the hole," Peter said. He and his Point stopped and knelt, each crouching around their blazers to put the bulk of their armor between their weapons and the threat. The battlesuits were proof against shrapnel and small arms fire, but lasers were notoriously fragile. Peter would have preferred a good rifle—even one of the dead Robe's AX-22s—but they left such a staggering amount of evidence behind: shell casings, bullets, powder burns and residue. Lasers were so much cleaner. Isotope cataloging could tell whether it was an argon or boron laser, but the proliferation of lasers in the Inner Sphere meant that narrowed it down to around a hundred generic weapons. No rifling to match to a smoking gun.

The gate exploded.

Dom's Point was through before the heavy armored door had finished falling half-open. Peter led his troopers through on the other Point's heels. Once inside, the ten troopers formed a half-circle with their backs to the gate. Each scanned eighteen degrees of that ring. Behind them, Major Kormenski's Omni stalked up and planted a kick against the gate, sending the already-shattered assemblage to the

ground. The fifty-ton 'Mech stepped forward and deliberately ground its heel on the massive broadsword insignia of the Word of Blake. A short scratch of static blared from the Omni's external speakers, and Kormenski spoke one word.

"Vengeance."

The *Black Hawk* turned and leapt, its fusion-powered jets incinerating the laser-burned, gate-crushed corpses of the Blakist sentries. Peter stared at the smoking cinder of a corpse and grinned. A chuckle might have escaped his lips when the man's ammunition began to cook off, but he was already back to scanning his sector.

"We're officially not here," Peter said. "Let's make sure." He raised his left gauntlet and pointed. "Dom. Go."

The second Point fired their jump jets and clawed their way to the roof of the nearest barracks. The doors swung open to reveal a flood of half-dressed but fully-armed infantrymen. Peter chinned a preset signal and turned his Point to face them. "We're at Feral," he said, and fired.

The doorway was a natural bottleneck. The combined fire from the five Nighthawk battlesuits and their blazers ripped through the Blakist soldiers. Torsos and bandoliers exploded as the red-tinged fingers touched them. The bodies piled up until a blazer shot touched a grenade and cleared the doorway. Peter dropped the power pack from his rifle and replaced it in a fluid motion borne of long hours of practice. The doorway smoldered; no more infantrymen rushed through, although a few unaimed shots rang out. Peter ignored the shot that ricocheted off his breastplate. The armor shrugged the kinetic shock away, and Tara fired a burst through the doorway. A prearranged signal bleeped in his earphones, and Peter and his Point ducked away.

The barracks exploded.

The target was the cathedral. Wolfnet had learned that there was a new development in the Blakist's plans in the Chaos March. The Commander—The Wolf—had ordered Seventh Kommando to get those plans. Major Kormenski had spent the last four months on New Canton building toward this raid. He knew the local Robe commander would send his 'Mechs against the AMC demonstration across town. The news out of Hall was still fresh enough that everyone dreaded a repeat of South Harney. Peter had the cathedral schematics glowing on his HUD, off to one corner where he could reference it if he got lost. It didn't interfere with his targeting, or his vision. The pleasure of the Nighthawk suit was its control interfaces. It was better than an Elemental suit at communications prioritization. Peter had spent time in both suits, and despite the lack of armor and weaponry, he preferred the

Nighthawk. He might wear an Elemental suit, but he *fit* a Nighthawk.

"Let's go," he said. His Point charged down the main boulevard formed by the rising buildings. The cathedral's spire loomed before them, the crystal-steel sheathing of the HPG transmitter cleverly hidden in the latticework. "Dom. Report."

"Covering positions reached, LT." His Point would be atop buildings where they could cover the entryway Peter's Point would use to enter and exit the cathedral. They would hold the way open for Peter's intrusion team to exfiltrate after they downloaded the data.

"Status?"

Dominguez managed to send a smile through the voice-only link. "Feral, LT."

"Feral," Peter whispered. When he was a boy, a feral coyote had slaughtered one of the tribe's sheep. The Elders had set a young hunter after it as a test. Peter had caught the coyote, and killed it. He'd had the pelt when the ComStar 'Mechs had come. "We're going in."

Another Robe sentry stood his post at the cathedral gates. Peter didn't bother slowing his run. He brought the blazer up from where he carried it muzzle-down to the left, with the butt protruding over the Nighthawk's right shoulder, and fired. The pulse took the sentry in the face. His body fell with a steaming mass where its head had been. Peter glanced down at it as he passed. "Blake be with you, pal. No one else will be."

The schematic on his HUD pointed him toward an access stair off the foyer. He and his Point trooped past the sculptures of Blake and Toyama, their rubber bootsoles squeaking against the marble broadsword inlaid in the floor. Another explosion rocked dust from the ceiling as Dom's Point used up more of their demo. Peter let his smile widen; the rules of engagement when Feral was declared would be murderous under other circumstances. The death of The Wolf changed all that. Outreach Command wouldn't have called Feral without some evidence. The Robes deserved what they got. And more.

Peter had dreamt of little else but 'more' since he was a boy.

"We're starting to get a reaction out here," Dom called. "Platoon-strength infantry moving in units, along the walls. They haven't noticed us yet."

"Diversions," Peter whispered. His voice wouldn't carry outside of his helmet even if he shouted, but he whispered nonetheless. The radio would pick it up and transmit. The doorway he was watching for loomed up before him.

"Keep them away, Dom." He blinked his right eye three times and

his left once. The Nighthawk's reactive laser system switched his vision systems to IR. He beckoned to Esai, two fingers at the door and then a fist against his chest.

"Go."

Esai nodded to Tara, who ripped the door from its hinges and tossed it down the hallway. A trooper knelt on either side of them, lasers leveled, watching the corridor. Peter didn't look where they looked. Countless hours on the close-quarters battle course in the Fortress had honed his team into a CQB nightmare. He trusted them.

A pair of flash-bang grenades went bouncing down the stairwell. Esai followed those immediately with two thick-bodied smoke charges, then pulled his blazer around and followed the canister down the stairs. The thick black smoke roiled around him, swallowing the battlesuit. Peter followed, then Tara. Only the IR scanners in their helmets let them see.

"Clear," Esai said from the bottom of the stairs. He took a step into the corridor and stopped, going to one knee and training his weapon left. Peter stepped out behind him, looking right.

He looked right at the barrel of a fat-coiled gauss gun as a man stepped from a side room. The Robe infantryman triggered his weapon. Static washed across his display as the high-capacity electromagnets surged barely a meter from his head, and Peter wondered at the time he had, how it stretched, how he had time to call upon his ancestors once more to welcome him when he came.

The sonic crack was strong enough to rock his armor, but it was the wash of the projectile tearing past that spun him around and let him see the round take Esai in the back of the head. The decapitated Nighthawk fell into a sparking, twitching pile even as Tara leaned around the corner and set the Blakist on fire with her blazer.

Peter pushed himself to his feet and turned around. His blazer poked into the shadows, through the smoke, but the Robe had been alone. Reaching down, Peter lifted the straps of the Thunderstroke from the dead man's shoulders and settled them over his own. His blazer swung around behind him on its sling.

"Let's go," he said. Tara and the two remaining troopers stepped past Esai's body and continued. Peter paused over his fallen man. He knelt.

"You will be remembered in the Halls," he said, touching the body on the shoulder. It was all he could offer. It was all Esai would ask for. He was a Seven, after all. It had been good enough for Anton Shadd. It would be good enough for Peter. He chinned for the codes and activated Esai's self-destruct. The armor began to smoke. Peter watched for a moment, then stood.

The corridor they were running was a hundred meters long. Every two meters an office door broke the cold steel monotony. Out of most poked a head or a shoulder, to see the commotion. Many must have taken the smoke grenades for a real fire. They were half-dressed, but kept their heads down and one hand on the wall as they moved toward the stair.

A slender woman wearing the robes of an Adept and the silver flash of Rho division walked directly into Peter. She looked up through tear-streaked eyes and wiped at the inky smoke stains on her face. She took in the armor, and the weapons. She frowned.

"Peace of Blake," Peter said, and blew her in half with the Thunderstroke.

A storm of fire broke out behind him as the rest of his Point opened up. Feral made their options much simpler. There were no longer any non-combatants, not if they wore the robes of the Word of Blake. Peter raked the corridor until the ammunition gave out, then dropped the heavy rifle to the floor. The flux of the heavy magnetic firings had heated the barrel so much that it deformed when it touched the cold tile, sagging like a wet towel.

"They were not armed," Tara said, still covering the bodies with her blazer.

"Who cares?" Harbison asked.

"I did not become a warrior to kill civilians."

"They're Robes, Tara."

"Tara Novacat is no murderer."

Peter looked at her. He pulled his blazer around. His foot caught on the woman's outstretched hand and he kicked it away. "Neither am I, Corporal. I'm a soldier. I follow orders. Right now, our orders are simple. Destroy all threats."

"These people were not a threat."

Peter looked around him. He saw his family's house burning, the corpses of his father, his brothers, scattered in the yard where the explosion had tossed them. He saw his mother's body still buried in the wreckage of the house. He saw the smuggled trivid footage of the bone-white *Lancelot* firing on his house.

"They're zealots, Tara. They threaten everyone."

Hasegawa died in the corridor. Peter was coming to the end, getting ready to call up the door codes when the precentor's gold insignia flashed at him. He knelt, nudged the body. A laser had taken the man in the throat. It hadn't been quick, not when the laser cauterized the wound even as it caused it. Hasegawa must have felt pain as he suffocated, at least until his brain died from the lack of blood from the singed-closed arteries in the neck. Peter grunted as he stood. He had thought it would feel different than this, to see the *Lancelot's* pilot dead.

"Better than you deserve," he said.

"The door, LT," Harbison said. He and Tara crouched on either side of it while Dumont covered behind them.

"Right." He walked forward and canceled the active ECM on his suit. His right gauntlet cracked open to reveal a small interface, and the universal jack Wolfnet provided fit perfectly. The computer ran through the series, trying every combination it knew before starting a random search. It pinged almost before it finished the first cycle, and the door access flashed green.

"Erinyes," Peter read.

"What's that?" Harbison asked, not looking away from his sector.

"Beats the hell out of me," Peter said. He shouldered his blazer and stepped back. "Go."

Tara's hand fished the door open while Dumont turned and tossed another flash-bang. Peter followed the grenade into the room, his visor darkened and his audio pickups deadened. A burst of needles scattered off his armor just before the grenade detonated. Even with his preparations Peter felt the concussion. He was used to concussions, though.

Two steps in put him beside the Adept who'd fired. The man forgot reaching blindly for his needler when the two-hundred-kilo weight of the Nighthawk's right foot came down on his chest. He screamed as Peter let the myomer release more and more of the armor's mass onto the man. Feral or not, he needed information.

"The codes." The Adept snarled a curse and spat. The blood-tinged spittle ran down the shin of Peter's Nighthawk suit, marring the flat-gray armor. Peter smiled and stepped down. Bones snapped in the man's chest until he screamed. "I asked you a question."

"If you weren't a heretic, you'd already know the codes," the Adept said.

"I'm not a heretic," Peter said. His voice was calm. "You have to be a believer to be a heretic."

"All who defy the Word of Blake are heretics."

Peter laughed. He knew the helmet speakers would digitize the sound and make it sound something less than human. He'd heard himself laugh; it wasn't human without the speaker, either.

"I need the server access codes. I need the special passcodes to get into the encrypted partition." He twisted his bootheel slightly. Another rib popped. "I won't ask again."

The Adept smiled through bloody teeth. "Blake's will cannot be stopped. I don't care what the Puppet Primus has told you. I don't care what Focht or that little Davion you've taken in think. You can't stop us." His smile continued after his voice stopped. Peter had seen the belief in that smile before.

He smiled back. "Tara."

His Point second stepped through the door and slung her rifle. Two catches secured her helmet, and both released at a touch. The hiss of escaping air continued until she deactivated her environmental systems. She knelt by the man's head and pulled a small leatherette satchel around from her back. Gleaming chrome steel flashed in the light as she unrolled the bundle.

"I'll be in the hallway," Peter said. "Call me when you know something."

"I am Tara Novacat," Peter heard. "Blake does not know me." The Adept said something that Peter didn't catch, but Tara just laughed her musical laugh.

"Very soon, Blake will not know you, either."

In the hall, Harbison and Dumont knelt to either side of the doorway, weapons trained out. Each had piled the white-clad corpses nearest them into makeshift cover. Even Nighthawk armor had its limits. Esai had reminded them of that.

"Dom," Peter said, blinking for a separate channel. "Report."

"It's a bright-looking show," Dominguez said. "The Robes are still watching the Major."

Peter breathed deeply, ignoring the dry taste in his nostrils. Major Kormenski had promised him fourteen minutes before the defending Blakist 'Mech forces reached the HPG. He had promised another four minutes once they were engaged. There were two Epsilon Level II units within march of the HPG—a company of 'Mechs, in common terms—and only a lance of Dragoon 'Mechs. All were Omnis, of course. But there were still only four of them.

It had been nine minutes since tone.

"We're working on the data," Peter said. "Tara's with a captive."

"Bet she's laughing," Dom said. "Have you found your friend yet?"

Hasegawa was one of the bodies piled in front of Dumont. "It's taken care of," he said. He backed up until his back was against the armored door, then knelt between his troopers. "At fifteen, start the show."

"I know the plan, LT."

Peter checked the charge in his rifle before replacing it with a fresh cell. The slightly-expended power cell went back into his bandolier. Not full, but not yet empty. He'd been in situations before where that distinction had saved his life.

"No plan survives," he whispered, and blinked the channel closed.

"Movement at the end of the hall," Harbison said.

"Deal with it."

The trooper reached behind him and drew a slender tube from behind his back. He extended both ends of it. A small rectangular tab popped up on the fore end. Harbison settled it on his shoulder, sighted a moment, and pressed the button-like trigger set into the side. A slender rocket shrieked out of the tube, its exhaust flash-burning their armor black and melting loose strands of their webbing.

The explosion at the other end of the corridor blew debris back two-dozen meters.

"LT," Tara called.

Peter stepped back into the room. The Adept's face was peaceful. His eyes wandered unfocused across the ceiling—he was in shock, Peter realized. Tara knelt next to him, rolling her bundle of tools up. "I have the codes," she said.

"How?"

"I am very persuasive," she said. When she stood and put her helmet back on, her armored gloves left bloody fingerprints on its sides. "He told me what I need to know to access the mainframe servers." She pointed to his left. "Those are the workstations."

"Do it." Peter slung his blazer and knelt. "What's with him?"

"He is missing several glands and nerve connections," Tara said. Her fingers began tapping keys. "I removed them."

Peter noticed small bloody nuggets of tissue on the floor by his knee. He jumped to his feet, his hands automatically finding his rifle and bringing it around. "Is he dead?"

"Very soon," Tara said.

Peter drew in a deep dry breath and stared at the Adept's face. His mind was far away, watching his family's home burn and collapse. He stared at the flashes on the Adept's collar; Epsilon. He'd been a Mech-Warrior. The Robe's eyes faded. His chest rose and fell and did not rise again. Peter nodded and turned to the workstation.

"Have you got it?"

"I am currently downloading anything related to the keywords in the mission briefing. I've gotten hits on Gabriel, Waco, St. Jamais, Kernoff, Blane, Outreach, Chaos March, and several others. A separate core is doing a general sort-and-dump." Tara tapped a key and swapped crystalline data cores when a port opened. "A second copy."

"LT," Harbison said on the Point channel. Peter turned toward the door, his right hand unconsciously coming up to cup the right side of his helmet. He was two steps away when a rocking concussion threw him on the floor. He watched the heavy armored door scythe overhead and destroy the workstation next to Tara. Smoke filled the room.

"Report!" he called, dragging himself to one knee. His ears were ringing and his vision was blurry. He blinked his eyes, confusing his suit computer and opening and closing a series of windows on his HUD. A hand gripped his armpit and lifted. Tara waited just long enough to make sure he wouldn't fall again and then headed for the doorway.

"Harbison! Dumont!"

"They are dead," Tara said.

"We've got to move." He blinked for the Point commander's channel. "Dom. We're coming out hot. Three down."

When his subordinate replied, the heavy static of weapons fire filled the background. "We're holding the door, LT. Two platoons of Blake infantry just spotted our observation post. We're holding them back, but only just."

"We're coming to you," Peter said.

"It is not as easy as that," Tara said, ducking back inside the room. She shucked her blazer and reached over her shoulder for her sword. The rich hum of the vibrokatana filled the small room.

"Unity," Peter whispered. "It's that bad?"

Moving with a grace that should have been impossible in armor, Tara brought the sword up over her head and waited. Her helmet turned to face him. Through the still-billowing smoke and the periodic flicker in his HUD raster, he could have sworn he saw her eyes through the thick transpex.

"Purifiers."

Peter looked down at his blazer. "Shit."

▲▼▲

There was only a squad, a short Level I as the Robes would put it. Peter watched them creep down the hall from a sensor patch he'd

braved their fire to place outside. The Purifier battlesuits crept along, giving their mimetic armor every chance to hide their approach. The heavy pall of smoke that whorled and filtered along the corridor made them stand out though, if Peter watched for where the smoke seemed the blur and shoot off in another direction. There were four of them.

And only two Dragoons.

"Spirits of my fathers," Peter whispered. "Watch over me. Guide my blades and my hands." He let his blazer fall, let the sling carry it around behind him. It might come in useful once they got outside. If they got outside. He drew the paired vibroblades at his waist and thumbed them on.

"And you are always telling me that Nova Cat mysticism is pointless," Tara said.

"Nova Cat mysticism is," Peter said. He worked his arms around, flashing a shimmering arc around himself with his blades. The actuator he'd fretted over the day before hung a little. He suspected debris from the explosion in the rotator rings. It wouldn't matter. Not in the next few moments. Either it would move or it would not. Either he would live or he would not. In his mind he sang his death song. If his ancestors called him to the table this day, he would go prepared, with his blades wet from his enemies and his soul singing.

"Feral," he whispered. A shape rolled through the door, shedding color like water. He pounced, wolf-like. Ferally. The Nighthawk light powered armor suit was a marvel of technology, and the finest battlesuit Peter had ever worn.

He'd never worn a Purifier.

The Word of Blake battlesuits carried three times the armor protection of the Nighthawk. Instead of being restricted to weaponry not unlike those carried by standard unarmored infantry, each suit could and did mount a massive anti-'Mech laser. They were fast. And they were hard to see.

Peter stabbed at the neck of the suit from either side. The vibroblade in his right hand struck something hard and snapped, the broken end destroying itself his armored gauntlet as half its mass suddenly disappeared. The left-hand blade stabbed through the flexible gaiter around the Purifier's helmet. Steam hissed as the vibrating blade touched flesh and blood beneath. The suit jerked in a spasm, then fell still, the black maw of its laser pointed at the wall.

"One down," Peter said, and turned.

A second Blakist powered suit stood in the doorway, its right arm extended. He let his hand fall, let the hissing, steaming vibroblade fall to the floor. The mimetic trooper took a step into the room. His laser did not move from its covering position over Peter. He looked to his left.

"*Salaam*," Tara whispered from his right. Her vibrokatana slashed downward, taking the Purifier's bulky right arm off at the elbow. The laser fell to the floor and rolled to the side. Blood leaked from the severed arm within, mixing with the sparking power conduits that fed the weapon. Peter dove to the side, still watching.

With her sword point still by the floor, Tara pivoted so her shoulder was to the Robe power suit. She twisted, slashed. The humming tip ripped through the Purifier's faceplate, and the suit fell back into the doorway. Peter scrambled to his feet and jerked the heavy armored door from where it had embedded itself in a workstation. Tara stood and stepped beside the doorway again, her sword held out to the side. Peter moved to stand opposite her, still dragging the heavy door.

With half their number dead, the Word of Blake troopers abandoned any plans of capture. Stinging scarlet shafts of laser light whisked through the doorway, blackened the wall there they hit.. A glance at his environmental controls showed the temperature in the room rising rapidly. They'd not be able to stay long.

"Dom."

"Two down out here, LT. Marks and Arbuthnot." The heavy rattle of a machine gun echoed over the channel. "Two companies. We're out of time."

Peter closed his eyes. "We're pinned down in here," he said. "Purifiers."

There was a long silence before Dominguez spoke again. "I can't come get you, LT."

A grenade rolled through the door, a fat black cylinder Peter knew was packed with pentaglycerine. He strained, felt his muscles spasm as the servos in the Nighthawk fought to respond, and brought the door down on top of it. Together, he and Tara kicked, trying to shove the explosive back out the doorway. They succeeded. Almost.

The charge exploded while they each still had a foot on the door. The heavy armor plate absorbed most of the explosive force, redirecting it back into the corridor, but the heavy door itself imparted incredible kinetic energy directly onto the Dragoon suits. Peter felt a moment of weightlessness, and then a crashing blackness.

He blinked. His suit's bright green LED chronometer showed he'd only been out a few seconds. He shoved back with his elbows, forcing himself out of the cavity his Nighthawk had crushed in the wall.

Putting his left foot down, he screamed when his knee exploded in pain. The sequence to freeze the armor's leg straight took all of his concentration, and he triggered the medipack built into the armor's torso while he did so. By the time he could stand and look around, his knee was a just a dull ache.

"LT," Tara said from the doorway. The explosion had stripped the left gauntlet of her Nighthawk off. He saw her pale fingers, blue-tinged with the intricate tattoos she'd had since childhood, wrapped around the haft of her vibrokatana. The bundle with the data cores was clutched in her left gauntlet. "The Blakists are down, but moving."

Peter looked around. He saw a jagged piece of rebar jutting from the wall. Working it enough to break it off heated the end almost white. He limped to the doorway, his improvised club held in his right hand. He paused at the doorway, let his IR scan the smoky fog in the corridor. It was a charnel house of burned bodies and debris. He saw the two Purifiers. Both were down, but moving an arm or a leg. He looked at Tara.

"We're leaving," he said. Rebar held tightly, he stepped out of the room.

▲▼▲

The scene outside the cathedral was quiet when they emerged from the foyer. Three Dragoon Nighthawk troopers squatted outside, weapons trained outward. Dom was one of them. He flashed the all-clear signal to Peter before going back to scanning his zone. Peter stepped farther out, and looked up at the shape blocking the morning sunlight.

"Major Kormenski," he said. "I thought you were east of here."

The *Black Hawk* was scarred and missing its left arm. Its left knee was fused where a PPC hit had caused the armor to run like water before it cooled over the actuator. Behind it stood two other Dragoon BattleMechs, a slender *Ryoken* and the hulking mass of a *Masakari*. Both were in similar condition.

"You got what we came for, Peter?" Kormenski asked.

"Two sets," he said, holding up a memory core. "The mainframe is trashed, though. We won't get anything else out of it." He looked at Tara, who stood beside him, leaning on the tip of her broken vibrokatana. The missing piece was stuck in the throat of a Purifier suit two levels below ground. "I've got men down, Major. Self-destructs have been activated, but I don't think the Robes will have any trouble identifying us."

The *Black Hawk* turned away. "They will be remembered in the halls, Lieutenant. We've got a DropShip to catch."

Dom and his Point stood and ran for the Omnis. Tara hit her jets and landed at the foot of the black *Masakari*. Peter didn't move.

"DropShip?"

The *Black Hawk* waved its right—it's only—arm. "Get on, Pete. We're going to finish this."

A damaged turbine icon flashed red on his HUD when Peter tried to engage his jump jets. There was crap in his intakes. Using the rebar as a crutch, he limped toward the OmniMech. "Vengeance?"

A brief scratch of static told him Kormenski had switched to a secure channel. "We're meeting up with them in transit, Pete."

His leg began to hurt as he climbed the *Black Hawk's* ankle to reach the battlesuit alcove built into the Omni's torso. He anchored his hand around a handhold and locked the gloves in place. His fingers relaxed, and he sagged as much as he could inside the form-fitting suit.

"You taking that with you, Pete?" Kormenski asked.

Peter looked down. His other hand had locked around the haft of the rebar. The end was still stained and tacky, and he saw flecks of dust in the rapidly congealing blood. The heat from the *Black Hawk* was drying it like a kiln drys clay.

"We're going to Terra?"

"If we make the rendezvous."

"I might need it," he said, and closed his eyes.

ABOUT THE AUTHORS

Phaedra M. Weldon is the author of several *BattleTech* stories/novellas (available via www.battlecorps.com), including the continuing Sandoval Saga: *En Passant* and *Epaulet Mate* and the Isis Marik series, *The Art of War*.

Her other publications can be found in various DAW anthologies, as well as works in the *Star Trek* universe for *Starfleet Corps of Engineers*, and *The Next Generation* series, *Slings and Arrows*. She is also the author of the Zoë Martinique series from ACE Fantasy.

Jason M. Hardy is a beloved storyteller, international peacemaker, and revered philosopher who always enjoys the opportunity to write his own bio. He is the author of the *MechWarrior: Dark Age* novels *The Scorpion Jar*, *Principles of Desolation* (with Randall N. Bills) and *The Last Charge*, along with the *Shadowrun* novel *Drops of Corruption*. He's contributed a number of stories to the *BattleCorps* website and, with the editor's indulgence, will continue to do so. He lives in Chicago with his wife, son and daughter.

Jason Schmetzer has been writing and editing fiction professionally for more than twelve years, in both print and electronic markets. When not making things up, he is also a full time marketing copywriter and holds an MFA in fiction writing (he didn't make that part up). He lives in Indiana with his daughter and the menagerie of voices in his head.

Steven Mohan, Jr. lives in Pueblo, Colorado with his wife and three children and—shockingly—no cats.

He has sold more than twenty stories to *BattleCorps*, including the Jihad serial "Isle of the Blessed." He appeared twice in *Total Warfare*, and has done work for several upcoming *BattleTech* sourcebooks. His original fiction has appeared in *Interzone, On Spec, Polyphony, Paradox*, and several DAW original anthologies, among other places. His stories have won honorable mention in *The Year's Best Science Fiction* and *The Year's Best Fantasy and Horror* and he was nominated for the Pushcart Prize for his alternate history tale, *A Monument More Lasting Than Brass*.

Kevin Killiany has been the husband of Valerie for over a quarter of a century and for various shorter periods of time the father of Alethea, Anson and Daya. Since the late nineteen-sixties, Kevin has been an actor, a drill rig operator, a photographer, a warehouse grunt, a community college instructor, a drywall hanger, a teacher of exceptional children, a community services case manager, a high-risk intervention counselor, and a paper boy. He is currently a writer, with stories published in a variety of universes—including *Star Trek, Doctor Who, MechWarrior*, and of course *BattleTech*. He is also an associate pastor of the Soul Saving Station in Wilmington, N.C.

Ben H. Rome is officially titled Assistant Line Developer for *BattleTech*, a post he's held since 2008. While waiting for Herb to nuke himself into oblivion, Ben typically rambles around the nation's capital like some kind of photojournalist, taking pictures and writing articles about various exhibits, museums, people, events, and hockey, the king of all sports. He recently achieved one of his personal *BattleTech* goals, to write the climactic story of the Clans; *The Wars of Reaving* was published in 2011.

Chris Hussey is a local TV marketing director in the real world and his spare time is spent as a beloved cohost for *Fear the Boot*, an RPG podcast. Chris' *BattleTech* credits stretch back to the days of FASA (among others). Chris lives in Iowa with his wife and four kids, and a dog with digestive issues.

ABOUT THE AUTHORS

John Helfers is a full-time freelance writer and editor. He's published more than fifty short stories in anthologies such as *Schemers* (Stone Skin Press) and *Shattered Shields* (Baen Books), and written a lot of tie-in fiction, including for the *Dragonlance, Transformers, BattleTech, Shadowrun* and *Warlock II* universes.

Philip A. Lee is a freelance writer and editor whose many contributions to the gaming industry include more than a dozen short stories for BattleCorps.com and sourcebook/fiction writing for the *BattleTech, Shadowrun, Cosmic Patrol* and *Valiant Universe Roleplaying Game* universes. He lives in Dayton, Ohio, with his significant other and their three cats. To learn more about his work, look for @joechummer on Twitter and visit philipleewriting.com.

Christian Grainger lives in Massachusetts with the hope of becoming a full-time writer one day. An avid gamer of the video and pen and paper type (*BattleTech* anyone?), he has published three works with the *BattleCorps* website. He owes his success to his ever patient wife, step-son, the boys and Joe.

Blaine Lee Pardoe is an author of science fiction and military history books. He has written numerous *BattleTech/MechWarrior* books and books on Count Felix von Luckner (*The Cruise of the Sea Eagle*) and Frank Luke Jr. (*Terror of the Autumn Skies.*)

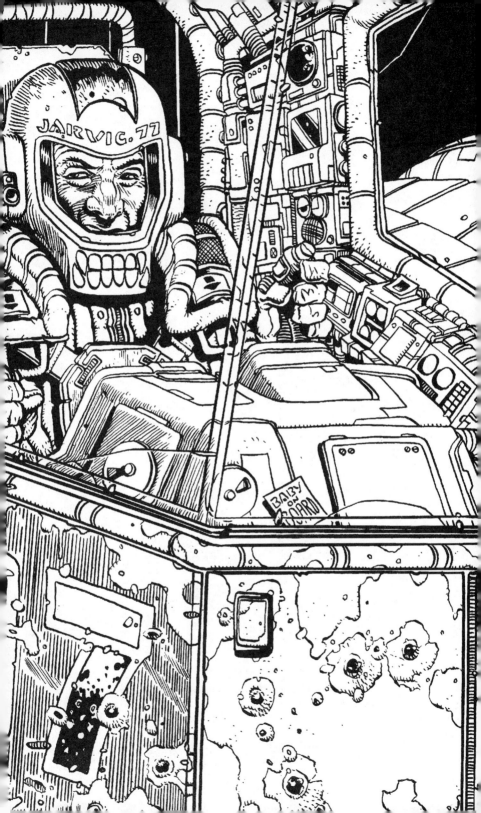